TAKE THE LONG WAY HOME

Susan Gordon Lydon

TAKE THE LONG WAY HOME

Memoirs of a Survivor

HarperSanFrancisco
A Division of HarperCollins*Publishers*

Grateful acknowledgment is made to Fifth Floor Music for permission to reprint lyrics from "A Sweet Little Bullet from a Pretty Blue Gun" by Tom Waits/Fifth Floor Music. Copyright © 1978 Fifth Floor Music.

Dragon's Milk and Psychocalisthenics are registered trademarks and Psychoalchemy a service mark of the Arica Institute, Inc.

The author wishes to express her appreciation to Bob Dylan for providing a soundtrack for this book, and much of her life.

FIRST EDITION   .

Library of Congress Cataloging-in-Publication Data

Lydon, Susan Gordon.
Take the long way home : memoirs of a survivor / Susan Gordon Lydon. —1st ed.
    p.   cm.
ISBN 0–06–250550–5 (cloth : acid-free paper). —ISBN 0–06–250723–0 (pbk : acid-free paper)
1. Lydon, Susan Gordon.   2. Narcotic addicts—United States—Biography.   3. Recovering addicts—United States—Biography.
I. Title.
HV5805.L93A3 1993   92–56400
362.29'3'092—dc20[B]   CIP

93 94 95 96 97 ❖ HAD 10 9 8 7 6 5 4 3 2 1

This edition is printed on acid-free paper that meets the American National Standards Institute Z39.48 Standard.

For my mother and father, Eve and Samuel Gordon, who never gave up on me, my daughter, Shuna Lydon, who endured it all, and my sweet soul sisters, Diane Wood and Rhoda Creamer, who saved my life and made it worth saving.

CONTENTS

Book 3: Getting Free 217

If you don't believe there's a price
For this sweet paradise
Just remind me to show you the scars.

Bob Dylan,
"Where Are You Tonight?"

THAT WAS THEN, THIS IS NOW

There's an abandoned synagogue on Norfolk Street, on the Lower East Side of Manhattan. The steps of the building are littered with rubble, and it's an easy climb over the broken concrete onto a raw wooden scaffolding platform just high enough to be hidden from the street. It's late summer of 1986. The Lower East Side is in the process of becoming one of those gentrified New York neighborhoods that gets cleaned up and renovated, gains in economic status, and loses its soul. But the housing developers haven't yet reached below Houston to Norfolk Street, and this particular makeshift rooftop commonly serves as an outdoor shooting gallery for some of the scores of junkies who roam the neighborhood on a daily basis searching for dope to feed their habits.

I myself am one of those lost souls. By now I've been fighting a losing battle with heroin addiction for close to fifteen years. Some of these Lower East Side streets are as familiar to me as my own veins, and my relationship with my veins is one of tender and intimate, almost sexual, knowledge. For the past few months, I've been on methadone maintenance at a private clinic near Gramercy Park. Once I've had my dose for the day, I can't feel a normal amount of heroin very well, so I've been shooting a lot of cocaine, and recently I've added crack smoking to my daily menu of drugs, as indispensable for my survival and vitality as food is for the non-addicted.

Right around the corner, on Stanton and Clinton streets, is the center of the neighborhood cocaine trade. The stuff is sold in nickel, or five-dollar bags, an almost unimaginable bargain to drug users in other cities, and I've come across nickel bags so strong that you couldn't shoot the whole thing without OD'ing. That's the tricky part about shooting coke. You want to give yourself a big enough hit so it explodes in your brain, lit-erally making bells ring, and slams into your heart with a rush of pleasure that rocks you from your head to your toes. On the other hand, put just a dab too much into the spoon and it's easy to freeze your heart and shut down your respiratory system, killing you quicker than a stray Uzi bullet.

But it doesn't matter how cheap the stuff is, because you can never get enough. I can't tell you how many times I've bought my coke one bag at a time, shot it up, and gone right around the corner to get another one, only to repeat the same routine until I'm totally out of money. On this particular August day, however, I've just copped six bags at the same time, and I'm up on the scaffold roof dispatching them one by one. All my stuff is arrayed around me: bottle cap cooker, disposable syringes, cotton, water for mixing with the coke and for cleaning the needles, full and empty bags, and a belt from an old bathrobe, splotched with blood, which I use to tie off my arms as I search for a vein. I keep my parapher-nalia in a big red leather bag I carry to work each day, with my books, my type gauges, all the tools of my legal occupation as a typographical proof-reader.

I'm not a pretty picture shooting coke. My hands shake so violently I can hardly slide the needle into my veins; my breathing becomes labored and gasping, as though I were having an asthma attack, and my eyes have the wide and startled look of someone about to be mugged. Unlike with heroin, I don't enjoy the high from shooting coke, if you can call such an overwhelming sensation of desperate compulsion, stripped nerves, and raging paranoia a high, but I love the rush. I love the cold chemical smell that rises into my nostrils when I mix the coke with water, and spreads down the back of my throat as the drug hits my bloodstream. And once I start I can't stop myself from doing more.

Today my friend Martin is up on the roof with me. He's a black Jamaican who sells heroin for one of the brands around here, a "worker," as they're called, and he's helping me clean my needles and keep from freaking out. I've just about finished jacking the sixth bag, pumping blood in and out of the needle over and over again to reexperience the rush, when a blue hat crests over the edge of the platform, followed closely by a fully uniformed beat cop from Manhattan South. With super-human stealth and those lightning reflexes junkies develop as part of their stock-in-trade, I manage to spirit all my paraphernalia out of sight and into my red leather bag before he can spot them. But of course I can't disappear myself.

My heart is already pounding from the coke, and with the added measure of fear, it feels like it will explode right through my ribs. I'm terrified. I'm on felony probation for stealing, with three years' jail time hanging over my head; and if this cop busts me on a drug charge, I'll be extradited back to Minnesota to serve my time in prison.

The cop takes in the rooftop scene. It's around noon, sunny, muggy, slow, and hot, and Martin and I are up there all alone.

"You," he says to me, "you got any identification?" I reach my trembling hands into my bag and fish out my wallet. I'm trying without success to control the violent thumping of my heart, and silently praying that blood doesn't seep from my punctured arms onto the long sleeves of my pale yellow Oxford cloth shirt, which I wear, despite the weather, to cover up my tracks.

I pull out my ID and hand it to him. I have a press card from the *Village Voice*, where I've been writing freelance articles for years, another from the *New York Daily News*, where I once worked as a feature reporter, an ancient temporary press pass from the *New York Times*, where I also wrote freelance, and a California driver's license with an uptown New York address, expired since 1982. The cop looks at my press credentials with some surprise, then back at me.

"What the hell are you doing up here?" he asks.

"Research for a story," I say, with as much professional nonchalance as I can muster under the circumstances. Fieldwork, officer, for an anthropological treatise on drug addiction.

"Why are you shaking like that?" he asks suspiciously.

"I'm nervous," I say. "You scared me, popping up like that out of nowhere."

He barely gives Martin a glance; black men who sell drugs on the street are so common and interchangeable around here that the cops don't even consider it worth their while to bust them.

"I was just interviewing him," I add for good measure, "about the neighborhood."

But the cop seems satisfied with my story. He hands me back my ID.

"You be careful now," he says to me. "It's not safe around here for a girl like you."

"Don't worry, sir, I'll watch out for her," Martin calls out to the cop as he climbs back down the scaffold. When he's out of sight, I nearly collapse with relief.

I'm supposed to be at work in ten minutes, to start a new job uptown, but instead I pull twenty dollars out of my purse and send Martin off to buy us two bags of heroin. "You better cop," I say. "My high is completely gone. I'll never be able to work like this."

By the time I get uptown to the type shop where I'm supposed to start proofreading today, I'm half an hour late.

"Don't bother starting," the foreman says. "If you're late for your first day of work, it's clear we can't expect much from you." So I'm fired before I begin. It's the third job I've been fired from in as many months. I'm scared I'm becoming unemployable. Once again my addiction is spinning out of control, my life spiraling downward toward another inevitable catastrophe. Impressing the cop with my old ID was a stroke of luck, but thinking about it now, all I feel is remorse for the person I used to be and shame for the one I am now.

Fear follows the loss of the job, and right on cue, my familiar companions, the gloom and doom sisters, strike up a chorus inside my head.

"You shouldn't be throwing your life away like this."

"You didn't go to Vassar to become a junkie."

"How will you explain this to your mother? You're on your last chance now with her as it is, and when she hears about this, you'll be out on your ass for sure."

"Look at you. You used to be a writer, and now you can't even get a job as a proofreader."

"You're such a mess, your own daughter doesn't even want anything to do with you."

"Your man is living with another woman." And on and on.

It's all too much to face right now, so I get back on the subway and ride downtown. Maybe I can hustle up a trick or two on the street, and buy myself a few more bags of dope. Quiet down the voices, get some peace. I'll look in the paper tomorrow, find another job, lie to my mother, get some sleep. If I can only get enough dope inside me to feel all right, everything will be A-OK.

Fast forward to the fall of 1992. "My name is Susan; I'm an addict." I am speaking at a Twelve-Step meeting, "sharing," as we say, my "experience, strength, and hope" with other addicts. It's been over six years now since I've had a drink or a drug, six years of recovery, meaning struggle and plain hard work. I still can't believe that I'm here sometimes, that this is real, that I got out, that I'm living the life of a so-called normal person. And then at times my old life seems unreal. But I have to remember how it was.

I used drugs for twenty-five years. At the end of my addiction, I was hopeless and in despair. I wanted to die; it seemed like the only way out. I thought I could never get clean, and I was too beaten down to try. By all rights I shouldn't be here now. I should have been dead many times over. But I'm not. I believe I lived so that my experience, painful as it was, can benefit others, offer light to those who live, as I did, in perpetual darkness. I've gone through a lot of growth and healing in the past six years. I'm better now than I ever was before I used drugs. I've gotten to the point where I'm grateful for being an addict, because otherwise I wouldn't have had the opportunity to recover.

I share my past partly in a quest for self-acceptance. I have to make sense of what happened, forgive myself, and move on. I'll never stop being an addict, but today I have a choice: I can choose to be a recovering addict rather than a practicing addict, and for that freedom I'm more grateful than I can say.

I'm also a mother, a Jew, a mystic, a feminist, and a writer, not necessarily in that order, but that's not how I identify myself in meetings. After six years without a drink or a drug, the addict's story is the one that still haunts me, that holds the mystery, the unexplainable, the source of endless questions. It's the story of my addiction I tell in this book, perhaps because it still has the power to keep me awake nights watching pictures

from my past like late-night TV rerun movies. How did it happen? I wonder. How did the sweet little child who was me, a regular girl from a nice
Jewish family, become the monster I was on the streets: a thief, a prosti-
tute, a liar, a con? Why did it happen? What was it for? And most of all, I
wonder how I got through it intact. Ultimately I believe it was by the
grace of God that I survived. And that is why I tell this story now.
Because a survivor is one who lives to tell the tale.

February 1993
Oakland, California

book 1

THE MAKING OF AN ADDICT

chapter one

What would happen if one woman told the truth about
her life? The world would split open.

Muriel Rukeyser

A LOST WORLD—1943

The world of my childhood is lost now, shrouded in memory and destroyed by time and urban renewal. The South Bronx in the early forties. My father was in the Army, stationed in Iceland, fighting World War II. My mother, a singer, was going to entertain the troops with the USO, but then she got pregnant with me, and it wrecked her plans. She was crazy about the movies. On the night her water broke, she was at Loew's Paradise Theater watching *Holy Matrimony,* and when I was born in Bronx Hospital on November 14, 1943, she named me Susan, after Susan Hayward, her favorite actress. That night my father's younger brother, Freddie, who worked at the Morgan Annex post office, sent a message on a stack of military newspapers, The *Stars & Stripes,* bound for Reykjavik, Iceland, addressed to my father's commanding officer. "Tell my brother, Staff Sergeant Sam Goldenberg, that he has a new baby girl," it read.

I came into the world as Susan Carol Goldenberg. My great-grandfather had defected from the Rumanian army. On the night he walked his first wife and nine children over the border into Austria-Hungary and freedom, he changed the family name from Thaler or Thalmann, no one knows which, to Goldenberg to cover up the desertion. Later my father would change the name again, to Gordon, in an effort to combat the anti-Semitism that he said prevailed in the business world. So like many Jews of the Holocaust years, I had no real name, no traceable history, only what I could salvage in bits and pieces from older relatives.

Since my father was away overseas, my mother and I lived with her parents in a large, dark railroad flat not far from the police station now known as Fort Apache. My grandmother, whom I called Bobish, was the moon and the stars to me. She was a short woman, under five feet, with straight black hair, graying in patches, that stuck out from her head, and one wandering eye. Bobish dressed in faded, baggy housedresses, but had the kind of beauty that shone from within; she was psychic. She could see the future in dreams, and neighbors often came to her to read their fortunes from her special deck of cards. She claimed to be part gypsy, a *diddikai,* and even as a child I knew she possessed a rich trove of mystery and magic. Pregnant with my mother, her fourth child, she had gone to get an abortion and instead had had a vision: her own mother, long-dead, appeared to her in the waiting room and told her to have the baby, which would be a girl, and to name it Chava, after her. From Bobish I inherited a tendency toward ESP and prescient intuition, a matrilineal legacy running through my mother to me and my daughter, as well as a taste for mysticism, a proclivity toward depression, and an ability to immerse myself so totally in an activity that I would appear to be lost in another world.

Ours was a Yiddish-speaking household, warm, close, and chaotic, full of stories and songs and jokes. Bobish cooked me homemade *lokshen* (noodles) and potato *latkes,* which I loved, and fed me slices of *challah* spread with *schmaltz,* the fat she rendered from chickens. We often sat on the windowsill looking out on the street; together we sang Yiddish songs and had long, nonsensical chats. Later my mother told me that I would talk to passersby on the street only if they were black. My grandfather worked in a fish smoking place and came home from work with tasty, fat whitefish chubs and succulent smoked butterfish. A dramatic storyteller, he regaled the neighborhood children with tales but refused to speak of "the old country," Poland, where he'd grown up seeing things too terrible to remember, only hinted at with dark words like "pogrom" and "Cossack." The born-in-America generation, my mother's three brothers, were in and out of the house constantly. Puzzling over the strange word "father," I concluded it must mean my uncles—Buddy, Sid, and Lou.

I was the first girl grandchild on my mother's side of the family, and the first grandchild altogether on my father's side. My whole family called me "Suseleh" and made a tremendous fuss over every little thing I said or did. My paternal grandparents, whom I named Mama Yetta and Papa Joe as soon as I could talk, came to visit with my aunts, Sylvia and Blanche, and their brother, Freddie. Uncle Freddie, the baby of the family, was blond and blue-eyed, drop-dead handsome in his crisp white sailor's uniform, and a favorite with the ladies. My grandparents' generation of the Goldenberg clan, furriers by trade, formed a huge, extended family. Throughout my early childhood, before they all started dying off, great aunts and uncles and my father's distant cousins came and went in a confusing blur of faces and furs and exotic smells, bringing extravagant presents and their propensity for loud arguments, punishing silences, and grudges that lasted to the grave.

My mother, who'd Americanized her name to Eve, was young, beautiful, and glamorous; I adored her. She fixed her hair in an elaborate arrangement of rolls and pompadours and wore suits with short skirts, and imaginative hats that she made herself. Best of all she sang to me in her incredible voice: "There's a song in the air, but the fair señorita doesn't seem to care for that song in the air." But my mother had her dark side too. She was high-strung, nervous, frequently worried and distracted, and given to violent outbursts of emotion. During the war, like most young wives, she worried about whether or not my father would come home safe, and wondered if they'd still love each other when he did. She chafed under the restrictions of living with her family, bristled at her in-laws' interference in her life, and resented all the unsolicited child-rearing advice she received from well-meaning relatives. Fiercely independent and accustomed to making her own decisions, she'd been on her own since her early teens, when she first started singing professionally in the Borscht Belt hotels in the Catskills.

My mother's maiden name, Samberg, like Goldenberg, was also made up. When my grandfather and his brothers passed through Ellis Island, immigration officials had difficulty understanding what they said and gave all three brothers different names. This was commonplace at the time. So one brother ended up as Simberg, one Zimberg, and my grand- father as Samberg. They came from Argentina, where they had worked as gauchos after leaving Poland. All of the brothers were alcoholics. My grandfather was highly intelligent and could converse in eleven lan- guages. In Poland he'd been a *yeshiva bucha,* studying to become a rabbi, but he lost his faith in God shortly before his ordination exams and re- mained antireligious to the end of his days. He was a bear of a man, phys- ically strong and also graceful; he hefted crates of fish around for a living and could dance on china plates without breaking a single one. But he could also be boorish and violent when drunk, and abused Bobish to a point of such despair that she frequently ran up to the roof and threat- ened suicide. At those times it was my mother who ran after her and begged her not to jump, just as it was her job to pick her father up off the floor and put him to bed when he had passed out from drinking.

Bobish had come to America alone from Russia when she was four- teen. Newly arrived in New York, she lived with an Italian family—gang- sters, according to my mother—and found a job sewing at the Triangle Shirtwaist Factory. One Saturday she wasn't feeling well and didn't go to work. Later in the day, a neighbor came to tell her that the factory was burning. She ran down to the docks and saw her friends, girls she worked with every day, jumping out of windows with their hair and clothes on fire. My mother never knew this story—it was told to me by Uncle Lou— and yet, when my sisters and I were little, her one overwhelming fear was that we would burn to death in a fire and she wouldn't be able to save us. So it is that family traits—fears and sorrows, secrets and shame—are passed on in an unbroken line even as the original impulse that created them is lost. I sometimes wonder if the atmosphere of deprivation my siblings and I grew up in, and which brought us such grief, came from my parents having lived through the Depression. The critical events of our lives cause our attitudes and outlook, which we then apply to every- thing that follows, to harden like crystals. Even as a second-generation American, I was born into a history of pogroms and persecution, the re- membered shame and deep sufferings of generations of victims of violent crimes. I inherited fear and fatalism as surely as if it had been imprinted in my DNA. We are born into our own time, but we carry our ancestors in our bones.

Since my mother was so nervous and distracted, my grandmother took care of me a lot, which was fine with me because she gave me pure, strong, undiluted love. My mother has told me that Bobish had the ability to lose herself totally in whatever she was doing. "When she was sewing," my mother said, "the whole world could fall down around her and she wouldn't even notice. She was in the *yenne velt* (the other world). Just like you, Sue, when you're doing something." So she turned her attention on me, and I in turn loved her above anyone else on earth. I learned to sew on my grandmother's treadle Singer. And I learned her deep concentration as a way of avoiding pain. I can knit myself into a state of meditation, dredge up memories, solutions, and serenity with repetitive movements of my hands. Along with the problem, it seems, we receive the means for its resolution. Everything in balance. Inside me run the streams of all my grandparents, their good and bad qualities, their gifts and liabilities, the singular embellishments of both their beauty and their scars.

My mother's father, Grandpa, was an alcoholic. I didn't learn this until much later in life, although I sensed as a child the constant crises and secret shame that surrounded this *"shandel* for the *goyim,"* my grandfather's drinking. If we inherit a genetic predisposition toward alcoholism or addiction, as some scientists contend, then my grandfather passed on to me what my friend David Getz calls "the wayward gene." If alcoholism and addiction are learned behavior, as other experts believe, he provided the alcoholic family atmosphere that my mother unconsciously recreated with her own small brood.

But there's more to it than that. Both my sister Lorraine and I now believe that he sexually molested us as children. I couldn't swear to it in a court of law, because I was so young when it happened that the memories are neither visual nor verbal but sensory and vague. I am still piecing them together, bit by bit, slowly, because each degree of memory brings an agony of pain. Whatever happened was so traumatic that I blocked out any knowledge of it for over forty years. Incest. Hard to believe.

Every fiber of my being wants to deny it. It couldn't have happened; I must be making it up. How will I ever know for sure? But the evidence that it did happen is too overpowering; the particular corrosion of spirit that incest brings too present in me, the healing that's gone on too dramatic and telling to be repudiated. For what it's worth, I don't believe he did it because he was bad and sought to damage a little child. He may have been repeating something he learned in his own childhood; perhaps it was part of the horror that made him reluctant to talk about "the old country." Or he may have shown his affection for me in an inappropriate way. I can't pretend I know the answers or have reached a final resolution. It's possible that more will be revealed to me in the future. So far, this is what I've been able to reconstruct:

I'm taking a nap on Bobish's bed. The bedspread is pink taffeta, many times washed; it feels soft and silky against my face. I'm wearing a cotton dress and underpants, something new; I've only recently been toilet-trained. Grandpa comes into the room. He smells of cigarettes and schnapps. He lies down on top of me. I can't see anything because my eyes are covered by something itchy. Maybe it's his wool sweater; maybe his pubic hair. He puts his finger inside my underpants and plays with my vagina. I can't breathe. My chest feels like it's being crushed. I'm so scared my heart is pounding. I love my grandfather, so I do what he says. Then I don't remember. I roll myself into a little ball and go way deep inside myself to hide. There's a place in my lower belly that's black-dark and safe. I make myself very small and hide there. I don't come out until I hear Grandpa leave the room. He goes in the kitchen and hollers something at Bobish in Yiddish. His voice is loud and gruff. Bobish sounds scared. The door slams. I wait until I'm sure he's gone and won't come back. Then I toddle into the kitchen, holding my arms out for Bobish to pick me up. She's sitting in a chair at the kitchen table. She leans over to lift me, puts me on her lap, and folds her arms around me, pressing me close to her heart.

I was two and a half when my father came home from the war. The first thing I did, according to my relatives, was tell him to take his hands off my mother's pajamas, and this was how our troubles began. My father, sensitive as a child, seething with feelings he couldn't express, believed I had rejected him, a wound to his heart that would take years to mend. I, in turn, felt rejected by him. My father didn't treat me the way the rest of my extended family did. He didn't fuss over me, spoil me, or make me the center of his universe. He required my mother's time and attention, which I wasn't used to sharing. And in that delicate readjustment so many soldiers experienced postwar, he wasn't conversant in the psychological knowledge that it might take time and patience to bond with a small child who viewed him as a stranger. So the tragic misunderstanding of our first awkward moments together haunted us both for half a lifetime, years we wasted looking warily at each other across an unbreachable chasm, each waiting for the other's acceptance to make it safe to express our enormous strangled love.

Shortly after my father returned, my whole world turned upside down. We moved into a small apartment on Hunt's Point Avenue, where we formed our own nuclear family—my mother, my father, and me. My mother was pregnant, and soon my sister Lorraine, named after Lorraine Day, was born. I was puzzled and upset and felt out in the cold, my former paradise lost. I missed Bobish; I missed my uncles; I missed all the relatives making a fuss over me. I didn't understand what had happened, why no one seemed to care for me any more. Left to my own devices, I took refuge in fantasy. I sat on a little chair in the middle of the living room and made up songs; I told myself long, complicated stories. I invented an imaginary playmate named George. George didn't like the baby either.

The web of relationships in our family—interwoven strands of passion and hatred, rivalry and resentment—was so complex and impenetrable that the older I get, the more difficult it seems to untangle or understand. Papa Joe and Mama Yetta didn't live together because they couldn't get along. Mama Yetta was unrelentingly critical and sarcastic; Papa Joe prone to towering rage. I remember Mama Yetta always cloaked in darkness and melancholy. Many of her relatives had been killed in Europe, and when I visited her, she would sit me down at the big mahogany dining room table and show me their pictures. She cried when she looked at the photographs and impressed me with the tragic word, *refugee*. I identified with the sad-eyed refugee children whose faces I saw in the newspapers, and I felt like an outsider, not a real American. This feeling of being on the outside looking in would become a hallmark of my life and my addiction, recurring like a musical refrain: "I don't belong here."

It was important to Mama Yetta that I have some knowledge of my religious heritage, to counter the bad influence of my mother, whom she called a *shikse* because she didn't keep a kosher home. Mama Yetta was the traditionalist in the family, the bulwark of convention and respectability, but she fought a losing battle. Papa Joe, her husband, was a staunch assimilationist. Educated in England, he spoke without a trace of an accent and had served in the cavalry regiment that chased Pancho Villa into Mexico. He was in love with America, with the horse culture and wide open spaces of the West. Papa Joe made me a leopard skin coat and bought me clothes, a riding habit and a bright red cape. The materialist and assimilationist strands of the Goldenbergs were firmly at odds with the crazy artist nonconformity and alienation of the Sambergs; and though I couldn't identify those differences as a child, I felt torn between the two families and troubled by the contempt Mama Yetta and Aunt Sylvia showed toward Bobish and my mother.

As I got a little older, I idolized my father; I thought he was the smartest, strongest man in the world, a veritable magician. When he played with me or rode me on his shoulders, I was in seventh heaven. But he was short on patience and quick to anger; he hit me a lot, which made me think he didn't love me. That was the great sadness of my life. When my mother yelled at me and hit me, I was sure that she'd stopped loving me as well, and that I'd end up alone in the world, an orphan. Since I already believed my father didn't care for me, and had lost the security of my earlier years, my mother was my last hope against total abandonment. And she was shaky too. One day my mother stood in the kitchen screaming and flinging plates against the wall. They crashed into pieces on the floor. "I want my Bobish," I howled, but my mother ignored me and went on throwing dishes until all of them were smashed. Now I can imagine that she was probably feeling trapped and in the throes of PMS, but then it was just terrifying. I felt there was nothing I could count on in my world, and that my parents' unhappiness had to be my fault.

When I was five, we moved to a bigger apartment downstairs, where Lorraine and I had our own bedroom. Within the year my mother was pregnant again. When she went to the hospital to have the baby, I stayed at Mama Yetta's and Lorraine went to Bobish's. I cried bitterly that it was unfair; I wanted to go to Bobish's too. My mother had another girl, my sister Sheila.

At the beginning of first grade, my mother took me to the library to get a library card, and I felt like I'd been given wings to fly. I took out the biggest book I could find, a biography of Johann Sebastian Bach and his family. It was boring, but I read the whole thing. Reading came easily to me because I loved it. Books may have been my first addiction, an escape into fantasy to numb my inner pain. But they broadened the reaches of my world, and I realize now that by reading constantly throughout my life, I also was teaching myself to write.

My teachers thought I was smart, but my father was always telling me how stupid I was. "How come you're so smart in school and so dumb at home?" he would ask me. When he called me "stupid" in front of other people, my whole body burned with shame; I wanted to sink through a hole in the floor and disappear. As a child, I remember longing with all my heart for a cape to make me invisible. The humiliation and stinging shame of my father's sarcastic barbs were worse than the physical pain of his spankings. Being smart in school was my one source of pride. I hoped that one day my father would learn to respect me. Each new putdown added to my feelings of rejection and worthlessness, eroding my fragile self-confidence.

There didn't seem to be enough to go around in our family, not enough money, not enough attention, not enough love. I was jealous of the toys and clothes other children had, especially my cousin Carole, an only child. When I told my mother I wanted those things, she said I shouldn't be jealous; I should be grateful. I had sisters; Carole didn't. In retrospect I know she was right; my sisters have been two of the great treasures of my life; but as a child I got the message that my feelings were bad and I shouldn't have them. I learned to hide my feelings because they were never the right ones. I tried to talk myself out of them, to ignore them. I grew quiet and withdrawn, learned how to suffer in silence. In becoming distanced from my true self, I believe I set the stage for my later addiction.

I was seven when Bobish died. I remember lying in bed at night in velvet darkness, trying to understand what *dead* meant. I could understand how a person's body could die, but not her thoughts and consciousness. I felt certain Bobish's spirit was still alive. I believed in reincarnation (which I had probably read about in my cousins Ira's and Stevie's EC comics, *Tales from the Crypt*), but was confused about the details. I thought perhaps part of Bobish was in the schoolbag she had given me before second grade. When I chewed on the plastic strap, I worried that I might be hurting her, as if I were pulling hairs out of her head.

She had been very sick with diabetes and was going blind, but didn't want anyone to know. My mother wasn't aware that Bobish couldn't see until she went to visit her in the hospital. Bobish took my mother's hand in hers. "Suseleh?" she said. Then my mother knew. She didn't let us go to the funeral because she wanted to protect us from death. I don't remember how or if I grieved for my grandmother, but I know that her death somehow sealed my sense of abandonment and loss. To this day her death still breaks my heart.

The part of the Bronx where we lived was dangerous. My mother was always telling me not to talk to or take candy from strangers or get into cars with strange men. One day I saw a headline in the *New York Post* that said a girl my age had been taken to an abandoned amusement park and raped and killed. I didn't know what rape was, but I was scared of it. I thought it meant kidnapping, that someone would take me away from my mother. Downstairs from our building there was an alleyway leading to the concrete yard in the back. I loved the morning glory that grew there, the deep blue-purple of the flower and the way its vine broke through cracked cement to climb over the entranceway, but the alley itself gave me the creeps. I kept having the same nightmare over and over: that some older men kidnapped me and hid me in a room over the alleyway, and I couldn't go home to my mother. I wonder now if those nightmares were connected to the incest, if memories of something that had actually happened were surfacing in my dreams, or even if the claustrophobia I sometimes experience now is related to having been molested as a child; but at the time it was all a mystery. Whatever the trauma was, I had already suppressed it, erasing it from my conscious memory.

I knew the Bronx was dangerous, but I liked it anyway. Everyone was different. The first thing you asked another kid when you met them was, "What are you?" meaning, Italian, Irish, Puerto Rican, Jewish, or what? Gypsies lived in storefronts in our neighborhood, and my Uncle Sid worked in the Hunts Point produce market around the corner. "That's my uncle!" I bragged to the other kids when he rode by on his banana truck. My best friend was a black girl who lived next door, and I had an Irish friend in my building who was always telling me about Jesus. A taste for ethnic diversity was imprinted in my psyche; and in later years, when I roamed the Lower East Side in search of drugs, I felt more at home in that polyglot neighborhood than I had since leaving the Bronx. I was proof of that well-worn cliché: you can take the girl out of the slums, but you can't take the slums out of the girl.

My teachers wanted me to take an admissions test to get into a special grade school for gifted girls at Hunter College, but I never took it because when I was nine, my parents found a house on Long Island. It was a long way away, in a new housing development called Harbor Isle. There were no trees there, or even sidewalks. It was an entirely different world from the Bronx. The island was a mile square and connected to the main town, Island Park, over a small bridge; water surrounded it and tall reeds grew in the vacant lots. Harbor Isle was almost all Jewish, and Island Park almost all Catholic, so the kids in school made jokes about where we lived, calling it "Hebrew Isle" and "Passover Place." Although my father and grandmother talked about anti-Semitism all the time, I had never before experienced prejudice in kids my own age. It was not only scary, it made me feel different and ashamed of what I was.

Because I had gone to a city school and read so many books on my own, I was way ahead of the kids in my class at Island Park School and frequently bored. I constantly created disturbances and got in trouble, until one day my sixth-grade teacher told me to go to the office and make a newspaper. I drew a picture of Pilgrims for the cover and cut it out on a Gestetner stencil. Then I wrote the stories, printed the newspaper on a mimeograph machine, and handed it out to all the different classrooms. Everybody liked it, especially me; I didn't know it yet, but writing and editing would become my lifelong trade.

My life changed in Harbor Isle. I still had my paper dolls in a cigar box, still designed clothes for them, collected stamps and read lots of books, but there was far more space to play outside, vacant lots and open land to explore. Now there were no elderly relatives around speaking Yiddish or heavily accented English; no exotic food smells coming from other apartments, no jumble of people speaking different languages on the streets or in the park, no dangerous strangers hanging around the schoolyard to lure young girls away. My mother seemed more relaxed and happier, our lives more normal. I wanted to be like the kids I went to school with: blond, freckled, agile, and physically strong. I went ice skating in the winter and swimming in the summer, stayed outside till it got dark, and played baseball in the schoolyard. I'd finally glimpsed the real America and wanted to be part of it. But I couldn't quite do it. My identity had been forged in an earlier environment, and deep down inside I still felt like a displaced person, a little refugee child in my heart.

My father was a "do-it-yourselfer." Undaunted by the fact that he had fathered three young daughters when what he wanted was sons, he enlisted Lorraine and me to help out with major house chores like gardening and construction. On the weekends Mama Yetta and Aunt Sylvia came to visit, and we all dug up the backyard with shovels so a garden could be planted. Mama Yetta and my father argued incessantly. *"Hab nicht con sachel,"* she said about my father: He has no brains.

My father owned his own business. He was a master electrician and knew every aspect of construction: electrical wiring, plumbing, carpentry, masonry, cement work, and landscaping. We learned how to mix cement, hang wallpaper, lay bricks for a retaining wall, pull weeds from the garden, shovel snow from the driveway in winter and mow the lawn in summer. My father's perfectionism made him a hard taskmaster. No matter how carefully we checked everything we did, there was always something wrong with our work. Once, after we had spent a whole day weeding the lawn and flower beds, my father came home and asked why we didn't pull the weeds from the curb on the gutter. Under the constant criticism, Lorraine and I, who'd started out eager to please, became resentful, reluctant helpers. We developed stomach aches on gardening days and fevers when we had to shovel snow.

Because he had very little money to work with, my father collected his building materials from other construction sites. One time he appeared with a wheelbarrow full of bricks he'd gathered from a questionable source. He piled the bricks on the back patio and then told Lorraine and me to take them through the crawlspace and stack them along the far wall, all the way in the back. The crawlspace made our skin crawl; it was full of spiders and God knew what all else. But we couldn't beg or con our way out of this job because no one else was small enough to do it. We took many trips through the crawlspace on our hands and knees, holding one brick in each hand. A few weeks later, when my father thought he might build something with the bricks, we collected them from the crawlspace and stacked them back up on the patio. When the project didn't materialize, we had to take them back to the crawlspace again. I felt like we were building the pyramids, like when the Jews were slaves to the Egyptians. The arbitrariness of my father's absolute authority made defiance grow inside me like a weed; to this day I have trouble doing anything I have to do and resent taking any kind of orders from a man.

One day Lorraine and I were helping my father fix up a playroom downstairs in our basement. Our job was to hang the wallpaper, which was light green with a horizontal texture like bamboo. We tried really hard to do it right; every minute we checked it with the level. I just knew that this time it was going to be perfect. But my father came downstairs to check our work and flew into a rage. "Can't you kids do anything right?" he yelled. "I never saw such a bunch of morons in my life." "But, Daddy," I said. "Shut up!" he yelled, and smacked me hard across the face. I ran upstairs to the kitchen, sobbing hysterically. "Why doesn't Daddy love me?" I asked my mother. "Don't be ridiculous," my mother said. "Of course he loves you. He's your father." I desperately needed my father's approval and attention, which I never seemed able to get. If this was love, then love came mixed with a big dose of violence; that was the message I got. Love meant rejection and brutality; ultimately it was unattainable; you had to work to get it, and chances were, you'd fail.

It was obvious that we were not like the other Jewish kids in Harbor Isle, whose parents spoiled them with expensive clothes and toys. Our daily lives resembled more closely the working-class Christian kids we knew in school. For one thing our mother was a nonconformist. She played mahjongg with the neighborhood ladies, but unlike them she had no cleaning lady, didn't drive, cooked regular meals, and never went to the beauty parlor, preferring to style her own hair. She was a free spirit and didn't care what people thought of her. Her look was distinctly sexy; she dyed her hair jet black, wore bright red lipstick, and dressed in off-the-shoulder gypsy blouses, full skirts, and big gold hoop earrings. To see my mother, you wouldn't for a minute doubt my grandmother's claim that there were gypsies in her family in Russia.

My parents' marriage was highly romantic and sexually charged, which we children were aware of from a very young age. All the boundaries in our family were fuzzy and confused. My parents' sexuality crossed over our boundaries and excluded us at the same time. My mother was so involved with my father that she frequently ignored us when he was around; consequently we got to lead very independent lives. I liked that, of course, but I often felt puzzled by my mother's easy betrayal of our interests when they conflicted with my father's; it was clear to us all that he was far more important to her than we. My father talked to my mother in a mean and condescending way and often called her stupid, as he did me, but she never answered him back or disagreed with him, even when what he was saying was patently wrong. Sometimes when he upset her she took it out on us.

I learned from my mother that a woman's worth was determined by her sexual attractiveness, her ability to cater to a man and keep him happy, no matter what. Yet observing the balance of my parents' relationship, where my father had all the power and my mother had none, I found it impossible to model myself after my mother. I wanted to function in a larger world than the one I'd grown up in, to wield at least an equal amount of power to a man's, to have the freedom to speak my mind and determine the circumstances of my own life. If my mother's martyrdom was the price marriage exacted from a woman, then I wanted no part of it. Although I suffered from my father's misuse of his power, of the two roles offered me, I preferred his. This set up a tremendous source of internal conflict for me, conflict I grapple with even today. By rejecting my mother's values, which I couldn't help but internalize, I went to war not only with society, but with my inmost self.

When I pursued my own interests, my mother said I was selfish; it was a woman's role to sacrifice for others, especially for her husband and children. I learned that intimacy could only be had at the cost of giving up my independence. Paradoxically, I had intense cravings for love and attention from boys and later men. I felt I had been damaged by men, and thought that they could repair the damage. Emotionally unavailable, rejecting, withholding men attracted me because they were so familiar, in the most literal sense of the word. I didn't feel entitled to the sanctity of my own body; I felt ashamed of my femaleness, confused about the difference between sex and love. I didn't think I had the right to say no to a man. I had no memory of the incest, so I didn't realize the way its

specter hung over my life. Incest is one of those crimes that lasts a lifetime because unconsciously you seek to victimize yourself over and over.
In that way it parallels racism; after a while the self-esteem of its victims
is so low that they don't need an outside perpetrator, they oppress themselves. Filled with shame, I became my own worst enemy.

Both my parents, raised during the Depression in families with unhappy
marriages and soul-destroying economic struggles, shared the same
opinion about bringing up their children. From their point of view, so
long as we were housed, clothed, and fed three square meals a day, we
had nothing to complain about. Since our lives were so much easier than
theirs had been, they found the expression of emotions other than gratitude puzzling and distasteful. My parents succeeded in keeping their
marriage intact and in building a family that, despite everything, remains
close and loving and supportive to this day. When I think of them now,
the phrase that comes to mind is from Keats's letters, "the holiness of the
heart's affections." As a parent myself, I know that my mother and father
loved me, and did the best they could with what they had. What happened later in my life was not their fault. But there's no doubt that a
childhood filled with shame, grief, and an overwhelming feeling of inferi-
ority fertilized the soil in which my addiction could take root and grow;
or that the adversity of my early life honed the skills I would need to survive it.

chapter two

It's got a back beat you can't lose it
Any old way you use it

Chuck Berry,
"Rock and Roll Music"

ELVIS IN THE SUBURBS—1955

I was twelve when a new kind of music appeared on the radio. "The Make-Believe Ballroom" had had a regular rhythm and blues segment for a long time, but this was different—stuff like "Rock Around the Clock," "Blue Suede Shoes," "Maybelline," and "Hound Dog." There was excitement in this music, a feeling of rebellion, power, and raw sexuality that expressed all the inchoate longings of my confused adolescence. Writer Greil Marcus has said that hearing Elvis Presley for the first time was like a jailbreak when you didn't even know you'd been in jail. Bored to death in bland suburbia, I wanted to go where I'd never been and do what I hadn't done, but there was no place to go and nothing to do. Rock and roll was a way out. I bought all the records in '78s and played them at top volume on my phonograph. Lorraine liked the music too; it was something we had in common. And unlike the mothers of most of our friends, our mother didn't mind if we listened to it. Sometimes she even sang along.

School was too easy for me. Even when I didn't do my homework or pay attention to the teacher, I ended up with high grades in all my classes. A behavior problem, I was constantly in trouble for talking or passing notes or cracking jokes. When my teachers tried to discipline me, I resisted. I'd had enough with authority and control at home. My report cards were full of high academic marks with U's, for unsatisfactory, in conduct, and it seemed like those U's were all my father could see. I didn't care much about school, though. Like most adolescent girls, I was interested in three things: boys, clothes, and music.

Throughout sixth grade I babysat almost every night for fifty cents or a dollar an hour. After school I worked for a woman who was a professional roller skater. We would go to the Hillside Rollerdrome in Queens, where she'd twirl around the rink, practicing dance routines with a partner, while I watched her two young sons. I saved up my money to go shopping for clothes with my girlfriends. We'd take the train to Lynbrook and spend the day smoking cigarettes, eating White Castle hamburgers, and looking around in the stores. A budding sociopath, if I saw something I wanted and couldn't afford, I'd hide it under my clothes and take it. I have to admit it gave me a thrill.

I'd started smoking cigarettes at eleven. I suppose I would mark this as the beginning of my addiction because even now, though the drugs are gone, I'm still hooked on nicotine. When I was a child, my father smoked a pipe. I loved the smell of the pipe tobacco; and sometimes, when my father wasn't home, I would inhale through the empty pipes just to taste it. Later on, when my mother's father lived with us, the smell of his Pall Malls made me sick. But in the fifties everyone smoked; smoking was cool, and I wanted to fit in with the crowd. I remember my first cigarette, a Lucky Strike, and the way it made me cough. As I would do with later drugs that came my way, however, I quickly overcame my revulsion and developed an instant habit. I was never one to employ halfway measures when it came to substance abuse.

I think the cigarettes helped me deal emotionally with the changes of puberty. My father had stopped being physically affectionate with me. When I was younger and my father came home from work, I used to say, "Daddy, kiss me like a movie star." He would bend me over backward and embrace me like they did in the movies. Sometimes I would stand on his shoes and he'd dance me around the house. My father could be a lot of fun when he was in a good mood. Often at night we'd lay on the couch together and watch TV. But after my body started changing and I began developing breasts, he wouldn't kiss me or hug me at all. I'd try to hug him and he wouldn't respond; it felt like he had turned into a piece of wood. Though our relationship was problematic, we had always been affectionate with each other, so the change left me feeling somewhat bereft.

"Susan is a good student, but she is entirely too boy crazy," my eighth-grade teacher wrote home to my mother. My father had called Lorraine and me "tramps" when one of his friends saw us hanging out in front of the candy store with some boys from town; but the truth was I was too scared of getting a bad reputation to really do anything with boys. We did the usual, had make-out parties in the basements of friend's houses, where we'd slow-dance to songs like "Earth Angel" or "To the Aisle." When I really liked a boy, I loved to make out. It made me feel all tingly inside. I imagined I would find a boy who was different from my father, who would give me all the love I'd never had. But just as my mother's ideas of romance had been formed in the forties, when women waited for their soldier boys to come home from overseas, my fantasies had a distinctly fifties flavor: James Dean or Marlon Brando, bad boys in jeans and black leather, tough on the outside, tender within; the kind of men who would only reveal their innermost selves to that one special woman I hoped would be me. Why do good girls like bad boys? A question for the ages. Erica Jong once said that writers fall in love with characters rather than suitable mates, and that certainly applied to me. I wanted someone exotic and different, someone who wouldn't grow up to be even remotely like my dad.

My mother let Lorraine and me take the train to go to Allan Freed's rock and roll shows at the Brooklyn Fox and the Brooklyn Paramount. We saw Mickey and Sylvia, the G-Clefs, the Clef-Tones, the Moonglows, Screamin' Jay Hawkins, Clarence "Frogman" Henry, and Chuck Berry. I wore tight black pants tucked into two pairs of elephant socks with saddle shoes, and put my hair up in pin curls with a black chiffon scarf tied halfway around to cover the back, a tough, slutty style I'd copied from some older girls I admired. The bands wore loud-colored satin suits with wide, sequinned lapels; when Mickey and Sylvia sang "Love Is Strange,"

Sylvia's breasts nearly tumbled out of her low-cut strapless gown. There were two shows, with a movie in between. We started dancing in the aisles and tried to go up to the stage, but the security cops got mad and began pushing us back, hitting people with billy clubs. They were screaming at us, too, calling us "cocksuckers." The cops were drawn from the generation that believed rock and roll led to frenzied sexuality and moral decay; they probably feared a riot, which in retrospect could easily have happened. Still this seemed like excessive brutality toward a bunch of unarmed kids. I advised Lorraine not to tell our mother about the cops; otherwise she might not let us go again. If we wanted to go water skiing or somewhere with our friends, the first question my mother would ask was, "Isn't that dangerous?" We always said no, but this time it really was.

When Elvis Presley first appeared on "The Ed Sullivan Show," my friend Flossie and I had watched it together and screamed in front of the TV. They called him "Elvis the Pelvis" and would only show him from the waist up. My mother understood how we felt because she had cut high school to hang out at the Paramount and scream over Frank Sinatra. But Flossie soon decided that Elvis was too wild for her; she wanted to marry a nice, Jewish guy and be a housewife in the suburbs. Flossie, who lived in the house behind mine and had been my best friend for several years, acted like she had all of a sudden lost her brains. "Boys don't like it if you're smarter than them," she told me. Later psychologist Carol Gilligan would do groundbreaking research on this subject: the time, usually around eleven, when young girls give up their independence and spirit and begin conforming to a subordinate role. I watched it happen, one by one, to nearly all my childhood friends.

Mama Yetta was taking care of us when my mother went to the hospital to have another baby. She woke me up early in the morning. "Thanks God," she said, "your mother finally had a boy." When my mother brought Ricky home from the hospital, I was standing outside the house waiting for her. She got out of the car with the baby. "Sue," she said, "go get a sweater. It's cold. How can you be outside in shorts on a day like this?" "Oh, you're home already," I said, real sarcastic. I thought she would never forgive me for hurting her feelings like that. Mama Yetta was sarcastic too; that must have been where my father learned it. Just before they were going to say something mean to you, they got a funny smirk on their faces, a little sadistic smile. My mother complained that I was too sarcastic, but I was really just mimicking what I'd seen in my family. I wasn't a pleasant teenager; I was incorrigible and behaved like a lazy, self-centered brat. I went out of my way to avoid helping my mother with the housework, and acted out my anger and unhappiness in a hundred different ways at school.

One day my mother was hanging laundry on the clothesline in the backyard. I went to ask her if I could go out that night to a party on The Block in Oceanside, where all the really cool guys hung out. Usually I had to babysit for my sisters and brother, but I was hoping she'd let me off this time. "Can I go?" I asked her. "You said I could last week." When my mother turned around, she was crying. "Leave me alone," she said. "Can't you see I'm grieving?" She'd just found out that Grandpa had died of a stroke. When she saw that I didn't break down at the news of his death, she said, "You never think of anyone but yourself." If I wanted to go out instead of babysitting, or got mad at Lorraine because she borrowed my clothes without asking and messed them up, my mother called me selfish. No matter how I felt, it was always the wrong feeling. "Stop crying," my mother liked to say, "or I'll give you something to cry about."

I never cried about Grandpa dying, though; of all my grandparents, he's the only one I never grieved. It seems telling to me that on some deep emotional level, below the plane of conscious thought, I knew what had happened and held it against him, withholding my tears for revenge.

Not too long afterward, Papa Joe died too. My mother told us he'd been in the Veterans Hospital for a long time before he died. "Mama Yetta took him in when he was sick and nursed him back to health," she said. "Then she got mad at him and threw him out to die." When my mother told me the news, I went to my parents' bedroom to say something to my father, who was lying on the bed crying. I had never seen my father cry before. "I'm sorry, Dad," I said. My father told me that Papa Joe had once fallen off a horse, which then rolled over on top of him. "He was never the same after that," my father said. "He never recovered."

I didn't feel anything about Papa Joe dying for a few weeks; it didn't seem real. We hadn't seen him for a while anyway, because he'd been sick. But one day we went to Mama Yetta's apartment in Queens. She lived in Jackson Heights, in a complex called Northridge. Aunt Blanche had gotten her the apartment and furnished it. Over the couch in the living room was a print of a Diego Rivera painting. You could tell it came from Aunt Blanche, because no one else in the family would have known who Diego Rivera was. My father and Uncle Freddie took all of Papa Joe's suits out of the closet and started going through them. Seeing his clothes like that, it hit me all of a sudden that Papa Joe was dead and I was never going to see him again. I ran into the bathroom and broke down crying. My father came in, dragged me out of the bathroom, and began hitting me. "You're always making trouble," he yelled at me. Lying on the floor while he hit me, I looked at the plants on top of Mama Yetta's bookshelf and concentrated on the fish tank where she raised her black-and-white striped angel fish; then it didn't hurt so much. My mother was too scared to try and stop him, and everyone else just ignored it like nothing was going on. But I was really confused. Just a few weeks ago, my father had been crying for Papa Joe; now I was doing the same thing and getting a beating for it.

When my father's rage was spent, I grabbed my jacket and walked over to Aunt Blanche's. "I hate my father," I told her. "He is so mean to me all the time, and for nothing." I thought Aunt Blanche was the smartest one in the family; she had even gone to college. I felt like I could confide in her and she would understand me. But she didn't. "You shouldn't hate your father, Sue," she said to me. "It isn't nice. He works so hard; he's just under a lot of pressure." "But all I was doing was crying about Papa Joe," I said. "He beat me up for crying because my grandfather died. I loved Papa Joe too." Aunt Blanche just turned away.

I went in the living room to listen to Aunt Blanche's records. She had a record by the Weavers that I loved, with songs like, "Round, Round Hitler's Grave" and "Tell me what were their names, tell me what were their names, did you have a friend on the good *Reuben James*?" I'd heard my father say that Aunt Blanche used to be a socialist. My favorite of her records, "Meadowlands," was the anthem of the Red Army. Listening to the music, I thought about Papa Joe. He had made me a gray mouton coat that I had to wear in eighth grade. I cried every time I had to wear it because it made me look fat and was so different from what everyone else had. "I'll never wear a fur coat when I grow up," I screamed at my mother. Now I was sorry I had hated the coat. Papa Joe would never make me another one. I felt numb inside, too drained to cry any more.

Recently I asked Aunt Blanche about this incident. "You know your father loved you now, don't you?" she said. "Yes," I answered, "beyond any doubt." Then she told me about a time when Papa Joe had beaten her so badly with a strap that her dress was torn and her legs were bleeding; she'd had to escape over the rooftops to a girlfriend's house. "In those days everyone hit their kids," Aunt Blanche said. "It was normal. Nobody talked about 'child abuse,' like they do now. We thought that was the way to be a parent." In my mind that didn't excuse it, but it helped to explain why no one had ever tried to stop my father from hitting us. How many generations back did it go? Aunt Syl had once described Papa Joe's father, her Zaide, as "a real son-of-a-bitch. He wore out three wives before he died, and terrorized his children to the end."

Some of the saddest memories of my life are connected with my father, and also some of the happiest. For my thirteenth birthday, I got a brand new Schwinn bike. It was maroon with gleaming chrome fenders, the finest bike I had ever seen and the best present I could have imagined. My father was beaming when he gave it to me, and when I think now of how little my parents could afford this splendid gift, it brings me to tears that they bought it for me anyway. Now I had wheels and could go anywhere I wanted.

All summer long I rode my bike to the big beach in Island Park, over the bridge to Long Beach to the movies, and to the library to take out books. I had read almost everything in the young adult section of the Island Park Library, including all thirty-two volumes of the *Nancy Drew* mystery series. My favorites that summer were *My Friend Flicka* and *Thunderhead;* I thought when I grew up it might be nice to live on a ranch in Montana and raise horses. I read all the time, at the table at every meal, and in the car when the whole family went someplace. Most of the summer, I didn't even go to the beach; I just stayed home and read. My mother teased me by calling me "Sheena the White Queen," after a character in Brenda Starr, because I wasn't as tan as the other kids. When I was reading a book, I forgot about everything else; the characters seemed more real to me than my own family. I even had fantasies of being a writer; as I pedalled my bike around the neighborhood I described what I saw in my mind, as if I were writing it down for a story.

I never thought my fantasies would amount to much, though, because I'd never met anyone who wrote for a living.

In ninth grade I had my first serious boyfriend, Bob Morgan. It took a lot of work to get him to go out with me. My friends Linda and Joanne, who knew him from grade school, dropped endless hints before he got the message that I liked him. We plotted our strategy for weeks, in notes we passed back and forth to each other in biology class. Even though Morgan was startlingly handsome and a star of the football team, he was very shy and had never gone out with a girl. I thought the best thing about him, besides his looks, was that he was smart. We spent hours on the phone talking about books. Both of us had read all of Kenneth Roberts's books, historical novels about the American Revolution.

When Morgan came to my house, we went down to the playroom that my father had made from the garage. The playroom had a bar for grownup parties, and a panel of numerous light switches that made combinations of different colored lights in the ceiling, giving the room a romantic atmosphere. My sister Sheila, who was eight, had a big crush on Morgan. She would stay down in the playroom and bother us until Bob gave her a kiss; that was the only way we could get her to leave.

Even though Morgan was Catholic, my parents didn't bother me too much about him, I guessed because he was so nice and smart and came from a decent family. My mother had had a talk with my father. She said, "Susan is too young to be serious, so let her go out with whoever she wants. It's just a phase; she'll get over it." That was what my mother said about everything. Lorraine used to joke that she could drop dead in the middle of the floor and my mother would say, "It's just a phase; she'll get over it." Lorraine was still in a greaser phase. She wore a tight black skirt to school with black tinted stockings. She was secretly dating a Puerto Rican boy named, of all things, Jesus, and climbed out of our bedroom window at night to meet him.

Morgan and I went steady all through ninth grade. We were the glamour couple of Oceanside Junior High. I was popular and got elected secretary of my class. I'd completely changed my way of dressing. Now I wore plaid pleated skirts and sweaters to match. My favorite outfit was a blue-and-white pleated skirt, which I wore with a royal blue vest that my mother had knitted for herself. My mother was flattered that I even wanted to borrow it. For years I'd criticized the way she dressed and tried to get her to change. She'd worn pink and red together, clashing colors, and I was embarrassed that she dressed so sexily. I had a horror of being sexy. I didn't want to have a body like my mother's when I grew up. My mother was proud of her big bust and liked to show it off. I wanted people to like me because I was smart. Of course I wished I were cute instead, like Debbie Reynolds or Sandra Dee, but I wasn't, so I would settle for smart. Morgan said I was pretty, but I didn't believe him. My stomach stuck out; I had no waist; my nose was too big and my hair too straight. In my opinion everything that could be wrong with someone's looks was wrong with mine.

Morgan and I went on dates to the movies. One Saturday, near the end of school, he put his arm around me in the theater and kissed me. I noticed that the old thrill was gone; I even felt a little bored. What we had together was too safe, too secure; all the excitement had gone out of it. When school ended I went to the beach in Long Beach. There was a new guy working there, with a beautiful deep tan, the kind you only get from being at the beach all day every day. I tried to talk to him, but he was quiet and shy. He seemed like a foreign country to me, exotic, impenetrable, and intriguing. I wanted to go out with him, so I broke up with Morgan, who was surprised and hurt. To celebrate my new freedom, I got my hair cut in bangs, which Morgan had never wanted me to do; and I went out with the new guy, who held my interest for about a week. Then I wanted to get back together with Morgan, but he felt betrayed and hurt and said he would never be able to trust me. Besides, he didn't like my bangs. He didn't speak to me again for several years.

Unbeknownst to me, with my first serious romance, I had set the pattern for all that would follow. I loved the chase, the conquest, the quivering insecurity of the "he loves me, he loves me not" stage of early attraction. What interested me was the longing for the unattainable; once I got it, I had no idea what to do with it. I suspect it wasn't really love that I craved, but excitement. Once a relationship settled down into stability and security, I got bored and wanted to run. I didn't want anyone to get too close to me, or too devoted. Intimacy reminded me of my parents' marriage, a trap I had sworn to avoid. Like many women of my generation, I spent my teenage years developing unhealthy ways of relating to men that would have me reading self-help books some thirty years later in an effort to change. I loved Morgan, so I pushed him away. I was cultivating a talent for self-sabotage, the knack of losing whatever it was I desired most, the fine art of leaving whomever I loved before he abandoned me first.

chapter three

I saw the best minds of my generation destroyed by
madness / Starving, hysterical, naked / Dragging
themselves through the Negro streets at dawn /
Looking for an angry fix.

Allen Ginsberg,
"Howl"

THE BEST MINDS OF
MY GENERATION—1958

Some of my closest friends in Harbor Isle were what I later came to know as "red diaper babies." Carl Zeitz, Peter Mitchell, and Marc Goldstein, friends I'd grown up with on neighboring streets, all came from politically active left-wing families. I liked hanging around their houses because I aspired to become, like their parents and unlike mine, a bohemian intellectual. Marc's father had fought in the Spanish Civil War with the Abraham Lincoln Brigade, and both Peter's and Carl's parents had been involved with the American Labor Party in the thirties. Peter, in particular, was like an older brother to me, a trusted adviser who'd broadened my horizons by introducing me to stock-car races, old blues records, and Tex-Mex food. None of them was involved in the Oceanside social scene. Peter rode a motorcycle and was a borderline hood; Carl was pathologically shy; and Marc was older than all of us, almost ready for college.

I'd begun high school with my popularity intact. I was elected an officer of my class and joined the school newspaper, *The Sider Press,* where I was a cub reporter. Besides trying to excel in extracurricular activities so I could get into college, I was also making an effort to acquire what I thought of as "culture." I'd decided that since I was a total misfit in my family, I didn't have to grow up to be anything like them. I imagined I could create myself from scratch, modeling my new persona any way I chose. I changed identities with my clothes, trying to see which one would fit. I had quickly metamorphosed from hood to wholesome coed, which I stuck with for most of my sophomore year, until I began dating Mitchell Hall and turned into a beatnik.

Through my work on the newspaper, I'd gotten to know the two humor columnists, Maris Cakars and George Wilkerson. They specialized in making funny announcements that sounded like Bob & Ray routines over the school's PA system. Maris, a junior, whose family came from Latvia, became a good friend of mine. Maris's best buddy was Mitchell Hall, an aspiring poet. Mitchell and Maris were hip. They walked through the halls spouting passages from Kerouac and the beat poets, and their favorite quote, the opening lines of Allen Ginsberg's "Howl," became a personal trademark.

Despite my fabulous social connections, I had already failed to make the cheerleading squad; I couldn't jump high enough or touch my feet to the back of my head in a thrilling backbend leap. I was in all honors classes in school, but I was too social and popular to fit in with the grinds and too smart to fit in with the jocks. Hip was an alternative to both, which appealed to me. Instead of fitting in anywhere, you just decided to check out.

For most of my junior year of high school, I straddled two worlds, the normal-popular and the semi-hip. But I was leaning. My friendship with the red diaper babies had exposed me to left-wing politics, folk music, and the bohemian lifestyle. When the Civil Rights movement started up in the South, my friends and I joined it by picketing local Woolworth's lunch counters. We sang and played guitars at CORE (Congress of Racial Equality) benefits. I began dressing in black leotards, black turtlenecks, black skirts and pants, and funny-looking shoes I bought in Greenwich Village. My long hair was pinned up in a severe bun, and I drew a heavy black line on my eyelids, swooping it past the outside corners to make "doe-eyes."

Through intense political discussions with my friends, I had decided to become a socialist. I didn't believe in the private ownership of property and land. At the dinner table, I called my father a capitalist pig and accused him of exploiting his workers. For once he laughed. My father had one worker, a slightly dim-witted helper named Bernie. Because my father had to cover the business's overhead and payroll whether or not his customers paid him, Bernie often went home at the end of the week with a bigger check than his. My father told me that as a teenager he had seriously considered enlisting in the Abraham Lincoln Brigade to fight fascists in the Spanish Civil War, but couldn't go to Spain because he had to help support his family. This was big news to me. He told me to be careful, not to join any organization or have my name on any list. The specter of McCarthyism hung over us all.

In principle I believed passionately in "free love," but in actual practice I retained all the fifties' values I'd been taught about sex. Girls I knew from high school were already married and bringing up babies; that wasn't the life I wanted for myself. I was afraid of getting pregnant, scared I'd get a bad reputation. Mitchell and I had been going out for a while by then. We made out and progressed from light petting, above the waist, to heavy petting, below the waist, but I always stopped short of actual intercourse. I loved Mitchell; but no matter how much he begged me to go all the way, I wouldn't do it. Eventually he got tired of the whole thing and broke up with me.

I was devastated; my heart felt like it had been stomped on the ground. I called Mitchell on the phone, begged him to reconsider, offered to do whatever he wanted. But he was cold to me and said he had made up his mind; the breakup was final. When we hung up the phone, I ran up to my room, flung myself down on the bed, and sobbed like it was the end of the world. I lay there for hours, crying hysterically, inconsolable in my desolation and misery. The heartbreak was the worst pain I had felt since Bobish died; I didn't know how I could go on living in such anguish. Finally my mother got tired of listening to my hysterics and climbed the stairs to my room. She sat down on my bed and told me that I should stop crying, forget about it, and go on with my life. "Clean up your room," she said. "That always helps you forget a heartache." I could remember countless times I had caught my mother in the kitchen in the middle of the night, ironing furiously, with tears streaming down her cheeks.

I didn't cry any more tears over Mitchell, but in the middle of my senior year I began feeling bleakly depressed. Often, for no reason I could put my finger on, a black mood would come over me, and I'd feel so awful I couldn't even stand to go to school. My mother let me stay home so frequently that one day a school administrator called her and said, "Hello, Mrs. Gordon. What's wrong with Susan today?" On those days I would take the train to the city and hang around in Greenwich Village. I'd go to the Folklore Center on MacDougall Street and listen to who-ever was jamming in the back room. Or I'd browse around the different clothing or jewelry stores, read in the bookstores, or sit outside Cafe Figaro drinking cappuccino and eating pastries. On weekends all the folkies would gather around the fountain in Washington Square Park to sing and play; I went there almost every Sunday. I attended lots of con-certs in the city: Pete Seeger at Carnegie Hall; the Friends of Old-Time Music at NYU, where I saw Doc Watson for the first time; and Gerde's Folk City, whenever the Greenbriar Boys or New Lost City Ramblers played there. There were hundreds of kids around the folk scene just like me, teenagers emulating the older beatniks who laughed at us and called us hippies, which was short for baby hipsters.

Among the folkie kids I hung out with in the city was a guy named Richie. One night he came out to Island Park to visit, and turned me onto marijuana for the first time, down in the playroom. He showed me how to roll a joint, then toke it by holding the smoke in my lungs for as long as I could to get the full effect. I smoked reefer with him and got a bad case of the giggles. Everything he said seemed intensely funny. He said it was be-cause I was high. The light in the room changed color; even the air seemed tinged with orange. I loved the feeling I had on the drug. I acted silly, like a little kid. My depression disappeared as if by magic.

It was 1960, the age of *Reefer Madness*. Grownups said that smoking marijuana would lead to shooting heroin, but we knew that was a lie pro-moted by the Establishment to keep all us kids from having fun. Now when I went to the city, I always found some reefer to smoke. Sometimes I drank alcohol with it and ended up sick to my stomach. When I did go to school, I felt as if I had a secret other life that none of my straight friends would ever understand. I was now editor-in-chief of the school newspaper, belonged to Arista and the Honor Society, had gotten a big prize from the National Council of English Teachers, and achieved my goal of becoming Miss Everything. No matter how much I did, though, I couldn't shake the feeling that something was wrong with me; I couldn't stand the way I felt inside, except when I was high.

When the time came to apply to college, I chose Barnard, Cornell, and Vassar. I was accepted to Barnard and Cornell and both offered me scholarships. I would have liked to go to Barnard; but because I was within commuting distance, I would have had to live at home, which I didn't want to do. My mother and I took a trip to visit Vassar. For my interview I wore an outfit I was really proud of that I'd sewed from a *Vogue* pattern: a royal blue silk blouse printed with tiny pink flowers and a blue wool skirt with pockets lined in the blouse's fabric. Vassar was different from anything I had ever seen. To my eyes it looked like Fairyland. The campus was big and green, with soft rolling hills, huge old majestic trees, gardens, brooks, and imposing gray stone buildings that looked like they belonged at Oxford or Cambridge. Girls in Bermuda shorts and button-down blouses rode bikes along the paths to classes; they seemed confident and self-assured. I had decided I'd be better off at an all-women's college; with no boys around to distract me from my schoolwork, I might actually study. I was totally enchanted by the otherworldly atmosphere of Vassar. It represented the big outside world, away from where and how I'd grown up. Being there was like stepping into a magazine picture: the archetype of college life in the glamorous Ivy League. Best of all, Edna St. Vincent Millay, my favorite poet, had gone to school there.

I got into Vassar with a big scholarship. "That's where I want to go," I told my father. "What for?" he asked. "Why can't you just go to Hofstra or Adelphi and live at home? I don't see why you have to go to college in the first place. You don't want to be a teacher." At that time the big joke about women in college was that they were going for their "MRS degree," which obviously could be better obtained at a coed institution. "It's a really good school," I told my father, "one of the best in the country. And they're giving me a full scholarship."

We had a big dinner at Mama Yetta's, where my father humiliated me in front of the entire family by saying that I couldn't wait to get away from home and had picked a college that was too expensive for him to afford. In my family education was generally considered a waste of time for women, unless you were planning to teach, which I wasn't. I ended up in tears at the dinner table, as the whole family berated me in chorus with my father. "You have to go to fancy-shmancy Vassar?" Mama Yetta wanted to know. "Hunter isn't good enough for you? You have to bankrupt your father, he already works too hard?" "No matter how much you give them, it's never enough," said Uncle Freddie. "They always want more." "She always was like that," Aunt Sylvia added. "Nothing was ever enough for her." Finally I exploded. "He doesn't have to pay anything," I yelled. "I have a full scholarship. And I'm going whether anyone likes it or not."

As I look back on this scene, which I resented for so many years, from the vantage point of adulthood and recovery, it no longer makes me angry; it makes me want to cry. At the time I had felt so unfairly persecuted; to my mind I had pulled off a major coup, and expected my family to take pride in my achievement. I was crushed when they attacked me instead, and I couldn't understand it. Now I see it quite differently. My father, who I so fervently believed didn't love me, wanted to keep me at home because he would miss having me around. My mother was afraid that if I went to an all-girls school, I'd never get married. And Vassar, with its undeniable upper-class connotations, was a threat to them all. What if I became so hoity-toity that I scorned my own relatives? Differences of class and education had been breaking the bonds of immigrant families since the first ship sailed past the Statue of Liberty. And the prejudice against education for women, which I took so personally, ran deep in the grain of Jewish culture. Had I known the value of the family life I was leaving behind, I might have thought twice about going. But I didn't. As my Aunt Blanche likes to say, "We grow too soon old and too late smart."

The summer after my high school graduation in 1961, Maris introduced me to his college friend, Steven Antler, and we began dating. Steven belonged to the Young People's Socialist League, which everyone called YPSL, and I went with him to meetings in a small building near Union Square. The people in the meetings were grubby and unkempt; one woman there had such filthy bare feet that I couldn't help staring. The other members told Steven that I was "an elitist with Stalinoid tendencies," because I had long hair and played the guitar. Nevertheless I joined YPSL and got a membership card. I had already joined the Student Peace Union several months before. I was now an official card-carrying member of the lunatic fringe, and my father was not amused. Steven and I went on peace marches and to demonstrations. He schooled me in the intricate subtleties of Marxist politics, which involved inordinate numbers of splinter groups and bitter enmities among people who, it seemed to me, should have been on the same side. But he was older than I was, and more sophisticated, so I listened to him. He had already graduated from college and would be going to Columbia Law School in the fall.

I had a friend in the Village named Gino, a skinny blond guy who lived on Elizabeth Street and sold pot. He asked me if I'd like to sell some nickel and dime bags for him when I went away to school. He would front them to me, and I could give him the money later. He gave me a bunch of the small packages in a paper grocery bag. I packed the little manila envelopes all around my guitar, wedged in the narrow space between the instrument and the case.

One bright fall morning, my parents and I set off for Poughkeepsie. Finally I was going away to college. My mother had taken me shopping for some new clothes at Best & Co. on Fifth Avenue. I had made myself a denim wraparound skirt and brought my special beatnik sandals, handmade by a Greenwich Village cobbler from an outline of my foot. My father was in a good mood on the way up the New York State Thruway. He belted out his favorite song, "Heart of my heart, I love that melody," though it was a joke in our family that he could barely carry a tune; and he referred to my mother as "the doll here," which he sometimes did when he was feeling particularly expansive. "The doll here says she got you everything you need," said my father, "so we hope you'll be a credit to your old man and your family."

As much as I'd been dying to go away, when my parents had finally settled me into my dorm room and were getting ready to leave, I was seized by an acute bout of homesickness. My mother was trying to be brave, but I saw she had tears in her eyes at the prospect of leaving me there. I was the first of her babies to grow up and leave home. Suddenly I wanted to break down sobbing at the thought of being away from my family. I felt scared and alone. I wanted to get back in the car with my parents and go home where I belonged. But this was the life I had chosen for myself, and I'd fought hard to get it, so I stood outside my dorm and watched them go. Ready or not, my new life was starting. I didn't feel excited, I felt desolate and sad; but I acted like a big girl and swallowed my tears.

In my hand I was holding my guitar case, loaded with marijuana. I'd left home to become a Vassar girl, and if all went well, to deal a little dope on the side.

chapter four

So you went to the finest school
All right, Miss Lonely,
But you know you only used to get
Juiced in it.

Bob Dylan,
"Like a Rolling Stone"

LOCKED IN THE IVORY TOWER—1961

I had hoped that by changing my circumstances and geography, I would change the way I felt; but it didn't work. I was still depressed, only now my depression was compounded by loneliness, alienation, and homesickness. I missed my family, especially my five-year-old brother, Ricky. When he got on the phone to say hello to me, I broke down in tears. The beauty of Vassar's setting—the meadow of tiny purple flowers on the way to the infirmary, the tranquility of the lake, the cathedral groves of towering evergreens—was some consolation, but not enough for the massive shoring up of spirits that I would have needed to feel whole.

Since this was my first prolonged time away from home, I hadn't reckoned on how strange I would feel in such alien surroundings, hadn't anticipated the difficulty of adjusting. And whatever was going on inside me at the time—whether it was caused by faulty brain chemistry I'd inherited from my family, hormonal disturbances, fallout from my emotional losses and the tears I had failed to shed, or disaffection from the upper and upper-middle classes from which most of the students were drawn, all of which have since occurred to me as possible reasons for my despair—the paradise I had envisioned had failed to materialize, and I was decidedly not happy.

I lived on the eighth floor of Jewett tower. Sometimes I looked out my window and thought about jumping; I imagined the way my body would look splayed out on the asphalt parking lot below. The first woman I had met at Vassar, when we were both brand new students browsing the college store for books about Edna St. Vincent Millay, committed suicide during Thanksgiving vacation. She went home, locked herself in the family garage with the car running, and died of carbon monoxide poisoning, the first fatality of the class of '65.

Despite my occasional morbid fantasies, I wasn't quite that dramatic. But depression lay heavy on me, like a constant lead weight in the pit of my stomach. Sometimes I found myself hovering just outside my body, or up on the ceiling watching myself perform some activity but separate from it, distant and disconnected from my self. And I was frequently in tears, or just too dispirited to go to class or do much of anything else. Luckily I had a way to cope. I had planned to sell all my pot when I first got to school, but it turned out no one even knew what it was. I sat on the steps of the student union, in front of God and everyone, smoking joint after joint, and no one passing by so much as looked twice. Since my classes were boring, and I didn't much like the other students, I spent most of my time in my room smoking pot and picking guitar. My biggest fear was that I would get arthritis in my hands and wouldn't be able to play my guitar any more.

A couple of other women on my corridor were also into folk music, so we got together in the evenings and sang. Both of them, Daidie Matteson and Susan Kent, were a class ahead of me. Most of the women at Vassar were rich, WASP-y, and completely apolitical. I complained to Maris on the phone, "This place is a hotbed of apathy." We were reading *The God That Failed* in one of my classes—essays written by people who were involved in the Communist Party during the thirties but became disillusioned by the Hitler-Stalin pact. I couldn't believe how naive the girls in this class were; not one of them had ever heard of the Spanish Civil War. Fortunately my economics teacher, Mr. Franklin, was a socialist, a kindred spirit. Mr. Franklin made fun of his students a lot. He would put two columns on the blackboard, "Knowledge" in one; "Folksy Wisdom" in the other, or else "Economics" vs. "Home Economics."

Many of the Vassar girls were blond and blue-eyed, what I thought of as real Americans. They were the daughters of the ruling class. A lot of them knew one another from boarding school. The preppie girls wore outfits that were too cute for words—pastel, flower-printed McMullen blouses with Peter Pan collars and circle pins, matching wraparound skirts, and two-toned Pappagallo flats or Bass Weejuns with tassels. I did like some of the components, though, so I went out and bought a brown corduroy wraparound skirt, which I wore with my black turtleneck, and a pair of Weejuns I wore with knee socks instead of black tights. I did it partly to fit in. I felt intimidated by these girls; I envied their wealth and privilege and the sense of entitlement they carried around like a badge of belonging. But I would rather have hung by my thumbs than let anyone know how inferior and inadequate I felt inside, so I acted cool and above it all, like I was superior because I was so much more sophisticated, bohemian, and politically aware.

As I had for so much of my life, I again felt like a misfit. There were a few, very few, other Jewish girls there, most of them a lot richer than me, and a scant handful of blacks. One of the black women, Sylvia Drew, was a friend of mine. Her father, Dr. Charles Drew, had pioneered the collection and storage of blood plasma, but bled to death after an automobile accident when a segregated hospital refused him a transfusion. Sylvia had been assigned a single room although she'd requested a double; the college had no qualms about telling her that it would make many students uncomfortable to room with her. The whole setup reminded me of a Leadbelly song I liked to play: "Land of the brave, home of the free / I don't wanna be mistreated by no bourgeoisie / In a bourgeois town / It's a bourgeois town / I got the bourgeois blues / Gonna spread the news all around." Sylvia ended up rooming with a girl named Joan Cadden, from a New York leftie family, and we helped make up a very small cadre of students who would protest the college's policies of subtle but institutionalized racism. When another black woman was busted in a civil rights demonstration down South, we went to Miss Blanding, Vassar's president, to demand that the college support the jailed woman. Miss Blanding actually had the nerve to call her a "nigra" in our presence. Looking back, I can see that my discomfort and alienation at Vassar were well-founded. Though I made many lasting friendships there, I would never again choose to place myself in that kind of lily-white world.

On weekends I'd take the bus to New York to see my boyfriend, Steven Antler, at Columbia, or to stay with Maris in his apartment. We hung out at a bar called Stanley's on Twelfth Street and Avenue B. I felt like I was living a double life. During the week I was locked away in an ivory tower, and on weekends I ran the streets of the Lower East Side with Maris and his friends. I know now, though I didn't then, that Maris was shooting heroin during this time. His new friends struck me as the drug addict dregs of the universe, though of course they also fascinated me because they were such colorful, interesting, bohemian characters. I thought they were living "real life," as opposed to my rarefied existence, but I wasn't quite ready to join them yet.

I'd only been at college a few weeks when I lost my virginity. Steven had borrowed an apartment in the Village from a friend of his father's. It was a weird place; the bedroom walls were painted black. I stayed there with him for the weekend, and we made love. It hurt at first, but it felt good too. Steven was a thoughtful, considerate lover and cared for me a great deal. His attitude toward sex was healthy, with no shame or guilt attached to it, and he made me feel comfortable and empowered, not at all self-conscious or afraid. I was lucky to have had such a positive first experience. Sex was definitely another step toward adulthood, which involved a gain and also a loss. It felt peculiar to visit New York without going home to my parents, but I soon got used to it.

After that first time, I became obsessed with sex. Sometimes when I'd stay with Steven, we'd fuck ten or twelve times in a night; and then during the week, I couldn't stop thinking about it. In art history class, when they'd show us slides of naked men, Greek statues, I'd think I was going to lose my mind. Most of the students were virgins, so there was no one to talk to about these new, confusing feelings. But I did meet another girl who slept with her boyfriend on weekends too, and we became fast friends. Like me, Debbie Michaelson was a Jewish girl from Long Island. She had grown up in Rockville Centre, not far from Island Park, but in different class circumstances; she was what we called a princess, the daughter of a doctor. Debbie had an artichoke haircut and a pair of shoes to match every outfit. But she was down to earth and smart, and I really liked her. We're still close friends. She lived in another dorm, but we got together for coffee in the Retreat, a campus hangout, and usually ended up discussing sex.

Debbie had a stash of diet pills. One night I had to do a paper for English class, which I had left to the last minute. She gave me one of the diet pills and said if I took it, I'd be able to stay awake all night. It was great. I wrote the whole paper. Then I started using them to study for exams too, since I'd cut so many classes. I loved those little magic pills. They made me feel brilliant and motivated, and—icing on the cake— also killed my appetite. I could get as many as I wanted from Debbie; she had a whole drawer full. I offered her some of my marijuana, but she didn't want it. She had heard you could get hooked on it.

I considered dropping out of Vassar, but then I would think that if I weren't there, I'd probably be a junkie on the Lower East Side like Maris's friends, and so invariably I'd decide to stay. One reason I had gone to college in the first place was so I wouldn't have to be a waitress for the rest of my life, or check out groceries in a supermarket, as I had done all through high school. And there were some teachers I liked and admired.

Sometimes in the winter, when it was icy cold, below zero, and the snow formed a thick crunching crust on the ground and draped all over the huge evergreens like a picture in a fairy tale, I'd feel a pristine purity in the silence and a crystalline calm inside, as though I were in a monastery. I enjoyed knowing that all I had to do for the next few years was study and learn. I was grateful for this luxurious stretch of time just to worry about myself.

Vassar was a rigorously tough college, and for the first time in my life I had problems with my schoolwork. I'd always gotten high grades without making much of an effort, and consequently had never developed any discipline or study habits. But everyone at Vassar was at least as smart as I was, and they knew how to work besides. We had to do original research for all our papers; Vassar didn't believe in learning from secondary sources. And the teachers were top-notch. Because there were no opportunities for women professors at any of the major Ivy League universities, many great women scholars taught at Seven Sisters schools. These were the first women I had seen whose lives I admired and could envision for myself; they were a tremendous source of inspiration. I heard that my philosophy professor, Ria Stavrides, had fought in the French Resistance during World War II. She was captured by the Nazis, but when the interrogating officer was called out of the room for a minute, she picked up her papers from his desk and escaped. Even though we read a lot of boring stuff for philosophy, Debbie and I never cut that class because we loved being around Mrs. Stavrides.

Vassar put up "Fallout Shelter" signs in our dorms. One night Susan Kent and I ran around the buildings in the middle of the night and put up our own signs: "There is no shelter from fallout"; "Ban the Bomb"; "Peace Now." Nobody knew where they came from.

The Vassar chapter of SDS, Students for a Democratic Society, had three members: me, another woman who belonged to YPSL, and a senior who was engaged to some big labor politico in New York. I read Tom Hayden's pamphlet, *Revolution in Mississippi,* and was riveted by his firsthand descriptions of what was happening in the South. When he came to Vassar to speak about his work in the Civil Rights movement, some of the Southern girls got bent out of shape. They asked questions like, "But don't you think our nigras are happy with things the way they've always been?" "It hasn't even dawned on them yet that they lost the Civil War," I told Maris.

I had joined the Northern Student Movement, a group of Yale students who organized freedom rides and support for civil rights workers in the South. I went on a freedom ride with them to a rural town in Maryland. When I told my mother I was going, she said, "But don't you think it will be dangerous?" "If it weren't," I told her, "what would be the point?" I'd never thought of Maryland as being like the Deep South, but the place where we went was scary. We got off the bus and tried to have lunch at a restaurant. Local people stood around the bus and screamed at us, calling us "nigger lovers" and telling us to go back where we belonged. Looking in the eyes of those people and seeing how filled they were with hate scared me half to death. But I knew that what we were doing was right.

I broke up with Steven. He didn't take it too well; he said he had hoped we would get married. I felt I was too young to get married. I wanted to experience life first, and other men. I wanted my freedom. It ran contrary to my upbringing, but I wanted to sleep with a lot of men before I settled down with one. Besides, I didn't even know who I was yet. I was in the midst of an identity crisis. I didn't know what I wanted to do when I grew up; I couldn't even choose a major. So how could I decide who to spend the rest of my life with? "I have to find myself first," I told Steven.

By my junior year in college, it was beginning to dawn on me that I had a problem with drugs. I had moved into Debbie's dorm to be closer to her. Susan Kent had dropped out of school; now she lived with Maris on the Lower East Side. I fit in at Vassar better than I had before. I had learned how to play bridge, and Debbie had taught me how to knit, which would become a lifetime passion. I had a group of friends now with whom I felt comfortable, but it was only because I had changed; they hadn't. As Lucy Baines Johnson said when her family moved into the White House, "You can adjust or you can adjust."

Eventually it had gotten to me, living a double life, and I had opted for the more normal half. I now wore preppie clothes; I'd dated some Yalies; I was majoring in history; and I'd learned how to get along with the daughters of the ruling class. But I still took more drugs than anyone else I knew. I was sort of famous for it, considered daring by my friends; no one else they knew had even smoked pot. But I was beginning to get worried. The previous spring, during finals, I'd taken speed for a solid week. At the end of it, I'd felt so crazy and paranoid I was sure FBI agents were following me around the campus.

I had been really depressed at the beginning of sophomore year. It started with the Cuban missile crisis. One night I woke up all of a sudden, saw a bright light, and was convinced the bomb had dropped on New York and killed my whole family. I had a stack of letters from a Yalie folksinger I'd met on the freedom ride; we had written to each other all summer. When Debbie and I talked about what we'd save if our dorm caught fire, I said I'd take my down comforter and those letters. At the worst of the Cuban missile crisis, when it looked like we might not make it through the night, I called him to say goodbye. I also called Maris and Peter. "Thanks for the memories," I said. "See you in the next life." I'm still not sure what made me so accustomed to impending doom, whether it was all those air raid drills in grade school or the way I'd been brought up in my family; but this wouldn't be the last time I believed the world would be ending momentarily, or that the future wasn't something you could count on, a chancy business at best.

The bomb didn't drop, but I still felt depressed. I stayed in my room sleeping all the time, sometimes twenty hours a day. The only time I got up was for meals, and then I went right back to sleep again. I felt so bad that I made an appointment with the school psychiatrist. He sent me home for a couple of weeks, and I did a lot of thinking about my double life, which was tearing me apart. When I came back to school, my friends sat me down and had a talk with me. They convinced me to cut my hair shorter and made me get some preppie clothes (I stole them). Then Carlyn, a junior who lived upstairs, introduced me to a friend of her boyfriend's, and we started dating. Carlyn roomed with a girl named Nancy Konheim; they were both Jewish. Sometimes Debbie and I went up to their room and the four of us played a game we had made up, called "Who Would Hide You from the Nazis?" That was our way of judging the WASP-y girls. Out of fifteen hundred students at Vassar, we could only come up with a handful of names.

So I was dating Stephen Jones, "a nice normal Yalie," as Carlyn had described him, visiting him at Yale on weekends, and doing everything the way you were supposed to, except that I was sleeping with him. His parents didn't like it one bit that he was dating a Jewish girl, so they offered to send him to Europe the summer after his graduation, and he went. Debbie and another friend of ours, Ellen, were planning to go to Harvard summer school. I went up to Cambridge with them, got a waitress job at a restaurant in Harvard Square, and we sublet an apartment on Everett Street.

From the minute we moved in to the minute we left, there was a nonstop party in our apartment. It seemed like we were drunk almost every night. On weekends, when it was hard to buy liquor in Boston, we rode around in people's cars looking for someplace we could find a bottle. There were a lot of guys around, and I was beginning to wonder if there weren't a fine line between free love and promiscuity, because some of my casual sexual encounters didn't end up feeling too good. One night a guy got me really drunk in his apartment and, in today's parlance, date-raped me. I didn't want to sleep with him and kept saying no; but I was just too drunk to resist. And then the parties in our apartment got out of control. They got so wild, in fact, that at summer's end the apartment owners sued us for "wanton destruction." At our last party, I drank so much Scotch that I threw up for days afterward. It would be twenty-five years before I could tolerate the taste of Scotch again. I didn't remember what had happened before I got sick; the whole night was a blank in my mind. Now I know I was in a blackout, and it wasn't the first. I can't recall the first drink I took as a teenager, and I'm sure it's because I blacked out from the start. Years later a drug counselor I trusted would tell me that I'd probably been "born an alcoholic."

By the time Stephen came back from Europe, I was still angry that he had fallen for his parents' plan to break us up. He was in New York, at Columbia Medical School, Physicians and Surgeons, and we saw each other a couple of times, but it was over. One weekend when I was down there, I met a friend of Maris's named Alan Tobias. Tobias went to Columbia. He was a Jewish boy from Brooklyn, brilliant, neurotic and totally nuts. He came up to visit me at Vassar a few times, but could hardly stand the resident population. "They're not affected by the Civil Rights movement; they're not affected by the Vietnam War; they're the living dead," he railed. Tobias claimed that they had me at Vassar as some sort of performing seal, "a smart Jewish girl from New York to make college more interesting for the *shikses*, give them a taste of exotic bohemian life." He acted pretty crazy. I wasn't even sure I liked him, though I'd been sleeping with him and had had a bad pregnancy scare not too long before.

Debbie had the name of a doctor in Pennsylvania who did illegal abortions. The story was that he took the chance because his own daughter had died of a botched abortion. Some friends of mine had been to see him, but it wasn't easy to arrange. Luckily I got my period; it was just a couple of weeks late. During the time I believed I was pregnant, though, I had thought about how nice it would be if I were with someone I could actually have a baby with, which I would never have considered with Tobias.

I was a little jealous of my sister Lorraine, who was only seventeen but pregnant and planning to have the baby. She had wanted to go away to college, to the University of Wisconsin. My parents refused to let her go there; they had a big fight; and the next thing anyone knew, Lorraine had turned up pregnant with a boy she was seeing named Bobby. Now they were getting married. Lorraine was young and small, and Bobby looked as much like a child as she did. I had an image fixed in my mind of Lorraine and Bobby getting off the Long Island Railroad train at Island Park. It was snowing and Lorraine was wearing her brown mouton coat. She and Bobby were holding hands; they looked like Hansel and Gretel, innocent children setting out through the woods.

Late 1963 to 1964 was a strange time all around. It started in November 1963, when President Kennedy was assassinated. Like everyone else who experienced it, I'll never forget that day as long as I live. I was on my way across campus to a conference with Miss Mercer, my English teacher, when I noticed the flag flying at half-mast. Miss Mercer told me that the president had been shot, and she was too upset to go on with our conference. When I got back to my dorm, everyone was crying. Eight of us rented a motel room just off-campus and stayed there for three days watching the funeral coverage on TV. Even though I'd never been much of a Kennedy fan, I cried my eyes out watching the funeral, especially the prancing black horse with no rider, which looked like something out of the Lincoln era. The mood of the whole nation was so sad, you couldn't help but feel terrible about it.

Up the road from Vassar, in Millbrook, Timothy Leary was conducting experiments with LSD. He and Richard Alpert had been doing LSD experiments at Harvard; when they got kicked off the Harvard faculty, Alpert went on to become Baba Ram Dass and Leary set up shop in Millbrook. In Cambridge Debbie and I had met a Harvard student who'd been involved in their research. I'd been aware of LSD and wanting to take it for some time. Maris had some, but he wouldn't give it to me because of my history of depression. "You're not supposed to take it if you're mentally unstable," he said. "You could become psychotic. I don't want to be responsible. It's bad enough I started your sister smoking pot, and now look at her."

Maris had been initiating Lorraine into the esoteric mysteries of hipness since her early teens, when he'd developed a secret crush on her while I was dating Mitchell. My father considered Maris such a bad influence on my sister that for years afterward he referred to him as "that creep." The previous summer Lorraine had been with Maris and his friends in a car going to the Philadelphia Folk Festival. They turned Lorraine on to some pot, and she had an anxiety attack and couldn't breathe. "Take me to the hospital," she told them. They were all in a panic wondering how they were going to explain a stoned underage teenager to the cops, but luckily they talked her through it, and she was fine. She laughed when she told me the story.

Since I couldn't get any LSD, I stuck with my pot and diet pills. I was in a lot of trouble at school; I'd been caught breaking some serious rules. I had broken as many rules as possible during my whole time at Vassar, but this was the first time I'd ever gotten caught. One night I fell asleep in the student union and missed curfew. I had already used up both my late sign-outs for the semester, so I signed Debbie's name. Then a few weeks later, I snuck out of the dorm after ten o'clock at night to go to New York, and a sophomore who saw me turned me in.

I thought I was going to get kicked out of school. I wouldn't have minded that much. Ever since I'd seen the movie *Operation Abolition,* about student protests at the House Unamerican Activities Committee in San Francisco, I'd wanted to go to Berkeley and join the student movement there. I told my mother I was in trouble, but she already knew. The warden of the college had called and advised my mother that she shouldn't trust me because I was "inherently dishonest." "Mom," I said, "I might get kicked out of school. If I do, can I transfer to Berkeley?" By now she'd become accustomed to my being away from home, so she said that I could. I was looking forward to it.

First I had to stand trial before the student tribunals. While I was waiting to see what would happen, I got an unexpected phone call from a guy I didn't know at Yale. He said his name was Mike Lydon. We had a Yale picture directory in our dorm, so I checked him out. He didn't look too bad, kind of cute, although later I found out I had looked up the wrong guy. This Mike Lydon said he had heard about me from a girl in my English class who dated his roommate. He wanted to go on a blind date with me. He had just come back from Detroit, where he'd picked up a brand new red convertible Ford Mustang. As a promotional deal, Ford had given a few of them for a short time to editors of college newspapers, and he had snagged the one for the Yale *Daily News,* where he wrote a column. He asked if I'd go out with him Saturday night. "I don't know," I said. "I might not even be in school by then. I'm on the verge of getting kicked out." He asked where I lived, and when I told him Long Island, he said no problem, he'd pick me up there. We were going to see James Brown at the Apollo Theater in Harlem, which he called "the Aps."

By Saturday the results of my trial were in. I was not getting kicked out, or even suspended. They had decided instead to put me on freshman social privileges for my senior year. Also I was losing my scholarship for, as they called it, "forgery." So I was feeling pretty blue. It was a beautiful May day; we were having some group function; the whole school was out on the lawn in the quad. I hated these group affairs, but luckily I didn't have to stay because I was waiting for Mike Lydon to pick me up for our blind date.

As soon as I saw him walking toward me on the quad, a strange thought crossed my mind: "It would be nice to be married to him." It must have been a flash of that intuition I'd inherited from Bobish, because right away I know what was going to happen. Mike Lydon was tallish and skinny, with a freckled Irish face and wild sandy hair going every which way. We drove over to the Vanderbilt estate on the Hudson River and talked about politics. He was from Boston and a family of staunch Kennedy Democrats. He wanted to work in the mainstream of American politics. "Not me," I said. "I hate the mainstream. I'm strictly a lunatic fringe kind of girl." We also talked about literature, and I told him my theory about writing, which I'd recently developed after reading James Joyce's *Portrait of the Artist as a Young Man,* a book that had touched me deeply. Although the sentiments Stephen Daedalus expressed were often hateful, I felt that Joyce must have been motivated by an incredible love for other human beings to have exposed his innermost self to total strangers. Lydon disagreed. He was a writer, an aspiring journalist. He said love did not figure into his motivation to write in the slightest.

Since my pregnancy scare with Tobias, I'd been thinking a lot about the kind of men I dated. I was beginning to long for a real relationship, one that could develop into a life partnership, in which it would be safe to have a baby. Many of my Vassar friends were graduating and getting married; girls in my class were becoming engaged. I was feeling kind of lost and alone during this time. I could see the end of college looming, and I didn't have a clue what to do with the rest of my life. In the back of my mind was the nasty question of my drug problem. I sensed that I was heading for trouble, but I couldn't see a way out. At the same time, I was building some of the intellectual framework that would provide stable ground and sustain my interest for years to come. Even in my later addiction, as the rest of my life came undone, I continued to grapple with questions and issues that I had begun to explore in papers I wrote that year. I still consider Joyce's writing a gift of love and find something telling about Michael's refusal, even then, to recognize the metaphysical dimension and emotional underpinnings of a life's work in writing. It illuminates one of the major differences between us, one that would eventually drive us apart.

We drove down to New York on the winding Taconic Parkway. On the road people stared at the new Mustang, honked their horns, and asked questions. Michael reveled in the attention. By now the Beatles had invaded America, and I was interested in rock and roll again after my long folk hiatus. We went to the Apollo. I'd been there before with Lorraine and Maris to see gospel concerts, but this time Michael and I were the only white people in the audience, and it felt kind of tense. James Brown did his dramatic routine, cape on, cape off, leaving the stage, coming back. Black women screamed for him the way white girls screamed for the Beatles. They threw roses at the stage and sometimes their panties. After the show we drove back to New Haven; Michael took me to his room and played me his Duke Ellington records. His column in the Yale *Daily News* was called "In a Mellotone," and "the Duke," as he called him, "the epitome of suaveness," was his ultimate hero.

A few days after our date, I took some speed because I had a paper due the next day. Instead of writing the paper, I wrote Michael Lydon a twelve-page letter on a yellow legal pad, continuing our political argument from that day at the Vanderbilt estate, detailing all the reasons I hated mainstream American politics. After reading the letter, he called up and asked me out again. "You know," he said, "you're a really good writer." I was shocked; this was something that had never occurred to me. A writer, to me, meant Faulkner or Hemingway, another breed of human, something I could never aspire to. "You're kidding, of course," I said. "No," he said. "I really mean it. I'm impressed with the way you write."

We went out again that weekend, this time in Poughkeepsie. He told me what kind of writing he did. I had never considered the stuff that was in newspapers and magazines real writing. I didn't work on the Vassar newspaper because I had such a bad attitude about being there, and the one creative writing teacher, who I had for a class called "Nineteenth-Century Novel," didn't much like me. My friend Mary Peacock, who also became a writer, and I sat in the back of his class; his teacher's pets sat in front. If Mary or I raised our hand to speak, he called on us with great reluctance and contempt. Since he had to choose you personally to take creative writing, it had never been an option for me.

Michael Lydon had an ebullient spirit. Like me, he was a scholarship student. He was smart, interesting, ambitious, and he wasn't a freak, like the guys I hung out with in New York. It seemed he was going to have an interesting life as a journalist. He managed to be normal without being boring. At least he knew what he wanted to do when he grew up. I was sort of in a panic, because I was almost a senior and still didn't know. I most emphatically did not want to go to secretarial school, as had been suggested to me, in order to get a job. And I didn't want to teach. I'd toyed with the idea of going to graduate school, but I wasn't sure I was suited to academic life. But Michael saved me from my dilemma, because we fell in love; and almost from the beginning, we talked about getting married.

For my advanced philosophy seminar with Mrs. Stavrides, I did a report on *The Second Sex,* by Simone de Beauvoir. The book had stirred powerful feelings in me. De Beauvoir talked about so many things that I had thought myself about growing up female and at odds with what was expected of women in our society. I'd never read anything like it. I worked hard on my report. In my verbal presentation, I tried to convey my enthusiasm about de Beauvoir's concepts to the class, which was mostly juniors and seniors. To my surprise their response was overwhelmingly negative. "I think the most creative thing a woman can do is be a wife and mother," said one girl, and others agreed with her. "What's wrong with getting married?" asked another. "Bringing up children is very fulfilling work." "Hmph," said Mrs. Stavrides, "any fool can produce children." But she and I were clearly in the minority on this issue. Debbie and I had often joked that the purpose of a Vassar education was to be able to make interesting small talk at cocktail parties, but this class seemed to prove it was no joke at all. Anyway, who was I to talk? I'd already decided to marry Michael Lydon in the hope that marriage would solve my own "What am I going to do after college?" crisis.

Since Michael only had the car for a little while longer, we decided to take a trip to Canada at the end of the school year. I was missing my final exam in Italian, but I hadn't learned Italian anyway. We went with two of his friends from Yale. I insisted we stop at Marlboro College in Vermont, where I got some marijuana from my friend Joe Raskin, a folkie musician from Brooklyn who had once played banjo with a famous bluegrass band. I didn't know why, but something about getting the dope really bothered me. I was coming down from all the speed I had taken for finals, and didn't feel good about taking more drugs. It didn't fit in with the new life I had planned for myself. When we got close to the Canadian border, I threw the pot away. I'd decided that Michael Lydon was also going to save me from being a drug addict.

It was Freedom Summer in Mississippi. As much as I'd ever wanted anything, I wanted to go South and register voters. But I couldn't. It cost over a thousand dollars to participate, which I didn't have, and I needed to work over the summer to pay for school, especially since I'd lost my scholarship. Michael had convinced the *Boston Globe,* where his brother Christopher was a reporter, to let him go to Mississippi as a stringer. I was staying home on Long Island. I had two waitress jobs and was taking Italian in summer school.

The first week Michael was in Mississippi, three civil rights workers disappeared. Michael stood on a bridge over the swamp they were dredging for the bodies of the men. Rednecks hung around on the bridge watching the searchers, grousing and cracking jokes. "They'll never find those damn bodies," one of them told Michael. "They got mosquitoes in that swamp so big they could stand flat-foot and fuck a turkey." It was a tragic situation, but the *Boston Globe* was ecstatic that they had their own reporter on the scene filing stories. It was great for

Michael's career, a feather in his cap. Older hands like David Halberstam and Nicholas Von Hoffman adopted Michael as "the kid" and took him with them everywhere they went.

I juggled my two waitress jobs and summer school and wrote Michael long, searching letters about my emotional life. When he came home we talked about our plans to marry after graduation.

That fall I was rarely allowed off-campus. My favorite history teacher, Mr. Charles Griffin, got me a Ford Foundation grant to do original research for my senior thesis at the Roosevelt Library in Hyde Park. I read FDR's press conferences from typed transcripts; often I was alone on the magnificent estate overlooking the Hudson, with the trees in full autumn splendor and fallen apples scenting the air. Weekends Michael came to visit, and we'd find places around Poughkeepsie to have dates. By now I had a large group of friends and was comfortable with the routine of school. I felt secure knowing that I would be getting married after graduation; it took some of the pressure off having to figure out what to do with the rest of my life.

During final exams I took my usual megadoses of diet pills. I was going to stay with Michael in an apartment in New Haven over the winter break. I had been looking forward to it, but something was troubling me; I suspected I might be pregnant. Michael and I wanted to go to Europe after graduation. He had applied for a Clare fellowship to study at Cambridge. I'd thought of applying for a fellowship to do historical research, and I was working on my senior thesis about FDR's relations with the press. During the long intercession, I went down to New York and had Peter Mitchell, who worked in a lab at Bellevue, run a pregnancy test on me. He called me at my parents' with the results. "Hi, Mom," he said.

I was crying when I told my mother. "Don't cry, honey," she said. "Having a baby is a wonderful thing." I felt terrifically supported by her reaction. Michael said not to worry; we could just get married sooner. He had decided to turn down the Clare fellowship anyway, because you couldn't be married and have it. He came down to New York and told my father that we wanted to get married. My father looked at him with puzzled incomprehension. "What do you want to marry her for?" he asked. I felt rotten when I heard it. Then we drove to Boston to tell his family. At the news that we were getting married, his mother turned dead white and sank into a chair.

I had to see the warden at school for permission to marry. It was decided that I could take most of my classes at Yale and commute to Vassar for my senior seminar. Since Yale had not yet formally admitted women as undergraduates, my classes as the wife of a student would be unofficial, ungraded, and free. My closest friends at Vassar knew I was pregnant, but I kept it a secret from my teachers and the college administration. My friends gave me a wedding shower at Alumnae House. I asked for things like demitasse cups and spoons. I was living in a fantasy world; I'd imagined grownup married life as involving some kind of genteel entertaining that had never been part of my own reality.

We got married in Long Beach by a justice of the peace on a bitterly cold day at the end of January. I wore an orange two-piece wool dress. Since I was marrying a Catholic, my father refused to attend the ceremony, and instead went to work that day. It didn't really surprise me, as he'd disapproved of the marriage all along. A few months later, once the shock had passed and he'd accepted it, he was extremely kind and generous to us.

My friend from Vassar, Genie Edelman, and her soon-to-be-husband, Duncan McNaughton, were there. Icy winds tore into us as we dashed across the street, with a few family members, to the courthouse. The justice of the peace wiped mustard off his face from his recent lunch and said, "It's nice to see so many people here. Usually people who come to me have to get married." Everyone swallowed hard. Lorraine came rushing down the hall toward the ceremony, her long hair flying out behind her, the baby, my niece Maggie, bobbing up and down in her backpack. At the sight of Lorraine, clearly a teenager, and the baby, Mrs. Lydon again turned pale. During the ceremony Maggie threw up. I felt sort of nauseated myself; my morning sickness had already begun. The justice of the peace stated the traditional vows, "Till death do you part," and Michael and I repeated them. I said the words out loud, "I do," but I wasn't wholeheartedly sure. In my mind I was thinking, "If it doesn't work out, I can always get a divorce."

```
                                         Unreal City,
                      Under the brown fog of a winter dawn,
                  A crowd flowed over London Bridge, so many,
                  I had not thought death had undone so many.

                                                     T. S. Eliot,
                                                 "The Waste Land"
```

LONDON BRIDGE IS FALLING DOWN—1965

When I awoke in the hospital, the room was bathed in unearthly golden light, and Michael sat next to the bed, holding my hand. "Everything's going to be all right," I whispered, beatific. I was filled with deep peace and a sense of well-being so profound it could almost have been described as bliss. The atmosphere around me seemed suffused with grace, and I had never felt so calm in all my life.

The baby was dead; she was stillborn. Though I was seven-and-a-half months pregnant when my water broke, the doctors told me the baby had been dead for several months in utero. We were in London, where we had moved after graduating from college. Michael had a job in the London bureau of *Newsweek* magazine. I planned to wheel my baby carriage around the parks and get to know the city. We were staying in a small furnished room in Notting Hill Gate until we could get our own place. As I stepped out of the bathtub one night, I felt something give way inside me, and blood-tinged water gushed down my legs. I laid down in bed while a kindly neighbor called a cab and told the driver to take us to St. Mary's in Paddington, the same hospital where penicillin had been discovered.

I was in labor by the time we got to the hospital, in terrible pain and so scared I was crying. The nurses told me not to worry, they would try to save the baby. In a teary blur, I was wheeled to X-ray, then taken to a room, where they came and broke the news to me that the baby was dead. The sister, as they called the English nurses, said I would still have to go through a normal labor and delivery. By this time hot bands of pain were tightening around my uterus, and the torment of labor, agony of loss, and terror of the impending birth all heaped together into a crushing misery. A kind, young medical student sat up with me and offered consolation, but like the biblical Rachel, I had lost my child and could not be comforted. Tears rolled down my face in a steady stream. Finally, when I was just about to deliver the baby, the sister came in and asked if I would mind having some of her students observe, as this was a teaching hospital and mine an abnormal case. Then she gave me a shot of morphine.

So the worst ordeal of my life had just ended, and yet I found myself in a state of near-ecstasy. This was my first experience with morphine, and the part of my brain in charge of accumulating pharmacological data stored this information away for future reference. It was a skewed equation: misery plus drugs equals happiness. Unfortunately my bliss was short-lived. As soon as the morphine wore off, my tears began again, and I wept constantly for the next ten days.

The sister told me that the baby, a girl, was deformed. "We don't know why these things happen," she said. I had read that the first twenty-eight days of pregnancy were crucial for fetal development and remembered that during that time, before I knew I was pregnant, I'd been consuming diet pills to study for final exams. I wondered if the speed I took had damaged the baby, then quickly pushed this thought out of my mind. I had also had a car accident early in my pregnancy. I was on my way to Poughkeepsie in the snow, driving too fast, and spun my Volkswagen out on a curve, ending up backed against a stone wall. The baby could have been hurt then, too, I told myself. But of course only drugs, or a genetic defect, would have made her deformed.

They kept me in the maternity ward, next to a nineteen-year-old Nigerian girl whose perfect baby girl had died a few days after birth. I heard her crying softly through the walls. I grieved for my baby violently; storms of tears would wrack my body and then subside, only to begin again at the next sad thought. Nick Bosanquet, a friend from Yale, came one day and stood shyly at the door to my room. He brought fresh straw-berries, plump and red, with thick Devon cream. In all the years since, I've never had the equal of those strawberries. The hospital food was awful: bland, tasteless, virtually inedible. At night the West Indian nurse brought around a large bucket and ladle, carrying dessert. "What is it?" I asked. "It's pink, dear; that's what it is," she tartly replied.

I had large, painful shots to suppress my milk. When I could concen-trate, I read *The Once and Future King,* T. H. White's retelling of the Arthurian legends, a wonderful book that was a great comfort to me, a blessed escape from pain. After ten days the hospital released me. Michael brought me back to our room at Notting Hill Gate. The sheets I had bloodied when my water broke were still on the bed. I became hys-terical and blamed Michael for not changing them, for being insensitive to how I would feel seeing the blood. He seemed mystified by my out-burst; he had ways of ignoring what he didn't care to see. The incident seared into my memory; I never quite forgave him for it.

Michael was working at *Newsweek,* and frequently was out of town; a few days after I got out of the hospital, he went to cover a golf tourna-ment in the West of England. As a young wife, I was insecure, and usu-ally jealous of whatever took his attention from me: his work or his family. I suppose we didn't think we had much choice; he had just started work and wanted to make a good impression, and we were short of money. I was too dispirited to show my anger or know that I needed him to stay. One of the huge differences between us, and a source of trouble throughout our marriage, was that Michael could shut off his emotions and get to work, while I was more or less ruled by mine. I felt emotion-ally as well as physically abandoned and learned, though it wouldn't be-come clear till later, that I couldn't count on my husband for support.

We had rented a flat in Highgate with an outside garden for the baby. We canceled that and took a bedsitter room on Weymouth Street, near Marylebone High Street. It was tiny, just one room with a single bed, lit by a depressing overhead light. I had nothing to do all day: no school, no friends, no family, no work, no hobbies in this strange, new country. And I was wildly depressed, crazed with grief about the baby. Now I realize it was partly a normal, hormonal, postpartum reaction, but at the time I thought I was losing my mind. I desperately wanted my mother to come, but she didn't. I never understood why until recently, when she told me that I had seemed as geographically remote from her then as my father had been when I was born. My sister Lorraine was in a dream-world, writing me letters about how lucky I was to have a glamorous life in London.

I hadn't been there long enough to make new friends, and my old ones seemed too distant and inaccessible to call on for help. On my own, I wandered around the city in a somnambulistic daze. I could empathize with the kind of craziness that would make a woman kidnap another's baby; I was sure mothers could tell, from the numb, hollow look in my eyes, that I was capable of such a desperate act. And there didn't seem any reason I should be hurting so bad. I hadn't changed my life to accommodate the pregnancy; I had finished school, written my thesis, moved to England. Yet I was completely devastated by the loss of a creature I had never even known outside my own body. Nothing in my previous experience had prepared me for this measure of grief. The words *miscarriage* or *stillborn,* so cool and detached, did not seem to warrant the shattering emptiness I felt inside, the shock and damage I had sustained. I had joined the walking wounded, and each day I faced my pain alone.

I had only been out of the hospital a short time when Bob Kaiser, another friend from Yale, whose father was in the Foreign Service, invited us to a party at the American ambassador's residence. It was an elegant affair, presided over by white-haired David Bruce and his regal wife, Evangeline, in a large, white Georgian mansion on the plush, green rolling lawns of Regents' Park. Among the prominent guests, I recognized Adlai Stevenson, the distinguished statesman whom my leftie friends and I had admired. I even remembered his presidential campaign song (sung to the tune of "My Heart Belongs to Daddy"): "Ike's teeing off a game of golf, and Nixon is caddying madly / They're up on holes but down at the polls / 'Cause our hearts belong to Adlai." I watched him mingle in the crowd, too intimidated to speak with him. "Another time," I told myself. But the next day Stevenson collapsed suddenly on the sidewalk outside the American Embassy in Grosvenor Square, and died in the arms of his old friend Marietta Tree. Again I felt death hovering nearby, close enough to touch, while I watched without knowing. I was frightened; I no longer felt safe; day by day I could feel the ground slipping out from under my feet.

I also had doubts about my marriage. Michael, though I'm sure he felt his own sorrow, seemed unable to comprehend my grief over the baby and appeared oblivious to my deteriorating condition. He went about his *Newsweek* business as though nothing untoward had happened, while I gradually stopped cooking, cleaning, shopping, or functioning on any kind of normal level. I was desperately trying to get his attention, to signal that something was terribly wrong, and the more he ignored my cries for help, the more extreme they became. It was like an opposite version of *Gaslight;* I was falling to pieces, while the one person who knew me well enough to notice blithely pretended nothing was wrong. It occurs to me now that variations of this drama have been played out in countless male-female relationships; it had the effect of making me feel doubly crazy and isolated. One day I was wandering around the city by myself, in my usual numbed-out state, and tried to catch a bus. The lumbering red double-deckers slowed down near the stop; you were supposed to grab a pole and swing onto the platform. I grabbed the pole, then fell off the moving bus into the road. A stranger helped me up, then noticed the look in my eye. "What's wrong, luv?" she asked. I shook my head dumbly, unable to speak.

I began having nightmares. Death had touched me. If I couldn't feel secure about a baby inside my body, what could I be sure of? I dreamt that people I loved died suddenly for no reason. My nightmares became so frightening, I was scared to go to sleep at night. Once, in a waking vision, I looked at Michael's face and saw all the skin peel off, exposing the skeleton skull underneath. I couldn't bear the thought of sex; it reminded me of death. One night I dreamt I was waiting for a bus. My mother came and told me she had terminal stomach cancer and was going to die. I woke up sobbing uncontrollably. I was inconsolable; I wondered if I was having a nervous breakdown. Michael took me to the local clinic, where they diagnosed my problem as "acute homesickness" and gave me a psychiatric appointment two months away. Hours had gone by, and I still couldn't stop crying. Shew Hagerty, the *Newsweek* bureau chief, recommended an English doctor in Belgravia. The doctor's wife, Shew said, had just given birth to a stillborn baby; he would understand what I was going through.

Dr. Alistair Gordon was tall, thin, youngish, and upper class, dressed in an impeccably tailored and fitted black three-piece suit. He was a kind and sympathetic man. When I told him my story, tears welled up in his eyes, and he confirmed that the same thing had happened to his wife. He prescribed sleeping pills for me, so I wouldn't be afraid to lie down at night, and a kind of long-acting tranquilizer that in time would alter my brain chemistry and stop the depression.

Then he listened while I talked. Through the months I saw him, he acted as a combination doctor and psychiatrist; and from these visits and the pills he prescribed, I began to feel better. Much of my healing took place in a series of dreams I had, where I gradually acquired some mastery over my fear of death. I bought some woolly red tweed yarn at Jaeger and began knitting Michael a sweater. I read Dickens: the majestically somber *Dombey and Son,* and *Pickwick Papers,* which made me laugh so hard I savored it a few pages at a time. Gradually I became more myself. When I took sleeping pills at night, I noticed an interval of time between when they first took effect and when they put me to sleep during which I felt positively euphoric. I sat up in a chair, fighting sleep, trying to make the euphoria last as long as possible. It felt almost as good as the morphine afterglow I had experienced in the hospital, but I was so groggy each morning that Michael had to prop me up in bed to drink the coffee he'd bring me before I'd wake up.

During this time I decided that never again would I put my faith in another emotional attachment. I would pursue the cold, clear life of the intellect, I imagined, envisioning some hard, bright scholarly work I could continue to do into old age, work that would sustain me when people I loved disappointed me, left, died, changed, or moved away. I would wall off my broken heart, protect my inmost self from the terrible vulnerability of human love. Inside my mind I'd construct a safe place where I could control what happened. Never again would I be caught so unawares, so blindly unprepared. Casting about for something to do, I determined to try my hand at writing. In my lifelong love of books, I had deified writers as a rarefied breed whose Olympian feats were unattainable by ordinary mortals like me. But Michael had demystified this image for me. I knew that if he could write, I could too; I was at least as smart as he was. I had to do something with my life; it might as well be something I valued. So I gave up on emotions and found my life's work. In this way the baby's death transformed me—for the bad and for the good.

It was 1965, the era of "Swinging London." Women dressed in white Courrèges go-go boots and micro-miniskirts. "Satisfaction" blared from the loudspeakers of every boutique along the King's Road. The English sound took over the airwaves: the Hollies, Herman's Hermits, Spencer Davis, Jeff Beck, and of course the Beatles and Rolling Stones. English style set trends throughout the fickle world of fashion. That year London was the happening scene.

Beneath all this surface glamour, however, I found England somewhat dreary and depressing. On the underground people all looked alike, ethnically similar, except for discernible physical differences between the classes. Upper-class people grew a good deal taller and had markedly better teeth, as John Osborne had noted bitterly in *Look Back in Anger*. Compared to America, England seemed a decaying culture, lacking in vitality. In the States the antiwar movement was getting underway; students on every campus were becoming radicalized; and I felt I was literally dying without the infusion of American vitality I had always taken for granted. A mean-spirited wartime rationing mentality lingered on in London; an atmosphere of scarcity overshadowed all the new rock star, model girl, magazine glitz, and far more accurately expressed the country's real economic condition. It was difficult to make friends there, and despite the ordinary supposition of a common language, the two cultures were in fact so different that no one understood my sense of humor or I theirs. The constant damp seeped into my bones and stayed; I pumped shillings into the gas meter, but our primitive heating system did little to drive the chill away. At the age of twenty-two, I found myself with rheumatism, a constant aching in my joints. And to top it off, I was looking for a job.

British salaries were shockingly low. Through Nick Bosanquet's connections, I was offered a job at the Labour Party as an office junior, running errands and fetching tea for about twenty-five dollars a week. Prospective employers told me that four years of college had put me behind most people my age in work experience. I was also hampered in my efforts by a total loss of confidence. Constantly fearful and shaken to my core, I was no longer sure who I was, and lacked the ability to present myself in a positive light. I felt deep shame about losing the baby, as though it had confirmed my inherent defectiveness, and was shamed as well by my physical vulnerability and the depths of my grief. This lack of self-assurance went hand in hand with the desolation and loneliness I felt. My everyday life, like the weather, looked cold and bleak. And then I had an extraordinary stroke of luck. A college friend called and asked me to have a drink with her and her then-current beau, an American journalist working in London.

Jon Bradshaw was a fabulous character: blond, balding, handsome, dashing, a latter-day Hemingway. He knew everyone who was anyone in London publishing circles, and for some reason, which baffles me to this day, took me under his wing and made it his business to help me find a job. One by one he sent me to all the editors he knew to apply for work as a writer. After each unsuccessful interview, I reported back to him. We sat on chintz-covered easy chairs before the cozy gas fire in his Chelsea garden flat, drinking tea, and he coached me on how to embellish my fictional history as an American journalist ("The bloody British are so polite, they'll never ask you for clips or proof," he assured me) until my made-up resume was so impressive that a newspaper or magazine would have been foolish not to hire me. At first I felt peculiar telling these lies. Then I had an interview with an American editor who I was certain would know I was lying. I recited my Bradshaw-embroidered history, including the preposterous falsehood that I had worked as the Poughkeepsie stringer for the *New York Times*. He asked me what I wrote for the *Times*, and I made up a story on the spot. "Oh, yes," he said, "I read that. Good job you did on that story." After that I went for broke.

My months of trudging around finally paid off when I got a job on a magazine called *London Life*, the newly refurbished *Tatler*, at quite a good salary. Considering my past experience (!), they felt lucky to get me at such a bargain rate. I was elated. Michael and I decided to take a vacation in Paris before I started work, and I felt so good there I stopped taking my sleeping pills and tranquilizers.

By British standards Michael and I earned good money; and aside from paying back our college loans, we had very few expenses. I loved to shop and dressed us both very well. We moved to a one-bedroom apartment on Sydney Street in Chelsea, which I stuffed with as much Habitat kitchenware and furniture as would fit in the little flat. We had people to dinner; I prepared complicated recipes from *The New York Times Cookbook*. I was trying to live up to my image of a real grownup.

I liked my job. After a somewhat shaky start—I had interviewed Peter Ustinov about a new film he'd directed and taken him at his word without seeing the movie, an unqualified dud—I had an easy time with the reporting and writing. I wrote about Alfred Hitchcock, the National Theatre, Americans in London, five generations of graduates of a women's college, a lithograph factory in Manchester, strippers, Playboy bunnies, art shows—the interesting, varied beat of a general interest feature reporter. It wasn't literature, but it was exciting and fun. By this time Michael and I had an eclectic group of friends from both the British and American press corps and were beginning to feel at home. For a while life seemed almost normal. But it didn't last long.

Michael got sick on a trip we took to Ireland. He began feeling ill on the plane. I was finishing up a story for *London Life* on the painter Jean Dubuffet, which I had to cable back the minute we landed in Dublin, so I wasn't paying much attention to him. We'd been looking forward to the trip for a long time. Michael was finally going to explore his Irish roots, and I wanted to steep myself in the literary atmosphere of O'Casey, Joyce, and Yeats. Stepping off the plane in Dublin, I was struck by the pristine smell of the air, noticeably different from the diesel fumes and industrial reek of London. We were excited to be in Ireland at last. But on our first day there, Michael felt so sick that he flew home to London. I stayed in Dublin for three days by myself, walking on St. Stephen's Green, visiting James Joyce's lighthouse, driving out to the country in the rain to see the fabled emerald landscape, and worrying about my husband. Finally he called with the doctor's diagnosis: he had contracted viral hepatitis.

Michael turned a lurid shade of mustard yellow from the tips of his toes to the whites of his eyes, and proceeded to lose fifteen pounds from his already gaunt frame. I cared for him at home for a month; then he was taken to the hospital on Grays Inn Road and put in the care of a funny, little brisk English woman named Sheila Sherlock, reputed to be the world's foremost liver specialist. Michael's case of hepatitis was severe and life-threatening, and it was months before we saw any improvement. *Newsweek* continued to pay his full salary. I was still working at my job, doing freelance articles here and there, and running back and forth to the hospital, living on dry biscuits and containers of yogurt, my nerves frayed to the point of exhaustion. Shew Hagerty suggested we go home to America for the summer, so Michael could recuperate from his illness. Though it was a beautiful spring in London, with bright yellow daffodils bursting out all over Kensington Gardens and sunny, balmy days relieving the usual monotony of rain, we welcomed the chance to go home. Both of us had been through hell in our first year abroad.

My whole family came to meet us at the airport. I noticed that Lorraine was very pale, her chalky-white complexion set off by the black dress she wore. As we walked away from customs, she pulled me off to the side and lifted up her sleeve. The inside crook of her arm was dotted with tiny pinpricks covered with scabs and surrounded by bruised, discolored flesh. "Don't tell Mommy," she whispered. "Promise me you won't tell." Lorraine had long since left Bobby. Now she lived in an apartment on Grand Street on the Lower East Side. Maggie was two. She called us "SusieMichael"; the concept of "and" had not yet entered her vocabulary.

When we reached our parents' house, Lorraine and I went off to our old bedroom and she told me she was shooting heroin. I felt a shiver of fear at the very sound of the word: heroin. I was appalled at the thought of my sister as a junkie, and angry that she had dumped this problem in my lap after the year I'd just been through. It felt like an old pattern between us: no matter what kind of problems I had, Lorraine's were always more pressing. And I was also scared. Like most people who've never shot drugs, I had a horror of the needle. And heroin was a drug people died from. "Not my sister," I thought in a panic, "I just couldn't bear it." As the eldest in the family, I'd always felt responsible for protecting my younger siblings. Lorraine seemed particularly vulnerable; she had a Pollyanna innocence she managed to retain no matter what happened, and had been blindly wandering into bad situations from which I'd tried to rescue her for years, another of our patterns.

In the Twelve-Step programs, we have a saying, "Scratch an addict, find a codependent." I didn't have a clue what to do, but somehow decided I would handle this crisis alone and singlehandedly save my sister from drugs. Ironically, in view of what later happened, heroin addiction was so outside my reality that I could barely comprehend what it meant, much less find a way to deal with it. I didn't know anything about detox, rehabs, treatment centers, Twelve-Step meetings, or interventions—if indeed they even existed then, in 1966; as late as 1981, there were only twelve Narcotics Anonymous meetings in all of Manhattan.

Not knowing what else to do, I imagined I could talk some sense into Lorraine, threaten, wheedle, and cajole until she came to see the error of her ways and the wisdom of mine. I couldn't understand why my sister would want to throw her life away on such dead-end self-destruction. That's how innocent I was about drugs at the time, and how little I knew of myself. I was young and ambitious, intoxicated by the world and the small measure of success I'd achieved in it so far. Though I'd suffered with the baby's death, I hadn't yet encountered my own inner demons, and so I failed to understand what was happening to my sister. Later on, when I fell prey to heroin addiction, my mother, who wanted desperately to help me, would feel similarly hamstrung by her ignorance of the drug world, helpless against an evil so far beyond the realms of her own experience. And Lorraine would turn out to be the one who knew what to do.

At least now I understood why Lorraine had acted so peculiarly during the few days she visited us in London. She had arrived with such bad body odor that I drew her a bath as soon as we got to my flat. The inside of her suitcase smelled like cats had been peeing there for months. She was nervous and disoriented; at night she couldn't sleep. She begged me to give her some of my sleeping pills. Her face was covered with scabs, where she had scratched the skin off. Now she told me she'd been shooting speed before she came to London. Since then she had graduated to heroin. Jeremy, Tamara's ex-husband, had turned her on to it, and she was strung out pretty bad. Maris had introduced us to Jeremy and Tamara when I was in college. They were the first junkies I ever met.

I didn't tell my mother, but while Michael was visiting his family in Boston, I went to the city and stayed over in Lorraine's apartment. Tamara was there: drug-free, noticeably pregnant, and angry. She'd just broken up with the father of the baby. "These men," she said, "you try to talk to them, and they quote you a line of Bob Dylan." When I stayed at Lorraine's, I could hardly get any sleep. All night long the fire engine sirens howled as Lower East Side landlords torched their buildings for insurance money, attempting to salvage something from their invest-ments before the city redlined the decaying neighborhood. Years later I'd shoot dope in what remained of some of the same buildings that burned down that summer. Along with the sirens' wail, Spanish music drifted in from radios playing in open windows. At three and four o'clock in the morning, the doorbell rang, and people talked loudly in the living room. Every night there was a crisis: someone OD'd and had to be taken to the hospital; others got busted and their kids were left alone in the apartment and needed a babysitter. Tamara told me that sometimes Lorraine went into the bathroom and stayed for a long time, while Maggie banged on the door outside, begging her mother to come out. It was depressing and chaotic at Lorraine's, and there didn't seem to be much I could do to help.

In the fall Michael and I went back to England. Michael had a full month's paid vacation coming, and we planned to spend it exploring France. We now saw ourselves as professional journalists, sophisticated grownups, cosmopolitan citizens of the world. We were young, upwardly mobile, in the first flush of success. My life felt as different from my sis-ter's as night from day. I had failed this time to rescue Lorraine. At the end of the summer, when we returned to London, nothing had changed; and my mother, though she might have suspected something amiss, still didn't really know what was happening.

We had a wonderful vacation in France and a comfortable life back in London. *London Life* had folded, but I got lots of freelance assignments and would soon be offered a position as the London art critic for the *International Herald Tribune*. I was beginning to feel I could settle down and live in London for a long time. I had almost forgotten that during my depression the previous winter, I'd decided I wanted to study creative writing in graduate school and had convinced Michael to apply for a transfer to San Francisco. I wanted to go to San Francisco State to study with Mark Harris, my favorite writer; I loved the easygoing vernacular style of his baseball novels, *The Southpaw* and *Bang the Drum Slowly*.

Newsweek considered it an insane request; no one ever asked to be assigned to the San Francisco bureau; very little that was newsworthy happened in that pretty but sleepy little town. By now I had changed my mind; but the *Newsweek* machinery had been grinding away, and soon Michael's transfer came through. He was scheduled to start work in San Francisco in January.

One morning at about three o'clock, my mother called, furious. "Why didn't you tell me Lorraine was doing drugs?" she demanded. "She begged me not to tell you," I said. "We thought it would hurt you too much to know. I was going to handle it myself." It turned out that a few nights before, Lorraine had tried to kill herself by taking an overdose of Valium. Jeremy had OD'd in her apartment; Maggie found him on the couch and couldn't wake him up; Tamara had given her baby up for adoption. It all got to be too much for Lorraine, and she took a bunch of pills. My mother took her to Bellevue to have her stomach pumped. Then she took Maggie home to live with her. Jeremy, who survived, had joined the Hare Krishnas; they recruited him out of the Bellevue psych ward, which probably happened a lot in those days. Lorraine was going into therapy. She was angry with my mother for having her stomach pumped, and my mother was mad at me for not telling her what was happening. "Ma," I said, "It's three o'clock in the morning here; I'm asleep." For as long as I've known her, my mother has never paid attention to time zones. "Well," she said, " I hope I scared your sister enough that she'll never go back to drugs. But what if Lorraine had died? You would have been partly responsible. She said you knew everything." When we hung up the phone, I went back to sleep. I felt sort of relieved; at least my sister and Maggie were alive.

At Christmas we flew back to Boston. Movers had come and packed up our London apartment. We had Christmas with Michael's family, who made numerous unflattering comments about the length of his hair, and then went down to New York. We visited Maris and Susan on the Lower East Side. My old friend Alan Tobias came over with a new record: *Electric Music for the Mind and Body,* by Country Joe and the Fish. He said they were a San Francisco group, part of a whole new music scene that was happening there. It was strange music, spacey, otherworldly, with cryptic lyrics like Bob Dylan's. The band looked as though they were dressed up for a costume party; one wore a wizard's tall hat, and Country

Joe himself sported a gunbelt across his naked chest; he looked like a Mexican bandito, Pancho Villa come back to life.

We flew to San Francisco and arrived the first day of the new year, 1967. It was January, but the sun shone brilliantly. I was in culture shock, accustomed to the constant gray drizzle of London. Michael replaced Rick Hertzberg (later of *The New Yorker* and the *New Republic*) in the San Francisco bureau. *Newsweek* threw a going-away party for Rick and a welcome party for us. A cross-section of local characters showed up: scruffy Bill Graham, who lived in an apartment above the Fillmore Auditorium with his girlfriend, Bonnie; Eldridge Cleaver, the black ex-convict who'd just been released from prison, with Beverly Axelrad, the lawyer who'd gotten him out; Paul Jacobs, the radical journalist, and his lawyer wife, Ruth. *Newsweek* had put us up in a hotel. At the party Ruth Jacobs and I discovered we had both gone to P.S. 48 in the Bronx, and she asked if we would house-sit while they vacationed in Hawaii. So we moved into the Jacobs's large, beautiful house in Pacific Heights, with its stained-glass windows and spectacular view of the Bay.

I registered at San Francisco State. Unfortunately I had neglected to ask who was teaching in the writing program. Mark Harris, it turned out, was somewhere else, and Herbert Gold, a local novelist, taught my writing class instead; it was a disappointing experience. I did take a thoroughly delightful course in American Jewish literature, taught by Wallace Markfield. He was working on a novel, *Teitelbaum's Window,* and read us a chapter in class: a scene in a deli where elderly people complain about the younger generation with the refrain, "Today's kids. The kids of today." All the dialogue was a mixture of English and Yiddish, like the line: "As God said to the Wergin Mary when she said she wanted a girl, 'Nicht bashert [it wasn't meant to be].'" It was nostalgic, funny, and resonated with authenticity; Mama Yetta could easily have stepped from its pages.

A week after we arrived in San Francisco, the Human Be-In happened in Golden Gate Park. It was a glorious, sunny day. The park looked lush and green under a brilliant blue sky. Up on the stage, a shaggy, bearded Allen

Ginsberg chanted "Hare Krishna" and danced around in filmy white Indian pajamas, banging on a tambourine. Timothy Leary exhorted the crowd to "Turn on, tune in, and drop out." Michael McClure read a poem in beast language, all grunts and growls. A band called Quicksilver Messenger Service played a spirited rock and roll set. Someone read a passage from *The Tibetan Book of the Dead* to introduce another band, the Grateful Dead, who performed long, spacey, feedback-laden instrumentals and down-home country tunes.

In what was to become a familiar scene, long-haired boys and barefoot girls dressed in headbands, long skirts, old marching band uniforms festooned with braid, strings of rainbow-colored beads, and outfits fashioned from old lace tablecloths and velvet curtains, swayed unrhythmically, weaving their arms and legs in a private dance to silent music they seemed to hear inside their heads. Their eyes focused inward and burned with a kind of ecstatic intensity. The pungent smell of marijuana hung in the air, mixed with smoky patchouli oil and sandalwood incense from the stage. Brightly colored tie-dyed banners rippled in the breeze. Here and there a man walked through the crowd, offering "Lids, acid, speed." It was a feast for the senses, a colorful, noisy, anarchic celebration of life.

I watched the whole spectacle with journalistic detachment, but deep inside I felt a tug. These were my old cohorts from New York hippie days: the lunatic fringe. What was I doing in this audience dressed so plainly in a turtleneck and jeans, drug-free, standing still, observing as though I were researching a story? What had happened to the wild girl I used to be? How did I end up like this, married, with a career, staying in Pacific Heights? I couldn't even remember the last time I'd smoked a joint; maybe several years ago by now. I looked at Michael. His eyes were all lit up, journalistic antennae vibrating with pleasure at being in the right place at the right time for the hottest cultural story of the decade. I felt an invisible distance open between us. I imagined his pleasure was total, unsullied by regret. Events would prove I was wrong; drastic changes in Michael's life, as in mine, began to unfold from this moment in time. I later learned that he had similar thoughts about me, felt the same invisible gulf. But I didn't know, and believed this was all new to him; while for me it was a reminder of a life I had once known, an old intensity and freedom I had nearly forgotten and now suddenly craved. So

I stood there in the midst of this carnival of sunshine, people, color, light, and sound, feeling my whole life, all the things I'd been so proud of before, turn to ashes in my mouth. I was wondering if I'd made some terrible mistake and ended up somehow on the wrong side of the line.

chapter six

> Now if you're tired or a bit run down
> Can't seem to get your feet off the ground
> Maybe you oughtta try a little bit of LSD
> Eat flowers and kiss babies . . . LSD . . .
> for you and me.
>
> Country Joe and the Fish,
> "The Acid Commercial"

IF IT FEELS GOOD, DO IT—1967

The Summer of Love, as it came to be called, was an all-out media circus. Charter buses rolled through the Haight-Ashbury so camera-toting tourists could gawk at the hippies; and Joan Didion, one of the few reporters to recognize the apocalyptic edge that underlay what looked like a huge party in perpetual progress, wrote her celebrated essay "Slouching Toward Bethlehem." The mood was definitely "Eat, drink, and be merry, for tomorrow we die." Though it was an era of unprecedented prosperity, hippies viewed the future with an odd mixture of hope and despair.

I was part of the media and watched from a distance, a little too old and entrenched in my ambitions to turn on, tune in, and drop out to become a runaway flower child in the Haight-Ashbury. Michael and I lived on Telegraph Hill in an airy, spacious flat we found after months of looking. It was expensive but worth it, a real home. We were still fairly conventional, but the veneer had started to crack, and an attitude of hippie decay was seeping in through the chinks. Occasionally we smoked pot, and our values and view of life, in the language of the times, were "going through changes."

I quit graduate school because I was bored, having already become accustomed to writing professionally and seeing my work in print. Michael grew increasingly dissatisfied with *Newsweek*. He was too stylish a writer not to have his stories bylined; frequently his critical reporting points were lost in the New York rewrites; and more and more he found himself taking sides with his subjects rather than maintaining the dispassionate and somewhat snide reportorial stance the job required. His long hair was a constant thorn in the side of the *Newsweek* brass, and on one occasion his bureau chief, the crusty Bill Flynn, gave him both the money and the dictum to go get a haircut or else.

I managed to put together a little freelance work, writing query letters and doing assignments here and there for some London and New York publications. Locally I had my best luck with a little paper called *Sunday Ramparts*, started by *Ramparts* magazine to fill the gap during a local newspaper strike. *Ramparts* was a formerly Catholic journal that had undergone a metamorphosis into the leading radical magazine of the day, with tremendous credibility among the New Left; *Sunday Ramparts*, though small, partook of its cachet. The arts page was edited by a guy named Jann Wenner. He was young, brash, and a little on the pompous side, but I was grateful for the work he gave me. For my first assignment, I reviewed a Paul Klee show. Then I wrote a piece on *The Beard*, Michael McClure's play about a romantic encounter between Jean Harlow and Billy the Kid in heaven, a meticulously crafted and lyrical work that garnered a great deal of notoriety by being regularly busted, like Lenny Bruce, for public obscenity. The language and conception of the play so impressed Michael and me that we ended up becoming friends with the author and his family.

In an effort to wean himself from *Newsweek,* Michael took on some freelance assignments. His story for *Esquire* on the underground press was widely read and impressed a lot of people, including Jann Wenner, who tried to engage Michael in conversation when we ran into him one day. "I can't stand that guy," Michael said later. "Well, be nice to him anyway," I said. "He gives me work." Michael had everything Jann wanted: journalistic legitimacy and a hip cultural beat. Though we had moved to the city for other reasons, the explosive cultural transformation taking place in San Francisco was the story of the decade, and we felt privileged to be on the scene.

Michael and I went to shows and parties at the Fillmore Auditorium and the Avalon and Carousel ballrooms, and wrote about the local bands. At the time there were only a handful of journalists writing seriously about rock music, including Richard Goldstein, Bob Christgau, and Ellen Willis on the East Coast, and Michael and me on the West, and we all knew one another's work. Greil Marcus, a fine writer and later a good friend of mine, became the resident rock critic of Marvin Garson's *San Francisco Express-Times,* in my opinion the best of the underground newspapers. All of us still work in journalism, though not necessarily covering music, and today virtually every newspaper in the country has a rock critic on its staff.

In April our friends F. J. and Nancy Bardacke came to dinner bursting with news: Nancy was pregnant. She spilled over with enthusiasm and information about her pregnancy; she planned to have natural childbirth by the Lamaze method, and was already talking to the La Leche League about breastfeeding. I was happy for Nancy but also felt a pang of heartache; never again could I approach pregnancy with her kind of innocence and optimism. After they left, Michael and I talked about the possibility of having another child and decided to wait a few more months.

The Monterey Pop Festival was in June. Michael covered it for *Newsweek;* we had seats in the press section, up front with the performers, and a room at the Highlands Inn in Carmel, a picturesque honeymoon hotel loaded with genteel charm. I believe it was on our first day there that we conceived our daughter, Shuna. Once the festival started, our room became home to a motley assortment of characters, all of whom camped out on our floor and appeared with us each morning in the dining room for breakfast, to the horror of the management. Michael McClure stayed there, along with our friends from LA: Harry Shearer and Terry Gilliam, who'd developed a running comedy patter writing ads together for Anderson Soups; and Glenys Roberts, an English journalist who looked like Julie Christie and had become one of my closest friends. Glenys lived with Terry in Laurel Canyon. Years later he followed her to London and fell in with Monty Python's Flying Circus, which became his springboard to fame. This was a wild and funny crew, and we spent much of our time together convulsed with laughter.

In Monterey we ran into Jann Wenner. He told us he was thinking of starting a rock and roll newspaper. *Sunday Ramparts* had folded, and the printers had offered him free office space if he would start a paper to replace it. Back in San Francisco, we met at Enrico's, an outdoor cafe on Broadway, to discuss it. Jann wanted to call the paper *Rolling Stone;* he intended it to be professional journalism, not a part of the underground press. His ambition, he told us, was to become "the Henry Luce of the counterculture." Michael, with his *Newsweek* credentials and rock and roll connections, personified the style he was after, and Jann offered him the job of assistant editor, second-in-command to him. I felt left out, especially since I was the one who'd been writing for him, but decided to stay out of the whole affair. Then Jann asked me, "What do you do all day, Susan?" In 1967 this was a killer question for women, one that demanded we justify our existence or admit to lying around in bed eating bonbons all day. "Why?" I asked, instantly on guard. "We'll be needing someone to type the address labels to mail out the dummies," he said. "Go fuck yourself, Jann," I suggested. "I'm a writer, not a typist."

So Michael and Jann typed the address labels themselves, with a great deal of fanfare about how noble they were and how childish I was to consider such work humiliating and beneath me. They could afford to be cavalier about it, I thought. They hadn't had to struggle for professional legitimacy the way I had; no one had expected them to go to secretarial school after college so they could find themselves a job. I thought about my friend Lynn Povich, who'd graduated from Vassar with me, working as a secretary in the Paris bureau of *Newsweek*, while Michael worked as a reporter in London. Without knowing what to call it, I'd been fighting against paternalism and male chauvinism ever since I started working in journalism. So I thought I'd stay out of this one. But as *Rolling Stone* got rolling, there were so few people involved in its startup that I ended up working as an editor, staff writer, and production manager to boot.

I have to admit that I wasn't terribly impressed by the concept of the paper. I thought we'd probably put out a few issues and then quit out of boredom. How many stories could you run about bands breaking up and getting busted for drugs? Nonetheless we all worked hard on the startup. Officially I was supposed to be the movie critic. For the first issue, which came out in October 1967, I reviewed *The Graduate*. I also edited copy that came in from writers, rewrote stories from the English *Melody Maker*, worked with the typesetters, and fiddled around with this and that. It was so hot in the Brannan Street building—the typesetters melted hot lead right next to our offices upstairs—that I sometimes worked in just my half-slip pulled up over my bra. It was early in my pregnancy, and I was sick a lot. The only way for me to avoid being sick was to eat regularly. Michael worked at *Newsweek* all day and came down to the office at night. Jann was maniacally driven, a natural speed freak; with or without drugs, I was never sure which, he always wanted to work around the clock. And to my great despair, he managed to involve Michael in most of his manic schemes, so that I had to be practically fainting or in tears before we could break for a meal.

I was sensitive to being treated as a second-class citizen, which Jann did naturally as a part of his temperament. On one occasion I was working with the typesetters out on the floor while Jann sat in the office. The phone rang. "Get the phone, Susan," Jann called out to me. "Why don't you get it?" I said. "You're sitting right next to it." "Oh," said Jann, "I think the phone should always be answered by a chick's voice, don't you?" Another time I used the first person in a movie review. Jann flew into a rage, ripped the story into pieces, and jumped up and down on them like a crazed Rumpelstiltskin, screaming about journalistic objectivity and how the first person had no place in a newspaper. Jann's unreasonable treatment of women extended to his girlfriend Jane, later his wife, a gifted artist who was barred from having any input in the graphic design of the paper.

I expected Michael to defend me from Jann's abuse, to offer some protection, solidarity, or at the very least understanding, but Jann appealed to Michael's ego—"Just us guys against these impossible women"—and enlisted him as a collaborator. I was pregnant and emotionally vulnerable, far too anxious about the baby's health to take drugs when I couldn't keep going, hampered by physical frailty. Often I had to fight both Jann and my husband to maintain a semblance of self-respect and dignity. Though I didn't know it at the time, this disheartening struggle marked the beginning of the end of my marriage. The bonds were unraveling; in my heart of hearts, I never forgave Michael for this betrayal, for collaborating with Jann in my continuing humiliation and oppression as a working woman.

By late October the paper was finished, and we all trooped downstairs, where the printing was done, to watch the first issue roll off the presses. Jann cracked open a bottle of champagne. It was an exciting moment. Our hard work had finally borne fruit, and all enmities were temporarily set aside while we celebrated our common victory. We didn't set the world on fire with *Rolling Stone,* but we did well enough to keep going. A few people came and joined our skeleton staff, and our work settled down into some kind of normal routine.

In November I felt the baby move inside me for the first time, which marked a dramatic difference from my previous pregnancy. Assured that the baby was alive, I started to relax, a feeling that settled, as the fifth month progressed, into a placid, unshakable contentment. Suddenly my brain wouldn't focus on the printed word. I stopped reading and started knitting. I passed blissful days making tiny sweaters and blankets for the baby, listening to the stereo as I knitted, playing the same two records over and over: Mozart's Piano Concerto No. 21, the theme for the movie *Elvira Madigan;* and Bob Dylan's *Highway 61 Revisited.*

I kept going in to work at *Rolling Stone,* but gradually there were more and more people to assume the different responsibilities, and all I had to do was write. I wasn't all that interested anyway; the everyday miracles of my pregnancy consumed me more. Barbara Garson was also pregnant, and she, Nancy Bardacke, and I compared notes on a regular basis. Toward the end of my pregnancy, Michael and I took Lamaze classes; I planned to have the baby by natural childbirth. Baron Wolman, the *Rolling Stone* staff photographer, did some portraits of Michael and me as proud expectant parents. My stomach was huge; in my seventh month of pregnancy, salesclerks begged me, "Please don't have your baby in my store."

My due date was past, and I was going crazy waiting for the baby, so I bought something that would totally absorb my attention: a fifteen-hundred-piece jigsaw puzzle, which I set up on the living room floor. I'd been working on it for weeks and was almost done when my labor finally started. It lasted nearly twenty-four hours. My cervix didn't dilate according to the plan they had given us in Lamaze classes, and I became so exhausted from the irregular contractions that the doctor gave me shots of Valium so I could rest between them. I was in such horrific pain I wanted to jump out the window. "Let's just go home," I said to Michael. "The baby seemed like a good idea at the time, but I'd just as soon forget about it now." During the transition stage, I lost my grip on sanity and asked Michael why he wasn't at work. Finally the baby crowned. I watched her emerge in the mirror rigged above the table, and at the moment of her birth, the pleasure of seeing my long-awaited child and the relief of having the pain finally stop converged into ecstasy that broke over me like a wave and lifted me into a kind of rapture.

Born on March 20, the vernal equinox, my baby girl was a beautiful, chubby little thing, over eight pounds. With her round red cheeks, almond eyes, and full head of straight black hair, she looked Tibetan. Thanks to my natural childbirth classes, I'd been totally awake to experience her arrival into the world. While the doctor was stitching up my episiotomy, I called my parents to tell them the news and reached my father. "Mazel tov!" he said, with hearty good humor. He found it hard to believe that I had just that minute had the baby. Then I rested. That night, when the baby was brought to me to nurse, I held her in my arms. The bedside lamp cast a small circle of light around us. She looked up at me with her eyes wide open, helpless and full of love. Looking into her eyes I saw clear into eternity and fell deeply, hopelessly, totally in love with this little being in a way that eclipsed any feeling I'd ever called "love." I called her Shuna, after my Uncle Sid, who had recently died, and the name of a fashion editor I'd known. I was intensely happy. I felt as though I'd just fulfilled my destiny. And in a way I had. I'd found my cosmic traveling companion; together we would embark on a lifelong journey.

Tamara, who had moved back to San Francisco, came to visit me in the hospital, bringing a tiny, pale green flowered dress for Shuna. My mother and Ricky came out and stayed with us for a week. My mother brought me a long string of luminous pearls, a gift from my father that moved me to tears. She cooked for me, took care of her new granddaughter while I rested and slept, and helped me through my postpartum blues, those weeping spells that would erupt suddenly as a result, I believe, of hormonal readjustment and endorphin withdrawal.

Shuna was an easy baby. Soon after her birth, she slept through the night. Awake from a nap, she would lie peacefully in her little bassinet, waiting for me to come and pick her up for a feeding. She rarely cried. I loved nursing her and reveled in our physical closeness. I lay on the couch with her nestled in my arm and felt a contentment I'd never touched before. I had knitted her a bright patchwork blanket out of different color yarns. One day I put her in her car bed and drove down to *Rolling Stone*. When we got to Brannan Street, I held Shuna to my chest, with her head resting on my shoulder, and covered her with the patchwork blanket. My heart was full to bursting with joy and pride as I showed her off to everyone in the office.

Michael was thrilled with our baby girl, and couldn't wait to get home from work each day to play with her or watch her sleep. Her birth had catalyzed his unhappiness with *Newsweek* into a determination to quit. "I want my daughter to be proud of me," he would say. "For her sake I have to be honest and live with integrity. How can I face her if I stay in a job I hate?" He was particularly galled by a telegram we had received from the New York office. "Congratulations," it read. "Trust baby's hair is longer than Dad's." He began pursuing freelance assignments more aggressively, and both of us talked about how we would manage when he left his job. *Rolling Stone* offered us plenty of work, but no income.

For the first few months, I stayed home with the baby. My life had never felt so full, so complete. I took the opportunity to stop working at *Rolling Stone*, which I'd been wanting to do for months, and got a freelance job with a new publication called *Eye*, Hearst Magazines' attempt to cash in on the youth market. I was the San Francisco columnist for a section called "Electric Last Minute" that appeared inside a foldout psychedelic poster bound in each issue. It was actually "Electric Three Months Ago" due to the magazine's long lead time, but that didn't matter. I wrote about Janis and Big Brother breaking up, the "Free Huey" graffiti on every wall in Berkeley, the antiwar demonstrations ("Hey, hey, LBJ, how many kids did you kill today?"), the *Express-Times,* the early days of *Zap Comix* and its exotic cast of characters: Mr. Natural, Lenore Goldberg and Her Girl Commandos, Angelfood McSpade, the Fabulous Furry Freak Brothers; and included news of the real characters of the times, the Diggers, the Black Panthers, the Grateful Dead, and a politi-

cal organization called PELVIS, which stood for Postal Employees
Living in Sin, all in the kind of snappy "three-dot journalism" Herb Caen
practiced in the *San Francisco Chronicle*. It wasn't a very time-consuming job, but it was fun.

My other friends with babies—Nancy with Teddy, Barbara Garson with
Juliet, and Anne Weills with Christopher—came over to visit. While the
babies played, we shared information about motherhood and other aspects of being women in our particular historical time. On one of these
visits, Nancy told me that a group of women had begun meeting in
Berkeley to discuss their dissatisfaction with the subordinate roles they
played to men in the student antiwar movement. I begged Nancy to take
me to these meetings. I was pretty content with my baby, but my anger
over my treatment as a woman writer in the male-dominated world of
journalism had grown from simmering resentment to a smoldering rage
that threatened to erupt into flames and burn the house down. The idea
of voicing my feelings to other women and finding a name for those other
vague and ill-defined problems that nagged at us appealed to me instantly. Through Nancy I had met a tough-minded, intelligent woman
named Suzy Nelson, also from Berkeley, who worked not far from my
house. Full of anticipation I went with Suzy to my first meeting, carrying
my three-month-old daughter in her car bed.

The group met at Anne Weills's brown-shingle house on Benvenue.
The women at the meeting were vital and good-looking, intelligent, mili-
tant, angry, and confused. So as not to be mistaken for NOW, considered
far too moderate for this radical group, we called ourselves "women's liberation." Groups like ours were springing up in other cities around the
country: New York, Chicago, Washington, DC, Gainesville, Florida. We
talked about our personal lives and found numerous common concerns,
articulating a concept that would become a trademark of the women's
movement: that the personal is political.

I'd experienced stirrings of these feelings throughout my life: observing the unequal balance of power between my mother and father in
childhood, finding inspiration in the independent lives of my women
professors at Vassar, seeing the problem described in words in *The
Second Sex* and *The Feminine Mystique,* and struggling for recognition

as a writer; but this was the first time I'd had other women with whom to share them.

The energy in Anne's living room was explosive. It's hard now to reconstruct how powerful those first moments of self-revelation were. Although we lived in the sixties and outwardly practiced a different way of life, all of us had been raised in the fifties and internalized its values, as had our mates. In college, with both of us in school full-time, I'd insisted that Michael share equally in the housework, which appalled my mother. Later, after we split up, she would say, "What did you expect? The man had to cook his own food and wash his own dishes. Should I be surprised you're not still married?" I scoffed at her old-fashioned views, but not without conflict; inwardly I felt the same way. It was my mother, after all, who had molded my thinking.

In the early days of the women's movement, we felt like pioneers. This was the era before intimate disclosures in self-help groups became the norm; we were some of the original support groups. Before our group we had been isolated within our own homes; there were private areas of our lives we simply did not share. If we had problems in our marriages, we put up a front and hoped no one would notice, just as our parents had sought to hide their troubles from the neighbors in suburbia. Sex was rarely discussed. We were taking steps to free ourselves, but it was only a beginning. As each woman in turn began to bare her secrets, pouring out her sorrows and rage and frustration, other women in the room experienced what *Ms.* magazine later called "the click of recognition," that empathetic feeling of, "Yes, my life is like that too." A collective sense of outrage grew as we coalesced into a strong group and began to develop an ideology and debate possible courses of action.

Like the other women, I had questioned the value of my personal relationships; but I was the only member of the group who had come to it through struggles at work rather than in radical politics, and had a somewhat different perspective. Where the others wanted to focus on how to change things in the movement, I wanted our analysis to include broader issues, like equality in the workplace, and to delve more deeply into questions of identity. Traditional stereotypes of women and femininity had failed to provide me with a model I could live by. I argued that we should search for the essence of what it meant to be a woman; to explore what, apart from the obvious biological differences, had been provided us by nature rather than social conditioning. With that information we could begin to define ourselves and our roles in society from a more authentic core. I wanted to know how we differed from men in real, internal ways, so we could become more deeply ourselves, not imitate or compete with men or try to live up to some fake ideal of womanhood. I believed we needed a change of consciousness at the very deepest level where people's views were formed, though I also recognized the need for practical, constructive action in the real-life here and now. Although all this would later become part of the common dialogue in the women's movement, in my group those more "practical" concerns carried the day.

I put my ideas to work in my own marriage first. Two women in my group lived with editors of *Ramparts* magazine; Anne Weills with Bob Scheer, and Consie Miller with Sol Stern. *Ramparts* had already run one feature on the women's liberation movement, which our group considered trivializing and highly unsatisfactory; it had emphasized how beautiful the women in the movement were. Anne and Consie lobbied for me to be hired at *Ramparts*, which had no female writers or editors on its staff, and I was offered a job. Michael wanted to quit *Newsweek*, so we decided to switch roles for a while. He'd stay home with the baby and write freelance articles, while I went to work full-time and provided the major financial support for our family. I was still nursing Shuna, but we lived so close to the *Ramparts* office on North Point that it was no problem for Michael to bring her there for periodic feedings. We'd already begun dividing up the household tasks more equitably, inspired by my support group's growing contention that the traditional division of domestic labor perpetuated our oppression at home.

Our arrangement was daring but far from ideal. Shuna now woke up before six in the morning, ready to play. Michael and I fought constantly about who would get up with her; both of us were exhausted, starved for sleep. Michael had always considered himself the serious writer in the family; on some level, though I don't know if he would have admitted it, I think he viewed my writing as an interesting hobby, at bottom the work of a dilettante. Professional rivalries added tension to our marriage. I was exhilarated by my newfound freedom and the self-esteem I got from my job, though *Ramparts* was not exactly a feminist paradise. On my first day at work, Bob Scheer told me I could keep the job so long as I promised not to cry in the office or fuck Eldridge Cleaver, who worked as an editor there. He was warning me, he said, so I wouldn't meet the same unhappy fate as my predecessor, a white woman driven to constant weeping by her love affair with Eldridge. Then I got to work on my first assignment, editing "The Autobiography of Huey P. Newton."

Most of the stories I subsequently wrote for *Ramparts* had a feminist point of view. A piece on the movie *Isadora* was critical of its focus on Duncan's love life rather than her artistic creativity. I reviewed *The Four-Gated City,* the last volume of Doris Lessing's magnum opus, *The Children of Violence.* Lessing had a strong following in the women's movement, giving voice as she did to many of our concerns, anger and frustration, the difficulty of being a free woman in a world controlled by men. Her bleak depiction of the future, a ruined planet, widespread madness among the sanest of citizens from poisons in the atmosphere and food, moved me deeply and frightened me to my core. Nor did it seem far-fetched. Sometimes I wondered why people weren't running out in the streets screaming to prevent what was surely going to happen.

But my personal life was going to hell as well. As I'd been exploring my frustration with my role as a woman in our weekly meetings, I'd also had to face some unpleasant truths about my marriage. Although Michael and I had a good intellectual relationship, discussing and editing each other's writing and generating ideas for stories, I felt stifled emotionally and sexually. We'd often discussed taking LSD together, but I knew in my heart that our marriage could not sustain the deeper level of honesty I was sure the drug would reveal. An undercurrent of violence ran through Michael's feelings for me and had come out when we first dated. He had hit me, and I'd told him that I'd grown up being hit by a man and didn't intend to spend my married life that way, that if it happened again, all bets were off. So the violence went underground and surfaced in his dreams. I'd wanted to leave him in London after the baby died, but stayed because at the time I believed that marriage was forever. We skated along the surface of these emotional issues, but a powerful drug like LSD could blow them sky high.

Nonetheless I'd begun to long for the freedom to explore my own psyche with the drug. I craved sexual adventure and excitement, a break from the stable routine of domesticity and security. Looking back now, I

can see the hand of my addiction at work, orchestrating the events that
followed. The drugs were starting to call to me, along with their inevitable partners—boredom and restlessness—expressed in my craving
for romantic and sexual highs. With the heady nature of these tempestu-
ous times, the explosion of feminist consciousness, the feeling in the air
that anything was possible—you could create your own life in the certainty of liberation; the revolution was just around the corner—it seems
almost inevitable that something had to give.

Ramparts asked Michael to go on the road for a story on Johnny
Cash. This infuriated me. I was the one who'd been listening to Johnny
Cash since my teenage years. I knew all his songs and could play many of
them on the guitar. Michael had never showed the slightest interest in
country music. "They just gave you that assignment because you're a
man," I said. "They think it's too dangerous for a woman to go on the
road." Michael didn't understand what the problem was; in his mind he
was the better writer; naturally he would get the assignment. In the
course of our argument, something came out that stunned me. "I consider you my professional competition," Michael said. "So when good
things happen to you, I worry, and when bad things happen to you, I'm
glad." I burst into tears; how could I continue living with a man who
wanted bad things to happen to me?

At Thanksgiving all the women's liberation groups convened at a Girl
Scout camp outside Chicago. *Ramparts* sent me to cover the meeting; I
went with a woman from my group. It was cold at the camp and living
conditions were spartan. For Thanksgiving dinner we ate hot dogs on
buns. But our spirits were high and we thrived on adrenaline and sisterly
warmth. My breasts were full and I nursed another woman's baby, which
made me feel bonded both to her and to the child in a personal, visceral
way, our universal motherhood and humanity an incontrovertible fact. In
round-the-clock meetings, we talked and argued, sharing insights, exchanging mimeographed articles, hammering away at ideas and possibilities until our fledgling ideology began to take shape. I felt then, and still
feel, privileged to have been there; though none of us could anticipate
how large our movement would grow, how profoundly it would affect society, the gathering had the excitement of history in the making. I was
supposed to write an article on the convention when I got home, but I

felt too much a part of what had happened, too involved, to stand outside and analyze it. The editors pressured me; I was supposed to be there to write about the women's movement. "Don't worry," I told them; "the topic will come."

Soon after I returned, a woman at our women's liberation meeting began talking about sex. She had never had an orgasm, she said. No one knew, not even her husband. She'd planned to carry this secret to her grave. For the first time, we women talked honestly among ourselves about our own sexuality. To me these were the most extraordinary revelations that had yet come out of our group, and the idea for an article began to take shape in my mind. I suggested it at our weekly *Ramparts* editorial meeting. The editors, all male, laughed and poked fun at me, reducing me to tears. But I went ahead and wrote the article. It was called "Understanding Orgasm," later reprinted as "The Politics of Orgasm." I talked about the prevailing Freudian views of female sexuality, the insistence on vaginal orgasm as the only legitimate form of sexual enjoyment for women, the denigration of clitoral orgasm as immature or hysterical. Masters and Johnson had just published their research findings, claiming definitively that all female orgasms were based in the clitoris. Yet the old Freudian myths, which had served men so well, refused to die. In the end I argued that it was up to women to explore and define the forms of our own sexuality, a personal kind of liberation. I worked very hard on the content and tone of the article with my editor, Peter Collier, and when it was finished, I thought it was some of the best work I'd ever done. What I didn't know was how fundamentally this little article would transform my own life, in ways I couldn't imagine, ripping apart the old one and putting the pieces into an entirely new configuration.

Ramparts printed the article, hiding it in the back of the book; still it generated a tremendous amount of attention. For starters my father called me up. "Congratulations," he said. "I learned a lot from your article." He laughed. "And believe me, I thought I knew it all." I was shocked; this was not a man who dispensed compliments easily, but his next comment sent me completely over the top. "You know, Susan," my father said, "you're a better writer than Michael. I never can understand what he's trying to say, but you have the knack of expressing complicated things in a simple way that anyone can understand. I'm really impressed with your

writing." It had never occurred to me before that I could write as well as
Michael, let alone better, and I was barely able to assimilate this idea. In
the months after the article was published, women called me, crying, to
thank me for writing it; they said it had changed their lives. Years later I
ran into a Berkeley feminist who claimed to have a sign on her wall saying, "Thank God for Susan Lydon."

But the changes in my personal life were even more dramatic.
Thinking about sex, researching the article, questioning my beliefs about
women and sex, had catalyzed something in my mind. I wanted to explore
my own sexuality, have different lovers and adventures. I was too young to
be settled down in a marriage. I wanted to get out, to live, to have all the
fun I imagined everyone else was having in the wild and wooly sexual climate of the sixties. My attraction to Anne Weills's brother Tuck, who
worked in the *Ramparts* mailroom, had been growing steadily, as had my
dissatisfaction with my marriage. Michael and I were quarreling constantly, struggling to find some new equilibrium at home; the energy in
our women's group was heating up; one by one all our significant relationships were coming apart at the seams. The breakup of Nancy and F. J.'s
seemingly ideal marriage would be among the first of the casualties.

Ramparts was also breathing its last. Bob Scheer and Warren
Hinckle, the editors-in-chief, spent most of their time in New York, trying to raise funds to keep the magazine afloat. They rode around in lim-
ousines and hosted extravagant dinners at the Algonquin Hotel, while
the subordinate editors put each month's issue of the magazine together.
Then Scheer and Hinckle would return from New York and tear it all
apart, demanding cover changes at the last minute, throwing money
around like we had it to burn. So there was a lot of resentment and anxiety in the office, a feeling that the magazine was on the brink of collapse.

Toward the end of the year, Eldridge Cleaver got involved in a shoot-
out with the San Francisco police. This meant his parole would be re-
voked, and because of what had been happening between the Panthers
and the police throughout the country—including the murder of Fred
Hampton in his bed in Chicago—he was certain he'd be killed either in
police custody or prison. Eldridge was no friend of the women's movement: his "pussy power" philosophy, which held that women should only
sleep with revolutionaries, along with Stokely Carmichael's pronounce-
ment that "the only position for women in the movement is prone," had

enraged us. On the other hand, nobody wanted to see him dead. The *Ramparts* staff held an auction ostensibly to raise funds for Eldridge's defense, but really as a cover to divert attention while he was spirited out of the country. After he disappeared our office was overrun by FBI agents searching for hints to his whereabouts. Soon the Panthers appeared en masse. Bobby Seale, dressed in beret and black leather jacket, shouldering a machine gun, stood guard outside the little office I shared with David Kolodney. It was plenty exciting, but it wasn't enough to save the magazine from ruin.

Tuck and I began an affair. Naively I believed that Michael would tolerate my sexual experimentation. Some of our friends had open marriages; we'd all talked endlessly about smashing monogamy and the nuclear family. But as usual our misplaced idealism failed miserably when confronted by the explosive feelings infidelity engendered in our partners; and my marriage, like the relationships of all my sisters in the women's group, fell apart. I didn't leave gracefully. I picked a fight with Michael, almost identical in nature to the first argument we'd had in our married life as students in New Haven. Then I announced, to his astonishment, that I couldn't take it any more and was leaving.

I could say it was historical pressures of the times, the giddy excitement and revolutionary fervor that accompanied the beginnings of the women's movement, or how casually people fell in and out of relationships in those halcyon days before AIDS. But I have close friends whose marriages survived those times, so I wonder about my own. My behavior was impulsive and self-centered in the extreme; like any addict I wanted what I wanted when I wanted it, and damn the consequences. I wasn't thinking sensibly, compassionately, or ahead. Nor am I convinced it was a mistake to leave, though I wish I'd been more honorable. Now, when my grown daughter questions my morals, it's hard for me to justify what I did. But Michael and I have become such different people that Shuna can scarcely imagine her father and me on a date together, much less married.

And no one can alter what happened in the past. Which was that one evening in January of 1969, shortly before my fourth wedding anniversary, I found myself in the front seat of a moving van with Tuck, holding my ten-month-old baby in my arms, on our way over the Bay Bridge to Berkeley, where we'd rented a house. I'd left my marriage, taken up with a lover, and was crossing the bay to begin a brand new life.

chapter seven

Señor, Señor, can you tell me where we're headin'
Lincoln County Road or Armageddon?

Bob Dylan,
"Señor (Tales of Yankee Power)"

DOPE WILL GET YOU THROUGH TIMES OF NO MONEY BETTER THAN MONEY WILL GET YOU THROUGH TIMES OF NO DOPE—1969

Tuck and I moved into a little white house with a peaked roof on Monterey in North Berkeley. The yard was overgrown with wild onions bearing tiny, cupped white flowers and had a fairy tale wilderness look about it. *Ramparts* had folded. The day the magazine went into bankruptcy the editorial staff celebrated, in typical *Ramparts* style, with an enormously expensive lunch at Vanessi's in North Beach. I was doing some freelance work for the *New York Times*. I had written a celebrity profile of Ruth Gordon and Garson Kanin for the Sunday *New York Times Magazine,* and I regularly contributed smaller music profiles and reviews to the Arts and Leisure section, where I had a wonderful editor, Seymour Peck. He was the kind of man who would call to ask if he could change a comma to a semicolon. Michael also worked for him, so he was a friend of the family; I was afraid to tell him we'd split up.

As much as possible, we were keeping the news of our breakup to ourselves. I think we were both confused; the sudden split had taken us so much by surprise that we didn't know quite what to tell our families and friends. It was impossible to keep a secret from my mother, the psychic, who could tell by her dreams and the tone of my voice when something was up with me; but apart from my mother's suspicion, the knowledge wasn't widespread within our families. Nor did either of us know if the separation would be permanent. I missed Michael—despite everything, we had shared a deep friendship—and I could not, at this point in time, imagine that we would now be apart for the rest of our lives. In later years I would hear from others how crushed Michael had been by my leaving, but at the time he acted cool, as nonchalant as he could manage under the circumstances, and all the emotion we both felt was clothed in the "taking some space to do our own thing" rhetoric of the day. I didn't know it would take me years to sort out my feelings, and that someday I would have to face Shuna's as well. Even now I'm not sure I could give a coherent answer as to why we broke up or how I feel about it; and since Michael hasn't spoken to me for close to twenty years, it's a mystery to me how he resolved it for himself.

Tuck's family had a house in Nevada City, where his mother had grown up, a couple of hours away from Berkeley. Nevada City is an old Gold Rush Victorian town in the foothills of the Sierras; unlike the temperate Bay Area, it has all four seasons. We went up there soon after we moved in together, bringing Shuna and some tabs of LSD. It was winter; the smell of oak smoke from fireplaces hung in the crisp mountain air. The house was old-fashioned and cozy. The acid was mellow, a soft and gentle high. I crawled around on the floor with my baby, "getting into her head"; we played together like equals. At night, when it was time to go to bed, she said good-night to the furniture, unable to distinguish between animate and inanimate objects. When she said good-night to the furniture, so did I. I liked this drug. It opened my mind to different possibilities. It didn't feel nearly so dangerous as people had warned me it was.

I applied for unemployment. I had my assignments from the *New York Times,* but I wasn't really that interested in writing any more. My plan was to drop out of the rat race, become a hippie earth mother, and spend my time sewing and cooking and grooving on life. Tuck and his friends were carefree and easygoing. They did odd jobs, usually involving physical labor; and when they were through working, they cracked open a six-pack of beer and smoked a bunch of joints. I got stoned a lot and lay on the mattress-couch on the living room floor listening to music. With the enhancement of pot, music took on a heightened intensity and subtlety of meaning, revealing its secrets and discrete notes more readily than when I listened unstoned.

Sy Peck assigned me a review of the Band's new album, the one following *Music from Big Pink*. As soon as it came in the mail, I took up my listening position on the couch, with headphones over my ears and a stash of joints nearby. I thought the album was brilliant and wrote that the Band was a major presence in popular music, as important as Dylan, the Beatles, and the Stones. Their lawyer took the review to their immigration hearing—most of them were Canadian—and because the *Times* said they were so important, they were allowed to stay in the country. Meanwhile I had decided that reviewing records was stupid; one didn't require an intermediary between listener and music, I felt, and so I stopped writing music reviews.

My plan had been to groove on life, but it was kind of tough because I was still getting depressed. I went to doctors, and they gave me tranquilizers and sleeping pills. Michael had moved to Elk, on the California coast near Mendocino, and was dropping out as well. We had an informal shared custody agreement with Shuna, passing her back and forth between Berkeley and Elk. When she was in Berkeley, I took her to Anne's house. We'd started a play group for the kids, who would crawl around on the grass in her big back yard, naked and totally free. They were social creatures even at this young age; we fantasized that as they grew they would form their own kind of community: Shuna, Teddy, Christopher Scheer, babies who'd known one another since birth. Anne had split with Bob Scheer and was living with Tom Hayden. She and I spent a lot of time together. I lived with her brother, so she was sort of my sister-in-law. Often we got together for casual spaghetti or taco dinners at her parents' home in Berkeley, which everyone called "the Big House." These were lively, boisterous affairs with the six Weills siblings and their partners and friends, hearty, athletic types, native Californians.

On the weeks when Michael had Shuna in Elk, I went to LA to do the reporting for my assignments. Glenys had moved back to London; Terry followed her and hooked up with Monty Python's Flying Circus. Sometimes I saw Harry Shearer, but it wasn't the same as when the five of us had hung out together, cracking jokes and acting crazy. I missed Glenys; she was the only other woman journalist I knew, someone to compare experience with. Michael had a new girlfriend, Lyndall Erb, a hippie seamstress. I didn't much like her, but I loved the way she'd decorated their little house in Elk, with crocheted lace and strings of colored glass beads over the windows.

Our house on Monterey suited us fine, but our landlord kicked us out when he discovered we weren't married. Berkeley in 1969 was a city in transition from college town to countercultural haven, but the transition had not yet been completed. Still, I felt very much at home there. There was a lot to do, and the people were smart, varied, and interesting to talk to. My life felt much simpler and easier to manage than it had before. Sunny days flowed into one another in a happy haze of pot smoke and barbecues, and I acclimated quickly. Soon I took my green suit from Paris, my Hermes purse, my grownup clothes from London, and dumped them into a Goodwill box outside the Shattuck Avenue Co-Op. I shopped at thrift stores and the flea market. Mostly I wore T-shirts and jeans. When I got dressed up, it was in Victorian lace dresses and silk-embroidered piano shawls. I never wore a bra any more. I'd thrown them all away.

Tuck and I took a trip to the Southwest: Arizona and New Mexico. We camped out at Canyon de Chelly and visited the Navajo and Hopi reservations. We went to Acoma Pueblo, which sat atop a windswept mesa in the New Mexico desert. Acoma is said to be the oldest inhabited spot in North America. The achingly beautiful vista that stretched out for miles around—space so vast and open that silence itself had an echo— with strange, massive shapes growing out of the desert floor, looked more ancient than time. It's become fashionable now to study shamanism and visit power spots, places made magical by the presence of spirits, but we ended up in one quite by accident, or divine design. Tuck took me to see his old school, Verde Valley, in Sedona; and we decided to drop acid in nearby Oak Creek Canyon, a bucolic oasis of rushing water and deciduous leafy trees in the midst of the parched red desert.

There is a special hush that descends at the beginning of an acid trip, as though one were present at the very dawning of creation. I approached this newborn world with wonder and reverence, observing the desert landscape in minute detail, noting how each cactus had its own distinct insect companions, camouflaged to match the plant's precise coloration. I watched crows lighting in a scraggly tree, and heard their raucous cawing as a sacred secret call. I felt, deep inside the cells of my body, my interrelatedness with the complex of living things around me and my connection with the spirit who made us all. It was awe-inspiring and exhilarating. But as we walked in the desert, I became frightened. I could no longer remember my name, my home, or other details of who I was. I saw rattlesnake skins discarded in the gullies and sensed the presence of terrible danger. Panic struck me; I was sure I would never return from this trip; I'd lost my mind, my identity, my way back. I thought I was doomed to wander in the desert until I died. Tuck comforted me and carried me to the car on his back. Physically he was fearless, a rock to lean on in an unfamiliar world. Despite my overpowering fear, that trip in the desert transformed my way of thinking; my psyche had expanded to include this moment of cosmic consciousness and would never contract to its former size again.

We moved into another small house on Ensenada in North Berkeley. I painted the front room, a sunny glassed-in porch, bright red, and the bedroom a vivid purple. I got the colors from Anne; she had a good eye for them. Mark Switzer came over to help us paint the spare bedroom a clear emerald green. He was a Weills sister's ex-boyfriend and Tuck's good friend, part of the Big House extended family. Mark had bottomless blue eyes that sparkled with mischief and simultaneously revealed a certain deep seriousness. He and his brother Larry had just bought a sailboat, sailed it down from Washington state, and were planning to take it around the world. We went over to the Sausalito marina to visit Mark and see the boat, called the *Kialoa,* a handsome, trimly built ocean racer with teak decks. Tuck worked on the boat, so we went there often.

One day, six months after Tuck and I had moved in together, when I was beginning to think I'd made a grave mistake, Michael came to pick up Shuna and I asked to speak to him alone. We took a walk around my neighborhood, which was blooming all over with bright mid-summer flowers. I told Michael I had been thinking a lot about our marriage, how much I regretted breaking it up; I said I missed him and asked if we could get back together. He refused. Once he'd gotten over the shock of my leaving, he said, he realized how unhappy he had been in our marriage all along. After he got home, he wrote me a truly shattering letter: "In a primal, subconscious, vicious, and powerful way," he wrote, "I hate you while at the same time I want nothing more than to be delivered

from that hatred which corrupts my life and my desire to give and receive love." I was disconsolate. I felt that if I let anyone get as close to me
as Michael had, or get to know me as well as he did, then they would
grow to hate me as much as he did. When I came across that letter recently, I was startled by its emotional violence, but I also was glad to have
found it; it helped me understand that the breakup of my marriage had
not been solely the capricious and irresponsible action of a selfish young
girl, as I had thought all these years, but perhaps a rare moment of sanity
and self-preservation.

In May Michael and Shuna and I went East for my brother Ricky's bar
mitzvah. Michael and I were trying to present a united front to our families and didn't want to detract from the happy occasion. My sister Sheila
had married Peter Probst, a Catholic boy from a large Island Park family
we had all grown up with. Lorraine was living with Maggie in a co-op
apartment on the Lower East Side, editing books and playing music. My
parents seemed like they had been waiting all their lives to *shepp naches*
(Yiddish for deriving pride) like this from their children. At the bar mitzvah, however, Mama Yetta studiously ignored me. Finally I walked up to
her to show her the baby.

"What do you think of your great-granddaughter?" I asked.

"She doesn't look Jewish," Mama Yetta said, turning away and reducing me to tears.

This traditional bar mitzvah in the midst of the sixties was a sometimes humorous collision of cultures. Michael's and Peter Probst's heads,
incongruous in yarmulkes, towered over the rest of the relatives, and
Michael and I almost came to blows with my cousin Ira when he opined
that the way to end the Vietnam War was "to bomb them back to the
Stone Age and turn the whole country into one big parking lot."

I also had business to conduct in New York. Robin Morgan wanted
my sex article from *Ramparts* to be included in her anthology of writings
from the women's movement, *Sisterhood Is Powerful.* While I was at the
Random House offices editing it, John Simon, the radical editor and a
friend of the Jacobses whom I had met in California, offered me a contract to write a book. He more or less dragged me into his office to sell
me on the idea. "You can be the next Simone de Beauvoir," he told me.
"You'll write the definitive feminist work on sexuality." I was flattered but

confused by his pitch; I'd planned to drop out of writing altogether. But publishers were racing to come out with books on the hot new topic of women's liberation, and snapping up feminist writers who hadn't even thought of writing book proposals. He made me a very generous offer and I said I'd think about it.

I consulted my friend F. J. Bardacke, who was staying with Jerry Rubin and Nancy Kushner in their apartment on St. Mark's Place in the East Village. In 1969 what used to be known as the Lower East Side had become the East Village, a chaotic and colorful hippie enclave much like Berkeley. F. J. advised me to sign the contract. "I'll do the field work for you myself," he joked. John Simon had offered me the astronomical sum of ten thousand dollars. "Go on," said F. J., "take the money and run." I went off to the offices of literary agent Lynn Nesbit, who negotiated a contract for me. She was as excited as John Simon. "It'll be a bestseller," she said. "You'll be on Johnny Carson." An appalling picture of being on the "Tonight Show" talking about orgasms flashed into my head, and I almost ran out of the office screaming, but instead I signed the contract. I had no idea how to write a book or what kind of work it would entail.

F. J. returned to Berkeley before me. He was involved in the construction of what would soon be called People's Park on some land owned by the University of California behind Telegraph Avenue. He had written a leaflet, illustrated with a picture of Geronimo, called "Who Owns the Park?" I was still in New York when the news broke of a terrible street battle over People's Park; one man had been killed and another blinded by police gunfire. I couldn't get hold of Tuck. He'd been up on the Avenue trashing stores and throwing rocks in the wake of the incident. I went back home for the demonstrations. A cloud of tear gas hung over Berkeley then and for many months after. Often I walked Shuna in her stroller through tear gas that hung in the air. Governor Reagan called in the National Guard. Like a surrealist vision out of Eastern Europe, tanks rolled into Berkeley, an occupying army, turning off University and right up Grove, in front of City Hall, to occupy the city.

While I was in New York, Tuck had had another woman sleeping in my bed. Our lives went on much as ever, but something had clearly gone out of our relationship. In June we watched the moon landing up at the Big House. Mark Switzer and I stood out on the deck and talked about the moon walk. He was awestruck; he tended anyway to view the world with a kind of spiritual reverence. I liked the way he thought deeply about things. The more we hung around on the boat with Mark, the more I found myself drawn to his quiet, gentle nature. The initial sexual chemistry that had attracted me to Tuck had worn off; without it, we didn't have much in common. One Sunday I drove to Sausalito, found Mark alone, and told him how I felt. He was troubled by my confession, torn between his friendship with Tuck and his feelings for me. "I won't be around for more than a few months, Susie," he told me. "As soon as the boat is finished, I'm taking off around the world." I was the mother of a young child; she would not be safe on the boat. "We may like each other," Mark said softly, "but we have no future."

Nevertheless we spent the night together. The next morning I went home and told Tuck. Mark had invited him on the trip as crew, he said; now that it was over between us, he would go. He moved out the same day. Mark and I went away for a few days to Nevada City; we were blissfully happy. When we returned, he moved the *Kialoa* to the Berkeley marina, where we sometimes spent the night, lulled to sleep by the soothing rocking of the waves. Sometimes we stayed on Ensenada. Mark brought all his worldly possessions into my house, but emotionally he grew more distant, his mind focused on his coming departure. I was as much in love with Mark as I had ever been with anyone. For several months, while everything was being finished on the boat, I lived in a daze of happiness. When Mark came home at the end of the day covered with fiberglass dust and smelling of diesel fuel, the sight of him made my heart lift with joy. "I love you too, Susie," he would say, "but I love the Pacific Ocean more."

Too soon for me, the departure day arrived. Some friends took me on their trimaran to accompany the *Kialoa* out to the Golden Gate. It was a beautiful early autumn day with a brisk wind blowing on the bay. The trimaran rode smoothly over the waves. The *Kialoa,* looking regal with her white sails billowing, cut a sharp swath through the water with her narrow racing hull. I stood on the deck of the trimaran, with the small knot of people who'd gathered to see the voyagers off. We watched the *Kialoa* sail under the Golden Gate Bridge, silhouetted against the setting sun, crossing from the safety of San Francisco Bay into the wide Pacific

Ocean beyond. Holding my baby in my arms, close against my body for warmth and comfort, I waved goodbye to the man I loved, my heart breaking in pieces.

I missed Mark terribly. I wandered around my house at loose ends, smelling the clothes he had left behind and weeping constantly. Shuna followed me. Sometimes she watched me cry; other times she joined in herself. Once when Michael came to take her to Elk, we had a terrible fight. I don't remember what we argued over, but Michael flew into a rage, grabbed Shuna, and ran off down the block, with me in hot pursuit, all three of us screaming bloody murder. I was so depressed that I thought about suicide and secured the means to accomplish it: a full prescription of Seconal. Looking back on this time and the years of on-and-off depressions that followed, I sometimes think the only thing that saved me from killing myself was having a child to care for and to care about so much.

With Mark gone I could no longer afford my rent. F. J. and his girlfriend Gwynne were forming a commune with Sol Stern and Craig Pyes, another friend. They rented a big white house on Derby Street in Berkeley and named it Fisherman. Their motto was, "You don't need a fisherman to know when something's fishy," a takeoff on the Dylan line, "You don't need a weatherman to know which way the wind blows," from which the radical Weathermen group had taken its name. They invited me and Shuna to move in, but I didn't know if I'd like communal living. What really scared me was the thought of living on my own, which I had never done, and I decided to confront that fear head-on.

I traded my house for a rear cottage on Stuart Street, in South Berkeley, that rented for eighty-five dollars a month. It was a little five-room dollhouse with a pointed roof, gray shingles, and blue-painted trim. The large backyard had a fishpond and fig tree. A giant plum tree hung over the side. In front were a rose garden, an apple tree, a giant cedar, white belladonna that perfumed the night air, and some dogs belonging to the people in the front house, hippies who ran a light show. When it rained the yard smelled of cedar and dog shit. Suzy Nelson and her boyfriend lived across the street; they helped me move in.

Michael decided he'd stay in Fisherman when he was in Berkeley, and take care of Shuna there. He went on tour with the Rolling Stones, on assignment for the *New York Times Magazine.* I spent a lot of time at Fisherman, and at Anne Weills's house, pining away for Mark. In early December we heard that the Rolling Stones would give a free concert at Altamont Speedway to close out their tour. We discussed the news at Fisherman and decided to get a babysitter for Shuna and Teddy, rent a van, and all go to the concert together. Michael came with us; he was back from the tour.

I brought along some acid I had won in a poker game. We parked the van and started the long trek, over dried brown hills, to the Speedway. I took a tab of the purple acid and gave some to F. J. and Gwynne. From every direction people were streaming over the hills. It looked like a medieval trade fair; cripples, burnt-out speed freaks missing teeth, everyone in weird, colorful costumes coming to gather in this godforsaken spot. The Speedway was at the bottom of a natural round depression in the hills. We took seats on the ground fairly near the front. From the first of Sam Cutler's increasingly panicked pleas to the crowd to stay calm and maintain order, the atmosphere felt ominous, distinctly different from the harmonious "peace, love, and good vibes" feeling that had graced the Be-In, Monterey, and Woodstock. There was a pervasive sense of menace; it smelled metallic and slightly decaying, like the presence of evil.

Over 400,000 people had shown up. I don't know if the human psyche is designed to handle that many people in one lifetime, let alone one place, but mine couldn't, and my circuits blew out. In my acid-drugged state, it looked to me as if the entire population of the planet was there, all gathered together for the apocalypse. I was frightened and trembling. Even the music, Santana's pounding congas and guitars, sounded frightening to me. By the time the Jefferson Airplane took the stage, the Hells' Angels guarding the performers had turned restless and mean, going after people with flailing pool cues. Marty Balin jumped off the stage to break up a fight, and reappeared with his face covered in blood. A fat, naked man approached the stage. I watched the Angels circle him, knock him to the ground, then beat him mercilessly with pool cues until fountains of liquid spurted from his belly.

I looked around at the overwhelming number of people in the audience, packed together so densely that no one could come in or go out. Palpable waves of fear rippled through the crowd, but no one moved to stop the Angels. I imagined this was the end of civilization. "The planet is dying," I thought to myself. "The planet is dying." I was so freaked out that my friends took me by the arms and got me out of the crowd, stepping gingerly over and on top of packed-in bodies. They led me to a spot behind the stage, sat me on the ground, and went to the first-aid tent for help. They returned with a tab of Thorazine, which failed to stop the trip going on in my head but eventually put my body into near-catatonia. I had been so depressed in recent months that I'd taken to carrying a full prescription of Seconal in my purse at all times, so if the pain got too intense, I could kill myself. I reached into my purse to get it now, but it was gone. All I could find were some Darvon, hardly what I needed for a fatal overdose.

I desperately wanted to leave, to escape the bedlam I expected to break out at any second, but some of our party were lost in the crowd. I begged Michael to get us lifted out in a helicopter, but he wanted to stay to see the show. He was cool and unruffled, unmoved by my pleas or my frantic state of mind. I sat motionless behind the stage for hours. Night fell, and finally the Rolling Stones came on. I heard the chilling opening chords of "Gimme Shelter," like a theme song from hell. Melees breaking out in the crowd constantly interrupted "Sympathy for the Devil." First the Angels drove their motorcycles into the audience. Then I heard calls for a doctor from the stage. I fully expected that everyone who was at Altamont would die. I was sad about never seeing my baby again, but I quietly resigned myself to my fate. There was no question in my mind that this was the end of the world. Entombed inside my catatonia, I sat cross-legged on the ground for some eight hours. My body didn't grow cold; my legs didn't get stiff; I never even got up to pee. I just waited there to die.

Eventually all of our party reconvened, and we made our way back to the van and out through the traffic around the Speedway, back to Berkeley. I was amazed to be alive, overjoyed to see my baby again, but I felt broken inside by my terrible vision, which stayed with me long after the acid wore off. The next day we heard that three people had been killed at the concert, two run over by cars as they walked through a ditch, one stabbed to death by the Angels during the Stones' set. I didn't share in the prevailing outrage over the stabbing because I was surprised the deaths were so few; I had expected everyone to die. And the heartbreaking certainty I had that the planet was dying has stayed with me to this day, more than twenty years since Altamont abruptly ended the sixties.

chapter eight

I been sittin' in here for so darn long
Waitin' for the end to come along
Only those who are on the brink
Can take a choice to swim or sink

The Band,
"To Kingdom Come"

THE END OF THE WORLD DOESN'T COME—1970

I spent the better part of 1970 convinced the apocalypse was just around the corner. *Ramparts* had run one cover story about the death of the oceans. Sometimes, in our editorial meetings, Bob Scheer would wonder aloud, "What will we do when peace breaks out in Vietnam? What will be our next big issue?" I argued that we should focus on the environment, but it wasn't a popular view at the time. Mark and I had discussed the ecological crisis at length; it was one of his motivations for sailing as far from Berkeley as he could. In the months following Altamont, I lived with overwhelming fear and constant acid flashbacks. I didn't bother to find work because I was sure the world would end before my unemployment ran out.

Why did I react so strongly to Altamont? How much of my reaction was due to the acid? From a recovery perspective, LSD is one of the hardest drugs to deal with. It's not addictive, and it has the power to give you valuable, transforming insights. But acid is a drug that can throw open the doors to heaven and hell, and it greatly intensifies whatever you're feeling at the time. At Altamont I'd experienced profound fear, fear for my life, and it tapped into a well of paranoia I'd had imprinted on my psyche since childhood. Though I believe my vision of a dying planet was fundamentally correct, not everyone would have brought to it the same degree of fear and fatalism that I had. For one thing, I hadn't been raised to be an optimist. I was from the generation that grew up with the threat of instant annihilation from the atomic bomb; in public school in New York, in the late forties and early fifties, we'd been issued metal dog-tags, like soldiers wear, so our little bodies could be identified in the ruins. And I hadn't learned in my family that the world was a safe place; far from it. My grandmother Mama Yetta, used to show me pictures of her relatives who were being slaughtered in Europe. "This one the Nazis murdered at Bergen-Belsen," she would say. "This is my cousin Esther; she perished in Treblinka." As a child I had dreams that the Nazis were coming to take me out of grade school. Fatalism is my natural state of mind; even today I have to struggle to have faith in the future, any hope at all. And my first glimpse of the ecological catastrophe we were heading for, whether it was an acid-induced vision or a flash of that weird streak of psychic ESP I'd inherited from Bobish, both terrified me and filled me with such deep despair it was an effort just to keep on living.

One night I dreamt that a tidal wave of garbage rushed up from the bay and drowned all of Berkeley. Any day now, I imagined, rivers of blood would be flowing past my little cottage on Stuart Street. I covered my walls with patchwork quilts, hung thick velvet drapes on the windows, and carpeted the floors with rattan matting and Oriental rugs, trying to insulate myself from the horror to come. I put bits of lace and strings of glass beads on the window to catch the light, made jam from the tiny red plums that gathered ankle-deep by the side of my house, and took my two-year-old daughter to nursery school like any normal mother. But inside I was full of terror, waiting for the apocalypse, or possibly the revolution, whichever came first.

I was living on my book advance, which I had sent to my mother to dole out to me in dribs and drabs. My expenses were modest; my biggest extravagance was the junk I bought at the flea market to decorate my house or to put into fantasy costumes, which were another of my hedges against what I perceived as the unbearable harshness of reality. Since I didn't believe in a future, it was impossible for me to contemplate writing a book. When the fact that I wasn't writing it weighed too heavily on me, I would take a Darvon and fantasize that I *would* write it and it would all turn out okay in the end. In the meantime I sewed a lot and decided to become an artist, like the new friends I'd made at Woolsey Street, an artists' commune and home to the Floating Lotus Magic Opera Company, a ragtag mystical theater troupe.

As I'd waited for doomsday, I'd taken refuge more and more in imaginary visions of history and fantasy. I saw my patchwork quilts as windows to another time; the women who had made them, long dead, lived on in their handiwork. I wanted to join those legions of women who, in the midst of hardship, heartbreak, and joy, had conjured up beauty with their hands. I decided to cast my lot with the survivors. Comforted by the beaded, embroidered, pieced, and painted work I'd gathered around me, healing myself at my sewing machine, slowly I made up my mind to live. Outside my cottage was a rose garden planted by some invisible former denizen of the house. I decided that no matter what happened, I would be like one of those ladies who tended their rose gardens while the bombs dropped on England.

I had never before considered spiritual solutions to my problems or answers to my questions. I knew this was a difficult time for everyone in my generation. The high hopes we had held for transforming society had been dashed by the continuing carnage of the Vietnam War. Many of us looked to the old ways of American Indians for inspiration and fancied ourselves a tribe. I started reading books about Indians and gypsies; their nomadic lifestyle appealed to me. After all, I was a wandering Jew of the Diaspora, unrooted wherever I went. I didn't have to think about my Jewishness, or practice the religion; it was a permanent part of me, like my skin. Thanks to my ancestral history, I believed, I never quite felt safe anywhere, never felt really at home. I retained a persistent sense of being an outsider, marginal, rootless, and somewhat deprived. It was not too far a leap from there to my fantasies of life as an Indian or gypsy.

More than anything, perhaps, my generation had a terrible hunger for community. The move to the suburbs, the invention of TV, the assimilation into mainstream American culture by our immigrant families, had stripped us of comforting rituals of religion and family life, and so we sought to create our own. For us LSD was not so much a drug as a sacrament; we took it as the Indians took peyote to sharpen their inner vision and illuminate hidden spirit worlds below the level of ordinary consciousness. We viewed ourselves as explorers of inner space, pushing the frontiers of consciousness with our experiments on ourselves; and this experience bound us one to another like a tribal drumbeat.

People I knew were moving to the country to live off the land. Many were survivalists who believed they could protect themselves from civilization's coming breakdown by becoming self-sufficient: growing organic food, making their own clothing, dipping candles and spinning wool like the pioneers, weaning themselves from the comforts of industrialized society. Others outfitted school buses or makeshift gypsy wagons and took to the road, supporting themselves by selling handmade crafts or doing odd jobs as transients. With the death of SDS, and the splintering of the movement into factional groups, many politicos had joined the Weathermen and gone underground. I traveled in my fantasies but stayed at home; I was happiest exploring my inner life, which unfolded in a series of what Michael McClure liked to call "brain movies" as I wrote, or knitted, or planned a quilt. When the apocalypse came, I wanted to be holding my daughter's hand; I hoped by then I would have made something beautiful with which to grace the waning world.

Among my little group of hippie artisans, the pattern of our days was comfortingly familiar. Every morning we all assembled at the "Med"— the Caffe Mediterraneum on Telegraph Avenue—to drink coffee and find out the news of what had happened or was about to happen in Berkeley. The Med was cavernous, with two-story high ceilings, an iron-railed balcony surrounding a half-size second floor, a long espresso bar in front where people lined up to get their orders, a short-order kitchen in back, and faded paintings with vaguely ancient Greek motifs on the walls. The Med served the best coffee in town. Under a badly rendered Neptune with trident, the women of Woolsey Street: Susie Angelcloud, Iris, Maureen, an astrologer who lived in a cottage in the backyard, Polly Moon, a young, pretty ceramicist, and assorted other friends gathered around the marble-topped tables to laugh, gossip, flirt, talk, compare outfits, and pass the time. Christian and his friend Conrad, flute-makers and musicians, decorated the windows of Shambhala, the spiritual bookstore across the street. Wesley sold antiques at a store nearby.

Telegraph Avenue was the undisputed heart and center of Berkeley life. You were liable to encounter anyone in the world parading along the Avenue dressed in any manner of outlandish costume and spouting every sort of philosophy. One regular Avenue character dressed in a military uniform and called himself "General Wastemoreland." The chanting of Hare Krishnas with shaved heads, saffron robes, and bells and tambourines provided an unlikely soundtrack to his diatribes against the war. From my vantage point in the Med, I once saw a nude long-haired woman ride by on a horse, and several impromptu police riots erupt on the street without warning. Often Shuna would grab my large glass of caffe latte off the table, gulp it down, and then run up and down the Avenue visiting with her friends among the street people, as we called people who lived on the Avenue, in doorways or parks.

Carroll Perry, a light-skinned black man with one wall-eye, was the resident astrologer of the Med. My birthday was the same as his wife's, so he knew my chart by heart and gave me frequent extemporaneous readings: advice on how to organize my life and mother my child, whose needs he gauged from her astrological profile. A regular cast of characters hung out in the Med, and we all knew one another by face if not by name. Sometimes we'd stay there all day, and then spend the evening drinking wine at the Albatross or dancing in one of the many clubs that featured live music by local bands: the Joy of Cooking or Commander Cody and His Lost Planet Airmen.

I often chatted with Christian and Conrad on the sidewalk outside the Med. They were interested in all sorts of mystical things: Sufis, Tibetan Buddhism, Hindu myths, and esoteric practices. I asked them questions, but they prided themselves on never giving a straightforward answer; they liked to speak in riddles, like Zen masters and Sufi sages. Christian and his girlfriend, Diana, had been going to secret meetings and getting together tents and various supplies for a mysterious trip to Chile. "Why Chile?" I asked Christian. "What could possibly be there?" But he evaded me at every turn. I bought a couple of books at Shambhala: the *I Ching* and Swami Satchidananda's guide to the practice of hatha yoga. I learned how to throw the *I Ching*, but could never find the motivation or discipline to get to a yoga class or practice the postures from the books. Later my sister Lorraine found the book in one of my trunks, and it led her to a lifelong involvement with Integral Yoga. As for me, I may have been willing to experiment, but I still considered myself a rational-minded journalist; I really didn't think this mystical stuff had much relevance to my life.

I frequently spoke on the phone with John Simon, my editor at Random House. We had become friends. I felt guilty that I hadn't started my book, but he assured me again and again that he understood I was the mother of a small child and hadn't much time or freedom to write. In the spring he invited me and Shuna to visit him. He was staying in a friend's house on Hudson Street and had lots of room. I had a wonderful time in New York. I wheeled Shuna in her stroller all around the Village and the Lower East Side, visiting with family and old friends, exhilarated by the familiar rhythms and pulse of the city. At night I sang "Ding Dong, the Witch Is Dead" to my two year old, to put her to sleep and perhaps give chase to my grownup demons as well. I even began to feel like I was re-covering from my bad acid trip at Altamont.

Then one evening I went to have dinner at the Cauldron, a vegetar-ian restaurant on the Lower East Side. I met a guy there, and we started talking. He told me he worked as a drug counselor. We walked back over to Hudson Street, smoked a joint, and turned on the TV news. It was shortly after the invasion of Cambodia. Student protests had been erupt-ing all over the country. On campuses everywhere, chants of "One, two, three, four, we don't want your fucking war," and "Hey, hey, LBJ, how many kids did you kill today?" were ringing in the air. We watched one such demonstration on a bucolic campus somewhere in the Midwest called Kent State. All of a sudden, soldiers armed with guns came over a ridge and start shooting into the crowd of students, killing four of them. I could not believe my eyes. Was this America? The whole nation shared in this shock and disbelief, but in my case it was compounded by a drug reaction. Watching the soldiers come over the ridge was like one of my worst nightmares come true, and it plunged me right into an acid flash-back. I began to tremble and again felt present at the end of the world. My companion had to talk me down. Thank God he was experienced at this sort of thing. Finally, when I'd calmed down enough to stop trembling, I took a Valium and sent him home so I could go to sleep. I still wasn't out of the woods.

Anne Weills, Tom Hayden, and Bob Scheer had moved into some houses on Bateman Street and put together a revolutionary cadre called the Red Family. One of their projects was a nursery school, which Christopher Scheer named Blue Fairyland. Our kids had been attending a Montessori school we had organized with two teachers in the Berkeley hills. It was expensive, but the kids were happy there. The Red Family was afraid the Montessori school was instilling bourgeois values in the children, and they were convinced it would be better for the kids to form their own collective in a school where racism and sexism could be eliminated from the curriculum. After some hesitation I decided to send Shuna there.

Every morning a light green van came to pick up Shuna, and every afternoon she would return home from school, singing, "Ho, Ho, Ho Chi Minh / The NLF is gonna win." At school the kids played "meeting" and talked about Vietnam. Shuna's best friend was Seven Anne McDonald, the tiny, elfin daughter of Country Joe McDonald and his wife, Robin Menken, an actress with the Pitschel Players, a local comedy troupe. The girls liked to play together after school, giggling and cooking up mischief, either at my house or at Joe's and Robin's; and through the kids' friendship, we all became friends. Joe took most of the responsibility for child care in their family; he was the parent who attended the Blue Fairyland meetings. The Red Family lumped me and Joe together as "the hippie-cultural faction" among the parents, most of whom were intensely political. When George Jackson got killed, the Blue Fairyland kids went on a field trip to San Quentin to protest his murder; that's the kind of school it was.

I was terrified to take acid again. Though my mental state was improving slowly, I was still so emotionally unstable that one bad trip could have pushed me back over the edge. One night I went to San Francisco with my current lover, Wesley, to the place on the Great Highway where Chet Helms had moved his Family Dog Productions. The Floating Lotus Magic Opera Company was performing a benefit there for Timothy Leary, who'd recently been busted. Michael McClure was there, and we walked around the edges of the auditorium, talking. "Don't drink anything," Michael said, and made a point of turning down whatever people offered us. He wasn't with me backstage, however, when a Floating Lotus actress handed me a jug of apple juice and I drank freely from it, without suspicion. It had been spiked with LSD, and too late I realized I'd been dosed. In a panic I grabbed Wesley and told him we had to drive back over the bridge quickly before this stuff took effect. Wesley was infinitely kind and patient, and to my great surprise, we had a wonderful trip together, a sweet and playful time. I experienced a vision of myself as a bird-dancer in a Mayan temple; costumed in brightly colored feathers, I danced in a sacred ceremony. It was a pleasant fantasy, and at home with Wesley, I felt safe and cosseted, with none of my former terror. It was a revelation to me that the same drug could produce such vastly different reactions as I'd had, and I was relieved to know that I could take it again without fear.

I had started working on my book. I'd finally figured out a comfortable way to write it. Since I didn't consider myself any sort of authority on sex, I didn't want to write a theoretical book. Instead I'd decided to do a series of interviews with real people on some varieties of sexual experience. I had one subject who'd had incest with her father throughout her childhood, a man whose wife had faked orgasm for the whole of their five-year marriage, the lover of a woman with multiple orgasms, an ex-convict, and some of my close girlfriends: Tamara, and Susie Angelcloud, who described herself in the interview as "just a cuddly little Jewish girl who likes to fuck." Eventually I finished the book of interviews and turned it in to Random House, but it wasn't at all what they'd had in mind, and they never published it.

Among my friends we were all pretty free and easy with each other when it came to sex. We believed in free love, a reaction to the sexual repression we'd grown up with in the fifties. I had broken up with Wesley and now had lots of affairs: one-night stands, two-week flings, short relationships, and casual encounters. I longed to be in a serious, committed relationship, yet I couldn't seem to find one. It wasn't sex I was looking for, but love; however, in our way of doing things, the sex always came first and then you decided if it was worth it to have the relationship. Good-enough sex might keep you together until the initial passion wore off and you discovered you had nothing else in common. We didn't even date any more, just fell in and out of bed with people like it was no big deal.

Emotionally, though, it was a big deal. I found I was always falling in love with the wrong people: the cynical bums who hung out in the Med, flaky young musicians, dope dealers, hippie carpenters, guys I picked up in bars, all emotionally unavailable men who didn't return my affections.

I believed I was repeating the pattern I'd learned in my family with my father, whose love I had tried to win. The whole issue of sex and love was so charged and confused for me, it was a miracle I could function at all. And the rhetoric of the time only served to muddle it further. We behaved as though our easygoing sexuality were a means of political liberation. We thought we were striking a blow for feminism, or against racism and repression. Yet my mother's values, which I'd absorbed before I ever had the chance to question them or form my own, were alive inside me and a tremendous source of internal conflict. I tried to do my work and take care of my daughter, but in my heart of hearts, I believed that finding someone to love was the most important thing in life, and that at that I was a miserable failure.

I spent a lot of time immobilized by depression. My heart often felt so heavy that it was an effort to get out of bed in the morning. Nothing seemed to interest me; nothing seemed worthwhile. I carried this feeling of unhappiness around like an open, running sore. I felt low and dispirited for months at a time. Each new heartbreak, disappointment, rejection, or unrequited love sent me into a tailspin. Deep down I knew there was something terribly wrong with me, but I couldn't put my finger on just what it was. Most of the men I met liked to have casual sex; they didn't want to get involved. I was dying to get involved; it was lonely being a single mother. I felt constantly torn between my love for my child and my desire to go out every night to meet a man. I resented all the trouble and expense of getting babysitters; at the same time, I often thought if I didn't have a child to care for, I might just go ahead and kill myself. And I couldn't for the life of me figure out why I was so full of pain.

Alex the Hippie hung out at the Med. He had jet black hair down to his waist, wore a filthy fringed buckskin jacket, and carried an attache case filled with every variety of drug known to man. One day he asked if I had ever tried cocaine, and when I answered no, he promised to come over that night and introduce me to it. Sure enough, he did, and we spent the next few days in bed, snorting cocaine and having sex. I fell in love with this exciting new drug; "It's the first good reason I've seen to become rich and famous," I joked. I only got out of bed to feed Shuna and go sign for my unemployment check. I liked the exhilaration and joy I felt with coke. It turned me on sexually and made whoever I was with seem fascinating. I couldn't get enough. Finally, though, Alex ran out of drugs and went home so we both could get some sleep.

Alex had taken it upon himself to provide my drug education, so a few weeks later he came over to turn me on to heroin. I was sitting on the mattress in my living room, sewing a calico border onto the hem of a flea market dress I'd cut short. I sniffed a little heroin and promptly fell asleep. I wondered what the fuss was all about; this was not very thrilling at all. Alex told me you could do heroin without getting hooked if you didn't use it for more than three days in a row. This was his third day, he said, so he asked if he could stash the rest of his heroin in my house for a while. He hid it in a book, and I didn't even look for it; that's how unimpressed I was with the so-called high. I wondered why people sold their souls for this stuff.

Cocaine was starting to become popular in Berkeley, and men, in particular, viewed it as a drug of seduction. I liked to keep a little cocaine around because it gave me the energy and the motivation to clean my house. I liked to do it alone and work with the extra energy. But it was just a once-in-a-while thing for me. People said it wasn't addictive; you couldn't get a physical dependence on coke like you could on smack; it was just a psychological thing. I also had little stashes of pot and hashish and pills around the house, all for different purposes. I took speed when I needed to write or wanted to lose weight, popped downers for period cramps or to get a good night's sleep, and smoked pot to listen to music and try on clothes. I liked to have little dress-up parties where I played music on the record player, tried on different outfits, and danced around the living room by myself.

For my twenty-seventh birthday Susie Angelcloud and her boyfriend, Russell, brought me some cocaine. She laid out two fat lines of white powder on a record album cover, and I sniffed them both quickly. I noticed a slightly bitter taste, but the familiar metallic chemical trickle down the back of my throat reassured me that it was coke. We were going out dancing at Keystone Corner; I was all dressed up in a short blue antique velvet dress and a fancy glass necklace of red roses and green leaves. I had a crush on the musician who was playing. By the time we got to the club, though, I felt really peculiar; I had to go outside and throw up. "Uh-oh," Susie said to Russell, "you mixed up the dooge with the coke." Then she told me she had given me some heroin by mistake. It was a strange experience. When the coke hit me, I got up and danced. When the heroin hit me, I sat down and nodded out. Then I had to run outside and throw up. I went on like this all night. The guitar player I liked didn't even notice. At the end of the gig, he walked me to my car. He lifted my face up to kiss me good night and looked deeply into my eyes. "You have such beautiful . . . clothes," he said.

I spent the next three days throwing-up sick. I wondered if the heroin were mixed with strychnine; I felt like I'd been poisoned. Outside my house I ran into Suzy Nelson. "I hear you were nodding out at Keystone Corner the other night," she said. "People are talking about you; they say you're a junkie. I'm going to ask you myself: Are you?" I knew she was concerned about me. Janis Joplin and Jimi Hendrix had both died in the past few months of drug overdoses, and everyone knew there was a lot of heroin in Berkeley. My babysitter's boyfriend and his brother were both junkies. So was one of my ex-boyfriends. But that had nothing to do with me. I was astonished that my friends could even imagine such a thing. "Don't be ridiculous, Suzy," I answered her. "You know me better than that. I'm not the type to become a junkie. And besides, I don't even like the stuff. It was given to me by mistake."

It certainly was strange how heroin appeared all of a sudden, out of nowhere, and quickly became ubiquitous. One day you couldn't find it, and the next it was being offered to you backstage at the Fillmore and Avalon, being sold on Telegraph Avenue, and killing off people you knew.

One night I met Allen Ginsberg at the Woolsey Street house. He was in town working on an article for *Ramparts*, which some of the old editors had revived in a slightly different form. Ginsberg came up with documentation proving that the CIA was smuggling heroin back from Southeast Asia in the bodies of dead Vietnam soldiers. Many people believe that the CIA deliberately flooded the counterculture and music scene with heroin in the sixties and early seventies to co-opt the revolution. I have no proof to support this; it was an opinion offered up at

Woolsey Street that night as we all sat around the kitchen discussing Ginsberg's article, and one I've heard repeated many times since.

Sometime in late 1971 I went to Larkspur to visit Michael's old girlfriend Lyndall Erb, who was living in Janis Joplin's house. Albert Grossman, Janis's manager, had sent Lyndall out to stay with Janis in hopes of preventing exactly what did occur: the fatal overdose. I noticed a framed poem Janis had hung up on the wall: "It's raining in love," by Richard Brautigan. It was one of my favorites too, expressing the awkwardness and constant disappointments of romantic love.

Lyndall had a new roommate, Nancy Getz, the ex-wife of David Getz, the Big Brother drummer who my old friend Genie had grown up with in Brooklyn. David and Genie's ex, Hank Crystal, had a band that played the Catskills all through their high school days at Erasmus Hall. That day David was at the house, playing with his daughter, Alzara, on the floor. I watched him with his child and thought how nice it would be to make a family with a man like that. I was lonely again, and hanging around with Joe and Robin had somehow given me the idea that my life would be ideal if only I could settle down with just the right rock and roll musician.

Michael didn't come to see Shuna any more. We had quarreled in the past when he came to pick her up. I needed the child support we had agreed on. He claimed he didn't have the money, and never paid it to me. Then he got sick of our fights and just stopped coming over. He lived in North Berkeley, just on the other side of town, with his new girlfriend, Ellen Mandel, but he couldn't make it over to South Berkeley, where we lived. Shuna was distraught. "Where's my daddy? How come he never comes to see me?" she asked. I didn't want her to think her daddy didn't care about her, so I told her he was busy; he was working; he loved her very much. Then when I was asleep at night, I dreamt about cutting up his face with razor blades. Shuna was three, the age when little girls adore their fathers, and it broke my heart to hear her crying night after night, "I want my daddy. I want my daddy," and not be able to do anything to help. It reminded me of my own childhood, my painful relationship with my father. I had tried so hard to be different from my parents, to bring up my child a better way. And yet here she was repeating the same question I had asked my mother, the one that still tore me up inside, "Why doesn't my daddy love me?"

book 2

ABANDON HOPE, ALL YOU WHO ENTER HERE

I fell into a burning ring of fire
I went down down down and the flames grew higher
And it burns burns burns, that ring of fire.

Johnny Cash (Merle Kilgore and June Carter),
"Ring of Fire"

chapter nine

Love will make you drink and gamble
Make you stay out all night long
Love will make you do things
That you know is wrong.

Billie Holiday,
"Fine and Mellow"

IT'S RAINING IN LOVE—1972

Nick Gravenites, the blues singer whose composition "Buried Alive in the Blues" would provide the definitive description of Janis Joplin's life, was having a Christmas party in Marin County. I got dressed up in a long, black, slinky Betsey Johnson dress and my favorite black thirties coat, and went with Robin and Joe McDonald in their vintage Ford convertible. The party was full of glamorous Marin County types: tall, thin, blond women in skimpy, midriff-baring leather halter tops, and long-haired rock stars in fringed buckskins and velvet pants. Among them I noticed David Getz. "You don't know me," I said, when I spotted him alone on his way up the stairs, "but I know some old friends of yours, Genie Edelman and Hank Crystal." We spent several hours talking on the steps, and by the end of the evening, I was convinced I'd met my next old man.

Joe, who was sardonic by nature, took a dim view of my infatuation with David, as he did of almost everything. "He's perfect for me, Joe," I argued as we drove home. "He's Jewish; he's from New York; he's nice to his kid, and he's even got a brain." "Yeah," said Joe. "He's perfect except for one little detail. That band he's in is a bunch of junkies. The original bad news band. Janis is dead; James Gurley's wife is dead; and Sam's so strung out he might as well be. I don't know about David, but it's a good bet he's not Mr. Clean. I don't think you should get involved with them."

I laughed at his concern. "It's sweet of you to worry," I said, "but you really don't have to. There's no way I'm gonna become a junkie, no matter who I go out with. I don't even like heroin." By now, I'd decided that all my problems could be solved by finding the man of my dreams, and David filled the bill. We had exchanged numbers at the party, and I pursued him by calling on the phone. We had a lot to talk about, much in common, and our conversations were long and interesting. David was on the rebound from a disastrous affair following the breakup of his marriage; he was gun-shy, and I wasn't really his type. But I was determined to succeed, and eventually, after several failed attempts to get together, he showed up unexpectedly at my house.

I had just come back from driving a friend and her daughter to the doctor after some emergency or other, and was getting out of my car when David's beige BMW pulled into the driveway behind me. I'd about given up on him, disappointed that he wasn't interested, and now here he was in the flesh. Superstitiously, I chalked it up as a surprise reward for my reluctantly performed good deed. David had a big smile on his face. "I'd forgotten how pretty you were," he said. We went in the house and talked, and he ended up spending the night. He was so aloof that even while we lay in bed together talking, he couldn't look me in the face, much less directly into my eyes, and wouldn't be able to for several months to come.

On our next date, I went to visit him. He owned a house in Fairfax, up in Marin County, set high on a hill lushly covered in fragrant bay trees and purple flowering myrtle. A hundred rustic stone steps led up to the door, which his friend Bob Silverman had turned into a painting in bold primary colors and a primitive abstract design. The whole scene was funky, woodsy, and artistic, a verdant hippie paradise. David rented out the top floor and lived on the bottom, mainly in a large pine-paneled room that held his drums and piano and a long mahogany bar. He made me a grilled cheese sandwich for lunch, read my Tarot cards, and took me on a tour of his stuff, as he had carefully inspected mine when he came to Berkeley; both of us were avid collectors of flea market junk. With our New York Jewish upbringings and careers in the arts, we were temperamentally suited to being great friends, which we are to this day; but right from the beginning we had problems with our emotional connection.

Although David liked me a great deal, he wasn't in love with me. I was determined to overcome his reservations by being a model old lady, the best he had ever had. I knew he suffered deeply from the betrayals and abandonment of women he'd loved, but my fidelity, patience, and loving kindness in the face of his aloof reserve would surely win him over. In time, I convinced myself, he would grow to love me. If this was an embarrassingly familiar repetition of my jumping through hoops to win the love of my remote and disapproving father, I didn't allow myself the luxury of doubt this comparison would have occasioned. Blinders fixed firmly in place, I was hell-bent on getting what I wanted, no matter the cost, which would prove to be astronomical.

Several months into our relationship, in early 1972, David came down with hepatitis. He was cranky and irritable and insisted he wanted to be left alone, but like some perverse Florence Nightingale, I nursed him anyway. I considered David's doctor, Stephen McDade, one of the wonders of Marin County. A humanitarian part-time musician, Dr. McDade made house calls and involved himself in the lives of his patients. He told me David had serum hepatitis and asked me privately to stick around to take care of him and try to keep him away from drugs. During this time Dr. McDade and I struck up a friendship, like the one he already had with David; and even after the illness had run its course, he often came over just to hang out and play music.

David and I grew closer. Sometimes in Berkeley, sometimes in Marin, we began sharing our lives, becoming entwined in each other's worlds. My Berkeley world had changed quite a bit. In 1970 Christian and Diana had left Woolsey Street for Arica, Chile, where they studied with a Bolivian mystical master named Oscar Ichazo. Shortly afterward Susie Angelcloud had flown off to Afghanistan, where she stayed for a long time, teaching

English in an American school. Coming back through customs, she was busted for smuggling drugs in a false-bottomed suitcase. She had endured endless legal hassles before beating the charges, and then, for reasons never quite clear to me, had converted to Islam. Now she was an orthodox Muslim who wore long skirts and covered her head, and she had given up painting. Occasionally I saw her when she babysat for Seven, but her new persona puzzled me, and I missed the old spirited, whimsical Susie with her bizarre artistic vision and ready, tinkling laugh. Christian and Diana showed up briefly in Berkeley, looking surprisingly clean-cut, then went off to New York with the rest of the people from their Chile training to start a school called Arica. So I didn't have much cause to hang out at Woolsey Street anymore, though I remained and still remain friends with some of the other women.

Tom Luddy, a friend of Robin's and mine, opened the Pacific Film Archives in the University Art Museum. We went to showings of old movies there. Tom lived with Alice Waters, and the walls of their little cottage, like mine, were covered with patchwork quilts. A few times we all went over to Francis Ford Coppola's house in the city for special screenings. Robin dressed to kill for these occasions in fabulous designer outfits; Sonia Rykiel was a favorite. Joe had gotten a windfall from his accidental appearance at Woodstock, where he had replaced no-show John Sebastian at the last minute, and Robin was spending the loot from the movie as fast as it came in. Alice was busy preparing to open a new kind of restaurant in Berkeley called Chez Panisse, and Suzy Nelson was going to work for her. Berkeley was changing, losing its funky hippie charm and turning into a consumer culture based on hip aesthetics we'd developed in our own lives through the late sixties and early seventies; our flea market styles and preference for organic, natural foods had become chic and were on the verge of becoming big business.

But I was really only half-involved in these new developments. Often when I went to David's, I stayed for three or four days. When I came back to Berkeley, my house felt uninhabited, like all the life had gone out of it, and it took me days to settle down in it again. I wasn't all that comfortable with David's friends in Marin County. Once when I arrived there, a whole bunch of people had been nodding out in the living room, and David acted very strange and distant to me. People sometimes brought him heroin when I was there, and there were always other women, groupies and old and new girlfriends, who flirted with him in front of me. Sometimes he would come home to find a naked girl in his bed. Needless to say, this did not make me feel very happy or secure about our relationship. I got along fine with Bob Silverman, the artist/ photographer who was David's best friend; he was around so much that I felt like I was really involved with both of them. David's daughter, Alzara, was a sweet little blond girl who was a year younger than Shuna; I grew to love her a lot. Often the two girls would play together, and we'd cook meals and take the kids places, just like a regular family.

I got very uptight when people brought David smack or when his junkie friends were around, and David and Silverman teased me a lot about the bad vibes I sent out. "Try it, you'll like it," David would say, but I couldn't; I was terrified of heroin. The struggles I had gone through with Lorraine when she was strung out were engraved in my memory, and my own experimentation hadn't left me with much of a taste for it. David also smoked alarming quantities of pot. Before we went anywhere, he'd roll four or five joints just for the ride in the car. I didn't much like that either; smoking pot made me paranoid, but it didn't scare me like the smack did.

David was only a cautious, occasional user of smack. He liked it, but had seen enough of his friends go down to have a healthy fear of its power. He hated what it had done to Big Brother. I saw it myself once when he took me to a gig. The band was playing behind a singer named Kathi McDonald. David loaded his drums into the car; he had built a little tram that ran up and down the hill expressly for that purpose; and we drove down to Sunnyvale, about an hour away. Peter Albin, the bass player, far and away the most dependable member of the band, was the only one there. David told Peter they should change the name of the band to Big Bother and the Folding Company. People showed up late for gigs or didn't show up at all. Sometimes they were so high they forgot the words to songs or stumbled off the stage. When David introduced me to Sam Andrew, their Texan guitarist, Sam asked me, "Aren't you the lady who wrote all that nice stuff about us in the press when everyone else was putting us down? I've always wanted to thank you for that." I was flattered and touched that he remembered what I'd written.

In the spring I went to New York to visit my family. David joined me there, and we had our best, most romantic time together. He came to my family's house, and I stayed with him in the Chelsea Hotel. While I was in New York, I had lunch with my old editor at the *New York Times Magazine*, and he offered me an assignment to write a profile of Randy Newman, the quirky singer-songwriter with the bizarre sense of humor; he sounded like someone I'd like.

Back in California I flew to LA to interview him. I loved his music, which was literary and intelligent, full of allusions to movie idioms, popular music traditions, history, satire, and old rock and roll. Liking the music was one thing, however; writing about it another. The *New York Times Magazine* was demanding and exacting; often I had to rework my stories several times, and each one took months of effort.

I was still taking speed to write my articles, and after a few days of writing in isolation, I began having imaginary conversations with Randy Newman where we analyzed each of his songs and their possible meanings in minute detail. One weekend David and I went to a party at the Grateful Dead's ranch in Novato. A woman moved through the crowd dispensing tiny spoonfuls of ground, dried psilocybin mushrooms from a wooden box. The psilocybin put me in a state of heightened awareness, not characterized by hallucinations, as with LSD, but by a crystalline clarity. That night we met Greil and Jenny Marcus at a San Francisco theater for a Randy Newman concert. I might have been inclined to say it was the drugs, but Greil, who was stone-cold sober, agreed that the performance was a transcendent experience.

I was pleased with my finished article, and so were my editors at the *Times*. Buoyed up by success, I decided to write an article I'd fantasized doing since I became a journalist: a profile of Fred Astaire. I got an assignment from a magazine and flew to LA with Joe, who was doing a gig there. I spent a week in a screening room in Hollywood, watching every movie Astaire ever made, and stayed at the Chateau Marmont. The night before I was to interview Astaire, I dreamt that we were going to dinner at Chez Panisse. For some reason, all the tables had been pushed together. I stumbled and tripped at every turn, while Astaire floated through nearly nonexistent spaces with consummate grace. Despite my dream the interview went smoothly.

The magazine that had commissioned my Astaire article went out of business before I finished writing, and the story ended up in *Rolling Stone*. I met with Jann Wenner, who apologized for treating me badly in the past and offered to make amends. I asked that my article, which was long, not be cut or changed without my permission, and he gave me his word. By the time the article appeared in the magazine, though, it had been heavily cut and edited, and Jann had broken every promise he made to me; still I was happy to see the work in print. Now I was working and writing on a regular basis. I did short profiles for the Arts and Leisure section of the *New York Times,* as well as longer pieces for the magazine, and I wrote them all on speed.

One day Larry Switzer, Mark's older brother, dropped by my house with Artie Ross, a friend from Woolsey Street days. Both of them had taken the Arica three-month training in New York and returned to start a teaching house in San Francisco. They offered me a free training if I would write an article about it for the *New York Times Magazine.* Larry showed me some of the exercises they did in the daily gym, and told me about the meditations and mystical work of the school. He was full of enthusiasm, as he always was for any new trip he undertook, and the theory sounded interesting, but I declined their offer. I was still certain that mysticism had nothing to do with my life.

After David and I had been seeing each other for over a year, our relationship, while far from perfect, felt stable and secure enough that we thought it might go on for a while. We'd talked about moving in together and occupying both floors of his house. I was wary of giving up my little cottage in Berkeley. It was affordable, comfortable, and mine, a home I'd maintained for me and Shuna over all the years I'd been alone. But I wanted the relationship to work, and living together seemed like the logical next step. The timing was good; Shuna would be entering first grade in the fall. We decided to take the plunge.

Now I thought I had everything. My career was in full bloom. I had a great old man. We lived in one of the most beautiful houses in all of Marin County, a woodsy palace filled with antique furniture, art, and high-status hippie collectibles. Our two beautiful children played together naked on the deck outside. We had love, money, beautiful clothes, independent lives, and an idyllic home in paradise. What more could anyone have wanted? David built me a room downstairs to write in, wood-paneled, with a stained glass window. We hired a live-in babysitter for the children. We wrote songs together and started a small music publishing company. When two books on Janis Joplin's life were published close together, David and I collaborated on a review of them for *Ms.* magazine. Ellen Willis came out from New York to visit and helped me edit the piece. She and I spent hours in my writing room downstairs, absorbed in discussions of Janis's music and the tragic effect heroin had had on her life. David's friends came over to jam. The days were long and sunny and warm. It was a full, rich life.

But despite the time I had spent at David's before the move, it was still difficult for me to adjust to having left Berkeley, where I had had my own life and friends. I didn't quite fit in with the laid-back Marin County crowd. I was too intellectual, too much a feminist, too political, outspoken, and smart to be the perfect old lady I had aspired to. I didn't feel pretty enough to compete with the long-legged blond *shikse* beauties who peopled David's fantasies and constantly caught his eye. Almost from the first day I moved in, I felt the stirrings of something wrong. David was still cold and distant to me at times, self-absorbed and holding back from a full commitment to our shared life. Our babysitter, a cheerful young woman named Heidi, was horrified at the way he would leave the house without so much as kissing me good-bye. My sister Sheila, who had moved to Berkeley and spent a lot of time with us, used to say that David was *"too* cool." But I had a part in it too. All my life I'd suffered from boredom and a persistent feeling of emptiness. Something was gnawing away at my insides, some deep self-hatred and perverse inclination toward self-destruction. I felt like a chronic malcontent. I knew I should be grateful for my good fortune; after all, I had everything I'd ever thought I wanted. Yet often I would find myself alone in the house, sitting in the dark on the living room sofa, listening to the crickets chirp outside in the trees and wondering, "Is this all there is to life?"

David had lower back troubles as a result of an old car crash. One night, without warning, his back went out; he lay down on the floor and couldn't get back up again. Bob Silverman and I couldn't get him down the stairs to take him to the hospital, so we called an ambulance and rode with him to Marin General. Before David was even out of the emergency room, Silverman stood by the side of his bed asking, "What'd they give you? Is it good? Let me have some too." They'd given him Percodan, and when we got home from the hospital, all three of us took it. I was amazed by how good the pill made me feel: at peace, happy, whole, and complete, like there was nothing else I needed and no place in the world I'd rather be. "You like it," said Silverman, "don't you? Well, if you like this, you'd love smack. This is just synthetic smack. Maybe now you can understand why we do the stuff."

David was away on tour when Silverman called me one night. "My friend Jason is here, and we're just hanging out. Why don't you come over?" When I got there, Jason and Silverman were high, talking softly, drifting in and out of a nod. "We got some boss smack," said Silverman, and offered me some. I hesitated. "Try it; you'll like it," he said. "You liked the Percodan, didn't you?" I rolled up a dollar bill and sniffed a little of the bitter powder into each of my nostrils. He was right; I did like it. I felt comfortable and mellow, basking in the luxurious warmth of the drug's euphoria and the pleasant companionship and easy talk of the men. I didn't even get sick, like I had in Berkeley.

When David came home from Europe, we all got high together. We drove down to the Tenderloin and David went to a pay phone. Using the code name "Breakaway," he called a connection named J. D., who lived across the street. J. D. sent his assistant, a young boy named Ronnie, downstairs with a balloon in his cheek. The balloon cost twenty dollars, and when the knotted top was split open, we could see that it contained what looked like a hefty pile of whitish powder flecked with brown, more than enough for all three of us to get down.

We went home and sat around the kitchen table. I was teaching myself to crochet from a book, making an intricate multicolored sweater. I worked on my crocheting, while David and Silverman sketched and talked. "How'd you get her to do this?" David asked Silverman. "I told her, 'Try it; you'll like it,'" he said. "And sure enough, she did." We laughed. All of us were drifting pleasantly in a calm, easy state. David and I felt soft and loving toward each other, newly reunited in the cozy enveloping warmth of home, relaxed and congenial with our mutual best friend. For the first time, I wondered why this drug had such a bad reputation. I loved the feeling it gave me, the womb-like security and pacifying comfort of being held in someone's arms. When I took it, like when I first tried the Percodan, I felt like a normal person: content and happy, lacking nothing. All the demons that regularly tormented me—dissatisfaction, restlessness, anxiety, and depression—vanished into thin air. I was filled with happiness, love, creativity, and inspiration, pampered and protected, floating on a cloud of perfect bliss.

The next day I felt sort of irritable. I was short-tempered with Shuna, easily angered by the million tiny hassles of everyday life. But I didn't connect this feeling to the drug. David and Silverman used the drug sparingly, careful to avoid doing it too many days in a row and getting strung out. Under their guidance I didn't feel as though I were in any great danger. It was no big deal, just another drug, like the many we'd used for years to expand our consciousness, buck the establishment, explore the unmapped territories of inner space. I thought I was smart enough to be able to use this drug without becoming a junkie, even if it did make me feel better than I had ever felt in my life. I just wanted to do it again, and soon.

Ever since my miscarriage in London, I'd had fibroid cysts in my breasts. Now, at my routine gynecological exam, my doctor felt something suspicious in one of my breasts and sent me to have a mammogram, the kind where the lab technician fills the room with nitrogen and then takes photographs that show up lumps as hot spots in the breasts. On my thirtieth birthday, the doctor called. "I don't want to alarm you," he said, "but we found a hot spot on the mammogram. You'll have to check into the hospital for surgery right away. It's a matter of pressing concern. We can't wait. We have to do a biopsy of the lump immediately."

Naturally the first thing that crossed my mind was breast cancer, and mentally I prepared myself for death. To my surprise what I regretted most when I thought about dying was not that I would never write a book or leave behind some great creative opus, but rather that I would never be able to have another baby. I had hoped to develop a stable enough family environment with David that I could have another child. That was my heart's desire. At the hospital I had to sign a paper authorizing the surgeon to remove my breast if the lump were cancerous, and as I went under anesthesia before the operation, I was utterly panicked, not knowing what I would find when I woke up.

I found a large scar running across the top of my nipple, but my breast was intact. The cyst was benign, a great relief, but inwardly I felt profoundly changed by my confrontation with mortality. My daughter seemed more precious to me than ever; but I experienced a curious detachment from David and the emotional nuances of our relationship, which normally obsessed me and which caused me endless pain.

David had changed too. Faced with the prospect of losing me, he had realized how much I meant to him, and now had fallen in love with me. He was more affectionate and gentle toward me than he had ever been. I should have been happy; this was what I had always thought I wanted. But the change was so striking that by contrast I saw how little he had loved me before. I felt a growing resentment over how he had treated me in the past and foolish for having put up with it. Now the tables had turned. As I folded inward upon myself, focusing my energy on healing, David grew more loving and attentive; sometimes he even mentioned marriage. Now I was the remote and self-sufficient partner, and David the pursuer.

For Christmas David took me on a vacation to Jamaica. In Negril, where we stayed, we played out our new roles. I had brought along a stack of Joyce Carol Oates novels, and I mainly wanted to be left alone to sunbathe and read, while he was inclined toward a romantic honeymoon type of trip. On our way home, I got to chatting in the airport with a good-looking guy from Libya, and I found myself wildly attracted to him, so much so that after our return I made a date to meet him at my sister's house in Berkeley. David called there, crazy with jealousy. I knew perfectly well that David had been unfaithful to me many times in the course of our relationship, and I didn't mind getting even with him now.

After that it seemed as though we were always fighting. We fought about money, about dope, about who had done what to whom in the past, about who cared more about the relationship. Each of us blamed the other, full of anger and recriminations. During these exchanges David got mad, turned cold, and stormed out of the house, leaving me crying. Sometimes I collapsed in tears in Shuna's bed, where she tried her best to comfort me. I didn't really understand what had happened between us. I still loved David, and it was unbearable to me that this relationship, which had started out with such great promise, the answer to all my prayers, should be turning out so badly. More and more it seemed that the only time we felt good together, able to express our love for each other, was when we were high on heroin; and as time went on, we used it with increasing frequency to solve our problems and talk out our differences. At first a twenty-dollar balloon from J. D. kept both of us high for several days. Then we used the whole thing in one night. And then we bought more than one at a time.

David always did the copping, from the same phone booth on the corner across the street. I asked him for J. D.'s phone number, but he wouldn't give it to me. "J. D. would eat you alive," he said. "He'd make mincemeat out of you." We knew a woman so hopelessly addicted that all she did was go back and forth on the Bridgeway in Sausalito, giving blow jobs to strangers in cars until she had enough money to cop from J. D. I felt sorry for her, but without empathy; I couldn't believe that would ever happen to me. Now, whenever David asked what I wanted to do, I suggested we go to the city and cop, but we still weren't strung out and didn't get high often enough for my taste.

Bob Scheer had gotten me and Anne Weills jobs starting a women's studies program at a progressive college in San Francisco called Antioch West. The previous year I had done a big article on contemporary women writers. It was supposed to be a cover story for *Saturday Review*, but the day it was due, the magazine folded, and I had done so much research that I ended up with enough material to teach a course in the subject. So I taught women's literature and writing and I had students for independent study projects. Once a week, on Tuesday nights, I went to the city to teach my class. Often I was coming down from heroin, which we'd been using all weekend. I'd stopped being able to use speed to write. After I'd finished one short profile for the Arts and Leisure section, I had taken it to Western Union to cable it to my editor. The office was on Market Street, downtown. On my way home to Marin, I had started hallucinating monsters on the side of the road. It scared me, and now I didn't use speed any more. I supposed heroin was slowly taking its place; I noticed that it gave me creative energy and wondered if I could use it to help me write.

That winter was rainy and cold, and I needed a new winter coat. Cheryl, James Gurley's ex, had one I liked, a suede jacket lined with curly brown lamb. I called her to find out where she had gotten it, and she invited me over to the house in Woodacre where she'd stayed since leaving James. I had almost never gone out at night without David since I'd lived in Marin, but I drove over to Cheryl's. One of her roommates, who worked as a chef, offered me some coffee and cheesecake he had just made. Rocky was tall and thin, with long hair that he swung over his shoulder with a toss of his head, a rock star's gesture. He sat down next to me and looked straight into my eyes. "You can come over here any time you want," he said. Later he tried to talk me into staying. I felt drawn to him almost against my will, but was so confused and scared that I tore myself away and went home.

I thought about Rocky all the next day. Finally I called him at the restaurant where he worked; we made a date to meet in Fairfax and go for a walk. "I used to be a heroin addict," he told me. "I've been clean for three months now." "You're really lucky," I said. "You mean lucky to be alive?" he asked. "No," I said, "Lucky to have done all that dope." He gave me a strange look I couldn't quite interpret, but which nevertheless sent a shiver through my body.

A few days later, he called me on the phone. "Come down to the restaurant," he said. "I get off at five. Meet me in the parking lot." David had gone to play a gig; one of my students was living in the house in exchange for babysitting, so she would look after Shuna. I drove to Larkspur and met Rocky in the parking lot behind the Lark Creek Inn, a picturesque yellow Victorian house in a woodsy setting, which had been converted into a fancy French restaurant.

Rocky was wearing a white chef's coat and black-and-white checked pants. His long hair hung down his back in a single braid. "Someone brought me this today," he said, opening his hand to show me a folded-up piece of paper with some brown heroin inside. "I have works at my house. Let's go." I had never shot up before. I was scared, but also attracted, curious to see what it was I'd been missing. He got in the car and we drove to Lagunitas, where he'd just rented a room in a house with some women. The house smelled of incense. We went into Rocky's room and closed the door. From a drawer in his bureau, he pulled out a dirty paper towel. Inside there was a large, bent spoon with the bottom crusted black. An eyedropper, attached to a baby pacifier with a rubber band, had a needle stuck in the end of it. Rocky added some water to the dope in the spoon and lit a book of matches under it till the powder dissolved and the mixture started to boil, filling the room with a sticky sweet odor. Then he drew it up through a tiny piece of cotton into the eyedropper, jabbed the needle into a horribly scarred vein in the crook of his elbow, moved it around till red blood swirled into the clear brownish liquid, and injected it all with a gasp of pleasure. "Okay," he said after a minute. "Your turn." I closed my eyes and held out my arm. The needle was barbed and hurt going in, but the rush of the drug in my vein was exquisite. Warmth spread under my skin and moved deep into my stomach. My head fell forward and my eyelids dropped shut. I drifted into a peaceful dream space. Soon I was cushioned in contentment. Love and well-being oozed from my pores. Rocky started to kiss me, and I didn't resist. After all, I wasn't a virgin any more. I had just had my first shot of dope, had gotten my wings, and now I would fly with a lover.

David had rented the downstairs of the house out to a couple of his friends, Jim and Irina. Irina was a beautiful, statuesque Russian woman who had studied ballet and worked as a model. She wasn't strung out, but she liked dope. A few times she'd brought home some opium and cooked it over the stove on a bent-up wire coat hanger. I confided in Irina about Rocky and asked her what to do. "You don't have to feel guilty," she said. "David's slept with half the women I know in this town. Just be cool." Luckily David was so busy that he barely noticed my comings and goings.

Shuna noticed, though. She'd always been observant; now she was almost six, and not much got by her. One night I was putting her to bed. I had just come home from Rocky's and was high, nearly nodding out. "Mommy, wake up!" she said sharply. "What's wrong with you?" Another time she asked me how come every time I saw Rocky I talked in a different voice. Heroin lowers the register of your voice, giving junkies that characteristic gritty rasp so familiar from old blues records. When I was high, I spoke in a slightly husky tone, not at all like my normal voice. It's one of the things that happens, like the pupils of your eyes contracting to narrow pin dots, that gives you away to anyone who knows the signs.

I saw Rocky all the time now, as much as I could. I knew I was on a collision course with disaster, but I didn't really care. I couldn't stay away from him. When David and I were together, all we did was fight. Often he went to stay at his friend Herbie's house for days at a time. Sometimes we made up when he came home, usually by going to J. D.'s to cop a couple of balloons of dope, so we could stand to be around each other. When he was gone, I took Shuna to school in the morning, then I went to Rocky's job to pick up money from him, and drove into the city to cop from his connection, a musician who lived in Pacific Heights. Rocky fixed his own shot in the restaurant parking lot, and then I went home and waited until he got off work for him to come and fix me my shot. I was afraid to shoot up by myself, scared that if I knew how to do it, I'd kill myself by accident, like Janis. On the other hand, not knowing whether I was going to live or die after the needle went in my arm definitely appealed to me. Living on the edge and flirting with death was a big part of the drug's allure.

Sometimes when I was at Rocky's, I cried about missing David so much. Then when I was with David, I wondered how I could escape to be with Rocky. No matter what I did, I was never happy. And I was getting more strung out by the day. David thought I was shooting dope with Irina. That was what I told him, and she backed me up. I think he didn't really want to know. Things were so bad between us we didn't even know if we were going to stay together. But I still loved him; and with all my heart, I wished there were some way to make it better, a way for us to work things out.

I couldn't believe what had happened to me, the change had been so sudden and shocking. A few months before I had been a normal, wholesome woman, taking care of my child, writing articles, living with my old man, getting high once in a while but keeping things together. Now I was like a skeleton. I weighed about ninety pounds. My arms were so scarred up from Rocky's barbed needles that I had to wear long-sleeved shirts all the time, even in hundred-degree weather. I didn't do anything anymore but cop and get high. Sometimes Rocky and I went to Bolinas Beach to get tan, so people wouldn't notice the junkie pallor of our skin. But even at the beach we had to hold our arms folded at the elbows to hide our tracks. One day I came home to Fairfax. David was downstairs practicing drums. He stopped playing when I came in, looked at me, and burst into tears. "What's happened to you?" he cried. "I hardly recognize you any more. You look like a corpse." "You got me into it," I said. "You were the one who told me, 'Try it; you'll like it.'" "Yeah," he said. "But you like it too much. I'm really scared for you, Susan, and I don't know what to do."

I went out in the morning to take Shuna to school and cop for Rocky. When I got home, David was gone. In our bedroom my favorite dress, a long Indonesian batik I wore for a nightgown, was torn to shreds and tacked up on the wall. On the bed was a note from David. "If you have any love for me at all then please do not try to find me or contact me," it said. "I'm sorry if I led you to believe that what has been happening is OK. I never felt that it was. I will try to write you sooner or later and explain my real feelings." I got on the phone and frantically tried to find David, but everywhere I called, Herbie's, Silverman's, they said they hadn't seen him. Then I lay down on the bed and sobbed. What had happened to us? What had happened to me? I felt like my life was spinning out of control, toward some horrible catastrophe that I was powerless to prevent. I was in so much pain I couldn't stand it. The only thing I knew how to do was use more dope; then at least the pain would stop for a minute. But the dope had turned against me too, making everything worse. I cried until the bedspread was soaked with tears. I'd never felt so hopeless and alone. But at five o'clock Rocky got off from work, fixed me with my shot, and by that night we were off and running again.

·

```
I'll pack my bags and run so far from here
                              Goodbye, dear
           I feel the monkey in your soul.

                                 Steely Dan,
                         "Monkey in Your Soul"
```

REPULSE MONKEY—1973

Rocky told me he'd been sharing his rig with a girl who'd come down with hepatitis, so I went to Marin General and got a gamma globulin shot. When I got home, David was there. He felt as bad about the situation as I did; I could hear the anguish in his voice. "I don't want us to break up," he said. "Isn't there a way we can work things out, something we can do? I'm willing to try anything." I was happy to see him; he'd been gone for a week. In honor of our reunion, we drove down to J. D.'s and copped. It was the last time for a while, we agreed; after this we'd cool out. We got high together and talked things over. I told David about Rocky. "I can't stand for you to be with another man," he said. "If you want to keep seeing him, you'll have to move out of the house." I didn't want to lose my home, so I promised David I'd stop seeing Rocky.

I had never been dopesick, so I didn't know what to expect. I didn't even know enough to be scared of it. I didn't feel too well for a few days; I was grouchy, achy, cried a lot, and had trouble sleeping. I noticed that I sweated profusely and that the sweat had a peculiar acrid odor, but the symptoms were nothing I couldn't handle. I missed Rocky and missed getting high, but I was glad to have a break; I'd been worried about the hepatitis.

Everything went all right for a few weeks. Then David didn't come home one night, and I found out he had spent the night with another woman. I was hurt and angry. Here I couldn't see my lover, and David was still doing the same old stuff, sleeping around whenever he wanted. I called Rocky and arranged to meet him in the parking lot of the restaurant. He was sitting outside on the wooden back steps, waiting for me, when I got there. He picked me up off the ground and twirled me around and around in the air; that's how glad he was to see me. He'd cleaned up in the time I was gone, too, so we didn't cop; instead we bought a bottle of champagne and the finest cognac we could find, then joked about how much money we'd saved by not buying dope. When you do heroin, money ceases to have any conventional value; your whole perspective changes, so that buying something most people would consider a major extravagance is a money-saving bargain to a junkie. That night we got drunk. It was kind of nice without the dope; I didn't have to keep my usual vigil, picking up the lit cigarettes Rocky dropped on himself while nodding, in terror that he'd set the bed, the house, and both of us on fire.

Now that we'd cleaned up, we were sure we could get high again without getting a habit, so it was only a matter of time before we were back to our same old normal routine. This time things deteriorated between me and David faster than they had before, and soon we had another fight and he left again. I was too angry even to look for him. Instead I called Larry Switzer in Berkeley, and asked him to come over. "I need to talk to you about something really important," I said, "and I can't discuss it on the phone." He arrived in his mother's gold Porsche, and we took a walk in a park nearby. The leafy bay trees towered over us, scenting the air with subtle spice. It was truly beautiful there; I felt like a fool for being so miserable, in trouble in paradise, but I had to tell someone what I'd been doing, so I poured out my heart to Larry. "I'm strung out. I'm a junkie. I'm afraid I'm gonna die. I never thought this could happen to me, and now that it has, I don't know who I am any more, just that I'm not who I thought I was," I said. "Good," he said. "Maybe now you'll be willing to try something new." He told me there was an Arica training starting in San Francisco in April and suggested I take it. I said I would think about it. He said if I needed him again, not to hesitate to call.

This time when David came back home, I felt different, stronger, more detached. I'd more or less accepted that it was over between us and was determined to do what I could to save my own skin. David still wanted to try to work things out. He suggested we do some kind of therapy, primal screaming or gestalt. "I'm doing an Arica training," I told him. "You can do it too, if you want, but I'm going whether you come along or not." I called Larry in Berkeley. He wasn't home, but his mother, Elise, answered the phone. "Come on over," she said. "I need you to help me with something. Mark is coming back from Hawaii, and I want you to pick him up at the airport." I hadn't seen Mark in years, since our breakup. The *Kialoa* had been destroyed; it went up on the beach during a kona storm, and Mark was finally coming home. Butterflies fluttered in my stomach at the prospect of seeing him again, but I couldn't imagine he'd be pleased to spot me first thing off the plane. "I don't think he'd like it," I protested. "Never mind what he wants," said Elise. "You're doing this for me."

So Shuna and I were waiting for Mark at the airport when he stepped off the plane. He looked older and more battered than the last time I'd seen him, but of course I'd changed too. I was skinny, nervous, high-strung, and my arms, hidden under a gauzy Mexican long-sleeved shirt, were covered with bruises and tiny red scabs along the main veins. Mark was surprised to see us, but before long our old friendship took over, and we spent the next few days at Elise's house in the Berkeley hills, catching up on the story of his journey and my current troubled state of affairs. I told him I wanted to take the Arica forty-day training because I was desperate and didn't know what else to do. He asked how much it cost, took out his checkbook, and wrote a six-hundred-dollar check payable to Arica rather than to me. I returned home to Marin County with the certainty that however bad things got, help was on the way.

David had also decided to take the training. We asked Anne, my student and our babysitter, to stay with Shuna so she could continue going to school, and we arranged to house-sit for some friends in the City during the week. David had experimented with transcendental meditation, but I'd never considered any kind of meditation a possibility for myself before. At this point, however, I was willing to try anything that might save me from being a junkie. I knew if I continued the way I'd been going, on the be-bop with Rocky, I'd be dead within a matter of months.

The Arica training took place in a large, carpeted, serene room, part of a suite of offices in a modern building on Market Street. The trainers all had short hair, clean, open-looking faces, and supple, well-muscled bodies dressed in leotards and exercise clothes. They had a space-age "Star Trek" kind of appearance, and the training room, decorated with nothing but a large geometric painting, the purple carpet, cushions, a gong, and an incense holder, also looked sleek and futuristically modern. We learned physical exercises and simple meditations, and heard lectures on the theoretical basis of the Arica system, which was described as a marriage of science and mysticism, specially formulated for our fast-paced technological era.

Two things I heard in the lectures resonated with my own deeply held convictions. One was that the planet was dying and that humanity's only hope for survival was the attainment of a new, higher level of consciousness. And the second was that this jump in consciousness could not happen without complete equality between men and women. I noticed the democratic atmosphere that prevailed in the training, the seeming equality between the men and women trainers. On the whole, I was skeptical about a lot of what was in the lectures and found it immensely difficult to do the physical work, which included yoga exercises like standing on your head. Some of the long meditations bored me so badly it was all I could do not to run out of the building and never come back. But I stayed because I knew that if I left, I'd be copping dope and getting high within minutes, precisely what I was trying to escape.

At home in our borrowed apartment, David and I quarreled about the training. He was conscientious about homework and proud of his ability to do the physical work. I was flaky about the homework, had a bad attitude in general, and often hid in the bathroom during some of the more strenuous physical exercises. But I didn't shoot dope, at least not during the week, and by Friday, when my tracks had healed, I was able to wear a short-sleeved leotard to the training. The first Friday night, David had a gig to play in Sonoma County. I arranged to meet Rocky in the city, and we got high and went back to his house in Lagunitas.

This became the pattern of our weeks in the training. Sometimes I enjoyed the peaceful atmosphere in the meditation room, and more and more I liked the work and the trainers, who beneath their clean-cut exteriors, seemed to have come from the more marginal world that I knew so well. We had to do a walking meditation outdoors each day, and David and I started out from a fountain near the facility, where he smoked a joint before the walk. I was surprised to find that when I smoked with him, my meditation improved, and I didn't experience my former pot-induced paranoia. Through the Arica regime of exercise and diet, supplemented with a high-powered nutritious drink called Dragon's Milk, I felt some of my health and vitality return, and often I experienced a new feeling I could only describe as a lightness of spirit. Still, by Friday, I was so anxious to get high that I almost couldn't stand to be inside my skin.

In the fourth week of the training, I broke down in tears and told one of the trainers, a gay doctor named Richard, that I had to drop out. "Don't," he said. "We'll take you out to lunch today and talk about it then." Richard invited another teacher, an artist with the handsome face and sculptured body of a classical Greek statue, to eat with us. "Now then, Susan," the doctor said, when we were sitting down with our sandwiches, "why do you want to drop out?" I broke down crying. "I can't do this," I sobbed. "I'm a junkie, and all I think about during the meditations is how much I want to get high. When we imagine a large globe filled with light, mine has a big syringe sitting right in the middle." Jimmy, the artist, immediately perked up. "You're a junkie?" he said. "I'm a junkie too. I used to shoot heroin." I was stunned; far from judging me, they were actually sympathetic and understanding. "Don't drop out," said Richard. "We think you're fabulous, and we want you to stay." The acceptance and tolerance I felt from them, their attitude that it was okay for me to be exactly who I was, so encouraged me and helped me feel I belonged that I decided to stick around a little longer and see what happened.

We did some intensive work called Psychoalchemy that week, powerful exercises for the transmutation of sexual into psychic energy; and to my astonishment, on Friday night I was able to watch Rocky fix his dope and turn down my own shot. Every day in the training we did what was called "karma cleaning" in groups, recalling painful incidents from our pasts involving sex, money, and power. During the sex karma cleaning, I sat in a group at one end of the room and talked about Rocky, while David sat at the other end. I strained to hear what he discussed but couldn't make it out. By the end of the training, an all-pervasive feeling of unity, happiness, and exhilaration spread among the members of our group, so strong that its benevolence extended even to David's and my relationship. Now I felt uneasy having secrets from him, and in our new atmosphere of honesty, openness, and trust, I confided to him that I'd been seeing Rocky all along and lying to him about it.

We were sitting outside on the deck of our house in Fairfax. Both of us were planning to go to the Arica advanced training in New York later in the summer. I expected David to be tolerant and to view my confession for what it was: an attempt to clean karma with him so I didn't have to live with the guilt of my secret, and so we could start anew with a fresh slate. But that wasn't the way he saw it. "How could you do that to me?" he demanded. "How could you lie?" "You lied to me all the time," I said. "What about when you said you were going to the grocery store and on the way home you fucked the airline stewardess around the corner? You just lied by omission; it's the same thing." "No, it's not," said David. "I never deliberately told you a lie. When I said I was going grocery shopping, I came home with the groceries." Then he stormed off in a rage.

I looked different now. As a symbol of my new inner changes from the training, I had cut off all my hair, Arica-style, and it was in sort of a crew-cut. I had finally learned to stand on my head; in my opinion this monumental achievement was worth the entire price of admission. I felt stronger, happier, more hopeful about a life beyond my heroin addiction, and even, until this moment, about the chances of salvaging our relationship. But these hopes were quickly dashed as David, distant and angered beyond all reason by my confession about Rocky, made plans to fly to New York early and stay with his sister until the advanced training began. I wept and pleaded for him to stay, forgive me, work things out; but he was determined to go, and did so almost immediately. I felt shattered.

With David gone there was no limit to how much time I could spend with Rocky, and we stayed together every night, either in his room in Lagunitas or mine at the Fairfax house. Rocky had always paid for our dope before, with earnings from his job; now I began selling some of my prize antique possessions and using the money I'd saved for my airfare to New York and the advanced training to feed my ever-increasing habit. When I called David in New York, he refused to speak to me, and I cried my heart out to Shuna or Anne, and sometimes even to Rocky. Within a matter of weeks, I was strung-out, broke, and as desperate as I had been before the forty-day, with no apparent escape from my predicament. Then one day I was driving home from the grocery store with Shuna, and some young boys, in a hurry to get to their high school graduation, careened into my car on the driver's side from a blind, intersecting street. The one who was driving quickly handed me his insurance agent's card, and they took off again in a rush.

The next day I went to the insurance agent's office. He inspected the driver's side, where the door had never opened since I'd owned the car, and wrote me a check on the spot for the damages. It was just enough to pay for my airfare and training, the exact amount I needed. I quickly sent a check off to New York, bought a plane ticket, and called Joe in Berkeley. "I need your help," I pleaded. "Can you come over and take care of the kids and make sure, no matter what I say, that I get on this plane to New York next week?" He came, viewed the circus of my everyday life with his usual jaundiced eye, and when the day came, drove us to the San Francisco airport. Rocky whined and begged me to give him just ten dollars more, for just one more bag, since I was leaving him all alone, but his pleas fell on deaf ears. I couldn't wait to get out of there. Joe made sure Shuna and I got on the plane, and soon we were airborne, on our way to New York and safety.

My mother was horrified by my appearance. She'd never seen me so skinny, so nervous, and my short haircut didn't help; it made me look like an Auschwitz survivor. I was tan enough to cover my junkie pallor, and didn't stick around long enough for her to discover the scars beneath my long sleeves, but she was troubled nonetheless. A woman from my forty-day had offered to put me up in her parents' Sutton Place apartment during the training, so although I was broke, I lived for the next three weeks in the lap of luxury. I had hoped that David and I would get back together when I came to New York, so I called him frequently from her apartment, but he had taken up with one of his sister's girlfriends and wanted nothing to do with me; it was all over between us, he said. I begged him to see me, forgive me, love me again. "Too late," he said coldly, and hung up the phone.

The first day of the training, we had to wait on line to get our Dragon's Milk. I spotted David standing in line as soon as I walked in. In an instant all the anger, heartbreak, and frustration I had felt over the past few months came to a rolling boil, and without thinking what I was doing, I marched right over to an unsuspecting David and punched him in the face. Soon we were scuffling in the hallway, while everyone watched in rapt fascination. A trainer named Max, a tall guy with glasses and unruly brown hair, came running over. "Someone separate those two!" he yelled, then waded in between us and did it himself.

Neither David nor Max seemed to hold my momentary lapse into violence against me, and the rest of the training proceeded without incident. About four hundred people from all over the country had come to New York for the training. Each morning we streamed up the escalator, through the fabric-draped blue cocoon, into the sumptuous modern offices of 24 West Fifty-Seventh Street, to do our Psychocalisthenics exercises, breathe, meditate, and learn about mysticism and the internal workings of our psyches. We studied domains and dichotomies, Kabbala, Tarot, the enneagon of ego fixations, and various other aspects of Arica theory and practice. The atmosphere in the training was relaxed and good-natured. I ran into Christian, who was teaching, and we reminisced about old times in Berkeley, which now seemed as if they had happened a century ago.

I was fascinated by the Arica theory, the maps and measurements to define the parameters of the human mind, the complex meditations, the acceleration of personal process through the utilization of group energy. But I noticed certain awkward wordings in the instructional manuals, which I ascribed to their having been translated from Spanish, Oscar Ichazo's native language. After a morning session one day, I went up to the trainer and told him that I was a writer and maybe could help with the manuals. He referred me to Max, the guy who had broken up my fight with David, and Max took me to a Middle Eastern restaurant to interview me. I told him all my professional qualifications: *Rolling Stone*, *Ramparts*, the whole journalistic saga in detail. He nodded his head and took notes on a pad. Later I learned the exact nature of his recommendation, what in his opinion most qualified me for a job in this strange and mystifying mystical school: "She appears to have a very good spirit," he wrote.

After the training ended, I stayed at my parents' house on Long Island. I went to the beach and hung out with my family. One day I was at Long Beach, watching Shuna play in the sand, when I was seized by a restlessness so intense and sudden that I knew I had to return to California immediately. That evening I telephoned Rocky and told him to meet me at the airport "with a loaded gun." I was in such a hurry to get high that I brought Shuna along with me to Rocky's house in Lagunitas. We fixed in his room, behind a door that didn't quite close all the way, and from time to time I caught Shuna peeking in. Later she asked me, "What was that funny squirt gun Rocky had in his hand?"

Some guys from the advanced training stayed in Fairfax with David and me. I had my room; David had his; we led separate lives, seeing other people, while continuing to live under the same roof. Our house became something of an Arica commune, which eased the tension there might otherwise have been between us. Every morning we drank Dragon's Milk and did Psychocalisthenics together, and then we went our separate ways. Tamara came to visit and got involved with one of the guys in the house. Soon she'd decided to take a forty-day herself. Anne also wanted to take a training. She was intrigued by what she'd heard of Arica from David and me.

One day I took Shuna and Seven, who was visiting from Berkeley, to Devil's Slide, a nude beach in a secluded cove at the base of a cliff just south of Pacifica, with Michael and Steve, the guys from the house. It was a bright sunny day, warm enough for the kids to play in the water. Michael and I did our Psychocalisthenics nude on a blanket near the cliff. I was standing on my head, moving my legs around, and I discovered I could twist them into a full lotus. The brilliant sun shone down on my nude body, upside down in a headstand with my legs in a full lotus, and the glorious wild Pacific Ocean pounded the shore nearby. I had a sense of being in paradise and experienced a perfect moment of exquisite, ecstatic bliss. I knew beyond doubt I was one with the universe, a part of Creation, the cosmic unfolding of consciousness itself: perfect, eternal, complete. I had only experienced this feeling once before in my life, at the precise moment of Shuna's birth, and all my incidents of drug-induced euphoria paled beside its pristine intensity. I wasn't giving birth this day, nor had I taken any LSD, so I knew this feeling must be coming from the spiritual work I'd done in Arica. I lay back on my blanket, watched the girls run in and out of the water, listened to the gentle roar of the waves, and basked in the sun's warmth on my naked skin. Everything was the same as it had always been, and yet my view of it had been subtly altered. I was unaccountably happy, filled with awe. I had gone to Arica to stop using drugs, but this was more than I had bargained for.

I had glimpses of eternity from my spiritual work, but I still kept shooting smack. All that summer I bounced back and forth between drugs and meditation like a boomerang. One August night Rocky and I were in his room in Lagunitas. He was playing a J. J. Cale record on the stereo and eating a bowl of corn flakes. We'd just gotten off, but I didn't feel high. I was feverish, weak, confused. "I don't think that dope was any good," I told him. "I still feel sick." "I've got some money," he said. "We'll go cop some more." We bought more dope and fixed it, but I still felt strange. "You can't be dopesick now," Rocky said. "You've had more stuff than me." I went home to Fairfax and lay in my bed, too tired and fevered to do anything but sleep.

For the next few days, no matter how much dope I shot, the sickness didn't go away. "You don't look too good, Susan," David said. "Maybe you should call the doctor. Even junkies get sick sometimes." Dr. McDade came over. He thought I had hepatitis, the infectious kind, of course. "I think I got it from a needle," I said, picking up the sleeves of my night-gown to show him my arms. "How did this happen to you?" he asked, clearly shocked by my quick transformation from the wholesome woman who'd taken care of David. "I never imagined you for the junkie type." It had been six months since I had my gamma globulin shot, exactly the incubation time for serum hepatitis. Sure enough, that was what I had.

I was scared of this disease, had watched Michael almost die of it in London. And I knew what it took to get over it. No drugs, nothing. Now I wouldn't even touch a Valium. Rocky came over and offered to fix me, but I turned him down flat. Good food and rest, that was what I needed. Anne, David, my various girlfriends all came over and cooked for me.

Once a week Anne took me to San Rafael for my blood test. I didn't have a very severe case, but was sick enough that I couldn't do anything but lay in bed. Max called from New York to offer me a job in Arica, taking over the editorship of the in-school newspaper from him. "I can't come," I told him. "I'm a junkie. I've got hepatitis." "That's okay," he said good-naturedly. "Just come when you feel better." He taught me a meditation to help heal my liver, breathing in dark green. My room was all windows, surrounded by trees, so it was easy enough to do. Within a month I felt better, and my blood test confirmed the good news.

Now that I knew it was safe to get high, I went all-out on a farewell binge with a vengeance. I'd decided to move to New York and take the job working for Arica. David was renting out the house and leaving too. Our escape route was all mapped out. I began selling everything I owned, my bias-cut velvet evening gowns from the thirties, elaborately embroidered piano shawls, crocheted lace and patchwork quilts, all the antiques I'd so painstakingly collected, and used the money to buy smack. One night Rocky and I stayed in a motel. In the morning he left to go get us breakfast. I'd never injected myself before, but I picked up the wake-up, which we had saved for the morning so we wouldn't be sick, from the table next to the bed, and shot the whole thing. When he came back and saw what I had done, tears welled up in his eyes.

I dropped Rocky off at work, promising to return later with a fix for him, and started out for Fairfax, where Shuna was waiting for me to take her to school. In San Anselmo, stopped at a light, I nodded out and hit the car in front of me. The cops came. I had works in my purse, bent-up spoons, enough balloons of dope to lose custody of Shuna and go to jail for the rest of my life. I had bought some extra dope to take with me to New York; I was building up a stash. I asked the cop if I could make a phone call because my little girl was waiting for me at home. I planned to throw all the drugs and paraphernalia away near the phone booth, but the cop followed me there. "What's the matter?" he asked. "Have you been drinking?" "No," I said. "It's early in the morning, and I didn't have my coffee yet." I was terrified he was going to look in my purse. Instead he asked me to stand on one leg and swing the other back and forth, then reverse the two. I couldn't believe my luck. It was an exercise from Arica Psychocals, which I'd been doing every day for months. I did it easily now, to the cop's satisfaction, and he let me go. By the time I got back in the car, my leg was shaking so violently I could scarcely put my foot on

the accelerator, and I was stone-cold sober; the drug's effects had completely worn off. But I felt as though I had a guardian angel perched on
my shoulder, watching over me, who had just saved me from what could
have been a major disaster.

It was the fall of 1974. Ever since I had moved to California, more than
seven years before, I'd thought of it as my permanent home. In my
wildest dreams, I never imagined I would be leaving to move back to
New York. And I didn't really want to do it. But the way I saw it, I had no
choice. I had to get away from the drugs, or I was going to end up dead.
David was renting out the house, so I'd have nowhere to live either. And
maybe the change would do me good. It had been a long time since I'd
had a regular job. I was a little afraid of becoming so deeply involved in
Arica; on the other hand, the theory fascinated me, and since the day of
my epiphany on the beach, I'd been convinced there was something immensely powerful in the work of the school. So I made preparations to
go. David and I had a permanent yard sale. Every day people came over
to buy our possessions. Then we both took the money we had made that
day, put it together, and I went to the city to get us some dope from
George, a grizzled old connection in the Castro.

David and I were together on the deck, waiting for Rocky to come
over after work and get his share of the dope. Every once in a while one of
us had to go hang over the edge of the railing to vomit. In an odd sort of
way, David and I were friends again. I guess we always had been, but the
ups and downs of our romantic relationship, which we now both accepted
as over, had sometimes gotten in the way of our genuine liking for each
other. My books and stuff were packed in boxes. Anne was taking them to
Berkeley to be stored in Greil Marcus's basement. Anne was the strongest
woman I had ever seen; in Yiddish she would be described as a *shtarkeh*.
She carried her bicycle in one hand, and Shuna, who was six, in the other,
and hefted them both up our hundred-plus stairs like it was no big deal. I
still didn't feel completely recovered from the hepatitis, and I knew shooting dope wasn't doing my liver any good, but it was all going to end soon
enough anyway. Max had found me a room in an Arica apartment in New
York that I could move into right away. Shuna would stay with my mother
for a while, until I could get my own place and put her into school. David

planned to drive across the country with a trailer; he'd bring the stuff I couldn't carry on the plane. So this was the end of our long trail together, or at any rate a new fork in the road. It would be years before we'd connect up again, and then still as friends. By 1980, long before me, David had found his own way into recovery. When I finally moved back to California in 1988, he and his wife, Joan, were seasoned Twelve-Steppers who could offer me a rich source of experience and wisdom.

In New York many of the Aricans shared apartments in the Orwell House, on Eighty-Sixth Street and Central Park West. I had a room in the largest apartment, with six other roommates, most of whom sat around the table in the kitchen all day smoking joint after joint to the point of stoned oblivion. I quickly used up my little stash of heroin and promptly gained ten pounds. "I liked you better when you were lean and mean in 192," said one of my roommates. In the Arica theory, levels of consciousness are assigned numerical values; 192 is the level of suicidal panic, a high state because the intense pain propels you toward change.

To try to quell my craving for heroin, I was taking whatever pills I could get my hands on: codeine, Percodan, Valium to help me sleep at night, Quaalude that made me bounce off the walls. I smoked pot all day with the rest of them, sniffed coke when it was around, and went out to the bars in the neighborhood and drank till they closed or I passed out, whichever came first. I told everyone I met that I was an ex-junkie. I thought I was clean so long as I didn't shoot dope, that heroin was my problem and without it I would be okay. I didn't know I was an addict for whom any drug was potentially deadly, had no idea of the tentacles sunk deep into my psyche, or that the diabolical grip they held me in would take more than a change of scene to break.

One night George, my old connection from San Francisco, showed up unexpectedly at my apartment and took me over near the Museum of Natural History to get some dope. We copped from two black guys George knew, dime bags wrapped in tinfoil, which we did in their apartment. At the sweet smell of cooking dope mixed with burning sulfur from the matches, my stomach turned over in anticipation. I was accustomed to shooting forty dollars' worth of George's dope at a time, so I put a whole dime in the cooker and drew it up. The minute it went into my arm, I overdosed and fell on the floor. One of the guys picked me up gently and walked me around the room, then took me over to the Three Brothers restaurant and poured cup after cup of black coffee into me until I was able to stand up and walk home by myself. The next morning one of my roommates lifted up my sleeve to inspect the tiny red pinprick in the crook of my arm, but said nothing.

In general I was weak and disoriented. Sometimes I couldn't manage to get to work until one or two in the afternoon, then I wasn't sure what I was supposed to be doing. Max was unfailingly kind and tolerant to me, although I noticed he was quick to anger when he felt he'd been thwarted in some creative enterprise or other.

I had a desk in the back office at 24. One day an olive-skinned, black-haired woman with deep, dark eyes and a commanding presence appeared in the doorway and spotted me at my desk. "Aaaah," she said, with recognition and pleasure, then crossed the room to enclose me in a warm embrace and murmur welcome in soft, Spanish-accented English. Her name was Jenny; she was Oscar's second-in-command. Many of the Aricans feared her quick tongue and sharp criticism, but from that first mysterious moment of our meeting she took me under her wing and offered me protection. Over the years I would learn much from Jenny, how to work hard, to grow into leadership as a woman unashamed of my strength. She was a role model for me, a woman of stunning dominion and power. Strong, kind, compassionate, hard-working, Jenny offered me a glimpse of what in time I might become. Because of her, I stayed in the school.

chapter eleven

Good morning heartache, you old gloomy sight
Good morning heartache,
thought we said good-bye last night
I turned and tossed until it seemed you were gone
But here you are with the dawn.

Billie Holiday (Erwin M. Drake,
Dan Fisher, Irene Higginbotham),
"Good Morning, Heartache"

SLIPPING INTO DARKNESS—1974-1979

From 1974 to 1979, I stayed in New York working at various jobs in the Arica school. Gradually my craving for heroin disappeared, though I still got high occasionally, or whenever the opportunity presented itself. In the Twelve-Step programs, we call moving from one place to another to escape your addiction "a geographic cure," and for a while mine appeared to be working. When I first moved to New York, I'd get high on heroin every month or so, then it became every six months, then once a year when someone blew into town who had some, and eventually almost never. I went on something of a binge one summer out in California, and I even brought some to Rocky in Hawaii, where he had moved to clean up; but when I came back to New York, I hardly thought of it at all.

That's not to say I didn't do other drugs. At one point I got into so much trouble with cocaine that I had to go to my parents' house for six months to recover physically from a one-month binge. For a solid year, I snorted PCP every day before I went to work and got so high I could feel the planet moving under my feet and see light emanating from the pages of the book I was editing. How could I be part of a functioning mystical school and still be taking drugs? "Nothing is forbidden in Arica," Oscar once told someone who asked about the permissive atmosphere in the school, "because in Arica we play the whole game of consciousness." We didn't get high during trainings and meditations, but the rest of the time we were on our own and basically responsible for ourselves, with the understanding that there was a direct correlation between freedom and responsibility. Arica had always made it perfectly clear that it was neither therapy nor drug rehabilitation; outside help for psychological problems or serious addiction was strongly recommended. I didn't get any, though, because I figured I was okay; I hadn't had a heroin habit for five years, and although I got high on other drugs, I considered myself to have cleaned up and believed I was cured.

I began living with Max after we'd been friends and working companions for three years. He was the last person I ever thought I'd get involved with. Although Max and I argued all the time and disagreed about almost everything in our personal lives, we somehow had the ability to work together in complete harmony. Putting out newspapers, on high-stress deadlines, we traded off between cool efficiency and total insanity; when one of us became overwhelmed, the other took over, comforting the casualty with calm words, doing the work that needed to be done, and then we switched again. For two years we published a newspaper out of our apartment called the *No Time Times*. It wasn't an official publication of Arica Institute, but it was Arican in its outlook and nature. It came out of some writing classes I taught in my apartment; after a certain point, I thought my students would only improve if they could see their work in print.

My main partner on the *No Time Times* was a woman named Carolyn. I fell in love with her almost at first sight. Carolyn was like a beam of light and had the working capacity of ten ordinary humans; I supposed this was because, like me, she'd been trained by Jenny in the fires of Arica Development. Carolyn was so patient and good-natured that I went along with whatever she wanted me to do. From the moment we started the paper, I lived in a state of perpetual exhaustion. I didn't use hard drugs to keep me going because I couldn't sustain the punishing pace required day after day with the same uneven spurts of energy I'd used for short-term writing projects. When I was fatigued past all reason, I'd go to my acupuncturist, who would jab a hair-thin needle in the center of my palm, the point called the "Palace of Weariness," and restore my energy. For two years he patiently repaired the damage I'd done to my body with cocaine, and his treatments kept me balanced and functioning through the constant, unending work.

Shuna was in the fourth grade. We lived in an apartment on East Seventy-First Street and Second Avenue, and she'd been going to a public school in the neighborhood for several years. During my first years in New York, I'd dragged her from pillar to post, moving every few months; or was so unsettled that she had to live first with my parents and then my sister, attending different schools with incompatible teaching methods. Now it felt good to have her with me and in a stable educational environment. I didn't have much time to spend with her, what with the newspaper being laid out in the living room, manuscripts all over my bed waiting to be edited, and the phone ringing off the hook all hours of the night and day. But I was always home when she came in from school, and she thrived on the excitement, pitching in to help with the paper by writing a kids' column and drawing cartoons.

New York was now my home, its rhythms and sounds and smells as familiar to me as the beating of my own heart. In many ways this was a happy time for me. I was part of a community; my life had a purpose; I had work I loved, good friends, and my parents and brother and sisters lived so close by that we visited back and forth all the time. I'd written some articles for the *Village Voice,* working with my old friend Bob Christgau, the music editor, and the writing and editing work I'd done over the years for Arica gave me immense satisfaction.

The trouble was, I began to get burnt out. My rent was hideously expensive, over eight hundred dollars a month, and I lost many nights' sleep worrying about how to pay it. In Arica we lived communally in apartments but each had our own room; Shuna's alone cost me three hundred dollars a month, almost as much as we had both lived on in Berkeley. Michael had moved to New York a few years after Shuna and I did, and he saw her regularly but barely contributed to her financial support. He himself lived marginally on money he made from writing sporadically or playing music with Ellen. After several battles on the child support issue in California, over which he'd stopped speaking to me, I'd given up hope of ever getting any help from him. I was a single mother struggling to support a child in New York City at a time when the press was just beginning to recognize a new phenomenon they called "the feminization of poverty." Women, it was widely reported, were paid fifty-nine cents to every dollar men made doing comparable jobs. At one point during these years, in desperation, I'd worked as a three-dollar-an-hour typist until the work and money became too demoralizing. It was wearing trying to be both father and mother to my child, breadwinner for our family, and a human being in my own right. In this my life was not much different from many other working mothers, but it was a strain and left me with a lot of residual bitterness.

Michael sent Shuna twenty-three dollars a month—I don't know how he arrived at that sum—which I put into the household expenses. One Sunday afternoon Shuna returned from a visit with Michael and Ellen, and demanded to know why I was stealing money from her. "What are you talking about?" I asked. "My dad says he sends me that money, and you're stealing it from me." "What about rent and food and clothes?" I asked. "My dad says that you have custody of me," replied Shuna. "He wanted custody of me, but he didn't get it. He says custody means that the parent with it is totally responsible for feeding and sheltering and clothing the kid by themselves, and they shouldn't be asking the other person for help." I was shocked and outraged. Michael had never tried to get custody of Shuna, and because he wouldn't speak to me, he was putting a ten year old in the midst of financial stuff she had no way to understand. Hearing her talk like that was emotionally shattering for me. Here I was knocking my brains out to support her, with no help from her father, and he made me out to be the villain. What really stung was that she believed it. I tried to explain it, but she was too young to comprehend rent and bills. It hurt me deeply that she took her father's side against me. "My dad says there are no 'shoulds' or 'have tos,'" said Shuna. "He's sending me money because he wants to, and it's mine." The pain and disappointment I felt over this exchange with my daughter seemed to rankle beyond its importance, adding to my general feeling that everything I valued was coming unglued.

In the summer my friend Laurie, observing my exhaustion and the sorry state of my relationship with my daughter, gave us money to go on a vacation to St. Croix. Shuna and I spent three carefree, relaxing weeks sailing and sunbathing in the balmy, voluptuous air of the islands. My friend Sue Stone and I taught Shuna the fine art of rolling joints; to our way of thinking, pot, "the sacred herb," didn't really qualify as a drug. In St. Croix I finally had time to myself to think, and by the time I returned home, I had made up my mind to leave Max. Our bitter arguments and his never-ending affairs with other women had worn me to a frazzle. And on my first night back in New York, I met Hunter, a younger man so soft and gentle that he seemed the polar opposite of Max.

Far from making a clean break with Max, though, I found myself in yet another triangle, unable to give up either of the men, or decide between one or the other in any kind of permanent, committed way. It reminded me of the song my sister Lorraine had written about me when I was leaving my marriage: "Blue lady, so afraid to be alone / She wants to keep them both on hand / One for holding, one for loving / With two men down, she's still alone." On the other hand, it had often occurred to me that maybe I just wasn't cut out for monogamy, and sabotaged all my relationships as a way of evading commitment.

I was sleeping with both Max and Hunter when I got pregnant. At first I enjoyed the feeling, but it seemed impossible to go ahead with the pregnancy; I wasn't sure who the father of the baby was and could barely support the child I had. I was thirty-five years old and had never had an abortion, but after a great deal of soul-searching and indecision, it seemed like the only course.

I was lucky it was 1978 and abortion was legal. I went to a women's clinic, where "the procedure," as they called it, was performed under general anesthesia by a woman gynecologist I knew. Everything went smoothly, and my mother came to the city to take care of me afterward. But my follow-up tests showed I was still pregnant. On the night of Max's birthday, Hunter and I took a cab to a different doctor uptown; we were referred to him by the doctor whose abortion had failed. He performed the abortion in his back office with no anesthesia. It hurt so much I was screaming out loud, begging him to stop; it felt like he was vacuuming out my insides, stabbing my flesh with a knife. Hunter heard my screams in the waiting room, but there was nothing he could do; we were too far into it to stop. Both of us broke down in tears when the nurse brought me out, and I was so crushed by the experience that I didn't speak a word for the rest of the night.

I was depressed for weeks after the abortions, numb inside, unable to cry. I felt as though my spirit had been sucked from my body with the fetus. The *No Time Times* was falling apart. After two years the paper still wasn't earning enough to pay salaries to Carolyn and me, and the financial pressure, combined with the endless work, was fraying the bonds of even our rock-solid friendship. The fledgling paper had been like a child to me, and now I was losing that too. Shuna tried to cheer me up, telling me it was far better for me to have had an abortion than a baby I couldn't take care of, but nothing could shake me from my gloom. One day I was at 24 on some kind of errand, and ran into a man I knew named Nick. "Where were you the night of Max's birthday party?" he asked me. "I had something for you, something I know you like." "What was it?" I asked. "Put on the pigtails," he mimed. "Dance with the Chinaman." We made a date with each other for another time to get high.

Because I hadn't been a junkie for five years, and because I'd been able to get high now and then without getting a habit, I didn't worry about heroin showing up in my life again. I thought I could handle it. I underestimated the power of the dope and the extent of my vulnerability. And the heroin made me feel wonderful. It was "China White," high-quality fluffy white powder from the Southeast Asia's Golden Triangle. We sniffed some at Nick's apartment, and immediately I was filled with hope and inspiration. "Why don't you try writing again?" he suggested, and we spent our evening together at opposite ends of his long wooden desk, writing separately in companionable silence.

It became a pattern for us, a comfortable routine. We got together at his apartment, sniffed heroin, and had "study dates," where we sat and wrote together. It was a high-class affair; this was no street heroin bought in balloons and shot with a barbed needle; it was expensive China White, sniffed by two highly educated writers, in the interest of helping with creative inspiration. Nick and I had a platonic relationship; we talked about literature and other writers, critiqued each other's work. For us doing heroin was like belonging to a secret, exclusive club; there was nothing the least bit sleazy about it; we were as far from purse-snatching junkies on the street as New York is from Outer Mongolia. High, we socialized with Nick's friends, glamorous, successful people. We hung out at Elaine's with movie directors and pop stars, some of whom were discreet, occasional heroin users like us.

I was so unconcerned by this casual drug use that I even told my mother, who knew about all my past problems, that I was using heroin once in a while to help me with my writing. We were taking a walk around Harbor Isle; I can picture the corner where we were when I told her. My mother stopped dead in her tracks; her face looked stricken. "My heart just fell into my toes," she said. "How could you start that again?" "Oh, Ma," I said. "Don't worry. This isn't like it was before. I'm not a junkie anymore. I can handle it."

Nick and I went to visit a mutual friend one night. He put a big pile of China White on the table and told us to help ourselves, take as much as we wanted. I sniffed it like it was coke, in huge, fat, greedy lines; for once there was as much dope as I could possibly want. We stayed there all night, and when I went home, I was flying so high that I sat down at my typewriter and wrote sixty pages about my family and my life. I enjoyed this writing, which was unusual for me. It just flowed out of me, with none of the tortuous effort I normally associated with work. The writing was inspired, drawn from a well of imagination I hadn't known I possessed. Other people liked it too. My friend Fred thought it was the best work I'd ever done. He made a copy of it to show his boss, a literary agent. Maybe he could get me a book contract, he said.

I was branching out from Arica, writing articles for various newspapers and magazines and doing a little drug dealing on the side. One night I bought some coke from a new acquaintance named Margo. She was a writer too, and suggested we collaborate on a magazine article. She had a friend at her apartment, a chubby, jovial fellow named Paul who was a full-time drug dealer. He knew Nick, had been dealing to him for years. When Margo asked if Nick were my boyfriend, I said, "No, and I'd hate to be getting my emotional sustenance from him." The drug dealer shot me a piercing look of complete understanding. Then I noticed him studying me for the rest of the evening.

I didn't need to use heroin all the time because I'd convinced my acupuncturist, an MD, to write me prescriptions for Percodan. Margo and I got the magazine assignment, and took a trip to interview the subject of our profile. She brought along a photographer and the drug dealer, Paul, because she thought we needed a man with us in case we got into trouble. Before we left I took twelve Percodan. When I got in the car, Paul looked at me. "You better put on some sunglasses," he said. "Your eyes are red as fire." Margo and the photographer turned out to be nutty as fruitcakes, and our trip was like a traveling circus. For sanity's sake Paul and I stuck together, and I was surprised by how extraordinarily comfortable I felt with him.

One night Hunter and I went down to Paul's apartment in the Village to buy some weed. Paul and I got to talking and discovered we were both ex-junkies. Hunter left, and I stayed at Paul's for a while. It was all friendly, not romantic; I just enjoyed his company. Several times in the weeks that followed, I ran into Paul by accident. Sometimes we talked on the phone. I was always trying to get him to come up to my apartment and deliver some weed. I had found out he had something I wanted: a heroin connection of his own. He told me he could buy heroin in small quantities, a dime at a time. I was getting tired of begging drugs from Nick. I told Paul to bring me some heroin, and I'd give him the money. By the time he showed up, it was apparent that we were attracted to each other and were going to be together. We went downstairs to the neighborhood bar to have a drink. I had one, and Paul had five or six in quick succession. He downed them hurriedly, knocking them back like a desperate man with a bad case of nerves. I noticed this odd behavior, but no alarms went off in my mind.

I soon discovered this was Paul's normal way of drinking. In addition to drinking like a fish, he took Quaalude by the handful, smoked so much pot that the smell of it preceded his entrance into a room, and did a dime bag of heroin every day. This was nothing, he told me, compared to how much he used to do when he was a junkie. "I'm keeping it down to a roar," he liked to say. He didn't do any coke, though he sold it and sometimes brought me some because he knew I liked it. But he complained when I asked him to get me heroin too often. Paul wasn't an Arican; he was patently sleazy, slobby, and unkempt, and none of my friends—including Nick, who accused him of "poor character"—approved of our alliance. But he made me laugh; I had fun with him; and he had what I wanted most of all, more than love or spiritual fulfillment: a ready source of heroin. I campaigned for months to get him to introduce me to the connection; normally he made me wait outside in the car while he copped.

From the start our relationship was intense and stormy. Paul had the classic addict/alcoholic's Jekyll-and-Hyde personality. Shuna called the Quaalude he took "his mean pills." He often became verbally abusive and sometimes physically violent, and I was frightened of driving in the car with him when he was loaded on alcohol and pills. On one occasion, when I was about to put him out of the house, he threatened Shuna and me with a gun. I don't think the gun was loaded, but it made little difference to my terrified child, who still talks about the incident. Looking back I can see that I was growing more and more dependent on the drugs, and since Paul was my conduit to them, I was powerless to leave him. The fact that I introduced my young child into this world of drugs and violence is a source of pain and grief to us both even now. I was still laboring under the delusion, fostered by the countercultural ethos of the sixties, that drugs were hip and cool, and that it was better for me to be open with my child than to hide things from her. In fact I did try to hide my heroin use from her, until it became impossible to do so; and I attempted so many times without success to leave Paul that I finally gave up and accepted him as part of our lives.

My family was puzzled and somewhat horrified by Paul's sudden presence in my life; he was a real departure from any of my previous boyfriends. We ran around a lot and kept odd hours. I was trying to get my writing career off the ground again, so I frequently stayed up all night making deadlines I'd left to the last minute. After several months of this, I developed mononucleosis. Fred had gotten me a book contract from Farrar, Straus & Giroux, with a modest advance. But debilitated by the mononucleosis, I was unable to write and had to use the advance money to live on. Sick with mono, if I wanted to have any energy at all to accomplish even the smallest task, I had to sniff a little coke or heroin to get me going.

Shuna, who was eleven, watched me grow weaker and paler by the day, and was scared out of her wits. She imagined I had cancer, that I was dying. Finally I had to tell her the truth, that I was using heroin again. She was relieved that I didn't have a fatal disease, and I reassured her that the drugs were really nothing to worry about. Sometimes when I went to my parents' house high, my mother stared at me in a strange way. "What's wrong with your eyes?" she would ask me. "You look haunted."

Still, I didn't think it was a problem. I didn't get high every day, and I wasn't using needles. I knew I was using far more frequently than before, but it was still only chipping. "I may be a user," I told myself, " but I'm not a junkie."

Paul resented all the money we spent on drugs, but I preferred he do heroin than drink and take Quaalude; he was easier to get along with that way. He blamed me for his increasing habit, and I blamed him for mine; after all, he'd been the one with the connection. When he left town for a few weeks, he was forced to introduce me to the connection, Carlos, a black man who lived on Fourteenth Street, on the West Side. Now, finally, I could get my own heroin, all I wanted, without having to beg Nick or convince Paul to take me downtown. Carlos and I got on famously, like a house on fire. With his help I set up a little coke- and heroin-dealing business. He fronted me the drugs, and I came back with the money. Gradually, almost imperceptibly, I began using every day. "I'm worried," I told Nick. "I have a habit." "Nothing you can't shake with a codeine prescription," he said. "You can stop this whenever you want."

Through a friend of Paul's, I got a job on the *Daily News.* They were putting out an evening paper called *Tonight,* hoping to compete with the *Post,* and had hired a number of magazine writers for a special section called Manhattan. Nick and I were still having our study dates. "What are you planning to do about your writing?" he asked me. "I'll be writing at my job," I answered. "That's not writing, Susan. That's for wrapping fish," he said. But the job on the *News* paid fairly well, and from having to produce so much copy so quickly, my writing became looser, more humorous and flowing.

I tried to hide my drug use at work. I was just like everyone else, except I had a secret life. In the afternoon Paul usually brought me a couple of bags of dope, and when I got off work, I went right down to Carlos's and bought some more. For the first time in years, I could afford my rent and was able to provide for Shuna. One night I was staying late at work, sweating over my computer, trying to write a difficult story, when all of a sudden the door behind me opened and Shuna peeked her head in the room. "Hi, Mom," she said. "I missed you, so I came to visit you at work." In her hand she was holding a single pink rose. She had bought me the rose and then walked all the way down to Forty-Second Street, a good couple of miles, to deliver it in person. It felt great that she'd wanted to do that for me after all we'd been through.

Paul thought things were getting out of hand, so when Shuna went away to summer camp, we decided to clean up. We didn't use heroin for twelve days. I couldn't remember ever being as dopesick as I got that time. I couldn't sleep; I spent whole nights tossing and turning, going from one bed to another in a futile attempt to get comfortable. Anxieties crowded my mind like monsters in a horror movie, larger and scarier than in life. I was so depressed, I kept breaking out in convulsive sobs. My mind hurt, and my body did too. The cramps in my legs and arms were so acute that I couldn't hold my limbs still; I banged them on the bed to try to make the pain go away. I didn't have the strength to lift my hand up to answer the phone. I sweated all over my body, even on my forearms and calves, and the sweat stank like a foul-smelling poison was coming out of my pores. I burned up with fever, then shook with chills. I called in sick to work and told them I had the flu. Paul took me riding in the car; he claimed the constant motion helped the bone-aches, and we both smoked a lot of pot. He would drink till he passed out, but I couldn't stand to do that; it made me too sick. After a few days, I snuck a few codeine, and didn't tell Paul I had them so I wouldn't have to share.

Sometimes it seems as if the dope has a life of its own; it's like an evil, insidious person, maybe even the devil himself. You think you're done with it, that you've gotten away, and here it comes again, knocking on your door. At the end of twelve days, Paul and I were feeling pretty good about ourselves. We were clean, healthy, and even getting along passably well; we'd decided we wouldn't do any more dope. And then Rishi, an old friend of mine, showed up in New York and rang my doorbell. He had just come from India with a couple of ounces of Burmese heroin he'd smuggled in, and he needed to unload it. He was willing to front it to me if I thought I could sell it. I told him it might take me a few weeks to build up a business, but I already had some customers, and it shouldn't be too much of a problem. He gave me a sample; the quality was fabulous. My spirits soared; within minutes Paul and I were counting up the money we were going to make and had forgotten all about the suffering of the past few weeks and our resolution not to get high.

The *Tonight* paper folded and I lost my job. Without my salary to pay the rent and my daily dope bills, I was in financial panic. The money from Rishi's dope was long gone, most of it to pay for our own personal use. Rishi was in India; he was supposed to be back with more drugs before too long, but I wasn't counting my chickens. My only hope appeared to be a methadone detox. I took the subway up to Spanish Harlem and got on a methadone program run by Mt. Sinai Hospital. I had to show up every day, including holidays, drink my dose, dissolved in orange Kool-Aid, at the window, and see a counselor once a week.

My first few weeks on maintenance I did pretty well. I had a lot of energy, enough to turn out several freelance articles. The methadone kept me feeling good enough that I didn't crave other drugs. But I was bored. I missed the excitement of running around copping, missed the hustle of dealing. I settled into the routine of the clinic: going in the morning to get my dose, having coffee and glazed donuts on the corner, hanging around the park with the other clients, who might not do anything else all day. Getting on methadone to cure a heroin habit is like pulling yourself up on quicksand to keep from drowning in water. Almost everyone I knew on the program still used other drugs, and dealt them too. You could get any kind of pill around the clinic; people sold Elavil, Valium, even their take-home bottles of methadone if they were lucky enough to get them. When I looked at the people around me, bloated and sedated with legally sanctioned narcotics, I felt I was now associated with a truly hopeless segment of society. Toothless, battered, old before their time, these committed dope fiends resigned themselves to staying on methadone because it was just too painful to kick, worse than heroin. I was afraid I'd never get off it; I walked around feeling impending doom; an invisible guillotine hung suspended above my head. Trying to get out, I'd sunk further into the abyss. "Once a junkie, always a junkie"; that was what everyone said. From the looks of my companions, it seemed to apply, and now it was true for me as well.

After a few weeks, the methadone lost its desired effect, and I started doing opium and heroin again. Methadone is funny; it can make you nod out twelve hours after you get your dose, with no warning, and the other drugs I took didn't help. Every night, it seemed, I was nodding out with a cigarette in my hand, setting fire to my bed. "Wake up, Mom," Shuna would say, coming into my room every five minutes to check on me. "I wasn't asleep," I'd protest. It was the family joke between Shuna and Paul, but there was nothing the least bit funny about it; I knew my child went to bed every night scared I'd set fire to the apartment.

Carlos got evicted from his apartment, and Paul and I found another connection, named Willie. Willie was a black guy who dealt mostly to white women. He sold out of the bathroom of his place on First Avenue, little tinfoil packets filled with potent brown dope. We spent a lot of time waiting for Willie; there was always some kind of problem with getting the dope. Waiting is a big part of the dope game. As a friend of mine once said, "The first thing you learns is that you always gots to wait." The desire for heroin is so powerful, the hunger so intense, that you wait on pins and needles, tingling with anticipation, almost faint with desperation, alternating wildly between hope and despair. And sometimes you wait like that for hours, sick or knowing that you'll be sick any minute, with no guarantee that the person who has your last money will ever come back. Willie enjoyed having this kind of power over his customers, and I have to admit it was seductive; when I did a lot of dealing, I sometimes enjoyed it myself.

Rishi returned to New York with a large shipment of smuggled heroin. Before long I was making more money than I ever had at any legitimate enterprise. It wasn't unusual for me to take in ten thousand dollars for a morning's work. I had so much extra money lying around the house that I gave Shuna the fifty- and hundred-dollar bills to play with. "Roll around in them," I told her. "Rub them on your body. See what it feels like to have enough money." We lived on exotic, expensive food. I was still on methadone, and now I had a steady supply of good-quality heroin too, enough that I got what people on the program called a double habit: I needed daily maintenance doses of both drugs to keep from being sick. I gave Paul all the dope he wanted and did as much as I could, and still there was plenty left to make a handsome profit. I didn't sell to many people, just a few whom I was sure about and who could afford the high prices I charged for the stuff, about eight hundred dollars a gram. This was the glamorous, high end of the drug world; some of my customers were celebrities; the doormen of my building were awestruck when they came to call. I was a wholesale connection for other people, like my friend Bob from the methadone program, who bought my stuff, cut it, and resold it in the Bronx. Now I had power, just like Carlos and Willie; my customers waited for me.

Still, I wondered how long it would last. By now I was a full-time dope fiend, what the sociologists called "an occupational addict." I didn't do anything else but deal, get my methadone, and stay high. Sometimes I worried that my parents would find out I was dealing heroin; in New York the Rockefeller laws made it mandatory life for anyone caught dealing smack or coke, even though the judges were too overwhelmed with drug cases to enforce the penalties all the time. I wouldn't be able to continue if they knew. I'd sworn Shuna to secrecy, and she helped maintain Paul's cover around my family too. Paul told everyone he was a book salesman, and had many customers in the publishing business to back up his fiction. My mother knew that Paul dealt drugs; she also knew I was on methadone; that was why I couldn't spend the weekend at her house any more. But she went along with our lies to keep the peace. Lorraine had moved to Virginia, so we didn't see her very often; my sister Sheila and her husband, Jon, tolerated Paul as a harmless drunk, and my nieces and nephews loved him because he was funny and would play with them. Everyone did the best they could to pretend everything was normal, just like in a Cheap Trick song that was popular at the time: "Mommy's all right, Daddy's all right / they just seem a little weird."

With all the dope I had around, my habit increased by leaps and bounds. Now I had a dealer's habit. I didn't just have a monkey on my back; I was supporting a whole family of gorillas. Every day I owed Rishi more and more money, and less and less was profit for me. I kept the dope in a safe deposit box at a ritzy trust fund bank on Madison Avenue to try to control how much I used. When someone put in an order, I went up to the bank with my small portable scale in my purse and weighed out the amount I needed. I had started out stashing the dope under my mattress, but Paul kept stealing from it in the middle of the night. He'd wait till I went to sleep, then hug and kiss me to maneuver me onto the other side of the bed. Bob would complain that the dope had been cut, and I'd be mystified; I knew I wasn't cutting it. When Paul confessed, I got the safety deposit box. Sometimes, walking out of the bank with my dope stashed in my sock, I felt like a white collar criminal.

My lower back began bothering me, but I ignored it. Then one morning I woke up in agony. My mother said I had a slipped disc, like she'd had a number of times; it ran in the family. The burning sciatic nerve pain was intense and constant; it throbbed like a toothache and came through the methadone and all the heroin I did. Standing in one place was the worst. One day I had to wait in a long line for my methadone, and by the time I got to the window, I was crying. "I understand," said the nurse. "I've seen people try to jump out the window with that pain." I couldn't face standing in line any more, so I walked off my program. Even through my increased doses of heroin, I could feel the withdrawal symptoms from the methadone. I was irritable, restless, achy, and had difficulty sleeping, but I managed to get through it okay. I went to a Chinese doctor who treated many Aricans I knew, and after several weeks of electric acupuncture, herbal packs, and chiropractic adjustments, my back began healing on its own. I was elated to be out of pain and off methadone maintenance.

In order to pay my rent, I rented out the middle bedroom in my apartment. When the tenants paid me a deposit and a month's rent, I'd pay my whole rent with that. Then when my roommates moved out, I never had the money to pay them back their deposit. Rishi rented the room for a while, but he didn't like being so close to the business. I tried to be discreet, do everything in my room with the door closed, and so far I'd been lucky with my roommates. But I rented the room to a couple whose finances were shaky, and one month they didn't have enough money to pay their rent.

All my money was going for dope, so I couldn't make up the difference. I'd been battling eviction notices for years and was adept at the ins and outs of housing court, but this time I couldn't find a way to keep my apartment. I was so loaded all the time that I suffered from magical thinking: I imagined that as long as my stuff was in the apartment, they wouldn't be able to evict me. As the time grew nearer, I knew I had to pack; but all I could do was sit in the middle of my bedroom floor and cry. I had told Shuna we were going to be evicted. "What will happen to our stuff?" she wondered. "They'll take it out of the apartment and put it in storage," I said. "Will they take my stuffed animals?" she asked, heartbroken at the thought of losing her imaginary best friends. Both of us broke down in sobs, helpless in the face of losing our home.

My ability to lie had increased proportionate to my escalating drug habit, and so my mother believed that I had detoxed from methadone and was now opiate-free. I had told her I was dealing drugs, pot, to be specific, and had somehow convinced her that this was equivalent to people selling bootleg booze during Prohibition. I'd also told her that I was being evicted because my roommates stiffed me for their share of the rent. I had started squirreling money away from Rishi, giving it to my mother to hold until I could find another apartment. My debt to Rishi was now in the thousands, but I was still making him so many more thousands that he could afford to let me slide for a while. I knew that one day this house of cards would all come crashing down; but in typical dope-fiend fashion, so long as I could keep going from one fix to another, I convinced myself that everything was fine, or as fine as it could be with a seventy-two-hour eviction notice tacked to my door.

Sheila came over to help me do some last-minute packing and was dumbfounded to discover that I hadn't done anything; I didn't have a single cardboard box in the house. Despite my denial, however, or my inability to pack, the city marshals arrived on schedule, armed with guns, and began carrying all our possessions out to moving vans in the street. It was humiliating being forcibly moved from my home, standing by helplessly while strangers carted my personal belongings away, helping themselves to whatever they felt like taking. I paid them some ungodly sum of money to take my stuff to a private storage place in Harlem, rather than city storage on Staten Island; I was so frightened and disoriented that I couldn't bargain rationally or think what to do for myself. Then I gathered up a few shopping bags full of clothing. My girlfriend Toni, who was a customer of mine, had said I could stay in her apartment until I found another place. Shuna had already gone to my parents' house, taking her favorite stuffed animals with her to keep them out of the hands of the marshals.

When I first got on methadone, I had written a funny story for the *Voice* about being evicted from my apartment and having to do my writing on park benches and in the street. The *Voice* had just cut their freelance rates in half, so the humor seemed appropriate to the occasion. There were not yet so many homeless people on the street, as there would be a few years later, that any attempt at humor on the subject would be rendered tasteless and cruel. I had slipped the article under the editor's door for laughs, not thinking he would print it. It was called "Bag Writer," and was meant to be satirical rather than prophetic. But as I carried my shopping bags out onto Second Avenue, the story's bitter irony hit me like a hammer. I had joked about being a "bag writer"; now I was one.

chapter twelve

Lost in the barrio, I walk like an Indian
So callow who'd suspect something's wrong here?
I dance in place and paint my face
And act like I belong here.

Steely Dan,
"Throw Back the Little Ones"

ABROAD IN THE CITY OF DREAMS—1979

Carlos was out of business, Willie was in jail, and Rishi wouldn't front me any more dope to sell because I owed him so much money. Paul had moved in with an older woman on the Lower East Side; he lived rent-free in exchange for cooking her meals. The Aricans were at a summer training in Maplecrest, New York; they'd taken over a resort called Sugar Maples. I couldn't go because I needed to stay in the city all summer to look for a job and another apartment to move into in the fall. Somehow I had to make sure Shuna finished school in Manhattan; she wanted to go to the High School of Music and Art the next year and would have to apply from a city junior high. She was up at Sugar Maples babysitting for the young son of Max and his wife Christine, who'd married the previous year. I only managed to get to Sugar Maples for a few days, just long enough to be initiated into the Octagon, a new training Oscar introduced there. It was a meditation done in groups of eight that would remain consistent and meet on a regular basis, constituting the cells of the school.

During the three years that Paul and I had been together, almost every day of which we'd done heroin, we'd copped intermittently on the Lower East Side. The Puerto Ricans who lived there called it Loisaida. The out-of-town dope fiends who cruised the blocks with their Jersey license plates knew it as Alphabet City, after Avenues A, B, C, and D, which ran only between First and Fourteenth Streets, where Manhattan jutted into the East River beyond the numbered grid. In the sixties, during hippie days, it enjoyed a brief moment of glamour as the East Village, a hip extension of bohemian Greenwich Village. But to me it had always been the Lower East Side, the neighborhood where I used to come with my parents to visit Tante Schave when I was a child, where my father was born, where Lorraine moved when Maggie was a baby, where my grandparents and all the Jewish immigrants who crowded New York at the turn of the century had lived and worked and struggled to survive.

Now it was like a dope supermarket. You could buy heroin on almost any block. It all came with brand names, in folded-up glassine bags stamped with words and logos: Colt 45, General, Executive, 357, Wiz, Lucky Seven, E.T., Elegant, Original, C.O.D., Night Train, and so on. Each bag contained about a tenth of a gram (known as a tick in the higher-end drug trade) and cost ten dollars. Ten bags, one gram, made a bundle. The dope was heavily stepped on, cut with lactose, but would still get you high, and was cheaper and more plentiful here than anywhere else in the country. Uptown in Harlem black dealers sold bigger packages, called quarters, cut with quinine. Quinine produced a rush when you shot it but left nasty burns and skin ulcers, which scarred like craters if you missed the vein. Lower East Side dope could be sniffed or shot. The quality of each brand varied widely from day to day, sometimes even hour to hour, and up-to-the-minute news of what was strongest and best traveled through a grapevine as reliable as Africa's mysterious bush telegraph. Spots where dope was sold were known by their brand names, and there was a particularly scandalous corner at Second Street and Avenue B where hawkers competed for business, shouting out a cacophony of brand names like barkers at a carnival.

By the early 1980s, when I was spending a lot of time in the area, American economics had created a permanent underclass of chronically unemployed minority youths—in New York mainly blacks and Puerto Ricans—and many worked at various jobs in the drug trade. Dope was sold out of abandoned buildings by carefully supervised and disciplined crews, known as workers, overseen by invisible syndicates. The abandoned buildings, torched by their owners in the seventies as insurance companies redlined neighborhoods like this and the South Bronx, had smoke-blackened holes where the windows had been. And the dope fiends who ran in and out of them at all hours of the night and day had similarly blackened holes where their eyes had sunken in. It was a perfect aesthetic match between environment and inhabitants, though not exactly a match made in heaven. What it most resembled was a circle of hell straight out of Dante's Inferno. We liked to joke that if Jesus Christ came back to earth and went where people needed him most, his first stop would probably be the Lower East Side.

The scene that had spread through this landscape of devastation was violent and dangerous, full of desperate characters and pitfalls at every turn. Shootings, stabbings, muggings, and beatings were a daily occurrence; a local saying went, "If the stickup man don't get you, then the police will." Lorraine had moved out of the neighborhood when she came home one day to find a machete fight in progress in front of her building. It was more difficult than it appeared to get real drugs; guys who accosted you on the street or ran up to your car were usually rip-off artists who'd take your money and sell you bunk, some look-alike powder that could be anything from baking soda to rat poison but wouldn't be dope. Near the real dope houses, there was an electric buzz in the air, a sound that sent adrenaline coursing through your veins so you'd move properly: quickly, and with stealth. You had to walk fast, keeping your wits about you and your mouth shut. Lessons were expensive, and the stakes might be your freedom or your life. I caught on quick; it's amazing what a good teacher desperation can be. And then I got to like it. Street life is seductive. I enjoyed making it in this man's world, full of macho posturing, where a woman had to be strong to gain respect. I felt I'd become tough and fearless, and in my best moments thought of myself as a *macha desperada,* some kind of feminist heroine with the outlaw mystique of the Wild West, which this urban jungle so closely resembled.

Sometimes you ducked into a blind alley, where a lone seller waited in the shadows. Other times you slipped through a hole in the wall of an abandoned building and waited in line on broken staircases lit by dripping candles; when your turn came, you put your money through a slot in a steel door and a bag of dope came out of the slot. Or you put your money into a bucket that was drawn up a few floors on a rope, and the dope came down in the bucket. Often you lined up in plain sight out on the street. When the cops appeared, a lookout yelled *"Bajondo,"* meaning "coming down the street," and all the junkies scattered. When the cops were gone and the seller came out again, junkies came crawling out of every nook and cranny in the block, like cockroaches in the kitchen sink when you turned off the light at night. There were lookouts, sellers, managers, owners, and the bagmen, armed with guns, who carried the money and drugs. No one would sell to you unless they knew your face; sometimes they asked you to "show your ID," meaning your tracks. For survival you got in the habit of memorizing faces; buyers who made a mistake might end up dopesick, with their money gone; sellers who made a mistake ended up in jail.

When we had first started going to the Lower East Side to cop, I was scared. I felt like I didn't belong there and had to wear a disguise to fit in. In those early days, I would cop a few bags of dope and go to write at the *Village Voice;* my rationale was that I was spending fifty dollars on dope to make five hundred dollars writing. Or Paul would cop down there and bring the dope to me. He lived in a co-op apartment building on First Avenue and Fourth Street, so he was always around the neighborhood and could find out what was happening. But Paul was blond and beefy; he looked like a cop. As time went on, I found I could deal with the Puerto Rican workers better than he could. Sometimes they made special allowances for women; a couple of hundred dope fiends would be lined up on the street, and the sellers would come out and say, "Ladies to the front of the line." This didn't happen all the time, but often enough. And then I was more careful about what dope I would buy. I took the time to get to know the workers and brands, making sure we got the best stuff for our money. So I was the one who ended up doing most of the copping, while Paul waited for me in the car. I was proud of my ability to maneuver, and became as hooked on the rush of danger and excitement as I was on the drugs. It was funny in a way: the ultimate shopping trip. And that was how I made my money; most people I knew were too scared to go into those neighborhoods, and as strangers they probably wouldn't have been able to score. So they paid me to do it, one of the ways I supported my habit.

I'd developed a different, tougher walk and had taken to wearing men's clothes all the time so I wouldn't attract any sexual attention when

I was out on the street by myself late at night. I'd get my father's old flannel shirts, which my mother had washed so many times they were soft and comforting, and I wore jeans and running shoes and a black leather jacket with my hair in a ponytail tucked in the collar. I learned enough rudimentary Spanish to negotiate with the workers, who spoke a particularly slangy and abbreviated version of the already idiomatic Puerto Rican dialect. *"Como esta esso?"* meant, What's happening? and would be answered by, *"Tato bien"* or sometimes just *"Tato,"* which meant the spot was open and everything was fine, or *"Tato feo,"* which meant the cops or some other danger were close at hand so they couldn't sell any dope. Dope was "D," coke was "C," *"negocio"* was customer; and if you knew how to count in Spanish, you could do business anywhere. I was, as they say, "in the mix," hustling money, exchanging information with the other addicts, fighting for a place in line, running and hiding from the cops when they were around, feeling a sense of accomplishment when I'd managed, against all odds, to nail down a decent supply for the day. It was hard at times, but never boring.

I already loved the neighborhood. Because of the low tenement buildings and vacant lots, there was more open sky than you usually found in Manhattan, and a different quality of light, almost burnished, as the sun reflected off the red brick buildings, coloring everything with a rosy sepia tint. I felt at home there; it reminded me of the Bronx of my childhood. Pockets of the old ethnic divisions still lingered; there were Ukrainian and Polish restaurants, and the yeshivas and synagogues, though for the most part abandoned, still lent an unmistakably Jewish flavor to the thick European atmosphere. I liked being among the ghosts of my ancestors, and could always imagine the streets teeming with pushcarts and newly arrived immigrants. I had a sense of connection there, in more ways than one.

New York addicts were a multicultural community that was democratic and integrated; we were all out there together, and the dope was no respecter of persons; you could be any color, from any class or economic strata, and still get as strung out and needy as the next person. I learned a lot about equality and human nature: how to distinguish the hopelessly selfish from those who would help me out; the cowards from the courageous; the strong who'd stand firm and the weak who would crack; and how to find, in a mob of hundreds, the scant handful who were trustworthy, making lightning-quick judgments in the heat of battle. A few years of this tempering and I felt ready for anything; I joked that I wanted a T-shirt reading, "Urban Combat Veteran."

You could always tell where the good dope was. There was that electric buzz in the air; the energy changed; you could see a taut tension in the bodies of people milling around, a sense of desperation and of risk. Paul and I drove around in the car sometimes until we spotted the place we wanted, or we talked to all the people we knew to find out what was good that day. No matter how much footwork we did, though, we still lost our money at times; there were as many con artists around as there were workers, and they knew how to think on their feet. "You graduated from Vassar, Little Suze," Paul used to tease me, "but any teenage Puerto Rican can outthink you on the street." He was right, in a way. I was in the midst of my third major education; the first had been liberal arts at Vassar, the second mystical studies in Arica; now I was learning street smarts in an entirely different sort of academy. So was Paul. He knew about dealing pot and cocaine, but street heroin was something else, a rougher game, where no rules applied. He got beat too; everyone did; it came with the territory.

I had an apartment at Ninety-Fourth Street and Broadway and a night job doing typographical proofreading. Every morning I woke up dead broke; no matter how much money I'd had the night before, in the morning it was always gone. I had an arrangement with the *bodega*, the Spanish grocery store downstairs; they would let me have a subway token, a pack of cigarettes, and a *New York Post* on credit in the morning, and at night I'd pay them back. I'd ride the subway downtown to meet Paul, and we'd go to the Lower East Side to cruise the streets and see what was happening. I collected money from people who wanted to score, sold stuff to other people, accompanied Paul on his pot rounds, and within a few hours I'd have enough to get my morning fix. I proofread in type shops because it was easy, transient work and paid better than writing or editorial proofreading. I was embarrassed to have a job in journalism as strung out as I was, though I still wrote freelance articles for the *Voice* and some other magazines. With the habit I had, thanks to dealing and methadone, I now needed more and more dope to do less and less work, and rarely seemed to find the time to do it.

Shuna was in her last year of junior high; she was fifteen. I left her home alone a lot; somehow I'd managed to convince myself she was old enough to take care of herself. I didn't like to take her with me to cop, though sometimes it seemed unavoidable; I've had some terrible times in recovery trying to deal with the guilt of having put my daughter in dangerous situations in my pursuit of the drugs. A few times, on our way to Long Island, she had waited in the car with Paul while I went into some buildings on Avenue B. She had been so scared that she made me promise never to take her there again. If I went downtown with her after that, I left her at the Kiev Restaurant with enough money to get a snack while I made the rounds of my regular spots. Michael lived on Ninth Street, near Second Avenue. I took pains to avoid his street; I was afraid if he found out I was a junkie, he'd try to take Shuna away from me, and I thought I couldn't bear that; I'd already lost too much.

"To be a junkie mother is to know guilt," Tamara once said, and that was an understatement of epic proportions. At the time I was unconscious, numbed to reality and morality by the exigencies of my need and the fact that for us it was everyday life; I would only come to know the extent of my guilt after I had finally cleaned up. I was really attached to Shuna, though I knew I wasn't much of a mother anymore, and lived in fear of losing her. I later found out that she had told her father what was going on; he warned her not to go with us to get drugs, but never asked her to live with him. It was a dreadful time for me; my addiction had accelerated and I was hurtling downhill at terrifying speed; but my daughter didn't even have drugs to buffer her awareness, just a lonely, depressing, frightening siege with a mother who slipped further away from her each day. I had found us a new home, but for most of the year we lived on Ninety-Fourth Street, I was hardly ever there. Between working nights and copping days, I never found the time to unpack the boxes I'd moved to our new apartment, and the place was a squalid mess, where a child would be ashamed to bring her friends.

Shuna kept her area of the house clean, but she'd given up on my room and was, I realize now, in the process of giving up on me as well. Sometimes if we were home at the same time, she'd come sit on my bed and try to talk to me. "Mom," she'd say, "What's happened to you? You used to be such a great dresser; you were the best ever. You looked so beautiful in your silk blouses that were such great colors I used to stare at them in your closet. Now you never even get dressed up any more; you just wear those men's clothes all the time. You used to be interested in so many things, but all you care about anymore is drugs. Can't you do something, Mom? I'm really worried about you." I heard what she was saying, but I was caught in the vortex of addiction, powerless to stop or even slow down. I had to run so hard to keep up that I couldn't hold a thought long enough in my mind to take positive action; there was always something more pressing to do; every day brought a new emergency.

I had gotten some of my stuff out of storage, but then I would plan to get some more and end up spending the money on drugs. The storage bill piled up so high, I lost what I had in there: a splendid old Gibson guitar, original paintings friends had given me, irreplaceable Arica notes, relics from my past. Most of the time, I was too busy even to worry about it. I spent my life at a dead run. I had a lot of customers I copped for, including one I'd had for years who sent me money from England every month. I sent the stuff to him by mail. Paul made me put it in the mailbox as soon as we got it; otherwise I would just chip away at it until there was hardly anything left. I had no time for friends any more; the only people I saw were my customers and connections. I still did some things I'd always enjoyed, reading, knitting, shopping for clothes; but the me who did them was a shell, a shadow of the person I'd been. My inner self had been eroded so gradually over the years by the drugs that, without noticing it, I'd ceased to inhabit my own life or even my body. I liked to get so high that I couldn't feel my body; I'd watch my hands moving at the end of my arms but wouldn't be able to feel them. I'd sought oblivion as a relief from pain, and I'd found it, but in the process I'd managed to obliterate myself.

I'd had two more abortions. I knew that with my lifestyle there was no way I could have another baby, so I just had the abortions and didn't think too much about them one way or the other. But Paul did. He'd been brought up Catholic, and the idea of abortion really bothered him. He'd offered to marry me the first time, but I'd said no. Then the second time he'd gotten furious with me because he suspected the baby wasn't his, which it wasn't, and had beaten me up, breaking one of my ribs. The abortions had changed our relationship so that we hardly ever had sex any more. We weren't so much boyfriend and girlfriend as we were dope partners; I'd noticed with other dope-fiend couples we knew that drugs could hold a relationship together more firmly than sex or love. Though betrayals were common, the awareness of mutual vulnerability and life-and-death stakes produced in these unions extremes of tenderness as well as brutality, forms of caring endemic to these particular circumstances: life during wartime, love in the ruins. I'd tried to leave Paul after he beat me up, but found that I couldn't; I depended on him far too much.

Sometimes when I went into those abandoned buildings in the dead of night, Paul was the only person in the world who knew where I was. Anything could happen in those buildings; people fell through holes in the rotted floors, and we heard all the time about customers who'd been tortured, stabbed, pushed out of windows. I had a close call one night when five teenage workers, young enough and brutal enough to be Khmer Rouge soldiers with no regard for life, surrounded and began menacing me. They circled like a pack of animals, trapping me on the stairs, taunting me with insults and sexual threats. No one else was in the building, and I was terrified. But the manager, who knew me, showed up and made them sell me my dope. I figured that if something had happened to me, Paul at least could have told my mother and seen about Shuna. Maybe he could even have rescued me, though I doubted that; he wasn't very brave. Paul and I looked out for each other because we had to. The life of a dope fiend was too hard otherwise. No matter how together you were, there always came a time when you didn't have money, couldn't get stuff, or got busted or beat, and would need your partner to bail you out. Another junkie would help you at those times, knowing he or she might need your help tomorrow.

One day I walked around the neighborhood for hours without finding anything. Either the spots were closed, or they had run out of dope, or they had the dope but couldn't open up because the cops wouldn't leave them alone. Finally I saw a familiar-looking guy who told me he could cop from a house connection, someone who sold out of an apartment rather than on the street. I gave him forty bucks and waited for him outside. Then I saw him running through the alley behind the building. I chased him around the block and caught up with him. "Listen, man," I said, "If you're so desperate you need to rip me off, then you can keep some of the dope. But you gotta give me a couple of bags too. That's my last money, and I'm sick." To my surprise he handed over two of the four bags in his hand. "You better watch out who you do this to," I told him.

"The next person might put a bullet through your head." "I wish they would," he said. "It would be a relief."

I knew how he felt. I had lost all hope of ever being able to get off the treadmill. Sometimes I wandered the streets in despair. "I don't give a fuck," I would say to myself, or "Fuck it," the two words I once heard described as "the junkie national anthem." But it wasn't true. I could feel my heart and spirit turning black inside of me. I loved dope, loved getting high, but some part of me, deep inside, knew that it wasn't right to be living this way. "I didn't receive all the advantages I have to become a junkie on the street," I would think to myself, but I didn't know how to break free of the stranglehold the dope had me in. I even considered moving to England, where they had legalized heroin for junkies, but that didn't seem like a solution either, because I would still be dead inside.

By this time Paul and I had tried to kick a number of times, but we always went back to getting high. He still talked about getting clean, but I'd given up trying. "I'm a realist," I'd tell him, "a pragmatist. We might as well face that we're hooked on this stuff and make the best of a bad situation." Sometimes it seemed that the only way I could ever get free would be to kill myself. I'd never seriously OD'd, and I doubted I could come up with enough money or drugs for an overdose even if I wanted one. Of course someone might shoot me or stab me on the street, or some worker with a grudge against me might give me a hot shot, laced with strychnine or battery acid, like they did to people who caused them trouble or ripped them off; there was always a chance of that. Otherwise I had to keep going; short of dying, there was no way out. The way I saw it, I was bound to the dope; we were in this together, till death did us part.

It was summer 1983. The hydrants were open on every block. We washed the car in the spray, cupped our hands for drinking water, and splashed ourselves to cool off, while crowds of neighborhood kids, squealing with pleasure, ran in and out to play. The streets were gritty, hot and alive; people spent evenings out on their stoops; all night long you heard the slap of dominoes and the syncopated congas and timbales of salsa blaring from the radios. Though I lived uptown, the Lower East Side was my stomping grounds. Even the stench of sun-baked piss in the alleys and the metallic dankness of the subway stations had become so familiar to me that they smelled like home. In the summer I spent all day and night, every waking hour I wasn't at work, running the streets. The warm weather seemed to exacerbate the violence. In the space of a couple of weeks, I'd had a butcher knife held to my throat on Twelfth Street and a gun shoved in my face in Williamsburg, but I was too far gone to care; sometimes I thought Paul and I were more scared of being dopesick than we were of being dead. Instead of stopping I did more dope than ever, whatever the traffic would bear.

On July fourth weekend, Paul and I copped some extra bags and went out to my parents' house to spend a few days. We got there late, around four in the morning; we were sitting in the kitchen, nodding out over the counter, when my sister Lorraine came out of a bedroom and found us. I might have been able to fool my mother, who believed at the moment my lie that I was clean, and explained to the family that I fell asleep at the table because I was tired from working nights. But Lorraine had been a junkie herself; she knew a nod when she saw one. She confronted me about it the next day. I told her the truth about what was going on, that I was hopelessly strung out and couldn't stop using. Just as she had done to me years before, I begged her not to tell our mother. Then I burst into tears. "Don't worry," Lorraine said. "You will be able to stop. Your days as a junkie are numbered."

Lorraine was preoccupied with her own advanced pregnancy, so Paul and I went on much the same way for another month or so. By now I was using about two bundles of dope a day, twenty bags. I needed six or seven just to be able to get up off the bed. I used to be able to save myself a wake-up, so I wouldn't be sick in the morning, but I couldn't seem to save anything anymore. I just did all I had and fantasized that money would fall from the sky so I could pay off my bad debts, or buy what I owed to my customers. Sometimes I nodded off with a cigarette and set fire to my clothes. A few times I woke up with my flannel shirt in flames. I sat up in bed, calmly muffled the flames, and sank back into a nod. I didn't have time to take showers or to wash my hair. I had some strange, painful infection on my feet; another junkie told me it was from not washing between my toes with soap and water. I cried all the time; I cried when I was dopesick and when I was high. I was in a state of total despair. I felt hopeless, helpless, and out of control. One night I was in Paul's room, trying to take a nap before my shift started at midnight. I couldn't stop crying. I was in so much desperation that I prayed to God to help me, to show me a way out. I didn't really believe it would work, but I didn't know what else to do.

Lorraine had the baby, her third son, Gopal. I received another eviction notice; since Lorraine was staying with my parents, I asked my father, who was working at my brother-in-law Jon's store, for the money to pay my rent. This created a big stir in the family; normally all of us went through my mother with any requests for money. My father insisted that she write me a check, so I paid my rent, but the gas and electricity got shut off. Lorraine told Jon that I was using heroin, and that was why I couldn't pay my bills. Shuna had a summer job working for Jon. He pressured her for information about my drug use, and finally she cracked. Jon told my mother, who called me one morning, catching me so dopesick, miserable, and crying that I told her the truth. Shuna came home from work the next day and informed me she was moving out. "You're not even my mother any more," she said. "You don't come home; you don't take care of anything; all you care about is drugs."

Of all the years of my addiction, that time seems like one of the most devastating. But when it happened, I was already so sunk in despair, so demoralized and beaten down by the drugs, that I barely could react to it at all. One crisis following on the heels of another was my normal, daily fare, and I had to hustle so hard to feed my habit that I could barely get through one before the next one was upon me. In all the confusion, I felt betrayed and abandoned. I blamed Shuna; I blamed Jon; I blamed everything but the drugs that had caused me and my family such anguish. I was incapable of making a rational decision, of feeling compassion for my daughter or of having any emotion not controlled by the drugs. I felt besieged and defensive, like a trapped animal, striking out blindly in a futile attempt to stave off certain death. Only the death had already happened. When I think about myself during this time, what comes to mind are Coleridge's chilling lines from "The Rime of the Ancient Mariner": "The nightmare life-in-death was she / That thicks men's blood with cold."

Michael and Ellen, who was now his wife, came up to the apartment and helped Shuna pack her stuff. Then she went to stay with my parents.

Both of us were dazed with shock; the enormity of what it meant for us to separate was beyond what we could afford to express at the time. We still had to keep going with our lives. The dope didn't allow me the luxury of stopping to reflect; and my daughter had been so deeply disturbed by the cumulative effects of the past few years that she took refuge in numbness to protect herself from being overwhelmed and unable to function. Eventually she got into therapy, in a group with other children of addicts; but even now, over ten years later, we still struggle to repair the damage the dope did to our relationship. I have to live with the fact that the anger and sadness she feels from her lost childhood will never completely be assuaged; the years I wasn't there can never be replaced. The normal twists and turns of the mother-daughter bond are difficult enough without complications; but between me and Shuna, both headstrong, intense individuals whose wills often clash, there is always the shadow of the invisible interloper that wrought havoc with both our lives.

Shortly after Shuna moved out of my apartment, my mother called to tell me I was to come to a meeting with the whole family, and that I could not bring Paul. Paul drove me there, dropped me off, and went back to the city. My whole family was sitting around the living room. They'd decided to have an intervention. Jon and Sheila had been going to some meetings for families of drug addicts, and learned about interventions and tough love. Each member of the family told me some incident about my behavior; Sheila talked about how I nodded out and nearly dropped her baby son the day of his *bris,* the Jewish circumcision ceremony. Most of what they told me I had done, I didn't remember at all, and I protested. Jon cut me off. "You can't be in this family any more if you don't do something about your drug problem," he said. My mother looked pained, like she was going to cry at any second. My father looked puzzled and acutely uncomfortable; I could read so much sadness in his eyes that I wanted to cry myself. I felt trapped. I wanted to cop an attitude and tell them that if I had to choose between them and the drugs, I would take the drugs, but I couldn't do it. I loved my family too much to give them up.

I had been reading in the newspapers about the black box, a new invention a woman doctor in Scotland had come up with to help heroin addicts over the pain of withdrawal. Normally when you abuse opiates for many years, your brain loses its ability to produce endorphins, the body's own opiate, which helps to kill pain and alleviate depression. Without endorphins as a buffer, addicts trying to kick heroin would experience so

much pain and depression that they'd be driven back to the drugs for solace before their bodies had a chance to readjust. The black box used
sound waves to stimulate addicts' brains to produce endorphins quickly,
and it had helped rock stars like Eric Clapton and Pete Townshend of the
Who to overcome their addictions. I suggested this as a solution, but my
family thought I was trying to con them. I wanted to live with my parents,
but there was no room for me, as Shuna and Lorraine were already there.
Shuna said nothing during the entire intervention and avoided looking me
in the eye. It was excruciatingly painful for both of us. Finally I promised
to go into a hospital to clean up as soon as one could be found, and the
family gathering broke up. Then I caught my mother alone in the kitchen.
"Now that you know what's going on, can you give me seventy dollars so I
won't be sick tomorrow?" I asked. She gave me the money.

Jon called the next day to say that since I couldn't see my family without trying to manipulate them for money, I was not allowed to talk to my
mother or my daughter until I cleaned up my act. He knew how much
losing my contact with these two would hurt me. Jon had promised to
look for a hospital for me, but there were very few in New York, and
none would take my medical insurance, the Blue Cross I had gotten at
my first proofreading job. I remembered that an old customer of mine
had recently cleaned up at a hospital in Minnesota. I called him and he
gave me the name and address of a drug counselor in New York who
could get me into the place he had gone, St. Mary's. In early September
of 1983, Paul and I went to see the drug counselor. He didn't believe we
were on heroin, he said, because we were both so fat from Paul's cooking. "You all are the two fattest junkies I've ever seen in my life," he
joked. It turned out that St. Mary's would take my insurance. The drug
counselor called Jon, and Jon said he would pay for a one-way plane
ticket to Minneapolis for me, if I agreed to go within a week. "What
about my stuff?" I asked; I was completely incapable of moving on such
short notice, if at all. Jon said Paul could pack up my apartment with one
of the workers from the store; then he'd store my stuff in his warehouse.
"It's only material possessions," he said. "You can always replace material
possessions, Susan; you only have one life."

The dope scene on the Lower East Side had become a public scandal. It
had always been a political football; the city government would clean up

the neighborhood before an election or when some big convention was in town; then, when no one was looking, everything would go back to hell. But recently some innocent bystanders and neighborhood children had been killed in crossfire from drug dealers' shoot-outs. The cops were starting an all-out offensive called Operation Pressure Point, busting workers and hassling customers all day long. A lot of my friends got arrested and charged with "loitering with intent to purchase drugs." Cops watched from the rooftops, armed with rifles and walkie-talkies. When they saw you come out of a building, they radioed the other cops on the corner, who picked you up while you were walking away. It was just harassment; there were so many junkies in New York that full-scale prosecution would have clogged up the court system to the breaking point. The *New York Post* was up in arms about one of the judges, "Turn 'Em Loose Bruce," because he let everyone off with a fine. But it was definitely getting harder and more dangerous to find any dope. Shuna would be starting high school at Music and Art soon; she was going to commute from Long Island. It was as good a time as any to be leaving.

I spent the next week in shock. I told my job that I needed a medical leave of absence; I was going to Minneapolis for a month and then I'd be back to work. The program was twenty-eight days long. I couldn't imagine staying off drugs for twenty-eight days. It sounded like an eternity; I could hardly go two hours without a bag of dope. I remembered how, when I had first started copping on the Lower East Side, I would look at the people who constantly stayed out on the streets, hustling and desperate, never going home, and think I wasn't a junkie because I wasn't like them. Now I was one of them. From a mile off, strangers could tell I was hooked. I was sloppy and unkempt, with big black circles around my eyes, and the slack features and waxy gray complexion of a heroin addict. I kept my drug use a secret from my job, but that was only because I worked graveyard shift, when none of the bosses were around to catch me nodding off and disappearing into the bathroom.

Paul decided he would go to St. Mary's too, a few weeks after me. He planned to rip off one of his big pot connections for the money, then drive out to Minnesota. I felt totally bereft. I missed my mother and Shuna desperately, and felt deeply resentful toward Jon for not letting me talk to them. I didn't want to leave New York. I didn't want to stop using heroin either, but I felt like I didn't have a choice. I was getting evicted from my apartment and didn't have the strength or money to find another place. Paul's place was out of the question; the woman he lived with hated me; she only tolerated having me around at all because she didn't want Paul to move out. In a numb fog, I packed what clothes I could fit into the few suitcases I had, leaving the rest of my scattered papers and possessions, and the still-packed boxes from the last eviction, for Paul to pack and bring to Jon's warehouse.

The night I was supposed to leave there was a huge rainstorm, one of those drenching downpours they have in New York where the raindrops pelt off the sidewalk, the air smells like ozone, and the daytime turns dark. There was nothing open on the Lower East Side, so on the way to the airport we stopped in Williamsburg, where I copped from a guy named Frenchie, who dealt out of his parked car. Frenchie sold seven-dollar bags packed in tinfoil; the dope was usually weak; we only bought them in a pinch when we were short of money or couldn't find anything else. I bought seven bags and stashed them in the pocket of my jeans jacket, the only dry spot on my body. I did the bags on the plane; to my surprise the quality of the dope was terrific. I got so high that in the cab on the way to the hospital I nodded out and began talking to people I saw in my nod. The cab driver looked at me like I was crazy; from what he could see, I was just another one of those weirdo nut cases from New York, having a heated conversation with myself. Maybe he was right, and I was crazy. I had no idea where I was, or why I had come there. For the moment I was still so loaded that it didn't matter—which was lucky, because if I had known what was coming next, I might have bolted from the cab and put out my thumb to hitchhike home.

chapter thirteen

Please, Sister Morphine,
Turn my nightmares into dreams

The Rolling Stones,
"Sister Morphine"

IN THE VALLEY OF THE SHADOW OF DEATH—1983

The next morning I woke up bewildered. I was in Minnesota with no drugs and no way to get them. How had this happened? I tried to reconstruct: It was raining; I copped; I got on a plane. I was high, and it seemed like a good idea at the time. Now I wasn't so sure, but there was nothing to be done about it because I'd come on a one-way ticket and didn't have the money to get back home. St. Mary's was a sterile-looking place—nondescript institutional rooms in a square brick building—but it was set on the banks of the Mississippi River, whose source was farther north in the state, at the edge of a lush green park ringed by enormous, leafy trees, which were just beginning to turn color, crimson, russet, and gold, in the warm Indian summer.

I was nervous as hell. I knew what was coming next, and I didn't want to face it. The intern who'd searched my bags the night before had confiscated the Dalmane I'd brought to help me sleep, the Ativan to take the edge off the jitters, and everything else in my suitcases with a prescription label affixed to it. I had an intake interview with the doctor. When he heard I'd been doing twenty bags a day of New York heroin and had barely spent twenty-four hours of the past four years without some sort of opiate, he decided to go against normal hospital policy and put me on methadone detox for three days. He assigned me a room directly across from the nurse's station. A large wooden cross hung on the wall above my bed; it made me shudder and laugh at the same time. I remembered my father's warning before I married Michael: "You marry a Catholic, you'll be sleeping with a cross over your bed." As it happened, I was the only Jew in the treatment center. I took the cross off the wall and put it in the closet. With all due respect, as far as I was concerned, Jesus hadn't helped me get here, and I couldn't imagine he'd be much help with the next twenty-eight days either.

The drug counselor who'd referred Paul and me to this place had told us we had a disease that was chronic, progressive, and fatal: chronic because it never went away, progressive because it kept getting worse, and fatal because it killed people on a regular basis. St. Mary's treatment was based on this disease concept, and recovery on the Twelve Steps of Alcoholics Anonymous. The counselors told us that the disease of alcoholism/addiction could not be cured, but it could be held in remission if one abstained from all mind-altering drugs. I could go along with the fact that I needed to stop using heroin, but in my book marijuana barely qualified as a drug, so I immediately exempted it from the list. I knew that if I could just smoke pot, I'd be fine. I made friends with two other junkies in my unit: a young man from Cincinnati who was heir to a metals fortune, and a jeweler from Massachusetts who had greeted me in the hall on one of my first days there with the Lower East Side password, "*Bajondo.*" "I have some pot," the jeweler whispered. Every afternoon, when we had a break between groups and lectures, the three of us went out to the park and smoked a couple of joints.

One of the first things they did at St. Mary's was administer the Minnesota Multiphasic Personality Index, or MMPI. It had literally hundreds of questions; I could barely pay attention, but did my best to answer them. When the time came to get my results, I was called into conference with a soft-spoken blond counselor. "Are you a rape and incest victim?" she asked me. "Not that I know of," I answered; I couldn't remember anything. "That's funny," she said, "you have the total personality profile of a woman who's been sexually abused in childhood." She went on to tell me that I had borderline personality disorder, a high degree of defiance and emotional immaturity, trouble with intimate relationships, and a tendency toward depression. I didn't understand what borderline personality disorder meant, but the rest of it seemed pretty accurate. As for the rape and incest, I simply thought she'd been mistaken.

I was introduced to a lot of useful information at St. Mary's, but I was in no position to assimilate it. I paid dearly for my three days of methadone detox. I couldn't sleep for three weeks straight, and the pains in my arms and legs were so bad that I spent whole nights in the bathtub, trying to soak them away. I begged the doctor for something to help me sleep. "Oh, you'll be able to sleep," he said. "One day you'll have peace of mind." "Fuck peace of mind," I would think to myself. "I want a Dalmane." But I didn't tell the doctor because my file already bulged with incidents of what they called "drug-seeking behavior." During groups I could barely pay attention; there was a constant burning behind my eyes from lack of sleep, and I fidgeted in my seat trying vainly to get relief from the pain in my body. I liked Cal, the drug addicts' counselor, but when he asked me in group, "How does that make you feel?" I got nasty. "How do you think I feel?" I answered. "I haven't slept in weeks. My legs hurt; my arms hurt; I hate it here." Of course he was asking how I felt emotionally, and the truth was, I didn't have a clue. Despite everything, however, with my exposure to the Twelve Steps, the seed of recovery had been planted; and though it wouldn't bear fruit for another three years, when it did I would realize that it represented the cumulative effect of all the information I had ever received and thought I didn't absorb.

Paul arrived during my second week of treatment and was put into a different wing, upstairs. He'd managed to smuggle some pot into the hospital, so he joined our little group outside and increased our supply. A new patient, an elderly black man named Vern, entered Cal's group. Vern had done hard time in various penitentiaries and was somewhat amused by the disease concept of addiction. "When we did it, it was a crime," he said. "Now that you all do it, it's called a disease." Vern had lots of visits from his family on weekends. We suspected they were bringing him drugs, but he refused to share with the rest of us. To pass the time and allay our cravings, we filled up on candy and desserts, played cards, and bragged about all the drugs we'd shot, the crimes we'd committed, adventures we'd had on the streets. The counselors called these "war stories" and told us we suffered from "junkie pride," but among ourselves we indulged these tendencies as consolation for the enormous loss and emptiness we felt without our drugs.

Except for Vern, who was almost sixty, everyone in my group was a lot younger than me, many in their twenties. Shuna called and asked how I was doing, and I complained, "Everyone here is twenty-four." "Mom," she answered, "that's because all the dope fiends your age are already dead." I missed my family, especially on weekends when the local people got visits and care packages from home. St. Mary's taught that alcoholism/addiction was a family disease, and that the addict's whole family needed to be involved in recovery. Our program included a family week, the last week of treatment. I wanted my family to come, but none of them would. I felt lost and abandoned, but I also felt guilty over the trouble I had caused my family and so was unable to tell them how much it hurt that they didn't participate in my treatment. In retrospect I'm glad they didn't come; I realize they were healing from their own trauma, and I wasn't ready to clean up yet.

St. Mary's had a halfway house around the corner, called Talbot Hall. I was scared to go back to New York after treatment; I knew I didn't have a prayer of staying clean there, and I didn't think my family wanted me back. I believed I'd have a better chance in Minneapolis, which had so many treatment programs and recovery meetings it had been nicknamed "Sobriety City." I arranged to live in Talbot and attend Twelve-Step meetings and aftercare groups. The day I was released, a friend and I went with Vern to a house in North Minneapolis, where he copped us some Dilaudid, which we shot in the car. Dilaudid is synthetic heroin, prescribed to terminal cancer patients. I'd never done it before. The high wasn't as good as with heroin, but shooting Dilaudid produced an intense rush that could knock you to your knees. In groups and meetings afterward, I told people that I'd had "a slip," and that it had really helped me to know how much I wanted recovery. I was still smoking pot, but didn't count that as a slip or even a drug; I'd accepted a thirty-day chip commemorating my clean time from St. Mary's without a pang of conscience.

When Paul got out of treatment, we drove up to Mille Lacs in northern Minnesota and went to a motel, where we had sex for the first time in two years. "Sex is okay, Little Suze," Paul said afterward, "but it lasts so short. It doesn't hold you for eight hours like a good bag of dope." We went out to a bar and had a couple of drinks, which I didn't mention to anyone. Then Paul took off for Atlanta to stay with his brother. I got a job at a type shop in downtown Minneapolis called Great Faces. I worked all day, then at night attended AA and NA meetings, aftercare groups, or our once-weekly halfway house get-together. I met the handful of Aricans who lived in Minneapolis and joined their Octagon, which met on Sunday mornings. Talbot Hall had very few rules and restrictions, except the one against using. Every week someone got thrown out or left because they'd gotten drunk or high.

One night I went to an NA meeting at St. Mary's and spotted a good-looking guy I'd never seen before, with a hospital bracelet on his wrist. He had straight black hair, high cheekbones, full reddish-blue lips, and eyes that looked like they'd seen the depths of hell. "Uh-oh," I thought to myself, "there's trouble." The next morning I was knitting in my apartment, still in my red flannel nightgown, when the jeweler, who'd relapsed and was now back in treatment, came over with the guy from the meeting, a Southerner named Blue. "I saw you last night," I told Blue. "I noticed your veins have that lived-in look." "That's funny," he said. "Some of them haven't been lived in for years." The counselors had warned us against starting a relationship the first year of recovery, but as usual I didn't think their advice applied to me. Blue had a distinctive Southern accent, a humorous way of expressing himself, and a deadly dose of charm. We carried on a flirtation and I convinced him to move into Talbot.

Blue and I commiserated on our homesickness. We considered ourselves exiles from home, banished by family pressure, adrift in an unfamiliar wilderness that might as well have been, and in climate resembled, Siberia. Without the excitement of drugs, we were bored and restless. One night we were downtown and ran into a guy who'd been in my treatment group. All of us went back to his apartment and ended up shooting morphine. I was so loaded when we returned to the halfway house that I walked around the block several times, hoping the cold air would revive me. But as I crept up the stairs to my apartment, another resident spotted me in the hall. The next day he confronted me in aftercare group about being high. I wanted to protect Blue, so I told a lie; I admitted to having smoked a joint.

We ended up getting kicked out of Talbot Hall anyway. I'd already made plans to move into a sober group house near Lake of the Isles, and

Blue sublet an apartment on Northside, a mostly black neighborhood, full of drugs. Often I stayed overnight at his house. We smoked pot, and I wrote pages and pages of stuff in my notebooks; I still believed the drug was helping my creativity. I was aware that Blue shot dope sometimes, but I didn't want to know the details and went out of my way not to ask. An unsavory character named Billy hung out at his house; I suspected him of being Blue's Dilaudid connection, and my suspicions were confirmed when he brought over some pills, which Blue and I shot. Unlike New York, there was very little heroin to be had in Minneapolis, and the local junkies mainly ripped off drugstores and got high on pharmaceuticals.

The sober people I lived with asked me to leave. I found an apartment on Hennepin Avenue, in what was called the uptown section, next door to some former Talbot Hall residents. Blue and Billy helped me move in. I had a single bed and a color TV a Talbot friend had given me when he got kicked out for drinking. The building manager had left one enormous armchair and a kitchen chair in the apartment. Blue and Billy set up the TV near the front door, turned the two chairs to face it, and watched a basketball game with beers in their hands. They looked like two Mafia thugs guarding the apartment. I didn't own so much as a fork, but over the next few weeks my Arican friends brought me dishes, furniture, and plants, and soon my apartment began to look livable. I still felt like I was in exile from New York, but at least now I had a place of my own where I didn't have to worry about being thrown out for using drugs.

At my job I walked around with a big lump of grief in my chest, but found it impossible to cry. I missed Shuna, my family, and Paul; I was homesick for New York and everything familiar, especially my drug life on the street. I went through the motions of living, attended growth groups at St. Mary's, saw people socially whom I'd met at meetings, and hung out with Blue, but inside I felt like that prison expression, "dead-man walking." I'd always been known as the crybaby in my family; now it had been six months since I'd shed a tear, the longest I'd ever gone that I could remember without weeping. Something strange was going on inside me, but I didn't know what it was or how to fix it.

I had just been through the coldest winter of my life. On Christmas eve of 1983, it was ninety-five degrees below zero with the wind chill, so cold you couldn't even sit near the window, much less go outside. Frost formed crystallized patterns on the glass, like the special paint my father had used on his tropical fish tank. The cold was so severe it was life-threatening; when you went outside your eyes watered, and before you reached your destination, the tears would freeze on your cheeks. Snow sparkled like dancing diamonds as it fell, cloaking the city in magic. It was startlingly beautiful, and I viewed the weather as a challenge to survival, like crime in New York City. I adapted to the climate with a big down overcoat and clumpy sub-Arctic boots, proud of my ability to survive. Now it was March, and spring was coming; though snow still fell, you could smell the thaw in the air and feel the underriding current of excitement. I wondered if my heart would thaw with the change in the weather.

Blue got evicted from his apartment on Northside and moved his stuff to my house. He'd met a bunch of local dope fiends and often stayed out all night with them or for days on end. Once in a while he brought home something to share: half a Dilaudid or a spoonful of coke, but I was trying to keep my drug use to a minimum. I smoked pot every day, but that was about it; I was afraid of being like I'd been before.

I'd gotten fired from Great Faces for showing up late for work too many times. Now I worked nights at Dahl & Curry, a union type shop just across the road from there. My shift was from six to two in the morning. Usually I brought a joint to smoke on my break, and after work I smoked another one and scribbled in my notebooks till the sun came up. It was a lonely life; there was no one to talk to when I got home. Since I'd cleaned up from heroin, I'd had vivid, compelling dreams such as I hadn't experienced in years; with opiates you have dreamlike visions while awake, but never sleep deeply enough to dream. My dreams were more interesting than my solitary waking life. I felt happiest when I'd come home from work to find Blue asleep in my bed, but that didn't happen too often.

I had made one friend at Great Faces, Carol, a typesetter who'd been a drug addict when she lived in California. She introduced me to T. J., a black guy who took me driving around every afternoon to buy pot. I'd started going to therapy. Tom, an Arican in my Octagon, studied neurolinguistic programming, a quick and deep method of therapy, and had recommended a practitioner. The therapist told me to try to get in touch with the little girl inside me, write about her, talk to her, ask her to visit me in dreams. He had asked me a weird question that sparked my thinking: "Where did you learn to disconnect?" After that session I'd had an image of myself as a two year old, toddling into Bobish's kitchen with my arms held out to be picked up, my little heart filled almost to bursting with love for her. I usually didn't have memories of that time in my life. When I reached back into childhood, I got to age two or three and then came up against a steel door that sealed off the area like a bank vault. I couldn't remember anything from that time.

Now that the weather was nicer, I often walked over to Lake of the Isles. I climbed down a big weeping willow tree that had fallen into the water onto a large branch, where I could sit hidden from view and look across the lake through the leaves. I would smoke a joint and imagine the world when it was still a wilderness, in Indian times. Sometimes I could conjure up silent canoes cutting through the water and the magnificent trees that would have surrounded the lake in the days when Minnesota was known as "the Big Woods." One day I walked to my secret spot and heard voices. Blue was lounging on the branch with his arm around a blond woman; they were kissing and passing a jug of wine back and forth, talking and laughing with the kind of easy, romantic intimacy I'd always wanted with him but seldom had.

I ran back to my apartment, got into bed, and pulled the covers up, consumed with jealousy and despair. Blue's friend Rick came over from next door and told me about the blond woman, Jane, an heiress with plenty of money and dope. I stayed in bed all weekend, too despondent to go out or do anything. Monday night Blue picked me up from work. We got in an argument in the car, and I screamed out all my rage and frustration with him. It felt oddly good, liberating, like breaking up a log-jam inside. To calm me down, Blue gave me a bag of New York dope he'd gotten from Jane, then dropped me off at my apartment. I locked the door behind me and shot the dope. I expected to feel euphoric, but instead a flood of tears welled up from behind my eyes and began flowing freely down my face. For the first time since I'd come to Minneapolis, I wept. The ball of grief that had been frozen inside me for months melted into warm, salty tears of release. All it had taken was one bag of dope, and I was back to my old self again: normal, crying, me.

There was a women's bookstore in Minneapolis called the Amazon Bookstore. It was right down the block on Hennepin Avenue. I would spend hours at a time in there, reading on the floor. One day I found that old essay of mine in *Sisterhood Is Powerful,* and a blurb from a book review I'd written for the *Village Voice* on the back of a novel. Here in this anonymous city, where I was nothing but a broken-down dope fiend struggling with my addiction, I'd forgotten who I was. I wrote in my notebooks, but for the first time in my grownup life I wasn't writing regularly for publication. My self-esteem, without the drugs to prop up even the false junkie pride I'd managed to retain, had sunk to an all-time low. I felt old and fat, self-conscious and unattractive; a horrible haircut I'd gotten at St. Mary's and Blue's defection to blond, willowy Jane hadn't helped. Seeing my byline in these books was like a glimmer of something only dimly remembered, like a foreign language I'd studied in high school and then forgotten. If I weren't a writer, or a mother, no longer a practicing junkie, then who was I? I simply didn't know.

As I'd been doing for as long as I could remember, I looked for the answer in books. *The Wounded Woman,* a Jungian exploration of the scars resulting from bad father-daughter relationships and the roles women played to cover them up, resonated deeply with my own experience. I read *Medicine Woman,* Lynn Andrews's first book, and was taken with her Cree medicine woman's teachings about reclaiming our lost feminine power, things like "Find the guarded kivas where you have hidden your heart." I studied my daily horoscope in Joyce Jillson's column for the Minneapolis *Star-Tribune* and threw the *I Ching,* looking for answers, omens, guidance, clues, whatever I could find to hold onto. I knew that in order to get better, I would have to heal my heart, but I didn't have any idea how to do it. So I lived in a world of fantasy and daydreams, looking for something to make me whole.

I smoked weed like I'd once used heroin. I spent all my money on pot. If I didn't have a joint to take to work, I was anxious and jittery; on my break I'd roam around Hennepin Avenue downtown, looking for someone to sell me one. I got in trouble at my job when someone smelled marijuana in the ladies' room; it had been raining too hard for me to take my normal smoke break outside. Then one night I ended up with a needle in my arm, shooting some Demerol that Blue's friends had stolen from a pharmacy, and returned to finish my shift in a semi-nod. Early one Sunday morning, T. J. called to tell me he was coming over with a surprise, which turned out to be a bag of brown heroin from a large quantity that he his brother, and a friend had brought back from Chicago. T. J. wanted to know if I'd be interested in dealing it for them.

No problem, I told him. The dope was good, and I already had a large potential customer base: all the junkies I knew from other cities who'd come to Minneapolis to clean up and were now paying fifty-five dollars apiece for #4 Dilaudid because they couldn't find any smack, not to mention Blue's friends. Everything started out fine, but over the next few weeks the dope grew weaker, while my tolerance grew higher. The three guys came over to my apartment to collect the money, which was short. They didn't say anything, but I started getting scared. T. J.'s brother had always been kind to me; he'd bring me dope at work if I needed it; but for some reason I was afraid of him. I was a woman alone, selling heroin out of a ground floor apartment on the main street of a city where I had no family and no one to protect me. Three men I didn't know very well were coming over to collect the money, which was starting to come up short. It didn't take genius to figure out what might come next in the scenario. What if something happened to me? Who would know? Who would care?

Before I could figure out what to do, the dope ran out. And the same day Ivy, one of the women in Blue's crew, came by to tell me that Blue was in jail. The cops had broken down Ivy's door and busted Blue on eight counts of armed robbery. She warned me that the police might question me. I fixed my last cotton and went off to work with dread in my heart. I was sad about Blue and worried about being dopesick at work. I felt alone, confused, and frightened. I wished I had never left New York.

I must have hit the jackpot that day, because on my way to work I met Hakim, a honey-colored black man with the green eyes of a cat, at the all-night grocery store. I had stopped to buy some food, knowing I'd be hungry when the dope wore off. Hakim struck up a conversation with me. He asked me why I looked so down, and I told him about Blue being in jail, but not about the dope running out, though I could see he had serious tracks on his arms. I wouldn't give him my address or phone number but told him where I worked, and he said he'd be there when I finished to walk me home. Late that night I spotted him from the window of the ladies' room. It dawned on me that he was probably a pimp, but he was al-most criminally good-looking, and I felt so lost and alone that I didn't care what he did; I was willing to have an open mind.

Hakim walked me home through Loring Park; we stopped to talk on a bench. He had an iron pipe hidden beneath his shirt, which he re-moved before we sat down. "Don't let that scare you, baby," he said. It didn't. I always carried a layout knife in my pocket, which I was famous for at work. The typesetters thought I was so tough they'd ask me, rather than the foreman, to walk them down to their cars at night. Hakim talked a mile a minute, which got on my nerves, and I only vaguely paid atten-tion. With that special radar addicts have, he'd spotted me for a dope fiend too. When we got to my house and I said I was starting to have withdrawal symptoms, he suggested we go out and cop. By now it was five in the morning; I'd gotten off from work at two. I didn't want to get more dope; all I wanted was to get rid of this guy and lie down in my bed alone. He asked me to fix him something to eat. The only food in my house was a container of yogurt and half a can of Carnation evaporated milk for coffee. I gave him a few dollars and told him to go get breakfast. He hugged me at the door. I was glad he was leaving; I never wanted to see him again. That was all I needed in my life right then, a pimp who carried an iron pipe. As if I didn't have enough troubles already.

But over the next few days, as my loneliness intensified, I became ob-sessed with seeing him again. When he finally showed up at my house, I called in sick to work and ran around with him all night. We copped some heroin and cocaine, and he showed me how to jack the cocaine over and over with the spike to keep repeating the intensity of the rush. Each time you drew back the plunger and injected your own blood mixed with co-caine, the drug slammed into your heart with a breathtaking hundred-mile-an-hour rush and bells went off in your head. I loved the feeling of the rush, but afterward I felt jangly and anxious. Hakim cured that with sex, endless, marathon tender lovemaking, exactly how I liked it, long, slow, and sensual. Within a very short time, I found myself living with him and totally under his spell. Out of the frying pan, into the fire.

Although I'd been a heroin addict for years, I'd never been in jail, done prostitution, or supported a man financially. I was completely igno-rant of the street-hustler scene on Hennepin Avenue or the rules of what

Hakim called "the game." But I became hooked on this man sexually, as well as on the drugs we constantly shot, and he appeared to have a great understanding of the psychology of women, though it had mainly been acquired for purposes of manipulation. Hakim had an uncanny knack of fulfilling every romantic fantasy I'd ever had in my life, at least at first. He started out protecting me from T.J. and his crew—soon after my dealings with them, T.J.'s brother got life imprisonment for murdering a coke dealer, so my fear had been well-founded—and then I needed protection from him.

I couldn't have been more shocked when Hakim showed his true colors. We'd been living a romantic dream for most of the summer, until the caretaker of my building, who didn't like having a black man around, demanded we move. I became stressed out working full-time and trying to find an apartment too, and one day, when PMS had stripped my nerves raw, I yelled at him about something. Hakim stood there for a few minutes and then, without warning, picked up a coffee table and flung it against the wall. "You wanna fight?" he shouted. "Okay, let's fight." He grabbed a leg that had broken off the table and began beating my arms and legs with it, fast and hard. At first I was too stunned to react. The whites of his eyes had turned beet red; he looked demonic. He was hitting me everywhere; I hardly knew where to put my hands to protect myself. I tried to fight back, but that just made him madder, so I fell to the floor and rolled into a ball, covering my face while blows rained down on my head, my feet, my back. He beat me until the table leg broke in half, then he dropped it and stood towering over me. "Don't ever raise your voice to me again, baby," he said. "I can't take it." I was sobbing on the floor. He turned away from me and left the apartment.

I didn't know what else to do, so I put on my sneakers and leather jacket and went to work. I had black and blue marks all over my body and a slight limp, but no bruises on my face. I didn't tell anyone what had happened to me because I felt ashamed to admit that I'd let a man beat me up that way. I struggled at work to keep my composure. I didn't want to go home, and I never wanted to see Hakim again. But two in the morning rolled around, and I had no money and nowhere to go, so I went home, hoping he'd stayed away. There were candles lit in the apartment, incense burning, and a vase of flowers sitting on the table. The whole place was spotless. Hakim sat in the armchair, his face in his hands, weeping. He rushed to embrace me. "Can you ever forgive me, baby? I'm so sorry. I don't know what came over me; I lost my head. I'll never do it again, baby, I swear, if you'll only just take me back and love me like you used to." He lay me down on the bed, undressed me, tenderly kissed the bruises, and made sweet gentle love to me, all the while crying and begging for forgiveness. I wanted to believe him, and I didn't have the will to turn him down.

The shop I worked for at Dahl & Curry went out of business, and under Hakim's tutelage, I learned how to support my habit as a booster—a professional shoplifter—how to turn tricks, and why women stayed with men who beat them. Everything that had never happened to me before as a dope fiend happened to me now, including going to jail. Within a year of meeting Hakim, I was well-acquainted with the black underworld of Minneapolis; the gamblers, pimps, hookers, thieves, and drug dealers who hung out at Moby Dick's bar downtown, frequented the after-hours joints and dice houses, and who bought my stolen merchandise or traded it for drugs. They called me "Gangster" or "New York, New York." Besides all these new friends, I'd also acquired three felony shoplifting cases, a massive drug habit, and a case of battered woman syndrome that at one time would have made my hair stand on end.

The first time I got busted, I was boosting silk dresses from Dayton's department store in one of the suburban shopping centers called the Dales. It was early in my career, so I hadn't, as musicians like to say, gotten my chops together yet; I was still using stealing techniques I'd developed as a teenager, taking things into dressing rooms and hiding them under my clothes. I had about five dresses stuffed into my clothes, just enough to put the total into felony range, and was so high that when the rollers grabbed my arms outside the store, I didn't quite understand what had happened. A police car soon showed up, and I was handcuffed and taken downtown to Hennepin County jail, where I was booked, fingerprinted, and put in a holding cell. I fell asleep or into a nod and wasn't all the way conscious when they brought me upstairs; the next morning, when I woke up, I didn't know where I was.

The big room was hazy, like the smoky atmosphere of a dream. Through the mist I could make out some shadowy figures moving slowly. I saw they were women; one was pushing a mop and hauling a heavy bucket across the floor; another was sweeping with a broom. I looked down and saw I was wearing the same uniform they had on: a dark blue short-sleeved shirt and pants. My jewelry and hair clips were gone, and I didn't have my purse. Light slanted down from high in the room. There were bars on the windows and in front of my bed, a metal cot. Someone had covered me with a thin woolen blanket. The women in the other cells stirred, and the place soon came to life. By the end of the day I was acclimated, playing cards and talking jive with the black women I knew from Hennepin Avenue. I stayed there five days. After that, jail would never again seem so strange and unfamiliar. By my third time there, the matrons were almost friendly. "Hi, Susan," one of them joked with me. "I see you've come back for the food."

After my first bust for shoplifting, I was offered a chance for drug diversion. If I entered chemical dependency treatment at the state hospital in Willmar and completed it, all charges would be dropped. At that point, though, I was caught up in the helter-skelter lifestyle of running around to maintain my habit. My days were so busy that I never got around to leaving for Willmar, and convinced myself, through a thick veil of denial, that it didn't matter. By my third bust, I no longer had a choice, or at least not much of one. The judge declared me "a danger to society and a danger to herself," set bond so high that I couldn't make it, and told me, "You can go to Willmar and play ball, or you can rot in jail." I was driven to Willmar, over three hours away, in handcuffs and shackles. It's the state mental hospital, out on the flat plains of western Minnesota, a sprawling complex with a small chemical dependency unit. I stayed there for three-and-a-half months.

Again I was given an MMPI, and again the staff psychologist, a Dr. Doweiko, asked me, "Are you a rape or incest victim?" I told him about St. Mary's, and we spent some time discussing the likelihood that something had happened in my childhood that I didn't remember. Even admitting the possibility was a major step for me. As I walked down the path away from his office, I had the physical sensation of a solid object in the center of my chest, like a large rock, breaking down and dissolving into warm liquid that spread through my torso, filling me with relief. I went back to my room and wrote in my notebook questions that I meant to explore: "Why do I hate myself? Why do I feel so ashamed?" I reflected that no matter how much I had accomplished in my life, a persistent sense of worthlessness and shame had never left me; my self-hatred seemed to run so deep that nothing could touch it.

In our women's group at Willmar, patients related stories of childhood molestation that were so painful and outrageous I thought they were making them up. The nun who ran the group told us that close to 90 percent of all prostitutes and women drug addicts had childhood histories of sexual abuse. It was the first chink in my armor of denial, allowing myself to acknowledge that those things could happen in families. But I still didn't have any memories of my own. And I was preoccupied with other problems. I was relieved that the criminal justice system had removed me from Hakim's tyrannical abuse, though my feelings for him were all tied up with my feelings for drugs, which I constantly thought about and missed. I smoked pot occasionally at Willmar, and fully intended to shoot dope whenever I had the opportunity; in that moment my addiction to the man I'd been living with seemed a more present danger to my life than my problem with drugs. In group the other clients would ask me, "So, Sue, are you going back to the beater?" I had already tried to leave him several times. Either he found me and brought me home, or I returned of my own accord.

Now I knew it was over for good. My treatment at Willmar didn't exactly get me clean, but it gave me the strength to leave Hakim. On one of the passes I'd taken to Minneapolis, I'd decided to go home. As I approached the back door of our apartment house, I was assailed by such overpowering fear that I couldn't bring myself to climb the stairs. I knew there was something wrong with feeling that afraid of walking into my own home, no matter how much sex and dope were waiting for me there. Besides, my three felony cases were still hanging over my head. In order to beat them, I had to go into a halfway house after treatment, and the one I'd chosen was in St. Cloud, an hour and a half's drive away from Minneapolis. It wasn't my first choice of where I wanted to live, but at least I knew I'd be safe.

First I went home to New York. I didn't know how long I'd be locked up and I wanted to see my family while I could, in my brief moment of freedom from Hakim, the drugs, and the criminal justice system. My old friend Bob from the methadone program picked me up at the airport and took me to the South Bronx, the neighborhood of my childhood, to cop. The building at 737 Hunt's Point Avenue where my family had lived still stood and was even inhabited, amazingly enough; women dealt cards at a table set up outside the front door. Around the corner the coral and turquoise row houses were like a landscape I remembered from my dreams, so strange and yet so familiar it made me catch my breath. It was two in the morning, but a bunch of black guys played conga drums on one of the stoops. Under the surreal glow of streetlights, in the thick humid summer night air, people were out wheeling strollers, buying groceries, doing laundry, selling drugs; the city was pulsing with life. My spirit soared and flew; I felt like I was high on acid. I realized how much I'd missed New York and how great it felt to be there, home at last.

The drugs were a bit of a disappointment. Because I'd been in treatment at Willmar for three-and-a-half months, I'd somehow developed the mistaken notion, a new delusion, that I now had brakes; I could still get high, I thought, and then I could stop whenever I wanted. But something strange had happened. I shot speedballs like I had in Minneapolis, but before I could experience the rush, I was already in a nod, an ambulatory nod, really scary. I got high at my parents' house while they were away and came to just before I walked into a plant, a glass door, or the refrigerator. I couldn't stay awake long enough to feel the dope. Like New York City itself, my addiction had been progressing just as if I'd never been away.

I returned to Minnesota to stand trial for my crimes. The judge said he believed I'd cleaned up because I was twenty-five pounds heavier than I'd been when I last got busted. I lived in the halfway house in St. Cloud, a mostly German Catholic farm community, where, as one of my counselors remarked, I was "not just a fish out of water but a fish in the desert." I made friends with Judy, another heroin addict who'd graduated from the program, and the one woman counselor, Sue. It felt strange to me to be around so many white people; during my relationship with Hakim, I'd spent so much time in the black community that they'd adopted me as a member. I felt bored and alienated in St. Cloud. Judy had come from a similar background and understood how I felt. She took me down to Minneapolis one night, and for old time's sake, we dropped into Moby Dick's. We ran into Little Larry, a black guy I knew, and he invited us over to his apartment, where a party was in progress.

At the apartment a Marvin Gaye album was playing on the stereo. I could have fainted from the sheer joy of hearing Marvin Gaye and the honeyed voices of black people talking jive and carrying on. I felt immediately at home. There was a tall, slim, good-looking man sitting at the table and Little Larry introduced us. "This here's Sue. She used to be Hakim's woman, but she caught a couple of boosting cases and had to go up north." The tall guy's name was Tommy. "You lucky you didn't get a bank robbery, messing with that damn fool," he said. "Oh," I said, "I see you know him." There was something about this man I liked, a presence he had, a way of looking directly into my eyes and smiling like he meant it. He was nice to me, treated me like an equal; later on in the evening he kept Little Larry from making any moves on me without making me think I couldn't have handled it myself.

I ran into Tommy the next day on Hennepin Avenue. I'd just shot some opium, and this time I felt like I was going to faint for real. "Don't take me to the hospital if I faint," I told Tommy. "I just shot some dope." "C'mon," he said. "I'll buy you a cup of coffee." We sat down and talked, and talked and talked. Tommy asked me about the halfway house where I lived. "I'd rather drink muddy water and sleep in a hollow log than live someplace where I can't have my freedom," he said. "But you have to do what you have to do to stay out of jail." We talked until Judy came to pick me up, and then he shook my hand goodbye.

Nothing romantic had transpired between us, but I couldn't stop thinking about Tommy for weeks afterward. Finally I talked Judy into taking me down to Minneapolis to look for him. Again I ran into him on Hennepin Avenue, and he took me over to the apartment. Before I got involved with him, there was one thing I needed to know. "Do you hit women?" I asked. "I'll quit you before I hit you," he said, with a broad beaming smile. He didn't seem to think it was strange that I had asked. We spent the night together. He was shy and sweet; I liked him immensely. And over the weeks that followed, when I took the bus down to Minneapolis as often as I could get away from the halfway house, the liking turned to love. His gentle nature soothed me and made me feel safe, and the way I relaxed and luxuriated in his presence reminded me of an American Indian expression I'd once heard describe the feeling: "My heart lies down." It felt like falling weightlessly through space, into a luminous black, deep well; inside it was soft and deliciously warm. A state of grace descended on me and clothed me in well-being; I had fallen in love.

In love and in trouble, I should have said, because that was the way it always was. Throughout my life and addiction, I could preface almost every disaster that had ever befallen me with the words, "Then I met this guy." My situation was by no means unique; over my years of recovery, I've heard it again and again in other women's stories. Looking back now, I feel embarrassed about all this falling in and out of love, and also compassion for the woman I was, so hungry for love, such a basic human need, and lacking a clue how to find it. From earliest years my mother had held romantic love up to me as the great goal of life; I had absorbed the words of countless love songs literally through my pores, and the plaintive wails of blues singers crying, "If you leave me, baby, I'll die," echoed in my ears and in my heart. I was addicted to men before I was hooked on drugs; the drugs were a relief from that; you could buy a bag of dope easier on the street than you could find a lover. I was looking for something outside myself to make me feel good inside, and it would take time and struggle before I knew that could never work. I had miles to go before I could live on my own.

On my forty-second birthday, I had to go to court to resolve the last of my cases. Since I'd completed treatment at Willmar and was in a halfway house, the judge gave me three years suspended sentence, provided I didn't use drugs, commit crimes, associate with known drug-users, or violate my probation any other way. If I did, I would have to serve the whole three years at Shakopee Women's Prison even if I only had a month to go on my probation. Tommy took me out for a drink to celebrate my birthday; then I had to go back to St. Cloud. I hated these goodbyes at the bus station; it was always painful to be leaving him. Now that my legal business was resolved, I wanted to move back to Minneapolis. I had a friend, Mike, who ran a fleabag hotel downtown; the place was so raunchy we called it "the hotel below the safety net." Mike and I shared an interest in Jewish history and culture, which we discussed for hours on end, smoking joints to sharpen our insights and fuel our enthusiasm. He let me stay in the hotel for free whenever I was in town.

I got a job working at another type shop owned by Dahl & Curry, and Mike said he would rent me a room. The counselors at the halfway house worried that I wouldn't stay clean in Minneapolis. "I'm madly in love," I told Sue. "That's far more important to me than dope." Tommy moved into the hotel with me. I was giddy with happiness, stupid with joy. Our room had a huge window. I would lie in bed and watch the gorgeous Midwestern sky as it turned from azure to shades of cobalt blue. Tommy watched the street below. He was a master of the streets, with tremendous intuitive judgment and careful powers of observation. I was intoxicated with him and with my newfound freedom. I never wanted to be in jail or treatment again so long as I lived, and I knew I wouldn't have to be, provided I didn't get strung out.

But how could I avoid it? I was still in denial, thinking I had the power to control my own drug use. I would shoot an occasional Dilaudid, maybe on the day I got paid from my job, but again I mostly just smoked pot. I was familiar enough with Twelve-Step lingo to talk it to my probation officer, and managed to keep her satisfied with my progress. I was too scared to steal or do anything illegal, but if someone I knew wanted to cop a Dilaudid, I'd go get it for them in exchange for a share of the high.

One day a friend I'd met at Willmar came over with a woman named Florence. Florence was middle-aged and frumpy, with thick gray hair and an honest-looking face. No one would have pegged her for a dope fiend in a million years, but she wanted a couple of pills. "Watch out for her, Sue," Tommy told me after she left. "That woman could get you into a world of trouble."

It turned out the gray-haired Florence was an accomplished con artist. The next day she showed up by herself at the hotel with a few hundred dollars to spend. And every day after that. I would cop the dope, and we'd split it down the middle. Before I knew it, I had another habit. And Tommy started spending more and more time away from home. By the time I discovered I was pregnant, I was so far gone in my addiction that I couldn't stop shooting Dilaudid and coke even though I wanted to have the baby. At first Tommy said it would be okay with him if I had the baby; "It's nothing we couldn't handle, Sue." I went to work walking on air, lost in fantasies of white-picket-fence domesticity, unfazed by my reality: that I was shooting dope out-of-control and living in a fleabag hotel.

Then Tommy changed his mind and pressured me to get an abortion. One day I picked up the pay phone in the hotel lobby and there was a woman on the line, waiting for Tommy to come down and talk to her. Jealousy hit me like a punch in the stomach; I was so weak I could barely make it up the stairs to our room.

A few years before, when I had done my fifth step ("We admitted to God, to ourselves, and to another human being the exact nature of our wrongs") with a chaplain at St. Mary's, what had troubled me most was the abortions I'd had; I'd felt that God would never forgive me. I loved Tommy with all my heart and wanted to have his baby; I was forty-two and knew this might well be my last chance to have another child. But Tommy didn't want the baby, and as much as I did, I couldn't stop using drugs. On the day scheduled for the abortion, my fifth, I went to the clinic and spent all day shooting Dilaudid in the bathroom, trying to decide whether or not to go through with it. I was confused, in pain, and doing what I knew how to do; I told myself I needed the dope for anesthesia; I didn't know I was anesthetizing my emotions so I could force myself to do something totally opposed to my values and desires. It never occurred to me that the dope itself was robbing me of the baby I wanted. At the last possible moment, I had the abortion. Afterward I was in such a rage that I literally stomped back through the streets to our new apartment on Harmon Street, in the building where I'd first met Tommy. It was quite a distance, and I was bleeding heavily, but all I could feel was that towering rage. I shot coke all night to kill the pain that followed it. Tommy and Florence both stayed with me. Florence and I fixed our coke in a spoon. Tommy cooked his in a bottle with baking soda till it formed into rocks, and smoked the rocks in a glass pipe.

Hakim, who preferred cocaine to heroin, had once warned me never to take up the pipe. "As much of a dope fiend as you are," he'd said, "that pipe would kill you. It's a motherfucker, baby. You think heroin is bad? The pipe is worse; it's more addictive than the spike, and you know how that spike can hook your soul." I'd been around people freebasing cocaine for over ten years, but it had never much appealed to me. I'd always preferred to take the downtown route myself. Tommy loved those rocks. He'd disappear for days on end, holing up in various base houses around the city (and other places I didn't know about), and when he came home his face would be so frozen he could hardly talk. By now Florence was more my partner than he was. I spent most of my time alone with her; but on payday, when I bought our dope to even out what she'd spent all week, Tommy would usually show up for a share. Our apartment became a shooting gallery for my friends, especially after I ran into Vern one day after seeing my probation officer, and he hooked me up with a reliable connection for heroin.

The apartment house where we lived on Harmon Place was the scariest place I'd ever been in my life. At one time I had thought Minneapolis had nothing to compare with the abandoned buildings on the Lower East Side or in Harlem where I'd copped, but Harmon Place had proven me wrong; it was worse. Winos drank out in the backyard; hookers brought their johns there; a bootlegger in the basement managed the place; and there was always some sort of violence breaking out in the alleyway or the halls. It was the kind of place where you could carry a loaded syringe through the hallway and no one would bat an eyelash. Shuna had visited me several times when I lived uptown on Hennepin Avenue, but I would rather have died than let her near this place. We'd moved there because our apartment had a kitchen and its own bathroom, an improvement over the hotel, where drunks threw up in the common bathrooms, but there the improvement ended. One friend of Tommy's called it "the devil's house," and that was what it felt like. A week after I moved out, my next door neighbor murdered his girlfriend by throwing her out the window. Most nights after work, I was home alone there and scared. Tommy had told me never to open the door to his so-called friends, but I was so lonely that when one of them, Blackie, knocked on my door in the middle of the night, I let him in. "Let me use your works, Sue," he said. "I'll give you some of my dope." Blackie shot coke. He'd had his eye on me for a while. He told me that Tommy was living with another woman, that I was the only one in town who didn't know.

Ever since I'd gotten the new heroin connection from Vern, my habit had been increasing steadily. After work sometimes, if I didn't have enough money to fix, I'd go over to Moby Dick's or Mousey's, across the street, to try and pick up a trick. Mousey's was where humanity's castoffs fetched up; its bar was home to the lowest of the low. Fat Al, a sometime connection of mine who hung out there, liked to taunt me by saying that in the whole history of Mousey's, I was probably the only Jewish woman who'd ever set foot there. And to make matters worse, when I did go in there I'd hear the waitresses whispering about what I was doing. I'd also gotten back into doing a little boosting, and I copped for a lot of people on the side. One night I came home from work to find my door kicked in. Tommy's leather jacket, our black and white TV, and the little Walkman Mike had given me were gone. I was terrified to stay in the unlocked apartment alone, so Blackie came over and spent the night. We'd been hanging around together anyway, though I was sure I was playing with fire; I didn't know what Tommy would do if he found out.

When Tommy let himself in the next morning, I was trembling with fear; in the same situation, Hakim would have beaten me to within an inch of my life. Tommy was mad and upset, but he understood why I'd done it; there was a limit to how many nights I could stand to stay there alone. I asked him about the other woman, the one whose voice I'd heard on the pay phone in the hotel. He'd lied to me about her, he said, because he loved me and didn't want to lose me. But he couldn't stand to love a junkie; it hurt too much; four of his brothers had died shooting dope. He said he'd had to get away; he didn't love the other woman; he stayed with her because it was convenient; he hoped I would understand. After he left I went over to the hotel to cry on Mike's shoulder. I was strung out, broke; my man had left me; all I could do was cry. "I'm such a mess," I sobbed to Mike. "I feel so hopeless." " But you're not hopeless," Mike said. "I know what you're capable of; you're a wonderful writer. You could redeem your whole life with just one good book." He loaned me fifty bucks to get a fix, and I went off to work. I needed the dope to get normal, but it wasn't going to get me high or make me feel better. A strange thing had happened recently; no matter how much dope I did, all I could do was cry. I knew there was something wrong with spending so much money just to be miserable, when misery could be had for free, but I didn't know how to stop.

I called my mother on the phone. She heard the pain in my voice and immediately asked what was wrong. "Can I come home?" I pleaded. I was sure she'd say no, that I'd had too many last chances with her already, but she didn't refuse. "Come home," she said. "I'll buy you a ticket." I didn't want to leave Tommy, but I knew if I stayed there, I was going to prison for three years and wouldn't see him anyway. My probation officer gave me permission to go home for a visit, and I got a vacation from my job. I was a wreck, hopelessly strung out again, and facing prison. The past few months had been my roughest ever: I'd been raped, robbed, jilted, degraded, demoralized, and hit what I thought was really the bottom, turning tricks with freaks from Mousey's. I didn't see how it could get much worse. I felt like the character in that Bob Dylan song, "Just Like Tom Thumb's Blues," a grim litany of despair that ends with the lines, "I'm goin' back to New York City / I do believe I've had enough."

chapter fourteen

It's raining; it's pouring
Old man is snoring
Now I lay me down to sleep
I hear the sirens in the street
All my dreams are made of chrome
I have no way to get back home
I'd rather die before I wake
Like Marilyn Monroe
And you can throw my dreams out in the street
And let the rain make 'em grow.

Tom Waits,
"A Sweet Little Bullet
from a Pretty Blue Gun"

GOIN' TO THE END OF THE LINE
JUNE-SEPTEMBER 1986

I was living with my parents on Long Island, in Island Park, in the apartment over the boatyard they had had for some twenty-odd years, and to which I had returned again and again in times of trouble. I was on a private methadone program, Medical M, on Twenty-Second and Third Avenue, near Gramercy Park, in the city. And I had a job at Photogenics, a high-quality type shop I had worked at several years before.

I had gotten on the methadone program and obtained the job during a visit to New York a few weeks before. I arrived from Minneapolis with a major heroin habit and a painful abscess on my arm. I went to see my old script-writing doctor on the Upper East Side to get some pills to kick with. I had a history with this doctor stretching back fifteen years, during which time he had written me more prescriptions for codeine, Valium, Percodan, and Dalmane than either one of us would probably have cared to remember. I liked and trusted him. In desperation, I asked his advice. "You're a hopeless junkie," he told me. "The best you can do is get on a methadone program and stay on it for the rest of your life." He told me some private programs to contact, and then refused to give me any more codeine. My mother tells me that while I was kicking heroin with the codeine, I paced the living room like a caged animal. I was extremely nervous, but also feeling somewhat hopeful about the future.

Once I got the job, convincing the owner of Photogenics that I'd been fired before because they had a crazy general manager who expected me to be perfect, I celebrated—of course—by copping dope on the Lower East Side. I went and shot it in the downstairs bathroom at Phoebe's; I had to be careful not to get blood on the white silk blouse I had worn to the interview. Then I sat at a table drinking iced tea and filled up a whole notebook writing about Tommy and how miserable I felt about his leaving me for another woman. All that remained for me to do was go back to Minneapolis for a few days to pack up my stuff and move to New York to start my new life. Best of all, I wouldn't have to go to jail.

I felt like a failure living with my parents; it was inconvenient commuting between Long Island and New York City, and I missed Tommy bitterly. But there were things I liked about living at home too. My mother's cooking, for one. I would come home from my night job and find a big, delicious salad waiting for me in the refrigerator. I don't know how she does it, but even my mother's raw salad ingredients taste different from anyone else's. I loved being back in New York; I felt right at home; and Photogenics paid me very well, as they had before. My mother had loaned me the money to move back to New York and was going to manage my finances for me, paying herself back and giving me allotments to pay my expenses. Every week she gave me a check for forty-five dollars to bring to the methadone program, and every day she made me lunch and gave me spending money to take to work. She bought me a monthly commuter ticket and kept track of all our expenses in a ledger she showed me from time to time.

For a few weeks, everything went fine. The methadone worked, and I was satisfied with my orderly life. Then I started getting lonely. One

Friday night around midnight, I was getting off work at Photogenics and had to kill a couple of hours before my train. It was a balmy summer evening and the end of the week. I was restless and didn't want to go home. I decided to walk over to the Lower East Side, maybe shoot a speedball, and then go home. What the hell? I deserved it. I'd been working hard all week; I'd been good; I wouldn't catch a habit because of the methadone; I only planned to do it on Friday anyway.

Being the addict I was, I could always think of an excuse to get high. I even got high when I didn't want to or didn't think I wanted to. I can remember times when I'd be telling myself in my head that I wasn't going to get high, and meanwhile my feet would steadily be carrying me toward the Lower East Side. One Friday night, anxious to get to my drugs, I refused to work overtime when the foreman asked me to. I'd been having a running argument with one of the typesetters, who was pregnant and objected to having me smoke near her. Like most addicts I got an attitude when I was high, and I'd been unpleasant to her. It must have been clear that I couldn't wait to get out of there, because I promptly got fired from that job. I was a little upset because I knew no one else in the city would pay me top dollar, as Photogenics would; but I told my mother that the typesetter had had me fired, so at least I had an excuse. I had worked there for about a month.

I had spent so many years running the streets of the Lower East Side that I knew most of the junkies and the Puerto Rican workers who sold the dope. But in the three years I'd been away in Minneapolis, the drug scene had changed. Now everyone was into smoking crack. The *New York Post,* which I read faithfully, published horror stories about crack every day. There was one story about a young man who had murdered his mother; a father who had pushed his child out a window; another who had thrown his baby against a wall when its mother complained that he was spending all the money on crack, leaving nothing for food. The *Post* talked about escalating crime and violence, and said crack was instantly addictive from the first hit. I had known a lot of people who freebased cocaine, but it had never much interested me. I was a heroin addict; that was my thing. But all over the Lower East Side, junkies were smoking crack too. The scene had changed. "Be careful now, baby," my old friend Red Dog told me when I ran into him, "these crackheads they got down here will cut your throat in a heartbeat. It ain't like it used to be here. Nowadays you can't trust nobody on the street."

Because of the methadone, I couldn't really feel any heroin I shot unless I combined it with cocaine into a speedball. I found myself shooting more and more cocaine, more and more compulsively. I'd buy a nickel bag on Stanton and Clinton, take it around the corner to the gallery where I did up, and plan to do whatever I had to do after my one hit. The minute I was done, I'd go right back around the corner and buy another bag, over and over until I'd used up all my money five dollars at a time.

I didn't believe the crack stories in the paper applied to me, because by then I was a long-time veteran of the drug scene and thought I knew it all. "I won't get a habit," I told myself. "It's not heroin. I can stop anytime I want." I had started hanging out with one of the workers from the brand Excel. Whatever money he made selling dope that didn't go to his habit went to crack. I smoked with him sometimes in a park on the Lower East Side. It was a much simpler operation than freebasing, which involved a large pipe, a butane torch, and apparatus to cook the cocaine into rock. The people who smoked crack on the street, which they called "beaming up"—as in "Beam me up, Scotty; there's no intelligent life on this planet"— used only a "stem," a thin glass tube usually attached to the large bowl of a base pipe, with a few screens jammed into the end, and a cigarette lighter. This could easily be carried, concealed in the hand, and was available for smoking in public places all over the city. But it still didn't do much for me, and I preferred to shoot my coke for the rush and the bells that rang in my head. Then one night I met someone who showed me how to hit the pipe correctly, so that I heard the bells, and I fell in love.

By this time I had been living at my parents' for a few months and had already been fired from my second job, which I also held for about a month. I got a new job on Seventeenth Street, on the West Side. Right around the corner was a really sleazy SRO building that was a shooting gallery for coke fiends. I was working nights. Even as small a dose of methadone as I was taking every day could make me nod out many hours later with no warning. Several times when I took the Long Island Railroad home late at night, I nodded out and missed my change at Jamaica, or I changed at Jamaica and missed my stop, which necessitated taking long and expensive cab rides home. I also nodded out at work. My excuse to myself for going and getting cocaine on my half-hour lunch break was that I needed it to stay awake. Of course, once I started shooting it, I couldn't stop, so I was always in trouble for getting back late from lunch.

Then I would return so nervous and shaky and in such a disheveled condition I could barely work. So I got fired from that job too.

I always had a good enough excuse for why I got fired that my mother didn't get suspicious. Somehow I had convinced her that even though she gave me lunch to bring to work and I had a monthly ticket for my commute, I still needed thirty dollars a day spending money. At Lower East Side prices, this covered two dime bags of heroin and two nickel bags of coke, my minimum daily routine. It's clear to me now that my mother is codependent. She grew up taking care of her alcoholic father and early in her life became practiced at denial. It was summer, and my parents lived right on the water. To cover up the tracks on my arm, I had to wear long-sleeved shirts every day. I wore old Oxford cloth blouses of mine, which I starched and ironed, and a tiny pair of black jeans that my sister Sheila had given me. I was very skinny at that time, which in itself should have been a tip off, but I said it was from all the walking I did in the city. I claimed I wore the long-sleeved shirts because the air-conditioning made me cold.

Up to now I had been keeping it together fairly well. When I first went home to live with my parents, my brother-in-law Jon had told my mother to hide her jewelry. My mother got angry with him. In all my years as a dope fiend, I had never stolen anything from her. She made a special point one day of showing me where she kept several hundred dollars worth of cash in the house, a vote of confidence in me in defiance of my brother-in-law's warning. She wanted me to know she trusted me. All during this time, my relationship with my mother was pretty good. Both of us enjoyed each other's company. We sat up talking and drinking coffee at the kitchen counter, attended my daughter's graduation from Music and Art, went shopping together, and lived in relative harmony. My mother didn't like me to smoke cigarettes in the house, but there was a glassed-in porch overlooking the bay, and I sat in a rocking chair on the porch smoking and reading magazines and books. I had always found the water around the boatyard to be healing and restorative; there was a wildlife sanctuary nearby and birds flying around. It was a pleasant and quiet life for me, and my mother was glad for the company.

My father wasn't around much because he was working hard at my brother-in-law's business in the city. Jon had recently bought a building to use as a warehouse, and my father was overseeing the renovations. He had two helpers in the store, Victor and Julio, Dominicans who lived on

Delancey Street. By this time in my drug use, thirty dollars, even on top of my methadone, wasn't enough for my daily use. So I had started turning tricks on the Lower East Side. I was so afraid of running into Victor and Julio that I couldn't walk the streets. But I often found tricks on Delancey Street and brought them to a little hole in the wall where you could pay seven dollars and rent a cubicle with a wash basin for twenty minutes. This was convenient for me because it was right near where they sold the coke on Stanton and Clinton streets. I'd walk on Twelfth Street and Third Avenue, over to Allen Street off Houston next to the park, and then via Eldridge and Rivington, another coke corner, where they sold the Jaguar brand, to Delancey. When I stayed out all night, I told my mother I was staying with one of my girlfriends in the city. Sometimes I did; I had one friend who invited me to house-sit when she went out of town on business, and another I had known for years who now sold coke for Cubans out of her rent-controlled apartment on the Upper West Side. Both of these women were cold-blooded dope fiends; there was nothing wholesome whatsoever in our so-called friendship.

One night at the coke house on Eighth Avenue in Chelsea, I ran into a guy who showed me how to cook up freebase. I spent all night basing with him in the bathroom. Then when the coke was gone and he had to go to work, I walked over to the East Side to try to hustle up a trick and get some more. Even on the "ho' stroll," I looked bad. One of the other girls jumped back when she saw me to let me pass by. "Ooo-wee," she cried, "you got some evil eyes there, girl. You scarin' me." I walked over to Tompkins Square Park. People were sleeping on every bench. I was looking around on the ground hoping to find an empty crack vial with some crumbs clinging to the edge. Crack makes you sweat copiously, and your hands get dirty messing with the resin in the screens, pushing them back and forth to squeeze out one last hit. The weather was hot and muggy. I'd been up all night, sweating through my clothes, and I was filthy. As out of it as I was, I still knew it was disgusting to be walking through that park at six in the morning looking for empty crack bottles. I knew I was a mess, but I couldn't see any way to stop.

When I started smoking crack, I could fool myself into stopping when it was gone. I would make sure to take a rock with me on the Long Island Railroad; it was the only way I could make myself go home. I would smoke it in peace when I got home, then go to bed, promising myself I could get more as soon as I got to the city the next day. One of my main crack spots was right outside Penn Station, on Eighth Avenue and Thirtieth Street. I slept with my pipe underneath the covers. When the crack was gone, I could feel how scared I was. I knew I was turning into a monster and that my parents needed protection from me. My father called me "the vampire" because I stayed up all night and slept during the day. I hated myself for getting high in their house. A couple of times I brought dope home with me. When I came in my mother was playing cards with her friends. I went into my room and propped myself up between the bed and the door so that if I OD'd and fell out, they wouldn't be able to open the door and find me. Then I shot all the coke I had till it was gone.

My mother used to lend me her car sometimes. It was a little beige Chevette. Sometimes I would drive it to the train station and leave it there for my father to drive home. I had a set of keys. I had convinced my mother it was okay for me to drive without a license (I'd been too disorganized to get it renewed); I had been driving so long that it didn't matter. I loved to smoke in the parking lot near the train station; it was anonymous, frequently deserted, and no one paid too much attention to what went on there. I would throw my empty crack vials and used-up screens under the train tracks.

I got a fourth job, at a shop called Manhattan Graphics, on Twenty-Seventh Street and Sixth Avenue, near the Fashion Institute of Technology. Far more important to me, it was only a few short blocks—easy striking distance—from my midtown crack connections. Better luck still, Manhattan Graphics, which was a great place to work, trusted their employees. You didn't have to punch a time clock to go out for a few minutes to get a cup of coffee or a snack. I could make it to Eighth Avenue and Thirtieth Street and back again in less than ten minutes, which I did on a regular basis several times a night.

There were two bathrooms in the shop, one upstairs and one down. I would come back with my crack, close myself up in the upstairs bathroom, fill the room with cigarette smoke, spray air freshener under the door, drop a rock in my stem, and beam up almost to my heart's content. Then I'd come out of the bathroom covered with sweat, with my hands shaking and fingers blackened from resin, constantly looking over my shoulder from paranoia, and sit down at my desk to do a little proofreading. Ten minutes later I'd go to the downstairs bathroom and repeat the same routine. In true addict fashion, I thought I was slick, getting over, and that no one would notice anything peculiar in my behavior.

There was one particular crack seller, named Chino, whose product was much prized in that neighborhood. Chino didn't come out to the street until ten o'clock at night. Though his rocks were bigger and more potent than anything else around, I didn't have the patience to wait until ten to start smoking.

I was very thin; I must have weighed about a hundred pounds. I felt physically very weak, and I was nervous all the time. I had been on enough drug runs to recognize the danger signals that preceded the end of a run. I knew I had got to the point where I was going to get sick, busted, or worse. I couldn't walk a block without crack. But the crack connections were right on the corner near Penn Station, so I could get a hit as soon as I got off the train. I knew all the sellers who hung out there. Some sold crack, and some just ripped people off. They sold cut-up Ivory soap, peanuts, bread crumbs, anything white and chunky they could disguise as crack. Sometimes they put a chunk of crack on top and filled the rest of the vial with wop. Groups of crackheads wandered around the neighborhood, smoking in various doorways, parking lots, the stairways of buildings, wherever they could hide out for a little while.

I got ripped off a lot, but I could usually manage to borrow money from someone at work to get more. Sometimes I was lucky enough to catch Chino. When I got my first paycheck from that job, I went to my friend with the Cuban connection to buy some regular cocaine and cook my own crack. I had about five hundred dollars, most of which I owed to my mother. I planned to spend about a hundred dollars and bring the rest of the money home. But once I started smoking and shooting the cocaine, I couldn't stop, and I spent my whole check in less than two hours.

I told my mother that since I had started working right before Labor Day, they had only paid me for one day. I was still managing to save one rock out of my crack to take home at the end of the night. One night, though, I finished smoking my rock and instead of going to bed, I decided to go to the city to get some more. I took fifty dollars from my mother's cash and got in the car, planning to be back in about an hour.

I got to Thirtieth Street at six in the morning. Chino was long-gone. A young boy sold me something that wasn't crack. I went to Ninth Avenue, near the Port Authority Bus Terminal, and the same thing happened. To get more money, I pawned my gold chain and a garnet pendant my mother had given me, which I wore all the time, for thirty-five dollars. I bought some jumbos in a crack house on Thirty-Eighth Street, and started driving home. In Astoria I discovered that only the top rock had been crack, so I turned the car around and went back to the city. By now it was too late to go home; I had to go to my methadone program. I called my mother and told her the car was at Freeport train station, then spent the day driving around with various people, from one aggravating, frustrating situation to another, until finally it was time to go to work.

I was on my way to my job when I ran into a crackhead I knew, who gave me a hit off the resin in his pipe. He told me he knew where we could get more without any money. I had to be at work in five minutes, but without hesitation I got back in the car. His plan was to rip off a crack dealer, ask for two vials to try, then drive away as soon as the guy put the crack in the car. When the plan backfired, he ran off with the crack, the crack dealer grabbed the ignition key from the car, and I ended up with my mother's car in the middle of Eighth Avenue. At first I didn't take it seriously; there were plenty of cops in the neighborhood. Normally you couldn't even fire up a cigarette lighter on Thirtieth Street without drawing a cop. But for some reason that night the cops were all busy transporting prisoners, breaking up robberies, doing whatever they do on summer nights in New York City; and though I tried to flag down a car, they all careened past me without stopping.

The crack dealer, Tony, kept returning to the car to taunt me with the key. He wanted twenty dollars for the crack, which I didn't have, or he wanted me to leave him the car, which I couldn't do. I called my job and told them I'd been the victim of a violent crime; they sounded skeptical. Then I got some unsavory guys who hung around on the block to try to hotwire the car. They jimmied the ignition and fooled around under the hood, but no one could get it started. My mother's little car turned out to be burglar-proof. Finally, in sheer rage and frustration, I started crying. Right out in the middle of Eighth Avenue, in crowded midtown Manhattan. I just stood there helplessly and bawled. My jewelry was gone; my money was gone; my mother's car was in the middle of the street; I couldn't get to work, and I couldn't leave. Everyone on the street was watching me. I was embarrassed and ashamed, but I couldn't stop crying. I felt utterly helpless. I had been up for days; I was exhausted, weak, and totally impotent. I stood out there and sobbed for hours.

In the middle of it, though, something strange happened. I had what we call in the Twelve-Step programs "a moment of clarity." From somewhere deep inside me, I heard a little voice. "Now, Sue," it said, "wouldn't you say this is kind of unmanageable?" It was the first Step, something I didn't even know I knew, much less remembered from all those years before when I had tried to clean up and gone to meetings: "We admitted we were powerless over our addiction and that our lives had become unmanageable." In all the time I'd been getting high since then, I'd never given the Twelve Steps so much as a passing thought. Now here they were popping up on me from out of left field. And then, how could I answer that little voice? "Unmanageable" was an understatement for the situation I found myself in.

By the time Tony's brother gave me back the key to the car, I was four hours late for work. The next morning I had to make up a story for my parents about being mugged in the Freeport train station to explain why the ignition was pried off and my jewelry was gone. I'd hoped that as I got more regular paychecks from my job, my mother would forget about the first one I had spent at my girlfriend's house; but the next day when I woke up, my mother told me my boss had called to say I was fired. That meant that the next week I would get my last check, and my mother would find out I had lied. I started thinking that maybe I could kill myself before then.

I knew I was now in the danger zone, completely, wildly out of control, and I was scared. But because of all the stories in the newspapers about crack, I couldn't tell my parents what was wrong with me. Losing my job, the fourth one in four months, also frightened me; I had always been able to keep a job before. I still had to go to my methadone program, so that day I went to the city as usual. I told my mother I'd be home early, since I didn't have to work that night.

What happened after this is kind of hazy in my mind. I can't recall if the events that follow took place over one day or three days or five days, or even where they fit in sequence. I think it was about three days, days with so much packed into them that they seemed to last a lifetime, and yet with time so speeded up, like a fast-motion movie, that it all might have happened in three minutes.

I remember what I was wearing: a red and black long-sleeved Indian print T-shirt, which a woman I had known for twenty-five years, since she was fourteen, had given me from her shop on the Lower East Side. I had a red cotton sweater over it, my black jeans, and my white Reeboks. I remember being in Times Square, running into one of the young crack dealers there, going to an abandoned building with him, and smoking until the stuff ran out; then walking down to Seventeenth Street, to the building where the coke shooting gallery was.

After that I remember going over to the ho' stroll on Third Avenue and Twelfth Street. I looked pretty bad. So bad, in fact, that tricks would drive by, slow down, look at me, and then shake their heads no. I had given up on trying to catch a trick and was walking over toward Houston on Second Avenue, when a cab driver stopped to talk to me. He gave me a ride down to Allen Street, and we got to talking. He was a nice Jewish guy, a single father, and he also worked part-time as a drug counselor. By this time Ray Charles could have seen I had a drug problem, and I think this cab driver wanted to take me under his wing and save me. He said he was driving out to Long Island later that night, and we agreed to meet about three in the morning near Allen and Houston.

I followed my normal routine near Houston Street, copping coke on Stanton and Clinton, going around the corner to shoot it, turning tricks, running uptown for crack, etc., etc. I remember going down Second Street, near Avenue B, to cop Dom Perignon, which was the hot brand of heroin on the Lower East Side at the time. It was about two in the morning. Almost no one was out. I saw some rats scurry across the street. Behind a fence, on one side of me, I saw more rats picking through garbage. I remembered how terrified I had been of rats when I first started going to the Lower East Side, years ago. Now they didn't even faze me. I could easily empathize with them. Slinking through the deserted street, I was just like one of the rats myself.

I copped the dope and started walking to meet the cab driver. On Norfolk Street I ran into some workers I knew from Lucky Seven. They offered to trade me some dope for my crack. I said no, I preferred the crack. In a weird way, that shocked me too; heroin had always been my drug of choice. Then I went to meet the cab driver. I talked him into giving me some money and taking me to midtown to get more crack. Then we started out for Long Island. He drove and talked. I sat in the back, shooting speedballs and smoking crack, sometimes alternately, sometimes together. I had a lot of drugs that night, and I was doing them all, but something wasn't working. I couldn't get high enough to kill the pain I was in. When we got to Long Island, I talked him into taking me to Freeport to get more crack. I had found the crack houses in Freeport after reading in *Newsday* that the cops had made some major drug busts there.

While the cab driver waited, I went with a man to a firehouse and turned a trick. Then I came back and bought more crack. By then it was time for the cabdriver to take his kids to school. I told him to drop me off at the Valley Stream train station, and I would get home from there. I called my mother from the station, with another cockamamie story.

"I met a drug counselor," I told her, "a nice Jewish boy. He says he's gonna help me get off methadone."

"Your father and I think you're back on heroin," she said to me. "Are you?"

"I wish it was just heroin," I said, "it's much worse than that."

She told me to drive the car home from the station, and we would talk about it when I got home. In a way I felt relieved, almost exhilarated; I had been looking for a way to tell her. Now I could let her know the truth about the check; I wouldn't have to kill myself before she found out. My good mood was also buoyed up by the fact that I still had some more crack, which I smoked on the edge of the platform while waiting for the train.

When I got home, I sat down with my mother at the counter. "You look the worst that I've ever seen you," my mother said. "Tell me what's going on."

"I've been afraid to tell you," I said, "because of all the stuff that's been in the papers. I didn't want to scare you. I've been smoking crack." I told her about the check. I told her about the other drugs. I told her I wanted to stop, was crazy to stop, but I didn't know how. I was crying with the relief of being able to tell her. We talked for a while, and then I went to bed.

I slept so long that I missed my methadone program. When I woke up, I was in a panic about being dopesick. I knew they sold heroin, as well as crack, in Freeport. I grabbed the keys and asked my mother for some money.

"Where are you going?" she asked me.

"To Freeport," I said.

"You can't," my mother said. "Your father said you can't take the car to Freeport any more."

"I have to go," I said, "I missed my program."

"I won't give you the money," said my mother.

"Then I'll take it," I said, "I know where you keep it."

I went in her bedroom, where she kept the cash. My mother was standing in the hallway, a look of absolute terror on her face. She didn't say anything to me, or try to stop me as I rushed past her; she just stood there watching me, with that look of fear on her face.

I went to Freeport and copped some heroin and cocaine in the square near the center of town. Then I went to the crack house and got some crack. I drove around, looking for a place to get off. By this time I had worn out my veins shooting cocaine, and it was difficult for me to get a hit. I was smoking the crack while I drove. Every time I found a place to stop and shoot my heroin, tied off, and started looking for a vein, paranoia overtook me. I thought people could see me from their windows and were calling the police. So I ended up driving around, with no license, in the car I had taken from my mother, with my pipe in my mouth and the needle in my hand, trying to find a vein while the car was moving. I was totally insane.

Just as I did in the city, I would hang out, run into someone I knew, trip around with them for a while, get some money, do some more dope, and then trip around with the next person. For a while I ran around with this guy who was going to find me some tricks, then I dropped him off and ran around with a girl I knew. Each of us had five dollars, and we were putting it together to buy a bag. She went inside to the crack house, and I sat outside in the car, waiting. It was dark outside, a black night, with that kind of street-lamp yellow overlay that makes everything look menacing and surreal, like a horror movie. Unlike the dope scene in the city, which was racially mixed, this scene in Freeport was all black. I was the only white person in sight, totally conspicuous to the cops. The other customers didn't like having me around, and neither did the sellers, who thought the way I drove down the main street with my pipe in my mouth was sure to get them busted.

I had been waiting quite a while for this girl to come out when I decided to go inside and find out what was happening. I locked the door to the car and left my regular pocketbook and my work bag, which had a complete assortment of drug paraphernalia in it, on the front seat. The girl was sitting on the stairs in the hall, outside the connection's apartment. I sat down with her, and we talked for a while. Then she told me to go back outside, because the connection might not sell to us if she saw me there.

I went back to the car. Both the front windows had been smashed out. There was broken glass all over the place, on the sidewalk and inside the car. My pocketbook and work bag were gone. I was stunned. I hadn't heard the noise from inside. It had happened so quickly, and so casually.

The windows must have been smashed out with crowbars, maybe by someone walking by, maybe by one of the guys hanging out in front of the dope house. There was no way to tell. And there was something about all that broken glass in the yellowish black night that gave me the creepiest feeling I have ever felt. All of a sudden, I felt the hatred surrounding me, and the danger, which I had always ignored. I saw how casually those same crowbars might have smashed in my skull. In a flash I saw myself broken and bleeding, my head smashed in, brain-damaged beyond repair. I saw myself dead. I looked at the broken windows of the car and saw death itself, as close as my own shadow, no more than a flicker of a heartbeat away.

I was terrified, but I was still a dope fiend. I wanted another hit, now more than ever. I didn't want to feel what I was feeling. The guy I'd been riding around with earlier came back and said he had found me a trick. We just needed to go down to the square. It would only take a minute. We brushed the glass off the front seat and got into the car. I parked in the parking lot near the square.

In a minute the guy came back with the trick, a Mexican. He looked at the car; then he looked at me. "Where?" he motioned to the guy. Both of us pointed to the car. That's how sick I was, how crazy and desperate. I was willing to lay down on a bed of broken glass in a car with smashed-out windows, just to get another hit of crack. But the trick said no and walked away.

After that I gave up. I drove home as fast as I could, hoping somehow I'd run the car off the road or get killed on the Meadowbrook Parkway. I didn't want to live any more. I didn't want to face my parents, face my life; I didn't even want any more drugs. I just wanted to die.

When I got home my mother was waiting at the door with her hand out. "Give me the keys," she said, "You can kill yourself if you want to, but you're not gonna do it in my car." I think it was somewhere around six in the morning, because I had brought the car back so my father could drive to the station.

I was afraid of what my father would do to me when he saw the car with the windows broken out of it. I started crying. My mother just watched me cry; her eyes were cold as ice. "Too bad all the tears you cried couldn't save you," she said.

I went out on the porch to wait for my father. My mother sat at the counter in the kitchen. My father came in from outside and sat down at the counter with my mother. He didn't even look at me. He said something to my mother that I couldn't hear, and then he left for work.

My mother came out to the porch looking grim. "What did Daddy say?" I asked her. I was still crying. I knew it was the end. Living with my parents had been my last-ditch attempt at some kind of normal life, and now I'd failed at that. I had nowhere left to go, and I had hurt the last two people in the world who cared about me enough to try to help me.

"Was he mad about the car?" I asked.

"You're lucky he had his morning sex," my mother said. "It could have been a lot worse. But you can't stay here any more."

"What did he say?" I asked her again.

"He said, 'Get her out of here.'"

"I'm sorry," I said. "I fucked everything up." I was crying uncontrollably now.

"Look," she said to me, "I know you're not a bad person, Sue. You're not doing this to hurt me. I know it's because you're sick. You're a very sick woman. I've done what I could to help you. Maybe I hurt you more than I helped; I don't know. What kind of mother gives her daughter money to buy drugs so she can kill herself? It's my fault too. But I can't help you anymore. You need professional help, people who know about drugs. I've been talking to Lorraine on the phone while you were gone. She says there's a place you can go to for treatment. That place where she works in Virginia. They have other places too."

"Treatment doesn't work on me," I said. "I tried it. More than once."

"Lorraine says they can help you," my mother said. "I can call them and they'll come pick you up right now. Do you want me to do that?"

"I'm so tired," I said. "I need to sleep. I haven't slept for days. Let me sleep for a while and then we can talk about it, okay?"

I went to my room and slept. My mother spoke to my sister Lorraine on the phone again, and they set up an intake interview for me at the New York office of the chain of treatment centers she worked for.

When I woke up, my mother made me breakfast. I was scared she'd be angry, but she seemed sort of peaceful, like she had come to some kind of resolution. And as she had done so many other times in my life, she tried to give me comfort and inspiration. Drinking a cup of coffee at the counter while I ate my French toast, she told me, "I know you don't believe this, Sue, but there's hope for you. It's a miracle you even survived this far. By all rights you should have been dead many times over. I mean, think about it. Somebody up there must have other plans for you. There must be a reason why you had to go through all this, a reason why you're still alive. Maybe there's something you're supposed to do. You could clean up and become a drug counselor, do something to help other drug addicts. Lots of other people do it, why not you?" Then she told me when we were going to the interview.

She was right about one thing. I didn't believe there was any hope for me at all. I didn't want to go to treatment. I knew it couldn't possibly work for me. I was just too hopeless a case. I tried to listen to my mother, but I was too numb, too dead inside to respond. I felt burned out, exhausted, weak, and utterly defeated, in total despair. Still, I agreed to go with her to the interview. I didn't have the strength to resist, and besides, I had nowhere else to go.

book 3

GETTING FREE

And if I cried, who'd listen to me in those angelic
orders? Even if one of them suddenly held me
to his heart, I'd vanish in his overwhelming
presence. Because beauty's nothing
but the start of terror we can hardly bear...

Rainer Maria Rilke,
"Duino Elegies"

chapter fifteen

> It's been a long time comin'
> But I know a change is gonna come.
>
> Aretha Franklin (Sam Cooke),
> "A Change Is Gonna Come"

HOPE SPRINGS ETERNAL— SEPTEMBER 1986

The next day my mother took me to my intake interview in the city. First we brought the car to Surf Glass in Long Beach to have the windows replaced. Al, who'd been doing business with my father for years, said it would be done that evening. "Too bad you can't get fixed that fast," my mother said. She was wearing a white top and a bright yellow skirt. I dragged along behind her as we walked to the train station. I couldn't keep up with her, and she was sixty-six years old.

I was weak and spaced out. I felt like a zombie. I just followed my mother like a helpless child. When we got to the city, we went to pick up my last paycheck at Manhattan Graphics, and then walked over to Eighth Avenue to catch a cab uptown. Unbeknownst to my mother, we were taking my usual crack route.

It was an early fall day, crisp and beautiful. Across Eighth Avenue I saw Panama, one of my crack connections. He waved to me, signaling that he had something and I should come right over. The thought crossed my mind to con my mother, tell her that since I was going to treatment she should let me get high one last time. I had my stem in the pocket of my jeans; I didn't leave home without it. But I didn't have the heart to bring my mother around the crackheads. Maybe if they'd been garden variety junkies, I would have tried it. But the crackheads were too violent and unpredictable, too dangerous. Gentle Panama, who could barely speak a word of English, was the best of the lot, but I didn't know who else was with him. So I let the opportunity pass. It must have been one of those frozen moments of grace, because in my mind's eye I can still see Panama to this day, smiling and waving on Eighth Avenue and Thirtieth Street, his head surrounded by red and yellow changing leaves, with the warm autumn sun shining through them, bathing the scene in eternal light.

We took a cab to Fifty-Second Street. At the interview my mother did most of the talking, trying to convince them to take me, telling them I was a Vassar graduate and a writer for the *Village Voice,* a worthwhile person. I was embarrassed and sat on the sofa crying. I was hoping they would turn me down. I told them I was a hopeless case. I'd been to treatment before. It hadn't worked then and it wouldn't work now. Apparently they weren't interested in my own assessment of my case, because it was their job to evaluate me. They said they were placing me in Conifer Park, in upstate New York, with an almost total scholarship. They gave me a list of what I was and wasn't allowed to bring there—no tank tops, bandanas, stuff like that—and they told me not to go to my methadone program that day or at all before I was admitted.

The pawn ticket for my garnet necklace had been in my stolen purse, but I took my mother to the pawn shop, near Penn Station, and we were lucky enough to be able to redeem the necklace without it. I'm wearing it now as I write this. Then we took the train home to Long Island, and my mother told me to pack my clothes to take to Conifer Park. I was such a basket case, I didn't know what to take. "Just bring a few sweatshirts and stuff, Sue," my mother said. "You're only going for a few weeks." "Mom," I said, "once those places get hold of you, they keep you for a long time, send you to halfway houses and God knows where else. It won't be any couple of weeks." In this case, I was right because I ended up going away for a couple of years, and I never lived in that house on Long Island again.

The next morning my mother took me on the train again. This time we went to Grand Central Station, preparing to take a long ride to

Schenectady, four hours or so away from New York City, on the line that runs to Niagara Falls. I still had my stem in my pocket, hoping I might run into something in the station or on the train. But my mother barely let me out of her sight. When she let me get a cup of coffee and a donut at Grand Central, she wouldn't give me more than a dollar-fifty to take with me. I felt like I was traveling to my own execution, a mixture of depression and dread. I still wasn't thinking too clearly. This was the first time my mother had taken me anywhere since my parents drove me to college in 1961, twenty-five years earlier.

I slept most of the way to Schenectady. By chance my mother had bought a women's magazine, I forget which, to read on the train. Hidden away in its back pages was a personal account of addiction and recovery by Martha Morrison, the doctor who later wrote the book *White Rabbit*. "There is hope," she said at the end of her story. "We do recover." It made an impression on me, I suppose because the timing could not have been more dramatically propitious if it had been scripted in Hollywood.

I was moved by my mother's taking me on the train, and by the tenderness of her care for me. I knew it was a big trip and a big deal for her to accompany me. She didn't like to leave my father alone that long, for one thing. Also she would be going straight back on the train—more than ten hours of traveling in one day—and arriving at Penn Station late at night, when it was full of unsavory characters and dope fiends. I knew how dangerous it was there that time of night from personal experience.

But she was cheerful and hopeful. Many times in my life I've thought my mother had access to certain psychic channels of communication, knew things I didn't know, and acted on intuitions that were invisible to the rest of us. This was one of those times. I think she knew that I was at the end of my addiction, and that I would find hope and help when we reached our destination. Perhaps it's just hindsight that makes me feel that way, but I like to think it was her mood and behavior on that long train ride to upstate New York.

When we reached Schenectady, my mother asked if I would mind if she stayed at the station and caught the next train back, and so I arrived by cab at Conifer Park alone. They searched me for drugs and paraphernalia and took away my stem. Then they checked me into detox, where I got my first shock of many at this treatment center. They were not going to give me any methadone. I was terrified of kicking methadone. The only way I'd been able to do it before was with some high-quality white

Thai heroin I was dealing. And even through large amounts of heroin, I'd felt withdrawal pains from the methadone.

The detox nurse said I would be given clonidine, also called Cat-apres, a medication to lower blood pressure that suppresses the most violent symptoms of narcotics withdrawal. I'd taken it plenty of times before; it made me feel even more robotic than I already felt. She said if things got too bad, they would also give me phenobarbitol to ease my anxiety and help me sleep. They took Polaroid pictures of me. I was so skinny that, as a friend of mine likes to say, my face was "sharp enough to chop wood." There was a kitchen on the unit, where I met some of the other patients. A beautiful young woman from Boston, with a glamorous hairdo and fashionable clothes, was trembling uncontrollably. "What are you kicking?" I asked her. "Freebase cocaine," she said. "You couldn't have based all that much," I said. "You still have your jewelry." She wore several rings, one a large, exquisite aquamarine, an expensive watch, and a heavy gold chain. "I had access to unlimited amounts of money," she said miserably.

It took a few days before I really started getting sick. My legs hurt, my arms hurt, I was twitching, anxious, angry, and couldn't sleep. I asked the counselor who came in to see me if I could have the phenobarbitol. He looked at the book I was reading, one I had brought from home, *Mustian,* by Reynolds Price. "Why are you reading that useless stuff?" he said, picking up the Narcotics Anonymous Basic Text they had given me. "Why don't you read something that will help you recover?"

I was edgy and irritable. I started yelling at him. "I've already read that book. It's very badly written. And now you're trying to tell me that all of literature, one of the few decent things in this fucked-up world, is just so much useless trash. Get the fuck out of my room." He left in a hurry, and one of the nurses came in to calm me down. "I need the phenobarbitol," I told her. "I feel terrible." "Oh, no, dearie," she told me. "We're going to wait till you get worse." "What do I have to do?" I screamed. "Jump out the window?" I picked up one of my shoes and threw it at the nurse. When it missed I threw the other. After that they gave me phenobarbitol.

That night one of the patients from downstairs, where the regular treatment programs were conducted, post-detox, came to see me. "I can't stand it," I told her. "I can't go through with this. It hurts too bad."

"I know how bad it hurts," she said. "I just kicked 120 milligrams of methadone myself. But look at it this way. If you go through this—and believe me, you can if I did—you never have to go through it again. This could be your last time kicking anything." The patient's name was Sue B. She was a Jewish woman, like me, but from New Jersey. She too was a junkie who'd been on methadone, shooting heroin and cocaine and smoking crack before coming to Conifer Park. She told me her detox from methadone had been agonizing. Now she felt great, and the detox nurses regularly enlisted her to give support to "the methadonians," as she called us, who were known to have the most painful withdrawals.

The night Sue B. came to see me was the worst night of my detox. After that I started to improve a little every day, and by the end of ten days I was ready to be transferred downstairs to a regular treatment unit. I was still on phenobarbitol and still experiencing cramps in my legs, as well as overall restlessness and anxiety; but I was bored with detox and wanted to get involved in the regular program, although Sue B. had warned me that the schedule was rigorous and demanding, and that I shouldn't start before I was sure I could handle it.

Each patient was assigned a case manager, who worked with the counselors in the various groups, with continuing care, and with the nursing staff. I was assigned a popular counselor who was leaving shortly to run a treatment center in Hawaii. I had one meeting with him. "Wow," he said, reading my drug history. "Twenty-five years. Your addiction is all the way progressed. Out of all the patients in here, you're probably the most far gone. That means one of two things. Either you're the most hopeless case, or you're the most ripe for recovery. You know you can't go anywhere farther with drugs; it's either dereliction or death at this point. I would advise you to get in touch with the little spark of God inside you, with the tiny little part of you that wants to live, and work on growing that part."

At Conifer Park each patient was given what they called "a group statement," something you said along with your name when you identified yourself at the beginning of every group and meeting. These group statements were made up by your treatment team: case manager, therapist, medical staff, and counselors. Some of them were quite funny, in a chilling kind of way, things like "Let me entertain you while I kill myself," or "What's a nice guy like me doing in a place like this?" or "I only lie when I move my lips." Usually they changed halfway through treatment. Mine, which the team was quite proud of, and which never changed the whole time I was there, went, "There's no place left in the world for me to hide. I'm scared to live and scared to die. When will I surrender?"

Since I had to say it five or six times a day, right along with "My name is Susan; I'm an addict," I thought about it quite a lot. Looking back now, I can see I surrendered that night I drove the car with the shattered windows back to my parents' house at top speed, hoping to run it off the highway. Although nothing that dramatic had happened to me on the face of it—smashed-in windows, after all, are not that unusual an occurrence in the real world—my vision of death right there beside me on the street had radically altered my internal perceptions. In some very deep and unconscious way, I knew it was all over. That is, I knew it was all over with the drugs, but in no way did I believe for a minute that there was any other way for me to live. I had surrendered in the sense of throwing my hands in the air in abject helplessness, but I certainly had not surrendered to the concept of recovery, which was nothing but a chimera to me at that time.

"What keeps me from surrender?" I wrote in my notebook. "False pride. I have fucked-up so much else in my life—home, possessions, financial security, relationships, career, family, respect, etc.—that all I have left is my false macho pride about being a tough street junkie. I can't seem to shake the image even though I am constantly victimized on the street.

"What I genuinely value—motherhood, my writing, my humanitarian instincts—is harder for me to cop to. I would have to take responsibility for giving love and care to myself and nurturing my talents. All my life I lacked the qualities of seriousness and discipline, the ability to make sacrifices and postpone gratification (I feel so sorry for myself, I need an instant reward) and to take orders from anyone else. So I sabotaged my education, my spiritual evolution in Arica, my health and my life. What Sue B. called 'a bad case of the fuck-its' applies to me too.

"I'm incredibly pissed-off that I can't take drugs and stubborn about giving up control. I'm intolerant, resentful, full of anger and rage, which I love to blame on anyone or anything around that annoys me rather than focus on what is going on inside. And yet . . . and yet . . . my pain is crying to get out. Inside myself I'm screaming for help. Inside of me is a nice, wholesome, ambitious, intelligent woman struggling to break out. But

I'm hurting and I'm scared. Who will win? Sobriety and life or the addict and death?"

Conifer Park was part of a whole chain of treatment centers owned by Avon, the cosmetics company. Like many other rehabs, their staff was made up of recovering addicts and alcoholics. Up until then I had never seen a recovering addict who could serve as a role model for me. When I heard other addicts qualify at Narcotics Anonymous meetings, I would think to myself: "He must not be a *real* dope fiend," or "She must not love drugs as much as I do," or "It's okay for them but not for me." There was one counselor in my unit, though, who had been a hard-core Harlem dope fiend. His arms were covered with quinine burns. He was as tough as any street junkie I'd ever seen. I knew beyond question that he wasn't any less of a hope-to-die dope fiend than I was. And a part of me knew that if he could recover, I could too. The only question was, how to do it.

I had lived without hope for so long that I had built a wall against it. I didn't like to set myself up to be disappointed. I lived with hopelessness and despair every day of my life. These feelings, though painful, were familiar; I knew how to deal with them. I didn't share the optimistic enthusiasm of other patients in my unit. Over the years I'd seen too many people leave treatment certain that they had their problem licked and would never get high again; within days they were back in the cooker or sucking on the pipe. So I held on to a certain cautious cynicism. But I did make one major change in my normal treatment routine: I didn't get high at Conifer Park; I didn't even look for drugs.

A few days after I got to Conifer Park, my mother called to tell me that my father had had an accident. He had fallen off his horse onto a rock and broken six ribs. She was running back and forth to the hospital, she said, but she wanted me to know that my father, though in pain, was okay, and that I shouldn't worry. By then my head had cleared enough for me to realize the enormity of what I'd done. I started to apologize.

"Mom," I said. "I'm so sorry. I feel so bad. What can I do to make it up to you?"

"Just stay clean, like you're doing," she said. "And take care of your daughter. She needs you." She gave me Shuna's phone number in New Paltz, where she had started college.

As soon as I could, I called Shuna. "Guess where I am," I said. "In treatment."

"I was wondering," she said. "You sort of disappeared on me."

We hadn't seen each other much in the months I lived at my parents', but we usually knew where the other one was. I told her about the crack, and about the car. I made it sound funny.

"Chunks of Ivory soap?" she said. "Cut up peanuts? I can't believe that my mother, the big-time New York drug addict, bought chunks of soap on the street. Wait a minute, I'm gonna tell my friends in college about this. Maybe they can make a little extra money when they go to New York."

We could joke around with each other on the phone, but there was an undercurrent of sadness in our relationship. Years of drug use, lies, broken promises, and failed attempts to clean up had nearly cost me the love, and definitely lost me the respect of my only child, the person I cared most about in all the world. I cried when I hung up the phone. I felt shame and remorse for how I had treated my daughter. But the counselors advised us to go slow with our families. It might take years, they said, to rebuild the trust that had been shattered in the course of our addictions. I knew I was in for a long haul with Shuna, and that for now there was very little I could do about it except to take care of myself.

I hung around with Sue B. and some of the other women. We went to groups and did our homework, but mainly we were preoccupied with flirting and developing crushes and intrigues with the various men in the treatment center. In lectures we wrote notes to each other and checked out "the googie eyes" we got from different men. It was a lot like junior high.

Ironically one of the main reasons I had agreed to go to treatment was that during the summer I had read *Women Who Love Too Much*. I knew I had an addiction to men, and the book had convinced me that it was progressive and fatal, following the same downward spiral as my addiction to drugs. Over the years, as my self-esteem plummeted, my relationships had gone from bad to worse. I wasn't sure if I wanted to be clean and sober, but I knew I wanted a healthy, loving relationship, and that I would have to make major changes in my life before I could have one. These changes, obviously, would not take place at Conifer Park, where men outnumbered women twenty to one, and provided a constant source of distraction, or "defocusing," as the staff called it.

By some miracle, despite our teenage antics during lecture, I managed to absorb a few salient facts. One of these was that you had to be willing to go to any lengths to recover. I had no problem at all understanding the concept of "any lengths," since there was virtually nothing I would not do to obtain drugs. I regularly prided myself on the fact that I would go anywhere at any time, face the gravest danger, in pursuit of drugs. I had frequently gone out to cop in Minnesota in seventy-below weather and never returned empty-handed. "Any lengths can sometimes hurt a lot," I also heard. Just how much it could hurt, I was soon to discover.

Once a lecturer caught my attention, I listened with desperation. I needed to hear some piece of information with the power to transform my thinking and turn my life around. If I heard it, I planned to hang onto it literally for dear life. I sat transfixed one day in a talk on sexuality and recovery given by a counselor named Helen. Sexuality, she said, was all about how we felt about ourselves. And the key to recovery lay in self-acceptance. "The road to self-acceptance," she went on, "is paved with a lot of storytelling." In a flash I saw a future for myself, the first I had glimpsed in many years. She spoke about freedom and responsibility, a theme I knew from Arica. "Responsibility," said Helen, "makes you a whole human being." I left the lecture filled with gratitude, awe, and the beginnings of determination. I wanted self-acceptance; I wanted to be a whole human being, and now I felt I'd been given the key. "I shall be free," I wrote in my notebook that day.

In our unit's communal kitchen, we had a blackboard where patients sometimes wrote treatment sayings as messages to the group. "U-Drink. U-Drug. U-Die. U-Dig?" appeared often; it came from Mitch, the Harlem dope fiend counselor. Patients' restrictions, silences, and phone messages were also posted there. One day soon after Helen's lecture, I wrote on the blackboard for the first time: "I can recover. I want to recover. I will recover. There is no recovery from the grave." Writing it marked a turning point in my treatment. It was probably the most positive thought I had had in twenty years.

I still hadn't given up my plan to get high when I went back to New York, though. My mother sent me money for cigarettes and sundries, and I had stashed away forty dollars. It was hidden in a secret compartment of my black leather jacket, accessible through its shredded lining and just big enough for bags of dope or folded up money. I wondered where I would stash my luggage when I got to the city; it was impossible to get a locker in any public train or bus station because so many homeless people lived out of them.

I got to know a big Puerto Rican dope dealer from the Lower East Side who arrived a few weeks after I did. This man owned a few brands, Elegant and Dom Perignon, which I'd been copping regularly on Second Street. He left his brother in charge of the business, and one morning he told me that his brother hadn't cut the dope enough and it had killed ten of their workers. I thought about my dope-fiend buddies and wondered if any of them were dead. Dom Perignon was one of our favorite brands. I knew if I hadn't been in treatment, there was a good chance I'd have been among the casualties. On the street I hadn't cared if I lived or died. But I was beginning to feel different about dying, and felt gratitude for having been spared, again.

The dealer had a crush on me and tried to convince me to come to New York with him when we got out of treatment. I had enough presence of mind by now, however, to predict the probable outcome of such a move. I'd go with him, get a humongous dealer's habit, and then when my true dope-fiend personality emerged, he'd throw me out on the street and I'd have to hustle up a thousand dollars a day to keep my sick off. It wasn't too appealing a prospect. I cursed my luck, though, that I hadn't met him at another point in my addiction, when he might have been the answer to my prayers.

Just as they do in jail, dope fiends in treatment obsess endlessly about the good times they had before and the highs they're going to have as soon as they're back on the street. Patients live a double life: they act one way in front of the counselors and another way among themselves. In the past I had always met new customers and made new connections whenever I went to rehab. At Conifer Park I became friends with a guy named Vinnie; the dope dealer introduced us. Vinnie was a white boy with heart. He sold crack cocaine in Harlem, where he was known on the street as "the Skinny Guinea." Vinnie and I would lie around in the grass outside, and his eyes would light up as he recounted his adventures in the drug trade. We planned to get together and have some fun when we got out of treatment.

During my first meeting with Jack, my new case manager, he'd told me that because of my long drug history, the team was recommending that I go to a halfway house after treatment. I said that was fine with me so long as they sent me back to New York. I didn't want to go to a new state and start over; I had done it too many times. In all our conferences, I was adamant on this point. We had conferences fairly often, because I was always late on my written homework assignments. Jack was a large, genial man with a warm heart and a sense of humor. In general he let me get away with murder.

The longest, most serious session we had in our daily routine was feelings group. Mine was led by a therapist named Judy Schwartz. One day in feelings group, I mentioned to Judy that both times I'd taken an MMPI, the psychologists had asked if I'd been a rape or incest victim. I told her I didn't remember anything like that. She led me back through guided imagery to scenes in my childhood, where I reexperienced the terror and shame of some sort of sexual assault. I was extremely shaken. But I still didn't have a clear memory of any specific person or event. "Is it possible I made it up?" I asked Judy.

"Possible," she said, "but pretty unlikely." She was very gentle with me. "Susan," she said. "You may never remember what happened. Or a memory may surface years into your sobriety. My experience, though, is that when a woman suspects something happened but can't be sure because she doesn't remember, something *did* happen. It's not so important to know exactly what happened as it is to explore the feelings and see where they led you, to drugs or certain kinds of abusive relationships. I strongly recommend that you continue to work with this and explore it further. And I'll give you as much support as I can."

That weekend my mother came up to visit me on the train. I was very moved. It was the first visit I had ever had from a family member while I was in a treatment program. We walked around the grounds and talked. I asked her if it were possible that I had been molested as a child, if there were some incident she could remember. "I don't think so," she said. "And you told me everything." She brought me news from home, about how my father was getting along in the hospital, and what my sisters and brother were doing, and what new trouble my nephew Darryl had gotten into. She said that everyone loved and missed me. They were proud of what I was doing. They couldn't wait for me to come home. I felt raw and vulnerable, like a child, and I appreciated my mother's presence with the passion of a child. Both of us were sad and teary when visiting hours ended and she had to go home.

The next Sunday Shuna surprised me with a visit. I was outside sitting on a bench with some friends when I saw her get out of a car. Her hair was chopped off short and dyed Raggedy Anne red. "That's my daughter!" I shrieked, and ran off to meet her. We walked around the grounds with our arms around each other, sharing confidences and giggling like schoolgirls. "This is so great," said Shuna. "I feel like I finally got my mother back." All of a sudden she turned serious. "Oh, Mom," she cried. "I thought I was beyond caring about you. It hurt too much to care, so I stopped. But I do care. I care a lot. I love you so much." I held her in my arms while she cried. It was a moment of such raw power and presence, so much a measure of our very real connectedness, that I was touched beyond words.

We ended up at a picnic table under the giant conifers that had given the place its name. I told Shuna what I'd been dealing with in group. Then she asked me about an incident from her childhood that she only dimly remembered. I told her I had left her with a neighbor one day. Her fourteen-year-old son had taken Shuna into the bathroom and was lying on the floor on top of her when my neighbor found them. She told me about it, said she had caught her son before anything could happen, and Shuna never went there again. For the second time that day, I held my daughter in my arms while she cried. Later she asked my advice about a problem she was having with her boyfriend. I felt like a mother again, a wonderful feeling of renewal.

About three weeks into my treatment, I began to feel tremendous anger. The Conifer Park psychiatrist had told me that heroin was particularly good at suppressing rage. Now I had no heroin and was spewing rage like an erupting volcano. Much of it was directed toward Pete, a young guy who had just joined our feelings group. My case manager got wind of it and called me into his office. He asked why I was so angry at Pete. I didn't know. He suggested I spend a day in silence, checking out my anger to see where it was coming from, and told me to keep a journal of my thoughts and feelings.

I spent the next day in total silence. I was feeling very vulnerable, and as I had so often in my life, comforted myself with clothes. I wore my mother's burgundy cashmere sweater and a black rayon skirt. I washed my hair and wore it down. I went inside myself, where it was quiet and peaceful, and wrote a lot in my journal. I wrote about my self-hatred and how I had to learn to love myself if I were ever going to recover. I knew that I had to make an investment in myself, do something so difficult that I wouldn't go back on it. I wrote about my longing for a better, decent life.

The day went fine till I got to feelings group. I had to pass Pete to get to my chair, and he refused to move his feet out of the way without my asking him out loud. "I feel like bashing Pete's skull against the wall," I wrote in my notebook. "I sense he has a mindless hatred of women that comes out in sexual violence. What makes me so angry is my own powerlessness against this kind of brute male strength. Guys like Pete can intimidate and oppress women because they know we're not strong enough to fight back. I'm feeling the rage of helplessness, and it makes me want to kill.

"Pete reminds me a lot of my sister Lorraine. He's always so angry and rebellious and transparently needy that he sucks up all the attention in the group. Just like Lorraine did when we were growing up because she acted out all the time. I was the quiet one, at a time when being quiet was equated with being good. I was just as needy as she was, but she got all the attention. I'm jealous too of people who can express their anger. I'd like to take my rage and pain out on Pete right about now. Some physical violence would be really delicious. But Pete's not the cause of all this anger; this belongs to my family, unresolved childhood stuff. God, this stuff is embarrassing."

My day of silence was almost over when I heard my name called on the loudspeaker to report to Continuing Care. The Continuing Care counselor, Ben, was partners and close friends with Mitch. They'd been dope-fiend buddies in Harlem, and had both cleaned up after the predicate felon, or habitual criminal act, threatened to put them in the penitentiary forever. I'd seen him before and liked him.

I went into his office expecting the same sort of aftercare plan most of the graduating patients received: NA meetings, continuing care groups on Fifty-Second Street, maybe a short stay in a New York City halfway house. I had been in silence all day, and my feelings were pent up inside me. Ben greeted me warmly and told me to sit down and make myself comfortable. Then he dropped a bombshell in my lap.

"The team is recommending that you go to Women, Incorporated, in Boston. It's an all-women's halfway house with an excellent reputation and high success rate. Judy in particular feels strongly about your going there."

I burst into tears. "I've said over and over again that I don't want to go to another state. Couldn't you find any place for me in New York? I wanna go home." I stopped just short of whining, "I want my mommy," but that was how I felt.

"What it all boils down to," said Ben, "is whether or not you're willing to go to any lengths. Look, we can't force you to go to Women, Inc. But will you do me just one favor? I had one hell of a time setting up this interview. I'd hate to have to cancel it now. So why don't you go there for the interview and take a look around. We'll discuss it again after that. Will you do at least that much?"

"Okay," I agreed. "I'll go to the interview. But in the meantime, I want you to look around for a place in New York for me."

"Deal," said Ben. "I'll see you when you get back from Boston."

I walked upstairs and slumped into a seat in the unit kitchen. I had some close male friends in my unit. One of them, Sam, who was in the Chronic Relapse part of the program, saw the look on my face and came over to comfort me.

"What's up, Sue?" he asked, putting his arm around my shoulders. "Did the silence get you down?"

"Sam," I said. "They want to send me to a women's halfway house in Boston. I wanna go home. They're letting everyone else in our unit go home. I'm the only one they're sending to a halfway house."

"Look at it this way, baby," said Sam. "You might be the only one who makes it."

Conifer Park was plush as far as treatment centers go. We had a pool, jacuzzi, steam room, maid service in the rooms, and fabulous food, including the occasional lobster dinner. But the rules were strict. Listening to music was forbidden except on social occasions, since it was considered conducive to thoughts of drugs. So I looked forward to a day away from Conifer Park, riding in a car and listening to the radio. Ben had arranged for a driver to take me to Boston and back, and though I wasn't too keen on going to Women, Inc., I relished the thought of all that freedom.

I had the phone number of a former patient named Rich, a heroin addict who had returned to Boston and was, it was rumored, getting high again. I carried his number in the pocket of my jeans jacket, in case I could get away from the driver long enough to call him and cop. Part of me may have wanted to recover, but I was still an addict, and that part of me, the one that was used to running the show, wanted to keep on getting high.

I had gained about fifteen or twenty pounds at Conifer Park; and in my first week out of detox, I'd had sex—which was strictly forbidden— with a guy I liked. I suspected I might be pregnant. I was thinking I might not be able to get an abortion easily in Massachusetts. Also, after five months, my probation had finally been transferred from Minnesota to New York. I was hoping that my New York probation officer wouldn't agree to my moving to another state; at the very least, that he would in- sist on my coming to New York to meet with him once. I really wanted to go home. My mother had already said that I could come home. She missed my company as much as I missed hers.

So I went to Boston on a lark, as a favor to Ben, and for a day's vaca- tion from treatment. We set out early in the morning, on a crisp, sunny day in mid-October. I was in a good mood, chatting with Kevin, the driver, and singing along with the songs on the radio. It was a beautiful drive too, up the Taconic, and across the Berkshires on the Mass. Pike, with the au- tumn leaves in full splendor. We arrived in Boston around lunchtime and stopped around Framingham to call Women, Inc. I was going to take that opportunity to call Rich, but Kevin never let me out of his sight. We went to a sub shop for lunch, and then he drove me to Women, Inc.

Women, Inc., was in an enormous white Victorian house, a little run- down around the edges, on the borderline of Roxbury and Dorchester, deep in the ghetto. I waited downstairs for my interviewer and noticed there was a day-care center on the first floor. "There's no way I'm going to take care of these little kids," I thought to myself. A white woman named Sasha, wearing a hippie-type dress, came down and took me up to the third floor for my interview. The room we sat in was a sun porch, with windows all around, surrounded by trees. Furniture was piled up here and there along the walls. Sasha sat behind a large wooden desk.

She asked me for my drug history, from start to finish, all the drugs I had ever taken, what age I had been when I started, how much I took, when I stopped. It took a long time for me to tell her everything, and in the process I remembered whole chunks of time and categories of drugs that surprised even me. She asked about my experiences in treatment, jails, halfway houses, other attempts to get clean. Then she took my med- ical history. I told her about my abortions and said I thought I might be pregnant. By the time we finished, I felt drained and discouraged; remem- bering my past in so much sordid detail had left a bad taste in my mouth.

A light-skinned black woman named Joy, dressed like a man, with her hair cut short, came into the room and sat on the desk. She read through my history and looked into my eyes with what I could only interpret as a hostile glance. "You've been through treatment before," she said.

"Yeah," I answered listlessly. Joy's arrogance made me uncomfortable.

"You couldn't get clean then," she went on. "What makes you think you can do it now? You just gonna come up here and waste our time? What's different?"

I sat with my head down, unable to look her in the face. "I don't know what else to do," I said miserably.

"She wants to know if she can get an abortion," said Sasha.

Joy looked at my medical history. "You've had five abortions already," she said. "Don't you believe in birth control?"

I didn't answer. If she was any indication of the counselors in this place, there was no way I was coming here.

Joy left the room, and Sasha asked me if I had any questions. "What's it like here?" I asked. "What kind of program do you have?"

"The women spend most of their time sitting around a big table in the dining room dealing with their feelings," she said. "It's difficult, but it's never boring. The first couple of weeks are the hardest. For the first few weeks here, you're gonna feel like you're in hell. But you'll experience relief like you've never felt before."

She told me to call her in two days, at one o'clock, and she would tell me if I had been accepted. She asked me how I was getting back to Conifer Park. "A driver brought me here and he's taking me back," I said.

"Wow," she said. "What is that? About a nine-hour drive? They're really going out of their way to help you. How come?"

"I'm a writer," I said. "They think I'm a worthwhile person."

"All our women are worthwhile people," she said. "Don't think you're so special."

She walked me downstairs. On the way I saw a big room at the other end of the hall. It had a shiny wooden floor and several beds along the walls. A woman sat on one of the beds. "I'll see you in a minute, Brenda," Sasha said.

Kevin was waiting for me downstairs. We left the house and got into the car. "What'd you think of it?" I asked him.

"I wouldn't send my worst enemy there," he said.

I didn't say a word all the way back to Conifer Park. I didn't listen to the radio. I rode in the car too despondent to move or speak, nearly paralyzed with dread.

"What did you think of Women, Inc.?" Judy asked me the next day in group.

"I hated it," I said. "They were really mean to me. Kevin said he wouldn't send his worst enemy there. Why do you think I should go there anyway?"

"Don't judge it by how the house looks, Susan," she said. "They're a community-based program; they don't have a lot of money. But they have one of the best success rates in the business. It's a very fine program with a terrific staff. I don't think you could find a better one in the country. We just sent another woman there, also a long-term heroin addict, and she's doing very well there. Think about it."

"Well, I don't know." I said. "I still want to see if I can find a place in New York."

I spent the whole next day in Continuing Care, looking through Ben's books of halfway houses for a program in New York State, even though he didn't think I could find one. "First of all," he said, "there aren't a lot of programs for women, period. Then the ones there are deal with alcoholic women. And many of these places have shooting galleries in the actual house. That's what the ones in New York City are like."

After looking through the books all day, I had to concede that Ben was right. But I still hadn't made up my mind to go to Women, Inc. I called there, a little after the time I was supposed to, and Sasha yelled at me for not calling precisely at one o'clock. Then she said they had accepted me. I had made the phone call from my case manager's office, and he talked to Sasha too.

"They can't take you till next Monday," he said when he hung up the phone.

"Great," I said. "I'll go there from New York." I was scheduled to be released on Friday. "Then I can go get my clothes from home."

"You can't get anything," he said. "The only way they'll take you is straight from here, delivered by one of our drivers with no stops along the way."

"But I'm supposed to go home on Friday," I said.

"I'll try to get you an extension," he said. "I can't promise, but I'll see what I can do."

"What about my probation officer?" I said. "He might not let me move to another state." I was hoping against hope.

"Call him now," he said. "I'm sure he'll okay it."

I called him, and he did. The man didn't know me anyway. He said it was no problem to transfer my probation to Boston.

That night I called my mother. I was crying. "They want me to go to an all-women's halfway house in Boston," I told her. "I don't wanna go. I wanna come home. I miss you."

"I miss you too, honey," my mother said. "But I think you should do what they suggest. They know more about these things than I do. Maybe you should do what someone else says for once. You and I haven't been doing too well with this so far."

"I don't have any clothes," I said.

"I'll send you whatever you need," said my mother.

"They said I couldn't get on welfare either, because I'm from another state. You'd have to pay my rent there; it's fifty-five dollars a month. Plus you'd have to send me spending money. I couldn't get a job for a long time."

"Sue," my mother said, "whatever I have to do is fine. Just listen to what they're telling you. It's your *life,* honey. It won't be forever. Try it. If you don't like it, you can always come home."

In the last week of treatment at Conifer Park, all the patients who were leaving had to stand up in meetings and say their name, their unit, and where they were going after their release. I would say my name and my unit, then I would say that I didn't know where I was going; I hadn't made up my mind.

On Thursday afternoon my case manager called me into his office. "I have good news for you," he said. "I got you an extension. This is the first time in the history of Conifer Park that a patient on scholarship has been granted an extension. The whole team went to bat for you. We feel very strongly that Women, Inc., is the best chance you have for continued sobriety. And we all want to see you get that chance. You deserve it." Jack was smiling from ear to ear.

"All right," I said, resigned. "I'll try it. I guess this means I'm willing to go to any lengths, huh?"

"I guess so," he said.

"And any lengths can sometimes hurt a lot," I said.

"Yes, it can," he said.

"Well, this hurts," I said. "It hurts as much as anything ever hurt. But I'm gonna do it anyway. I really don't know why."

"Because you want to live," he said. "That's why you're doing it. Because deep down inside, you want to recover. I'm happy to see it." He got up from his desk and gave me a big bear hug, then he held me while I cried.

The next day I met Vinnie outside at lunchtime. We were laying on the grass in a sunny spot near the gym. "I'm going," I said. "I can't believe it, but I am."

"I'll miss you in New York," he said.

"Do you have a car?"

"Yeah."

"Will you come get me if I can't stand it there?"

"Call me anytime. I'll come get you."

"Will you send me something if I need it?"

He laughed. "Sure, babe. Whatever you want."

"I'll be able to have visitors after a few months."

"Then I'll come visit."

"I hate I can't go to New York," I said.

"You'll be there soon enough," said Vinnie. "And then we'll really have some fun."

I needed a picture ID before I could go to Women, Inc. Kevin took me to the nearby town of Glenville to get it. I gave my brother's address in New York as mine. I thought I looked glamorous and healthy in the picture.

As my last exercise in feelings group, I had to read a list of forty secrets. I read things to my group that I had never told a living soul before. It was scary. When I finished reading, I was shaking. "You did splendidly," said Judy. Her eyes were misty. "I'm very proud of you. Make sure you keep in touch with me. Write me from Women, Inc." We hugged each other tight, and my eyes misted up too.

Vinnie and I hung out together over the weekend. I signed other people's NA books, and they signed mine, as was the custom there, and I said my goodbyes to all the counselors and patients I knew from groups.

Early Monday morning two of my men friends, Sam and Gello, carried all my belongings, in two garbage bags, to the car. "Lemme see your book, Sue," said Gello. "I have something I want to say to you."

He took my book and leaned on the hood of the car, writing. I looked around. It seemed unbelievable that only a little over a month had passed. I felt as though I'd lived there for years. Gello finished writing and handed the book back to me. "Don't read it till you're well on your way away from here," he said.

Kevin came out of the building and got into the car. I waved to Sam and Gello till I couldn't see them any more. Once again Kevin and I were on the road to Boston. I didn't feel happy or excited exactly, more resigned, but I was anxious to get there and begin whatever it was I had set out to do.

We were about an hour away from Conifer Park when I remembered the book in my lap and opened it to read Gello's message. "Lay down your guns," it said. "The war is over."

chapter sixteen

The sisters of mercy they are not departed or gone
They were waiting for me
when I felt that I just can't go on.

Leonard Cohen,
"The Sisters of Mercy"

WALKIN' TO THE FREEDOM LAND—OCTOBER 1986

I arrived at Women, Inc., on October 20, 1986, wearing my mother's burgundy cashmere sweater, black leggings I had bought from a New York street vendor, hightop Reeboks, and my black leather jacket with the money stashed in the lining.

Kevin dropped me off. A counselor came downstairs and led me to the second-floor office, where they kept my garbage bags to be screened for drugs and paraphernalia. I had to leave my purse and jewelry too. Whatever money I had would be held in the office; clients were not allowed to carry money in the house. Dorothy, an elderly, white-haired black woman, led me upstairs to take a shower. "But I just took a shower this morning," I said. "That's okay, dearie." said Dorothy. "You have to use some of this, and rub it in good." She handed me some K-200 shampoo for lice and crabs and told me to give her my clothing piece by piece as I took it off so she could search it for contraband. I had intentionally held back some of my money in the office. I figured if Dorothy found the money in my jacket, I would lie and say I had forgotten about it. But she didn't find it, and I didn't say anything.

When I finished my shower, Dorothy told me to wrap my head in a towel, get dressed, and follow her back downstairs. We went into the dining room, a large corner room with a badly patched paint job in shades of white, a discolored stucco ceiling, fluorescent lights, and gray linoleum floor. There was an open serving window to the kitchen and several windows to the outdoors. I stared longingly at the large, lush trees in autumn foliage and the views of distant houses, already regretting the loss of my freedom.

A group of women, mostly black, in all their marvelously varied complexion colors—black-black, blue-black, mahogany, cocoa, sepia, cafe-au-lait, with here and there a few white faces mixed in—sat around a big table made up of many smaller folding tables. I sat down near the door and began talking to the woman next to me, Michele, who had long, shaggy blond hair and wore a baggy Raiders T-shirt. We talked about getting busted for shoplifting, and where we had been in jail. Our conversation was getting pretty animated when a woman at the end of the table turned around to look at us. Her elegant tweed jacket and silk blouse were in marked contrast to the sweats and T-shirts of the other women. "You two know each other?" she asked. There was something challenging and a little sarcastic in her tone of voice. "No," answered Michele. "Then you shouldn't be talking to each other," she said. "You're both too new." Michele rolled her eyes at me and shrugged her shoulders, then she walked around to the other side of the table, sat down, and stared into space.

"I'll talk to her, Diane," said a dark-skinned woman in a bright yellow sun dress. She spoke with a distinctly Southern accent. "I'm Charlene," she said, as she came around and sat next to me. "I've been here for about six weeks. I'm from Orlando, Florida. New women aren't supposed to talk to each other 'cause y'all be so negative, just comin' off the street and all. It take some time to get used to bein' here. I'm fixin' to ask for Phase 2 soon's we have group." Charlene explained that since I was new, I would be on what they called "support." That meant I couldn't go anywhere in the house on my own, not even to the bathroom. I had to ask one of the higher-phase women to support me everywhere I went. "After you've earned the trust of your peers," she said, "you can ask to get off support. I was only on support for about two weeks."

Without my purse and jewelry, I felt like I was back in jail. I was frightened, disoriented, and bored. I couldn't imagine sitting around this table day after day, and I already felt resentful about the support business.

"Why is it so strict?" I asked Charlene. "I thought this was supposed to be a halfway house."

"A halfway house?" said Charlene. "Honey, who told you that lie? This is treatment. Long-term residential treatment."

"But I just finished treatment," I said.

"No, honey. You just finished *detox*. Otherwise they wouldn't have let you in here. This is treatment, and you startin' right at the beginnin'."

It was noisy, hot, and chaotic in the dining room. Disco music blared from the radio. In mid-afternoon three small children showed up and added their commotion to the general din. Another new woman, Debbie, had also come in that day. She looked as uncomfortable as I felt. I wanted to get away somewhere by myself to think, but apparently that wasn't possible in this place.

At around five-thirty dinner was served. Macaroni and cheese. Debbie and I weren't allowed to help ourselves to food because we hadn't had physicals yet. But since we were the newest members, the women served us first. I sat next to a small, dark, friendly woman named Linda. "I knew you's a base head soon's you came in," she said. "The way them pants is hangin' off your ass. Well, don't feel bad. I smoked up my ass too."

After dinner was cleared off and the dishes washed, all the women in the house gathered around the table and introduced themselves to us. They told us their names, ages, if they had any children, their drug of choice, how long they had been in the house, what phase of the program they were in, and then they each gave us little tidbits of advice. "It's hard here." . . . "A lot of women don't stay." . . . "The first few weeks are the hardest." . . . "Just hold onto your seat." . . . "It gets better." . . . "If you feel like leaving, or you feel like getting high, grab one of your peers and talk about it. Have the feelings." . . . "If you're really interested in saving your life, you'll do whatever it takes. If not, you'll probably leave."

After the introductions I saw Debbie sitting at the other end of the table, crying. A wave of homesickness washed over me, and I started to cry too. Two women came and sat on either side of me. They encouraged me to talk about what was bothering me, feel the feeling, "let it go." I said I didn't think I could stay. It looked too hard. They told me to describe what my life was like on the street and asked if I wanted to go back to that. By then it was late, and I was tired. I couldn't have found my way out of there if I'd wanted to.

The evening counselor, Mollie, a tall woman with regal bearing, came into the room and introduced herself to Debbie and me. She had red hair, a reddish-brown complexion, and tiny beauty marks high on her cheekbones that looked like exotic tattoos. Her nails were long and opalescent pink. "Cynthia will be your big sister," she told me. "She'll help you get settled and tell you the rules." Then she told the rest of the women it was time for "tighten-ups," the daily cleaning chores. "You go with Audrey," someone said to me. "You'll be sharing her tighten-up, the bathrooms upstairs." Audrey, light-skinned and pretty, with an odd, slightly skewed look that came from one wild eye and a missing tooth, was the mother of the little kids. She screamed at them to follow her, and we all trailed up the stairs.

There were two bathrooms and a separate shower room that had to be cleaned every evening. Audrey split the bathrooms with me and told me what to do: wash everything down, empty the trash, mop the floor. She finished her part of the job in what seemed like thirty seconds and was putting the kids to bed when I got done. "How'd you do yours so fast?" I asked her. She laughed. "I know what I'm doing," she said. "You'll catch on quick. Don't worry."

After tighten-ups we went back downstairs for morning meeting papers, on which we wrote answers to several questions: "How do I feel today? Where is it coming from? What do I plan to do about it? My goals for tomorrow." We each had to read everyone else's papers, and then we could go to the office and ask for permission to go to bed. At Women, Inc., we had to ask for everything, Cynthia explained to me, because as dope fiends we could not distinguish our wants from our needs.

I was assigned to Dorothy's room, the large corner bedroom with the shiny wooden floor I had glimpsed the day of my interview. Michele slept in the same room. Since there was no bed for me, Mollie said I could sleep in Barbara J.'s bed. She was in the hospital with back problems. Mollie was warm and kind, and I liked her right away. I felt safe in her presence. "I know it's all strange to you right now, baby," she said to me. "And you're probably lonely and homesick. But you'll get used to it soon and be right at home, I promise." She gave me a big, comforting hug and told me that they weren't finished screening my stuff, but I'd have it back, along with a bed and dresser of my own, by the next day.

I was exhausted, but I lay awake in the dark for a long time listening to Dorothy snore and missing my peaceful pink solitary room in Island Park. I was glad I had my secret stash of money; I could use it to split back to New York when I couldn't stand another minute at Women, Inc. I didn't think I could stick it out. I had never been able to follow strict rules. I couldn't stand the constant noise and lack of privacy. I hated housework, and it looked like there was plenty of it in this program. What did housework have to do with giving up drugs? I wondered. Why couldn't I talk to Michele? I missed the easygoing male companionship I'd come to enjoy at Conifer Park. Why had I come to this place? I was sure I had made a terrible mistake.

The next morning we had cold cereal for breakfast and then "morning meeting" in the family room on the other side of the kitchen. Like the dining room, it was large, shabby, and spotlessly clean. There were fluorescent lights and a brown and white linoleum floor with some chipped and missing tiles. Several couches in muted shades of brown sat along one wall, at the end of which was a pay phone and a large window opening onto a fire escape nestled in the branches of a large tree. A small flight of stairs to the kitchen led past two low utility sinks and a corner full of mops and brooms. Everything smelled of Pine-Sol, floor wax, and cigarette smoke.

We sat around a wooden table so heavy it took four or five women to pull it out from the wall. Diane, the woman who had reprimanded me and Michele the day before, sat at the head of the table. She had a light brown complexion, broad features, full lips, and dark, deeply expressive eyes. Her luxurious green satin blouse stood out incongruously against the utility sinks behind her. She exuded confidence and authority, an air of absolute dominion. There was a quality in the room that seemed oddly familiar to me, but I couldn't quite place it.

"Where are you at today, Vivienne?" she asked a large Jamaican woman with luminous skin. "Still fucked up, as usual?"

"I feel so sad, Diane," said Vivienne. "I miss my baby. I keep seeing the look on her face when the social worker come to take her from me. I wish so much that I can see her and know she all right."

"There's nothing wrong with missing your baby, Vivienne," said Diane. "Most of the women here miss their children. But when are you going to get past that and do something about your treatment? That's all you've talked about for weeks, your baby, your baby. What about you, Vivienne? Apparently you haven't realized yet that you're fighting a battle for your life, and that if you lose this battle, you won't be of any use to your baby or anyone else."

Diane addressed the group as a whole. "Maybe you think this is a game. You come here to waste our time and don't want to do the footwork to save your own lives. This is a life-and-death battle we're fighting here against the dope. Does anyone know what I mean by a life-and-death battle?"

"Yes," I said quietly, surprising myself; I hadn't planned to speak, but my mouth had opened and the word tumbled out.

Diane looked at me sideways, sizing me up. I was new and an unknown quantity. "Do you want to tell us about it?"

"I saw death on the street," I said. I talked about the night in Freeport with the broken glass. I felt extremely self-conscious and regretted that I had spoken up. I was frightened of what she would say to me; she seemed so powerful and intimidating.

"Well," she said when I finished. "It's a good start. You know what's in store for you if you go back to shooting dope. Now let's see what you're willing to do to save your life. Time will tell how serious you really are."

A small, compact woman with round mahogany cheeks that shone in the light came into the room trailing crisp, outdoor air. She wore a black-and-red checked flannel shirt and seemed agitated. "I need some space," she said.

"Come on with it, Rhoda," said Diane.

"I just had a blood test at Dimock. They couldn't get blood from my arm so they had to use a vein in my groin. It was the place where I used to get off. It really kicked up my addiction. I kept waiting for a rush. I want to get high real bad. I'm fucked up."

"You sound surprised, Rhoda," said Diane.

"I am," she said. "I was fine before I went there. I wasn't even thinking about any dope."

"You all kill me," said Diane. "Rhoda, you shot dope for twenty years and you're surprised that you still want to get high after four months in treatment? You think you're not a dope fiend any more? Stay aware, Rhoda. Remember, to be aware is to be alive."

Several more women asked for space and talked about how they felt. A few of them cried. I was relieved to sit back and observe in silence.

This confrontation stuff was scary, uncomfortable; during my brief one-on-one exchange with Diane, I had felt like squirming in my chair. And yet the women seemed to view her with respect, rather than fear or resentment. Beneath her harshness I sensed a hint of something else: understanding, maybe, or compassion. I learned a saying that day that explained a lot about Women, Inc.'s, treatment style: "Help doesn't always feel like help."

After morning meeting Diane left the room, and we continued the same routine among ourselves. I felt bored and restless. I wanted to leave. But something about the way Diane talked about addiction had impressed me deeply. She seemed to know things I had learned viscerally from being a dope fiend but had never heard addressed in treatment. I told myself I would stay for a little while more. I was hungry. I would wait till after lunch. Then I wanted to wait until the shift changed and Mollie came on. I would wait till after we got the mail, till it stopped raining, till morning.

Somehow, five minutes at a time, I got through the first few weeks. I was pretty much in a fog. My peers pulled me up regularly for spacing out and not paying attention. As much as I could get away with, I'd stare out the windows and let my mind wander. I had no other distractions. I couldn't read books; that was a Phase 2 privilege. I couldn't use the phone. There were no men around and wouldn't be in the foreseeable future. I could write and receive letters; that was my only contact with the outside world. When I got fed up and thought about leaving, which happened at least several times a day, the first thing that would pop into my mind was wondering where I could leave my bags in New York while I went to cop on the Lower East Side.

So I knew I wasn't ready to stay clean on my own. The women encouraged me to talk about how much I wanted to leave and how much I hated it there. The counselors told me to talk about how I felt about myself, and what I had done for the dope. "How did that make you feel?" they asked constantly, in the middle of my stories. Sometimes my answers surprised me; apparently I wasn't the cool, uncaring, thick-skinned tough I'd fancied myself on the street. Some of the things I'd done had really hurt, and without the drugs to take the edge off the pain, they hurt even more as I told about them.

But I still couldn't get in touch with my feelings, despite all the confrontations and peer pressure from my group. "Get real," the other women would yell at me. "Get out of your head. Where's the feelings?" Honesty, I learned, was more than truthfulness; it was emotional honesty, feelings, the messages you got from your gut. I had lived in my intellect for so long, rationalizing away my misgivings and justifying everything I did, that I was out of touch with my inner reality; emotionally I was numb.

"Dealing with feelings," meaning experiencing and expressing them in all their ragged glory, was the core of the Women, Inc., program. "You shoot dope to cover up your feelings," the counselors told us. "Learn how to deal with your feelings, and you never have to shoot dope again." It sounded too simple to be true. And it was a lot easier said than done. The main feelings I had in my first weeks at Women, Inc., when I had any, were anger and frustration. For the most part, I was bored and apathetic; I had to fight to stay awake in groups. I thought the other women didn't like me and I felt isolated and lonely. The best I could do was simply endure.

I was allowed out of the house earlier than most women because of my suspected pregnancy. I had to see a doctor at the Dimock Community Health Center in Roxbury, and while I was at it, the counselors said I might as well have a physical too. So I went to the gynecologist in the morning, supported by Dorothy, and went again in the afternoon, supported by Rhoda.

Rhoda was a highly respected member of the group who had progressed rapidly through the phases. She was standoffish and somewhat harsh in her feedback to peers, but everyone liked her and wanted to be her friend. I was a little bit afraid of her. Of all the women in the house, she was closest in age to me, and she was intelligent and thoughtful. Dimock was about a ten-minute walk from the house. On our way back, we began talking about proofreading and got so involved in our conversation that we didn't see Diane drive by in her car.

"You two sure were talking up a storm," she remarked when we returned to the house and signed in. She seemed surprised.

It turned out I wasn't pregnant, only gaining weight from the starchy diet we had, or "eating up my feelings," as Mollie put it.

I spent a lot of my free time with Cynthia, my big sister, who in reality was almost twenty years younger than I was. I had become close to

Debbie and Michele during my first weeks in treatment, but when Debbie dropped out precipitously, leaving me feeling hurt and abandoned, Diane told me I should try to get close with the women who had been there a while and had something to teach me. Cynthia was lively and funny, a natural mimic. She had been paroled to Women, Inc., from Framingham, the Massachusetts women's prison. She was in Phase 2 and kind about supporting me any way she could, including baking a cake on my forty-third birthday, which happened three weeks after I came to Women, Inc., and was a pretty dismal affair for me.

On weekends the regular staff of counselors took off, and the house was run by part-time coverage staff. One weekend counselor, Alma, was a large, tough woman who normally worked as a security guard. Over the course of a few weeks, Alma and Cynthia began a flirtation that escalated into a full-scale romantic intrigue. I observed its progress during our weekly card games. We played spades, a game I had learned in jail in Minnesota. Alma and Cynthia played partners against me and Barbara J., who was home from the hospital, and one of my roommates.

Liaisons between counselors and clients were strictly forbidden. It was okay to have feelings about a counselor, but acting on the feeling was grounds for termination. Cynthia was on parole and in danger of losing custody of her two children. At the time she was also dealing with an extremely painful incest issue. Week by week she became more vulnerable, agitated, and unstable. When the regular staff caught wind of the situation, Cynthia was called into the office. She admitted that she was in love with Alma. Alma denied playing any part in what had happened, and claimed that the infatuation was all a fantasy in Cynthia's mind.

I knew Alma was lying. I had seen her flirt with Cynthia and deliberately provoke her. Finally Cynthia cracked under the strain and left treatment, which meant an almost certain return to drugs, prostitution, and jail, if she were lucky, or possibly death. I felt sad for Cynthia and angry at Alma, who, in my opinion, had hounded Cynthia out to cover her own ass. Alma knew that I had seen everything, and gave me a very hard time the following weekend. I was afraid she would force me out of treatment too; I was in fear for my life.

On the Monday after Cynthia left, we were having morning meeting with Joanna, another treatment counselor. Joanna was a flamboyant Cape Verdean woman whose leather clothes and flashy jewelry were the envy of all the women in the house. I was terrified to reveal my feelings about Alma. She was a powerful black woman, in a position of authority in the house and an activist in the community. I still felt pretty insecure and out of place in my group at Women, Inc. But I had learned enough by now to know that I had to be honest and talk about what was going on with me.

"I need some space," I said. "Joanna, I have all these feelings about Alma. I feel like she fucked with Cynthia and then lied about it, and now she's fucking with me. I'm afraid she'll try to force me out of the house. I'm also scared because she's staff, and powerful, and I'm still new here."

"You did right to bring it up," said Joanna, "no matter how scared you are. Every woman in this house has the right to confront staff just like you confront your peers. I'll bring this to the rest of the staff and see what they think should be done about it."

A few days later, Diane called a house meeting. None of the women had any idea what it was about. We waited around the table to find out. After about fifteen minutes, Diane walked in. My heart sank into my toes when I saw Alma walk in right behind her.

I sat near the front of the table, close to Diane and Alma. "One of you has made certain accusations about a staff member," said Diane, "and we're here to deal with it."

I took a deep breath and summoned up all my courage. "I made the accusations," I said. "Alma, I feel like you fucked with Cynthia and forced her out of treatment. You lied when you denied your part in the romance. I feel like you use the women in this house for your own personal power trip. You're unprofessional. I'm afraid of you, too. I feel like you fuck with me, and you'd think nothing of making me leave treatment even though my life is at stake. I'm really angry at you and very scared."

Alma was leaning back in her chair, her pose a study in arrogance. She had a contemptuous sneer on her face. "Susan," she said, "every word you're saying is a lie. You're a very sick woman. I don't know how you dreamed all this stuff up, but none of it is true."

"I'd like to hear from the other women," said Diane.

We went around the table. Each woman gave her opinion. One by one they said that they liked Alma and had seen nothing provocative in her conduct with Cynthia. They believed what she was saying and wanted her to continue as staff. I grew more and more dismayed. Not one of my peers supported me. I was sorry I had spoken up in the first place. I was in terror of what would happen to me when the meeting ended. I thought I would probably be asked to leave.

Finally all the women had had their say, and it was Diane's turn to speak. "I want you all to know," said Diane, "that Alma has been terminated from the staff of Women, Inc. I called this house meeting to find out how many of you have the courage to stand up for yourselves and confront a staff member. Now I have my answer: one, and a new woman at that. And not one of you all supported her. What if Alma had offered you a bag of dope? Would you all shoot dope with her because she's staff?"

"Susan," she said, turning to me. "I'm proud of you. You stood for something today, and you were right. Remember this: if you don't stand for something, you'll fall for anything. The rest of you all better think real hard about that one before you find yourselves shooting dope." And Diane swept out of the room, Alma following close behind, considerably chastened.

I was stunned, in shock. All my life I had been fighting authority, and right or wrong, authority had always won the fight. For the first time ever, I had challenged someone misusing power in a position of authority and been supported by someone I deeply respected. I had gotten fair treatment. I wanted to shout it from the rooftops, "Life can be fair!" It was that big a deal. On the downside, I felt more paranoid and isolated from my peers than ever. But at least now there was one person who I knew I could trust to be fair, and I was so grateful for that, I could have wept with joy.

My troubles in the house, though, were far from over. Every Saturday we did "GIs," short for general inspections. We dressed in old clothes, tied scarves over our hair, and thoroughly cleaned our normal tighten-up. By now I had gone from the bathrooms upstairs to the dining room, which I shared with another woman. For GI we had to break down the folding tables that made up the big table, wash down the walls, and mop and wax the floor. I always volunteered to do the waxing, because it was the only time I could be alone. I took my time waxing the large, pale gray linoleum floor, and then I stayed in the room by myself while it dried.

Almost every woman in the house was better at cleaning than I was, so I was always having to ask advice about how to do something. Sandra, a mulatto woman who had come in about a month before me, kept the nicest bedroom upstairs. She had told me that she used a lot of wax on her floor. This suited my purposes too, because the more wax there was, the longer the floor took to dry and the more time I had to myself. I was waxing the dining room floor one Saturday, and had gotten about to the middle of the room, when suddenly Sandra appeared in the doorway. "You're using too much wax," she said. "You're wasting household supplies." "You're the one who told me to use a lot," I replied. "Yeah," she said, "but not that much. You just wanna keep everyone out of this room for as long as you can so you can isolate."

I didn't say anything. Sandra was getting on my nerves. I didn't like her watching me or telling me what to do. I had a very short fuse at that point, particularly on weekends, which were extremely difficult for me to get through. Sandra kept on standing there. "You're doing it wrong," she said. "You're supposed to wipe the rag from side to side, not do one square at a time like you're doing. You could finish this floor in half the time if you did it right." "Sandra," I said, "why don't you just shut the fuck up?"

Sandra went to the office and told staff that I had disrespected her. The weekend counselor came in and screamed at me, and then she gave me an LE, a "learning experience," consequences for breaking the rules or behaving inappropriately. There were three kinds: written LEs, physical LEs (more cleaning), and presentations, in which you had to stand up in front of the group and speak on a particular subject, such as "Why I Need to Follow My Gut," "Why I Need to Respect Myself and Others," "Why I Need to Keep My Commitments," and so on. After you finished speaking, everyone in the group gave you feedback and voted on whether or not to accept the presentation. If they didn't accept it, you had to do it again. For disrespecting Sandra I got a presentation, my first of many in the house.

I was still on support. In order to get off support or move from phase to phase, you had to get space in group and ask for what you needed. It was up to the counselors whether or not to grant your request. Many groups had another agenda, and requests weren't even taken. I considered support a major form of torture. I was used to being an independent loner on the street; now I could never get away by myself for even five minutes.

Every request I had made to get off support had been turned down, to my continuing humiliation. I think the counselors had decided that everything had always come too easily to me, and they endeavored to give me the hardest time they could. "You only appreciate something when you really work for it," they told us. "When you earn it, it's yours, and no one can take that away from you."

Saturday afternoons were particularly excruciating. The Phase 2 and Phase 3 women went out to an AA meeting; and since they had regular weekend visiting privileges with their children, all the children remained in the house to be "supported," or babysat, by the Phase 1 women. These included Audrey's three resident kids, plus her two older kids, little Audrey and a boy named Roy, who was truly hell on wheels; Lynn's two kids, Ellen's son, and Robin's baby boy all stayed in the family room with us. We watched TV, which by group consensus was usually tuned to a horror movie. *The Texas Chainsaw Massacre* was the house favorite. I was as out of place in this scene as I had ever been in my life, and I had to stay right in the thick of it every minute, because I had no freedom to move around at will. The boredom, tedium, and nerve-shattering noise were absolutely intolerable to me. By the time the women got back from AA, I was a nervous wreck.

In general I was sullen, rebellious, angry, and miserable. I didn't like the other women, and I felt like they didn't like me either. Every morning when I came down to face them all at breakfast, another horrifying moment that occurred day after day, I gritted my teeth and wondered how I would make it through the next twenty-four hours without going stark staring mad.

But I was learning things about myself. It wasn't particularly pleasant to find them out, but it was undeniable that they were real aspects of my character that had kept me shooting dope for years of my life.

One Saturday I was doing my dining room GI with a new woman, named Margaret. She was supposed to sweep and mop, and then I would wax. She did a lousy job sweeping, but I was too intimidated by her rough, belligerent manner to confront her, so I picked up the broom and gathered up what she'd missed. Then I swept it all under the bookcase in the corner rather than go looking for a dustpan. "Did you see that?" Charlene shrieked to Sandra and Vivienne, who were standing in the room. "She swept the dirt under the bookcase." "I did not," I said. "I saw you with my own eyes." Charlene said. "Are you really gonna stand there and tell me that you didn't? Are you calling me a motherfucking liar?"

When we had morning meeting with Joanna on Monday, she started off asking me why I had swept dirt under the bookcase in my Saturday

GI. She told me I had a lazy issue. Everyone already knew I was sleazy; now they knew I was lazy too. "Issues" were brought to your attention in group confrontations. Your issues were what had kept you shooting dope. So far they had told me that I was sleazy (I had always called it "resourceful"), thought I was better than anyone else, and acted like a victim who couldn't stand up for myself; and now they said I was lazy. It felt like the last straw. I had never done so much housework in my life, never tried so hard to do it right. So I protested.

One by one Joanna asked all the women in the house for feedback. All of them said I was lazy. I had the same feeling I had had when no one supported me in the meeting with Alma. I felt totally misunderstood and despised. I decided there was nothing for me to do but leave.

I had said I wanted to leave one time before, when we were going on restriction. I had heard that when the house went on restriction, your cigarette smoking ration, which was normally one pack every day, could be cut down. I didn't see how I could face a day at Women, Inc., without cigarettes. Joy, the counselor from my intake interview, told us about the restriction. "Who wants to leave?" she asked. I raised my hand. "You?" she said. "You wouldn't even make it out of Boston before you were in the cooker." That was a shock to me, the idea of getting high in Boston. I had always planned to get to New York before I copped. I sheepishly lowered my hand and stayed through the restriction.

I didn't have a lot of contact with Joy. One day soon after I got there, she came into the family room to look the group over. "You still here?" she said to Michele. "Why?" said Michele. "Did I have an appointment to be somewhere else?" Much to my surprise, Joy laughed along with the rest of us. I saw she had a human side to her. But I still didn't want to tangle with her in any kind of confrontation; I felt like she considered me a lost cause, someone who wouldn't be there long.

I spent the whole day after my confrontation about being lazy feeling depressed and lonely. I waited until some of my older peers came home from their day before I shared my feelings with anyone. Audrey, who had been my older sister since Cynthia left, came home, and I told her what had happened and how I felt. I cried. "Is there any truth to it?" she asked me. "Has it been a pattern in your life?" I wanted to say no; but during that same day, I'd had a disturbing memory of being asked to leave a communal Arica house in New York because I didn't help out enough with the household chores.

I saw that my laziness had damaged my relationships with other people for most of my life. While it was painful for me to admit that it was true, unless I did something to change it, the pattern would continue on its depressing course. "I feel like shit," I told Audrey. "Help doesn't always feel like help," she reminded me, "but all of us have it in our power to change." Then she told me about the confrontations she'd had about being lazy when she was new in the house. I remembered my first day's tighten-up with Audrey and how quickly she had finished her chores. She was every bit as lazy as I was! I laughed with her, and my desire to leave evaporated for another day.

By then I had begun dealing with my feelings. After weeks of confrontation from my peers about how intellectual and out of touch with my feelings I was, Andrea, one of the counselors, had hit a raw nerve of mine in group. I had claimed that I had no guilt about being a dope fiend all those years. "What about your child?" she asked me.

I described the day of Shuna's graduation from junior high. She had made Paul promise to take her out for a lobster dinner. Both Paul and I had been late for the actual graduation, then snuck off while it was happening to go down to Executive and cop. After the graduation we drove around in the car all day trying to get money to cop and pay for a lobster dinner. Finally Shuna asked me if she could get out of the car and take the subway home alone. In my mind's eye, I could still see her in her little white-and-blue graduation dress walking by herself to the subway. Suddenly, without warning, the floodgates burst, releasing a torrent of sorrow and guilt from a bottomless well of grief. Sobs tore out of me in spasms that rocked my entire body. "Ahhh," said Andrea. "That's the one. That's the one that really hurts."

It was a revelation to me when I got in touch with how I had really felt during those years. Inside of me were pain, rage, guilt, shame, and sorrow that I never even knew I felt; the dope had covered up all of it. "Talk about what you did for the dope," my peers urged me. "How did that make you feel?" they asked again and again. Under their prodding I discovered an emotional reality that the dope had blinded me to. It hurt like hell, but I recognized it as the truth, truth with the power to set me free. This was no simple antidrug dogma I was learning; it was my own internal truth, gleaned from my own experience, and validated by feelings that welled up from deep inside my own gut. I had to face the truth of how I really felt about myself and my life. It was a shattering realization. And I couldn't run from this knowledge either, because it was alive inside of me. Alive and growing.

"Dealing with the dope" was another core part of our treatment program. This is an incredibly powerful tool that I've only seen used at Women, Inc. "The dope" is a generic term we used to describe the disease of addiction in all its various manifestations. My addiction, I discovered there, spoke to me in my own voice, and I had to learn to stand and do battle with it when it called me to go get high.

The first time I ever saw women dealing with the dope en masse, I thought I had slipped into a scene from the play *Marat/Sade;* it looked and sounded, quite literally, like bedlam. A Phase 3 woman named Lynn, who had been looking for an apartment so she could regain custody of her kids and move out of the house, had started a chain reaction. It began when she asked for space in group and stated that she wanted to get high.

"My addiction is on," she said. "I wanna get high. The dope is telling me that I'm never gonna get an apartment, that I won't get my kids back from foster care, that I'm not shit and won't even stay clean for a minute when I leave this house. I wanna get high so much I can taste it. I want the escape; I want the good feelings; I want the relief."

"Come on, Lynn," said Joy, who was one of the counselors in group that day. "Isn't there any other way you can get relief?"

"The dope is telling me that I can't. I can't fight for my own life. I'm not smart enough. I'm not strong enough."

"Well," said Joy, "Are you gonna listen to the dope?"

"No, I'm not, goddamnit," said Lynn. "That motherfucker lied to me for years. Now it's trying to lie to me again. And I'm not gonna listen."

"Don't tell me, Lynn," said Joy. "Tell the dope."

"You motherfucker," yelled Lynn. "I hate you, you slimy motherfucker. You're the one that made me lose my kids in the first place. I was so busy chasing you that I slept in doorways and didn't even know where my kids were. You stinking bitch, you told me everything was gonna feel all right, that you would made me feel all right, and I didn't. I felt like shit. I felt like the lowest slime on earth. I wanted to die. I hate you, you fucking bitch; you took and took from me, and you're still trying to take from me. But this time I'm not gonna let you. You can't have me now, you bitch. I know too much to go with you. Fuck you, motherfucker! Fuck you, dope! Kiss my ass, dope! Kiss it! I'm through with you."

Lynn was screaming at the top of her lungs and pounding the table with her fist.

"You got any rights, Lynn?" said Joy.

"Yes, I do," said Lynn. "I got rights today, you motherfucker. I got the right to get my kids back and live with them. I got the right to be a mother. I got the right to respect myself. I worked damn hard for this. I got the right to live today. I got the right to live!"

The other women were cheering Lynn on. "Tell that motherfucker where to go, Lynn." Many had tears in their eyes. The minute Lynn stopped, another started. Soon there were five or six women screaming at the dope; others were sobbing and whimpering; then they would start yelling too.

I was sitting in the corner crying. All the counselors were in the room by now. Mollie came up behind me and put her hands on my shoulders. "You wanna deal, too, baby?" she asked me. "You can do it."

I added my voice to the commotion, but my heart wasn't in it. "I'll never be able to do that," I thought. Michele was on the other side of the table, her eyes wide as saucers. She was holding tight to Linda, another woman who'd come in the same time as us. Both of them looked terrified. I felt like we were in a mass exorcism. The idea didn't even seem that strange to me because many times, in the course of my addiction, I'd felt like I was possessed by evil spirits. "Maybe this is what it takes," I thought.

"Fuck you, you motherfucking dope!" yelled Dorothy. "You can kiss my ass at twelve o'clock in Macy's window."

Finally the screaming and yelling stopped, and for a minute a hush spread around the room. Then one of the women started singing a song to the tune of "Oh, Freedom Over Me." "No more dope," she sang. "No more dope. No more dope over me. And before I'd be a slave I'd be buried in my grave, And go home to my Lord and be free." All the women and counselors stood in a circle with their arms around each other singing spirituals with revised verses. "Ain't gonna let no dope turn me around," they sang, "Turn me around, turn me around. Ain't gonna let no dope turn me around. Keep on walkin', keep on talkin', walkin' to the freedom land." They sang with joy and spirit, clapping hands and swaying to the music.

By the time the singing ended, Diane was beaming. "Well, I guess we ran the dope out of here today, didn't we? We kicked the dope's ass, instead of vice versa, the way it used to happen." She was chuckling. "Sometimes I just love my job. Diane the dope buster, that's me!"

"I know all you new women must think we're crazy," she said, "talking to someone who's not even here. But sometimes you have to externalize your addiction in order to deal with the rage and pain that's been building up in you for years. Stick around for a while, and you'll be doing it too. You can believe that."

I used to think that once I started crying, my tears would flow like water and never stop. I thought that if I even got near all the rage inside of me, I'd blow the roof off a building or bust up somebody's face. Now I was tapping into my feelings, and they were coming to the surface in a rush that threatened to explode and blow the top of my head right off.

So it happened that one day, shortly before Thanksgiving, I was so full of anger and frustration that I could hardly sit still in my chair. "Will you see if one of the counselors will come in here?" I asked Charlene. "I feel like I need to deal with the dope. If I don't I'll never make it here through Thanksgiving."

Joanna followed Charlene into the room. "So," she said. "You're finally ready to deal. Well, come on with it."

"I wanna get high," I said. "The dope is telling me that I can't stay here for Thanksgiving, that I need to go home and be with my family. The dope wants to drag me out of here so I can go get high. But I need to be here. I need to be here to save my life. When I was with my family before, I needed twice as much dope to get through a holiday."

"I'm tired of this motherfucker fucking with me!" I yelled. "I hate you, dope! You took twenty-five years of my life! You took my kid away from me. You took everything from me! You dragged me through the mud for years! I can't stand you any more. Get out of my mind! Get out of my body! Get the fuck away from me! I don't want you in my life any more!"

"Come on, Susan," Joanna said. "Look at somebody and keep going. Get free."

I looked across the table at Vivienne. She was crying and nodding her head. "Fuck you, dope!" I yelled. "You're not dragging me out of here today! Get the fuck away from me! I can stay here! I'll have other holidays with my family, and without you, you sleazebag motherfucker! I don't have to get high today! I can want you, but I don't have to pick you up. Kiss my ass, you rotten cross-out bitch!"

"You got any rights?" Michele yelled out.

"Damn right I do! I got the right to live like a human being, not the animal I was on the street. I got the right to a decent life. I got the right to be a woman today. I got the right to live!"

Diane stood watching me from across the room. "Rage," she said. "That's rage. Now where's the other side?"

I put my head down on the table and started to cry. My whole body shook with sobs. Diane came around behind me and held me while I cried. I cried and cried, flooding the table with tears. "It's all right," Diane murmured. "Let it go. All of it. You're safe now. You can have your pain." I cried until I felt totally empty, drained, as limp as a rag doll. It felt like I was crying for everything that had ever hurt me all my life.

"Some people are just more sensitive than others," Diane said softly when I finished crying. "Some people are just born that way. And nobody understands. You're gonna be all right now, baby," she told me. "Just hang on in there. You're gonna be just fine."

By now I had recognized the feeling that had seemed so familiar to me my first day of treatment, but which I hadn't been able to identify. It was in the way the room felt when Diane came in to lead group, as if the electromagnetic charge in the air had changed. I recognized the phenomenon from my experiences in Arica, from the way the air became charged around Oscar. In a strange way, Diane reminded me of Jenny, the woman who had inspired me in Arica. Working with addicts was Diane's spiritual mission, her vocation, and the room took on a spiritual dimension when she did her work. That didn't mean she couldn't be as rough as the meanest motherfucker in the valley, but I felt her deep compassion, and an overwhelming respect. Whatever she had to teach me, I wanted to stick around to learn.

It wasn't easy. Women, Inc., insisted on absolute honesty. Honesty that went beyond truthfulness. You had to be real. You could tell if someone was being real, because you could feel their feelings right along with them. You could feel them in your gut.

"One thing I know," Diane said one day, "is that whatever is going on here, it will all come out in the wash." In group I thought a lot about the money I had stashed in my jacket upstairs. I was afraid now to admit that I had it. I thought I might get a massive LE or possibly be kicked out of

the house. Sometimes I would see those two twenty-dollar bills materialize in space as a vision over my head, and they'd be big as the sky. It was
my personal example of the sign that hung on the wall of the dining
room: "Guilt kills." I had guilt about that money, and I didn't know what
to do about it.

Diane was always asking us in group, "What are you willing to give up
to stay straight?" It was the Women, Inc., variation on the concept of
being willing to go to any lengths. Many women in the house, for instance, had to give up contact with members of their immediate families
who were using or dealing drugs. They dealt with their resentment and
grief often, particularly those women who had to stay away from their
own mothers. I didn't feel that kind of personal commitment. I was curious but cautious; I still didn't think it would work for me.

My mother had sent me a carton of cigarettes one week. We were allowed one pack a day, and I had no end of difficulty keeping to that ration. By evening I was usually bumming from my peers and risking their
ridicule and rejection when they said no. So I used the opportunity of the
new carton to get a whole pack of cigarettes one evening after the mail
was distributed. Margaret noticed that I had an almost full pack of cigarettes when we did morning meeting papers, unheard of for me, and reported it to staff.

When I went to the office to ask to go to bed, Mollie told me to stick
around. Brenda, a Women, Inc., graduate who worked as a counselor,
was in there with Mollie. Since I was still on support, Vivienne stayed
with me. After all the women had gone to bed, Mollie confronted me
about the cigarettes. She was angry because she felt I had manipulated
her to get over. "So you sleazed an extra pack?" she asked me.

"We'll have to give you some consequences," Brenda said to me.
Then she turned to Mollie. "What do you think her consequences should
be?"

"Put her on a smoking ban for twenty-four hours." said Mollie.

I burst into tears. "I can't do it," I sobbed. "I'll have to leave. I haven't
ever gone twenty-four hours without cigarettes. I don't think I can stand
it." I stood in the office and cried.

Mollie liked me as much as I liked her, and I know she wanted to
back down. But as a counselor, she had to give me consequences, and she
couldn't put her personal feelings for me before her job. "Well, you'll

have to stand it," she said. "Maybe next time you'll think twice about being so sleazy."

"I can't do it," I sobbed.

"Yes, you can," said Vivienne. "I'll help you. You'll just have to deal with the feelings: how much you want to smoke a cigarette and how much it hurts not to have one. You can deal with the feelings with me. I'll support you."

"You can do it," Mollie said. Brenda nodded in agreement. But I noticed that Mollie looked as doubtful as I felt.

The next day I dreaded getting out of bed in the morning. We had a long group. Audrey and Robin, who were best friends and nearly inseparable, were put on a speaking ban with each other because the counselors thought they should relate more to other women in the house. It took a long time for Audrey and Robin to get through their feelings, and then there were other dramas in the house that had to be dealt with. By the time group finished, it was time for lunch. The minute we got out of group, where we weren't allowed to smoke until we had dealt with our feelings, everyone lit up a cigarette.

In the afternoon we sat around the table. I asked for some space and dealt with how bad I felt about not being able to smoke. Audrey and Robin were down in the dumps. "I just can't take your feelings seriously," I said to them, "because at least you can smoke after you have them. I want a cigarette," I said. "I hate every last one of you motherfuckers who can smoke when I can't." I had to take space and deal with my feelings several times during the afternoon and evening. I felt a little foggy and spaced-out, but it wasn't as bad as I had expected.

I didn't even stay up till midnight so I could have a cigarette, but went to bed and waited until the next morning. I felt pretty good about myself. I was surprised at the degree of commitment I had shown myself by staying through the smoking ban. My peers had new respect for me too; most of them had thought I wouldn't make it. Shortly afterward I asked to get off support and my request was granted, since my peers and the staff felt that I was finally working on my treatment.

One afternoon in early December, Joanna came into the dining room to get me. "Your PO is in the office," she said, "and she wants to see you." The long arm of the law had caught up with me again. It had taken five months for my probation to be transferred from Minnesota to New York, and barely over a month for the transfer from New York to Boston. Many of the women in the house had been stipulated to treatment by the courts, as I had once been to Willmar, and I suspected that completing treatment at Women, Inc., might now be made a condition of my probation.

My new PO was a very pretty, well-dressed black woman named Kathy Tate. She asked Joanna if she might meet with me alone in a room where we could have some privacy. After asking me to fill out some forms and a little preliminary conversation, Kathy asked me point-blank, "This is a really tough program, isn't it?" "Yes," I said, "the toughest I've ever been in." "That's what I've heard," said Kathy. "I've never yet had a client who finished this program, so any time you want to leave here, just call and let me know." I was dumbfounded. Here I'd thought she would stipulate me to Women, Inc., and now she was practically encouraging me to drop out. Ironically, being thrown back completely on my own motivation had the effect of deepening my commitment. I'd taken what she said about the difficulty of the program as a personal challenge: I wanted to prove to myself that I was tough enough to stick it out to the end.

When it began to dawn on me that I might possibly be able to stay off drugs, I started worrying about my teeth. My addiction had taken a terrible toll on them. Except for dire emergencies, I hadn't been to the dentist for years. I had reasoned that I would probably die before my teeth fell apart. So far in treatment, I had been learning to deal with physical pain. In my first days at Women, Inc., I had gone to the office complaining of a headache. "Go back inside and deal with your feelings," the counselors told me. This was their normal prescription for getting through anything drug-free. They wouldn't give me so much as a Motrin unless I displayed a serious reason for needing one and had dealt with my feelings first.

The two kinds of pain I thought I couldn't get through without narcotics were toothaches and the kind of burning nerve pain I'd experienced with my slipped disc episodes. One morning in treatment, I woke up with a throbbing pain in my mouth. I had developed abscesses over three of my back teeth. I made an emergency appointment with the dentist at Dimock, who prescribed antibiotics and Motrin. He said that when the infection cleared up, I would probably need root canals and extractions. I went back to the house in a panic.

I had never had a tooth pulled before, and I could not imagine having a root canal without serious pain medication. I spent a lot of time in the office dealing with my terror of the pain. I wanted to call my mother, but since I was still in Phase 1, phone calls were out of the question. The day I was going to have two teeth pulled, I dealt with my feelings in morning meeting and got ready to leave the house. "Hey, Sue," said Rhoda. "If you die in the dentist's chair, can I have your new coat?" We both laughed, and then she got up and gave me a big hug, which helped my emotional state considerably.

I was allowed to lie down and nap when I returned from the dentist, a rare luxury in treatment, and I was surprised that the discomfort I experienced when the novocaine wore off was easily managed with Motrin. I was finding out that fear of pain is often worse than the pain itself, and that my normal habit of medicating myself before the pain even started (ten or fifteen Percodan, for instance, at the first twinge of menstrual cramps) was just so much addict behavior. Each time I got through a physically painful experience drug-free, I grew stronger. I was building up a reserve of strength that I could call upon with each new need.

The root canal, too, was less painful than I expected. The worst part was my fear that the dentist would hit a nerve when he probed the canals after the main nerve had been removed under novocaine. After one of these probing sessions, an hour of continuous terror for me, I was relieved to see Linda in the office when I got out of the chair. I grabbed her, pulled her into a corridor near the ladies' room, and sobbed all over her. The root canal was a tedious, time-consuming procedure, and I had to have weekly appointments for a long time. I loved having all the time out of the house. "It's a sad state of affairs," I told my peers, "when you look forward to having a root canal for entertainment." I was grateful, though, that I was finally in a position to see about my teeth and take care of my most pressing health problem.

I was allowed to invite Shuna, whom I had not seen or spoken to since Conifer Park, for a visit at Christmas. I called her at my mother's house. It was heartbreaking to hear my mother's voice and not be allowed to speak to her. Shuna came to visit for a few days, shortly after Christmas. We were happy to see each other but the visit was tense. She was angry at me, and held herself back from hoping that the treatment might work. "I will say one thing, though," she told me. "This is the first time I ever heard you talk about drugs where you didn't still think they were cool. It's a change. I like it."

At last I had a solution for what to do with my secret stash of money. I gave it to Shuna to buy herself a new pair of boots and swore her to secrecy. It was ironic giving Shuna my cop money to buy something for herself. All through my addiction, I had bought dope and let my child go without. I had a river of tears to deal with when Shuna left: guilt, grief, shame, and the pain of watching her go and having to stay there myself.

I became friends with Rhoda. It happened one day when the counselors sent all the women to the YMCA around the corner for some exercise. Rhoda, Charlene, and I all lay down in the changing rooms and took a nap while the other women exercised. Rhoda commanded respect from the other women and the counselors, and was somewhat exempt from confrontations. So the staff couldn't confront me too heavily about not exercising without giving Rhoda the same consequences. When we got back to the house and signed in at the office, Rhoda stuck up for me and made a joke out of the whole thing. Then she grabbed me by the hand, and we ran off somewhere to giggle about our escapade.

Rhoda and I had had some serious talks in the course of our treatment. Even before we became friends, we had confided in each other some of our deepest pain. It was Rhoda I went to with my river of tears over Shuna's departure; Rhoda to whom I spilled my grief about my grandparents and the lost world of my childhood when I wrote my autobiography in our "Who I Was" ("Who I Was, Who I Am, Who I Would Like to Be") papers; Rhoda who told me that I was able to stick it out through the hard times at Women, Inc., because I had "the gift of desperation." But some different kind of bond had been forged the day we napped at the Y, and from then on the two of us were fast friends, each other's greatest source of joy and support.

Having a true friend made all the difference in the world. Rhoda and I were close in age and education, a rarity in the house; and we had both been heroin junkies, in contrast to the other women, who mostly had cocaine-related problems. The fact that Rhoda had such a deep commitment to staying at Women, Inc., and changing her life around had a beneficial effect on me too. Not that our shared viewpoint was altogether positive. I felt that I could tell Rhoda anything, and vice versa, and both of us, no matter what it was, could expect each other's understanding and support. And we had a lot of fun too. Women, Inc., had saved my life, but my friendship with Rhoda made it a life worth saving.

I no longer felt so isolated and alienated in the house, but I had just as hard a time getting into Phase 2 as I had getting off support. The staff turned my request down four or five times, all of them painful, and Rhoda comforted me by letting me get through my feelings of frustration and rejection. The worst part for me was that I couldn't read a book until I got Phase 2. The counselors said I needed to become acquainted with reality, not escape from it, as I always had with books. It was difficult for me, as a prodigious reader, to accept this proscription, but I suppose it was okay because I didn't suffer any lasting harm. At the time Rhoda and I became friends, she had just gotten Phase 3 and was getting ready to look for a job. My big fear was that Rhoda would move out of the house in a matter of months, while I'd still be in Phase 1, unable even to talk to her on the phone.

Rhoda's tighten-up was Candace's office. Candace was the director of Women, Inc., and she had a large, beautiful office set off from the rest of the house. I was not allowed inside the room, so I used to stand in the doorway, leaning on the mop or broom with which I'd just finished my own tighten-up, and gossip with Rhoda while she finished hers. Somehow in treatment I remember myself always leaning on a mop or broom, like Cinderella, and I remember all the things Rhoda and I would find to giggle about. I loved Candace's office: a round room with three big windows. I began to dream of living in an apartment like that when I got out of treatment. I could visualize one big, sunny room with plants hung in the windows. It was the first concrete glimmer I'd had of a possible life without drugs.

I was grateful for the changes, though I still felt oppressed by Women, Inc. I didn't *want* to be there, but I knew beyond knowing that I *needed* to be there. I had been running in circles in the drug labyrinth for too many years. I wanted out. I wanted out of the living death of the dope-fiend hustle. I wanted out of my pain too. That's why I'd taken the drugs in the first place. But at the end, even drugs had failed to suppress my pain. I was so desperate for a way out that I was willing to do whatever it took. And I had taken to heart the favorite words of a new counselor we had named Julie, who liked to say, "The only way out is through."

chapter seventeen

Blackbird singing in the dead of night
Take these broken wings and learn to fly
All your life
You were only waiting for this moment to arrive.

The Beatles,
"Blackbird"

THE GREATEST LOVE OF ALL—1987

Snow was falling outside the dining room windows. I sat at the table lost in daydreaming and reverie, projecting myself into the landscape outside. I loved snow, its clean smell and diamond-studded whiteness, the sacred hush that came over everything as it fell, the safe seclusion in which it enclosed the landscape. When I lived in Minnesota I used to go out to cop in blizzards like this and come home to my snug hotel room to cook up my dope and get off, a true marriage of fire and ice. Then at night I'd snuggle up with Tommy in our single bed and watch fat, white snowflakes drift in blue darkness past our window. I was thinking nostalgically of those old days when Diane walked into the room.

"Well, it's snowing outside," she said. "Who wishes they were out in this blizzard looking for drugs?"

I raised my hand. "I do," I said.

"Go to the office and get your stuff then," she said.

But I hadn't really been serious, and I don't think she had either. Besides, where would I go and with what? I'd already given my getaway money to Shuna; I didn't know where Tommy was; and I certainly wasn't going back to Minnesota (and jail) on the twenty dollars or so I had in the office.

"I don't want to leave," I said. "I just miss being outside in the snow."

"If that's the case," said Diane, "You can go out and shovel the walk with Charlene and Undreea. Since your back is bad, you can pour the salt and sweep up."

That was the Women, Inc., prescription for whatever ailed you: hard work and dealing with feelings. I did feel a little guilty over my euphoric recall of those drug days in Minnesota. And I felt sad about Tommy. I missed him often. When I dealt with how bad I missed him, one or the other of my peers would say, "It's the dope you miss." On the wall over the staircase to the bedrooms upstairs, there was a sign that said, "What mask has the dope got on today?" I came to think of it as the dope wearing Tommy's face that made my heart ache so badly.

I thought a lot about my old dope partner Florence, too. Grieving Florence, who had lost everyone she ever cared for in this world and now was given up for crazy, with only heroin to console her. Since I had learned about experiencing grief and getting through it, I knew there was hope for Florence too. It hurt me that she had never contacted me, never written or called, just disappeared to California without a word to me. "When you're using drugs," one of the counselors said, "you don't have friends. You just have people who will use you for a bag of dope." I didn't want to believe it. Florence and I had become so close, closer in many ways than Tommy and me. But here was the proof. She had vanished from my life without a trace; I had just been her connection.

By now I was accustomed to daily life at Women, Inc., and there were even parts of our routine I had grown to enjoy. "Without a drink or a drug," Diane liked to say, "you learn to appreciate the little things in life," and I was finding it true. Within our small community of women and children, there was a lot of caring and intimacy as well as an appealing atmosphere of cozy domesticity. More than an institution, Women, Inc., was an extended family. I had formed affectionate bonds with some of my peers' children who lived in or visited the house, and with some of the staff's children, who were frequently around. When Lele came home from school, I liked to hold her on my lap and play with her; I sometimes babysat for Little Andrea, the daughter of a counselor, and I had a genuine friendship with Janelle, Vivienne's daughter, who started out visiting the house and ended up living with us. Andrea liked to comb and braid my long straight hair, as did Tamika, Mollie's youngest daughter. It reminded me of the closeness I had with my niece Dani, and did much to console me for the temporary loss of my daughter and family.

In the evenings, when we were done with our tighten-ups and before we wrote morning meeting papers, all the women and children lounged around in the family room, and the black women did one another's hair. They would oil one another's scalps, sectioning out pieces of hair with a comb and applying moisturizing lotion or Glover's mange to fight dandruff. Then they'd roll their own or someone else's hair up in rollers, and the mothers would put their daughters between their knees and braid their hair for school the next day. Every evening, no matter how tired she was, Audrey ironed all her children's school clothes. In the house we all wore sweats and comfortable clothes. We received bundles of clothing as donations fairly regularly, and there was much borrowing and trading of clothes, especially for outings and special occasions. Some of the women in the house who'd come from jail ironed everything, including their sweats.

I'd grown up in a family of sisters and attended an all-women's college, so I was fairly comfortable in the midst of a female community. It often occurred to me that many of my periods of greatest personal growth had taken place in the times I lived apart from men and used the energy I normally put into relationships to nurture myself. I had thought that I wouldn't be able to stand being deprived of my favorite distractions: books, shopping, and men. I thought I wouldn't survive; instead I thrived. I felt good at the end of a day in which I'd taken care of my responsibilities and honored my commitments to the best of my abilities; as the counselors often told me, I was growing despite myself.

Of course the growth was usually accompanied by a certain amount of pain. During this time I was almost always in some sort of trouble. The Women, Inc., rules were like a mine field, and every time you unwittingly stepped on a mine, you got an LE. I had to do so many presentations around this time that I used to joke that I wouldn't bother taking a seat at the table; I'd just stand up at the head so as to be ready for my next presentation. I did so many that I became quite adept at them. This was lucky, as it turned out, because I ended up having to give a presentation to get into Phase 2.

The day I gave it in group, all the counselors were there. I was a nervous wreck. I had already been refused Phase 2 several times, and the rest of the women who'd come in in my group had been in Phase 2 for months. It was late February; I had been in Women, Inc., for nearly five months. I was called on and stood up to speak. I talked about how I had felt on the street as a practicing drug addict: hopeless, wanting to die. I talked about how difficult it had been for me to stay at Women, Inc., at the beginning of my treatment, about how bored, frustrated, and angry I was. "It was worth it, though," I said, "because out of all that pain, I grew and changed. I got better despite myself. I'm a different person today, because today I have hope." Joanna and my peers had watery eyes, but when I said that thing about hope, Diane burst into tears. I had never seen her cry like that, and I was shocked, but I had to keep going with my presentation. "That may not seem like such a big deal to someone else," I continued, tears running down my face too, "but it's a big deal for me. I lived without hope for years and years of my life, but I don't have to live like that any more. When I was using drugs, I had to have them. I didn't have a choice. Today I have freedom; I have a choice. I can choose to live my life as a woman of dignity and honor. Today I have hope of becoming the woman I always wanted to be, 'beyond my wildest dreams.'"

I got Phase 2. It was a real accomplishment. Diane told me later that she'd cried because that morning she'd heard about a former client dying of AIDS, which she'd contracted after leaving Women, Inc., and returning to active drug addiction. "She had no hope," Diane said. "That's what was missing. So don't think it's a small thing. Hope can make all the difference in the world."

I had now been clean for almost six months and was going through an intense mourning period. One of the most useful things I learned at Women, Inc., was how to get through these periods of grief. They came, I was told, at predictable intervals: three months, six months, nine months, a year, and then on each succeeding anniversary.

I felt as though my heart were breaking. I missed getting high, missed my old life on the street, missed the old me, and felt like I had lost my best friend. This was normal, the staff assured me. I was letting go of the dope, and grieving for the loss was the way to do it. I thought back to the time in Minnesota when I'd walked around with all my grief balled up inside of me and no way to let it out. I had missed the dope so acutely and so painfully that I'd decided if I were going to feel that bad without it, I might as well go get high. Had I known what they told me at Women, Inc., about mourning periods and active grieving, I might have gotten through that time and been spared three more years of suffering with my addiction. This time, armed with information, I found it possible to miss the dope with all my heart and soul and still not have to pick it up.

Shortly after I got Phase 2, the whole house went on a house ban. This was the most severe form of restriction. No one could leave the house except to go to work or for appointments of extreme urgency. The counselors would not come in and have group with us. All activities were suspended. We had to sit around the table all day and work with one another until we pulled the group together. I was working in the kitchen during this time, and one of the conditions of the house ban was that we couldn't go grocery shopping. The three members of the kitchen crew made up endless variations on meals prepared with commodities, the surplus food we received from welfare. Cigarettes were restricted to two a day. Everyone was back on support. No one had any sort of privileges. It was a pretty dreary couple of weeks.

Toward the end of the house ban, Diane brought a shoe box with a hole cut in the top into the dining room. "This is a guilt box," she said. "Whatever guilt you give up into this box, you won't get any consequences for. It's a once-in-a-lifetime opportunity, so take advantage of it." I almost started crying from sheer relief. At last there was a solution for my guilt about the money. Getting it off the premises had been one thing, but I still lived with the guilt of withholding the information from staff. I wrote it down on a piece of paper and hurried up and dumped it into the guilt box, along with a few other things I considered minor, like stashing a couple of Motrin in my room when I'd had my teeth pulled. Later that day I was called to the office. I was rigid with fear. But what they wanted to ask me about was the Motrin; they thought if it were still there, it might endanger the children. No one mentioned anything about the money.

I received another unexpected benefit from the house ban. In order to get off it, we had to write and submit a group paper, like a written LE, but coming from the entire body of women. Up until that time, I had never felt wholehearted acceptance from my peers. Although I wasn't the only white woman in the house, I was white, educated, and older—

different. When we did our morning meeting papers at night, some of the women would ask me how to spell things; they called me "the dictionary," with an odd mixture of respect and contempt. In treatment I had frequently dealt with my feeling that I would never be able to write again without drugs. I had decided that if it came to a choice between my life and my writing, I would have to give up writing, but it hurt me even to think of life without it. Whatever tiny shred of self-esteem I'd managed to salvage from my addiction had come from my ability to write no matter how strung out I was.

When it came time to write the group paper, I took charge and organized it into sections, with work teams, like a newspaper. I edited the overall paper and wrote one particularly dramatic section. Not only did we have fun working on the project, but the paper was accepted, and as a result we could come off the house ban. After that my peers fully accepted me as part of the group, and I got a big dose of self-esteem back from seeing some of my positive attributes in action. It was especially nice to experience my newspaper talents again, this time clean and sober.

In Phase 2 I was able to read books, to speak with Shuna and my parents on the phone, and to spend more time outside the house. Phase 2 women were responsible for going on "bus run," where we accompanied the school bus driver in returning the kids home from day care downstairs. I loved going on bus run, seeing the neighborhood surrounding Women, Inc., and kidding around with the children. It was a far cry from how I had viewed the day care on the day of my interview. Dorchester and Roxbury were both formerly Jewish neighborhoods, full of synagogues that had been turned into churches. Traces of their former lives could still be seen in their structural decorations of Torah scrolls and Stars of David. There was one huge abandoned synagogue on Seaver Street, across from Franklin Park. I could see it had once been a magnificent temple with a prosperous congregation. "Not by might nor by power but by my spirit, saith the Lord" was carved into its stone walls. Chills ran up my spine whenever we passed this abandoned temple, overgrown with weeds like a Mayan ruin. I saw it as a metaphor for my own lost connection to Judaism, and for myself, "grand but ruined," as I wrote my brother Ricky.

As I earned more privileges and was granted more freedom and responsibilities, I gained in spirit and self-esteem. I knew my way around the house and the rules and rarely got into trouble any more. One day a new woman came into the house, and I was assigned to see her through her orientation. I took her to the shower and screened her clothes, as Dorothy had with me. She thought I was a staff member. I told Rhoda about it later that evening.

"She thought I worked here," I said in amazement.

"You do," said Rhoda. "And the new woman doesn't know it, but now she does too." We both fell out laughing in the kitchen.

I could now go on passes and to outside AA and NA meetings, where there were men. I got my hair cut and went shopping for new clothes. Margaret gave me a nickname, "Susan Lucci," after the soap opera actress. The name stuck. My peers all began calling me "Lucci," or sometimes "Looch" for short. The staff told me that I could continue my treatment in Boston, or I could transfer to a program in New York to finish up, as the woman before me from Conifer Park had done. I decided to remain in Boston, where I felt I had the best chance for continuing abstinence. I was now fully committed to my new life.

At this point the focus of my treatment changed. Where once it had been enough simply to live each day drug-free, I began to work on what Diane called "emotional sobriety," the attainment of inner peace no matter what dramas might be raging on the outside or feelings troubling me from within. And I had something new to work on, too. My parents had sold the boatyard and were moving to Florida. I was stunned by the intensity of the feelings this engendered in me. Although I hadn't grown up there, the boatyard had been "home" to me for the past twenty years of my life. It was a safe haven for me in times of trouble, a symbol of stability when my world crumbled like a house of cards.

Although I knew it was the best move for my parents, I felt betrayed and abandoned; like the rug had just been pulled out from under me. Against all my protests, I now had to grow up and make my own home; I would no longer be able to rely on my parents to do it for me. It underscored how critically important it was for me to continue on my course of recovery. I had to keep moving ahead now more than ever, because there was no home in New York to go back to any more.

On a practical level, I needed to figure out what to do with all the belongings I had stored with my parents. There was no way they could sort through my stuff and know what to keep and what to throw away. How could I get to New York to do it? Where could I store what I wanted to keep? It seemed I had no answers to those questions and no way to solve the problems from where I was, stuck in treatment. I went to the office and poured out my dilemma to Diane and Joanna, who said they would think about it. I continued to deal with my feelings around the table. I talked to my sister and brother on the phone. Shuna felt bereft and homeless too. It meant she had nowhere to go on her college vacations; her father's apartment, though she had often stayed there, had never been a real home to her.

In the meantime life continued at Women, Inc. As a Phase 2 woman, I had responsibility for supporting my Phase 1 peers in the house. Now I supported women to Dimock Street for appointments; I helped them adjust to life in treatment and showed them the ropes. More and more I felt staff trusting me with delicate situations. Rhoda said it was because they respected my maturity. Several times Mollie dropped hints in group that I should think about asking for Phase 3. With the change of season, I found more small pleasures in daily life. On walks to Dimock, I stopped to smell the lilacs and roses blooming in neighborhood yards. Evenings I liked to sit out on the fire escape beside the family room window and watch the sky. The fire escape was like a tree house, secluded and sheltered in green leafy branches. I found more opportunities for solitude and contemplation. I was thinking about my future now; soon I would be looking for an apartment and a job.

Rhoda was working full-time. I had observed her struggle first to find the self-confidence to look for work, and then to go out and find the job. Her job search had been preceded by a horrendous depression, during which she had often sat at the table with her hat pulled over her face, barely able to stay awake or participate in group discussions. In the upper phases, we all went to Mass. Rehab. for vocational testing and assistance. Rhoda had believed herself incapable of doing any sort of work in the outside world. "You name it, I can't do it," she said one day in group. But she had managed to find not just any job, but exactly the job she wanted, working at the Boston Public Library. It was inspirational for the rest of us when one of us succeeded. Many women in our group had never worked at all, or had worked at menial jobs that would not be able to support them in recovery.

One day Diane called me into the office. Out of the blue, she asked me, "Are you searching for universal truth?" I felt embarrassed. Joanna had once teased me in group by saying I reminded her "of some sort of mystic," due to my well-known habit of spacing out and mentally leaving the premises. Now my face turned red.

"Yes," I said, not knowing what was coming next.

"Well, if you are," said Diane, "you'll be needing all the information you can get. So I want you to organize the papers in my office and read as much as you can about alcoholism and addiction."

"Diane," I said. "You never fail to amaze me." I had thought that my inner beliefs were about to be ridiculed; instead they'd been validated and understood. I began to cry out of gratitude.

"You know, Suze," said Diane, "I really like you. You're a very likable person. Did you know that about yourself?"

"Not really," I said.

"Well, it's true," she said. "You've captured my heart, something I never thought would happen when you first came here. Underneath all that junkie bullshit, you turned out to be a real human being, very warm and loving. By the way, I'm searching for universal truth myself. That's how I know about you. Now get out of my office and go back to your group."

A few weeks later, she called me into the office again. She said the staff had been thinking about whether or not to let me go to New York. "We decided to let you go," she said, "but only if you get Phase 3 first. That doesn't mean we're going to make it easy for you either. Just like everything else in this house, you'll have to earn it legitimately by your own effort. But we think you can make it." Then she told me to sit down in a chair and looked me straight in the eye. "You know it's over, don't you?" she said.

"What's over?" I asked.

"The drugs," she said. "Your old life. The old you. It's really over."

I started to cry.

"Good," she said. "You have to realize that and mourn it, really let go of it. That's the only way you'll be safe when you go to New York."

"With the information you have now," she continued, "getting high is no longer an option. The guilt will kill you. It will cause you to kill yourself, even if you live through the drugs. I'm sure you've noticed that most drug addicts don't even make it to your age. And if they do, it's too late for them to clean up. They've already given up hope of ever being different. This is your last chance. And if you blow this, you won't be able to live with yourself. And even if you can, wherever you are I'll find you and kick your ass. I'll land on you with all fours. You won't be able to go far enough to hide from me. So don't even try it. You've come too far and worked too hard. You have too much of an investment in yourself now, not to mention all the work we've put into you."

By now I was really crying, hard.

"It hurts," I said. "It hurts a lot because now I care about myself. And it makes me see how little I cared about myself when I was shooting dope. It hurts coming back to life. Sometimes I feel like my heart is breaking in two. And I'm scared. Now I have something to lose. I know what you say is true, but I don't know if I'm strong enough to do it."

"You're plenty strong," said Diane. "Believe that. If you weren't, you never would have survived what you've been through. You were strong enough to make it here, too. And besides, you're a Women, Inc., woman. All this self-empowerment we talk about here, it really works. Look at the women who've graduated from this program. Everyone knows where they came from. We have a way about us, a vibe, that's different. We got some powerful women coming out of here. I know you can make it, Suze, otherwise I wouldn't even think about letting you go. All the material possessions in the world aren't worth your life." Diane gave me a big hug.

"I love you, Diane," I said.

"I love you too, baby," she said. "I can now, because you love yourself. No one can care about you more than you care about yourself."

I was approaching my nine months sobriety birthday, another mourning period, this one even deeper than before. I thought a lot about what Diane had said. Now I was not only grieving for the dope, I was grieving for the part of me that was dying, the old me. I knew there was no way to go back to where I'd been before; yet the way to my new life was still a mystery. I was caught in limbo; I couldn't go back and I couldn't go forward.

I had violent mood swings. I would cry for my loss, then feel totally empty inside; then fear would fill the empty space, only to be followed by murderous rage. I shared these feelings with Michele and Linda, who were going through them too. We thought we were going crazy. I felt fear such as I hadn't experienced since childhood: total, mind-numbing terror. One night I dreamt that my favorite plant, a string-of-hearts I had left with my mother, was being torn up by the roots. I woke up in the middle of the night in a cold sweat, certain that I had to get home that very instant, or something terrible would happen.

"That's the power of the dope," said Joanna the next day. "It will wake you up in the middle of the night with urgent reasons to leave here and go get high. That's why we have so many women sneaking out of here down the back stairs in the dead of night. The dope calls them, and they go."

My peers were amused by my dream, and concerned for me too. "What's really being pulled up by its roots, Lucci?" BJ asked me. "It's not your plant; it's you."

The counselors told us to hang on. All these crazy feelings, they promised, would be followed by a period of growth and peace. We were going through another time of transition. In the meantime there was plenty for us to do. We worked in the kitchen, from six in the morning to ten at night; we shopped for groceries, nine hundred dollars' worth, enough to fill up the entire van. One weekend, along with two hundred volunteers from a community service group, we cleared the vacant lot on the side of the house. Then we dug up ground for a garden. We went to meetings, cleaned the house, watered the garden, wrote papers, watched films, supported our peers, dealt with our feelings, went on passes, took care of our children, said our prayers, and fell into bed exhausted at night. Then we woke up early the next morning and did it all again.

At the beginning of June, I asked for Phase 3. Mollie had been encouraging me for weeks. "Your foundation is built, Lucci," she told me. "It's time for you to move on." I was sitting near the head of the table, next to Diane. As usual for me in these situations, I remember the day by what I was wearing: a green cotton blouse with black polka dots that my sister Sheila had sent me in a care package. In order to get Phase 3, I had to convince my peers and staff of my commitment to life and recovery. By Women, Inc., standards, I would be judged more on the feelings I transmitted than by my words.

None of the other women in my group had even asked for Phase 3 yet; I was the first. To my astonishment I got it. In contrast to the struggles I had had getting off support and moving from Phase 1 to Phase 2, this transition was easy and sweet. Diane said it was a measure of how much the staff had come to trust and respect me, and how much confidence they had in my commitment to sobriety. "And speaking just for me," she added, with tears in her eyes, "I'm very, very proud of you. You've come a long way from the sleazy little dope fiend who first walked through these doors. But that doesn't mean we're not going to strip-search you when you come back from New York."

I went to New York on the train. Most of the ride was uneventful, but about half an hour away from the city, my stomach suddenly turned over, my heart started pounding, my hands shook, and I felt that tingling mixture of anticipation and fear that always came before a hit. The closer we got to the city, the more I wanted some dope. I thought about my crack connections right outside Penn Station and how easy it would be to go out there and grab a hit. "Just one little hit," my addiction told me. "No one will know. It won't even be in your urine by the time you go back." But I was no longer helpless to resist these inner urgings. I knew how to fight back. I knew there was no way a dope fiend like me would stop at "one little hit." Crack cocaine doesn't come in that measure. One hit and you're gone. I had too much to lose. I had invested too much in myself, worked too hard, struggled too long for this recovery. So I grabbed the arm rests with my shaking hands, held on for dear life, and silently "dealt with the dope" until I got past the urge to get high.

I'd been homesick for New York City the whole time I'd been away, but by the time the train arrived there, I was too scared even to venture out of Penn Station. I got on the first train to Island Park and heaved a grateful sigh of relief as the train rolled out of the city. It had been too close a call.

I was happy to see my parents, but it didn't feel like home because the whole house was in a state of chaos and upheaval. Big piles of packed boxes stood in the living room, and my mother steadily added to the pile. I knew I had my work cut out for me. I had never been good at packing and moving. Facing this overwhelming task without the aid of drugs or the luxury of procrastination would be another first. I had to pack up what was in my room and the hall closet, and go through all my belongings that were stored downstairs in the old boatyard office. The boxes and trunks I had sent home from Minnesota, and which had never been opened since, held all my worldly possessions, everything I owned that hadn't been pawned, stolen, or lost along the way.

"How did I manage to keep so much stuff?" I asked my mother.

"You're your father's daughter," she said. "You come by it honestly. You should see what your father's been dealing with for the past few months. Forty years of electrical equipment, horse trailers, building stuff, don't ask."

My mother had already gone through some of the clothes in my bedroom closet. Most of my wardrobe was in sizes too small for me ever to wear again. I packed it in boxes to send to my sister Lorraine. Everything I looked at brought back some piece of the past for me. Some things had been stored in my brother-in-law's warehouse during the years I lived in Minnesota; some clothes had come from my shoplifting binges; lots of things had burn holes from my nodding out and dropping lit cigarettes on myself. I packed what I thought I could still use in suitcases and went to tackle the stuff downstairs.

There was no way I could store all those trunks and boxes at Women, Inc. I would have to make do with the absolute minimum. I had to keep my writing and family photographs, the same things I'd rescued from my house when I tried to leave Hakim, and get rid of most of the rest. In my trunks I had treasures I'd been lugging around for twenty years: beautiful old Chinese embroidered silks, handmade laces, Victorian buttons, silk embroidery threads, antique fabrics, paisley shawls, crocheted afghans, patchwork quilts, vintage clothes, old toys, Indian beads, pictures, and bits and pieces I'd been promising myself to "make something out of" for years. I had boxes of yarn and knitting books, half-finished needlepoints and sweaters needing only half a sleeve, a lifetime's worth of craft materials and art supplies left over from my old Berkeley hippie days. Painful as it was, I decided to get rid of all these unfinished projects. If I had creative energy when I got out of treatment, which seemed as if it would go on forever anyway, I determined to put it all into my writing. I dragged a big trash can into the room and started tossing things into it. I was trying my best to make a cleansing ritual out of ridding myself symbolically of my past.

The trouble was that every time I threw something into the trash can, my father would come along and take it out. These last vestiges of my once extensive antique collection were the things that had been most special to me, and they were extraordinarily beautiful.

"That's too nice to throw away," my father would say as I tossed a hundred-year-old baby afghan into the trash.

"Well, what am I supposed to do?" I would ask him. "I can't keep everything that's here."

"Put it in a box," he'd say. "I'll give it to the Masons for a garage sale."

Throwing away my books was just as hard. Since Sheila and my parents weren't speaking, due to an ongoing feud between Jon and my father, I couldn't get her to come over and take them off my hands. Again, these were treasured books I had held back from the various holocausts of my possessions that had taken place over the years. It hurt to let them go.

Several times I had to call Women, Inc., and deal with my feelings of loss with my peers, who missed me and were relieved to hear I was okay. To my great surprise, I worked on the task at hand with diligence and strength. Gone were my moving dramas of the past, when I would customarily sit in the middle of the floor and sob loudly rather than pack up anything to go. I kept working, threw out as much as I could, and took only one major break to attend an AA meeting with the other New York graduate of Women, Inc. In a matter of days, I was done with everything and ready to return to treatment. My father promised he would bring my things to Boston in a couple of weeks, the counselors gave me permission to store them in the basement, and I said good-bye to my family and took the shuttle back to Boston.

Just as Diane had promised, I was strip-searched and given a urinalysis when I returned. I felt proud that I had managed to go to New York and stay straight, and I was pleased with the growth I had shown in the way I took care of business. I talked about my experiences with my peers. The only thing I left out was my unsuccessful attempts to contact Tommy at his brother's apartment in Minneapolis after I found his phone number in my room.

When I came back from New York, the counselors gave me permission to begin looking for a job. I was ecstatic. The sooner I could get a job and save up money to get an apartment, the sooner I could leave Women, Inc. Most of the women who'd gone before me had had a hard time finding work, but I had a skill at which I'd worked steadily for the past ten years, typographical proofreading, and I was certain I would find a job without too much trouble. I was determined to start working before it was my turn to go back in the kitchen again. One thing I had learned in treatment, though, was that every gain involves a loss and every loss involves a gain. Mingled with my excitement about looking for outside work was the sadness of what I'd be missing in the house. Already the counselors were focusing their attention on the newer women in the house, and I felt a little like a baby bird being pushed out of the nest.

One day during group, Diane came in and sang "The Greatest Love of All." She had a powerful, church-trained voice, and she sang the song, which might have been an anthem for Women, Inc., with great depth of feeling and soul. When she got to the line, "Learning to love yourself, it is the greatest love of all," I broke down in tears. In a sense my whole recovery up to this point had been about learning to love myself enough to want to live. I'd been able to come this far, I felt, only with the support and guidance of this woman who'd come to mean so much to me.

Diane often said, "Caring is the only real antidote to addiction," and she had cared about me until I was able to care about myself. Now I was taking the first steps toward independence and away from the constant nurturing and protection I'd been given at Women, Inc. It felt good, but it also felt sad. And mixed in with those feelings were gratitude for what I'd received, excitement and anxiety about the future, and that old familiar grieving and loss. Once again I was leaving my childhood behind. I'd been growing up at Women, Inc., learning how to live all over again, this time the right way so I wouldn't need drugs to survive in the world. Now I was about to go out there and test my skills. Part of me couldn't wait to go, but another part suddenly couldn't bear to leave home.

Although I had confidence in my ability to find work, I hadn't worked in ten months and worried about how to explain the gaps in my resume. My vocational counselor at Mass. Rehab., who helped me a great deal during this time, suggested a solution used by many of her disabled clients, who told potential employers that irregularities in their work histories were due to "personal problems."

The counselors at Women, Inc., had imposed some stringent restrictions on what kind of job I could and could not get. Since I hadn't worked without drugs in a good ten years, they told me that my first job clean and sober would be a highly stressful transition. They advised against any sort of writing job, which would put too much pressure on me. Typographical proofreading was fine, but I absolutely could not work at night. Almost every type shop job I'd ever held had been on a night shift. The very nature of the advertising typography business, where agencies typically deliver jobs at day's end and expect them back first thing in the morning, demands that most of the work be done at night. I argued my position to Joanna, but she was adamant in her refusal.

"Your main task right now," she said, "is not to embark on a glorious career or make a lot of money; it's to support your recovery by earning a living and learning how to live a normal life. That means working nine to five and then going to meetings. Working nights would isolate you socially from your support system and put you at too much risk of resuming a dope-fiend lifestyle."

So newly clean and sober, with a history of "personal problems" (an understatement if there ever was one), and no possibility of references from my four most recent jobs (all of which I'd been fired from in short order), I set out to find daytime work in a nighttime business, all in an unfamiliar city. As far as the typographical business is concerned, Boston is a union town, which means you start out on second or third shift and move onto days only with seniority. The first place I went, a union shop in Watertown, offered me a job on the second shift, for a very good salary, which I had to turn down with great regret.

My second interview was an unqualified disaster. I applied for a mark-up position, writing specs (size, shape, and style specifications) for typesetters, and was interviewed by the boss, who gave me an on-the-spot quiz. Holding several pages torn from type books, he asked me to identify the faces. I hadn't worked in ten months, and I had always referred to books to identify typefaces, which differ from one another in minute details, so I guessed the first one wrong. After that, my confidence already shot to hell, I proceeded to guess all the rest wrong too.

"Well," he said to me, "it doesn't look good for you here."

I called the house in tears, expecting sympathy, and told Julie what happened.

"Good," she said. "You need a little humility. You were far too arrogant about your prospects."

The following Sunday I saw a job advertised in the paper at the Ink Spot, a shop in Quincy, a nearby town. Joanna said Quincy would be a workable commute, so I called the place. "Can you come in and take a proofreading test?" they asked. I made an appointment. I felt good; every time I'd ever taken a proofreading test to apply for a job, I'd been hired on the spot. I took a long ride on the Red Line to Quincy, a seaside town on the South Shore that reminded me of Island Park, and promptly got lost. I had to ask a passing policeman for directions to Oval Road.

"Hop in," he said, "I'll take you there."

"It was one of those times," I told my peers later that day, "when I knew I was really about change, because for the first time since I was a little girl, a cop was helping me out instead of arresting me."

The proofreading test was exacting and hard. It took me over two hours of concentrated work to finish it. Afterward I was interviewed by the boss, a slim, blond woman named Mary, who looked to be a few years younger than me. She told me that the Ink Spot was a commercial printer; that they did a lot of work for her husband's advertising agency, in the back of the building; and that it had recently become necessary for them to hire a full-time proofreader. Then she looked at my work history.

"You haven't worked in quite a while," she noticed.

"I had personal problems," I said, using my newfound strategy for evasion. She looked at me sort of strangely and then asked where she could call for a reference. I suggested Dahl & Curry, my last job in Minneapolis, "Although truthfully," I said, "I don't know what kind of reference they'll give me. I had a lot of problems when I worked there." I was thinking about how I had left Minneapolis without telling Dahl & Curry I wasn't coming back to work.

"I'll call them and let you know in a few days about the job," she said.

That night I worried obsessively about the interview. I wanted that job at the Ink Spot. It was a daytime job, doing something I was well qualified for, and it would pay me enough to save up for an apartment in a few short months. I kept thinking about the look Mary had given me when I said I had personal problems. The next morning I went to the office to talk to Julie about it.

"I'd like to tell this woman the truth," I said. "Personal problems makes it sound like I'm crazy or something. It could mean anything from schizophrenia to a prison term for first-degree murder."

"Go ahead then," said Julie, "Take a risk."

I called Mary on the phone. "I have something I need to tell you," I said. "When you asked me yesterday why I hadn't been working and I said I had personal problems, I thought you might think I was crazy. The truth is that I'm a recovering drug addict. I've been clean and sober for ten months, and I'm in a residential treatment program. I might not get a good reference from Dahl & Curry because I was using drugs the whole time I worked there. But I'm very experienced at the job; I'm committed to my recovery; and I'd very much like to work for you."

There was total silence at the other end of the line. "I'll call you in a couple of days," Mary said finally, her voice cold and impassive.

I went back to the office. "I blew it," I told Julie. "She didn't say anything. Now I know she won't give me the job."

"You don't know that," said Julie. "You'll just have to wait and see. Have some patience; you know, that quality dope fiends never seem to develop? Try it. It builds character." Then she smiled at me. "It'll be okay," she said, "either way."

I called Annemarie, my counselor at Mass. Rehab., and told her what had happened. "Don't worry," she said. "You just tried something new. If it doesn't work out, you can always do something different next time."

Annemarie was helping me find a job, and she was also working on getting me into school for the fall semester. Mass. Rehab. offered recovering addicts the opportunity to complete their education. I had often talked to her about my writing and my fears that I wouldn't be able to do it without drugs. Because I had finished college and had a degree, I wasn't eligible for full educational benefits. But we had worked out a plan whereby I could study a new kind of writing in school and have it qualify as vocational training. I had applied to take fiction writing classes at Emerson College, in the hope that through fiction, which I had never written, I might be able to make sense of some of my more horrifying experiences on the street as a drug addict. It was a longshot, but it had worked. "Congratulations," Annemarie said. "My supervisors just authorized me to pay your tuition at Emerson. So whatever happens with your job, you'll be going to school in September."

The next day the whole house went on a picnic to Lake Cochituate. I tried to get out of it, so I could wait for Mary to call, but Diane insisted that I go. I hung out by myself at the water's edge, trying to work up a tan, until Diane sent one of her daughters to get me. She wanted me to sit with her on her blanket so she could tease me. "Did you ever see that joke they have printed on the T-shirts?" she asked. "It says, 'If you were any lazier, you'd be in a coma.' I think they wrote it about you, Suze."

It was beautifully green and sweet-smelling in the piney woods near the lake, and as usual it was a pleasure to be out of the house. At all our Women, Inc., functions there was a lot of work to do: carrying supplies, barbecuing, looking out for the children, supporting the new women. Despite myself, I ended up having a good time and forgot about the phone call and the job.

Two days later another woman from the Ink Spot called and asked if I could come in for a second interview. She didn't say I had the job, but she didn't say I didn't have it either. So at least I hadn't been automatically disqualified for my drug-addict past. Again I got on the train to Quincy. It took a long time to get there, which I liked. It meant that if I got the job, I would be spending eleven hours, rather than the normal eight, away from the house. I missed one of my connections and arrived there late.

Mary seemed immensely relieved that I had gotten there at all and was pleased to see me. "Let's go into my husband's office, where we can talk in private," she suggested. She led me through the printing shop, where five presses were running full-tilt at a deafening clatter, to an elegant suite of offices in the back. "I want to tell you," she said, "that I appreciate your being so honest with me." Then she offered me the job.

"Since you were open with me," said Mary, "I'm going to be perfectly honest with you about a problem we have here." She warned me that her typesetter was extremely difficult to get along with, that in fact she had driven the last proofreader to tears on a number of occasions, and was so abusive to other typesetters who worked with her that they often quit without giving notice. "Also, there's a lot of pressure here," said Mary. "I would feel really guilty if it caused you to go back to using drugs."

I said I appreciated her concern but thought I could handle both the pressure and the prima donna typesetter. I had spent the last ten months learning how to stand up for myself and get along with all sorts of unpleasant people. We negotiated a salary, and she told me to start work on Monday.

I couldn't wait to get back to the house. "I got a job!" I shouted to my peers the minute I got in the dining room. They all crowded around me, jumping up and down and hugging me.

As I mentioned before, our group took personal triumphs as collective victories in our common struggle against the dope. In a house full of women, there were bound to be rivalries and jealousies, but these feelings were routinely addressed around the table, and once out in the open, they didn't linger long. I was most excited to tell Rhoda, but Janelle beat me to it. "Susan Lucci got a job! Susan Lucci got a job!" she yelled in her husky two-year-old's voice from the top of the stairs as Rhoda came in from work that night.

Rhoda and I sat up talking long after the other women had gone to bed, as we did almost every night, and I told her my fears about the job. I had been fired so many times in the course of my addiction that I didn't know if I was capable of keeping a job. I was afraid that the proofreading would bore me silly without drugs.

"I'm nervous about this typesetter, too," I said. "I'm afraid if she fucks with me, I'll go off. You know how we talk here. When I get angry, I sound like Eddie Murphy, and somehow I don't think that would go over too well in this lily-white office."

"I see," said Rhoda, "that you're still trying to pass for white. Well, don't worry, Sue. I'll never tell."

Then we both had our giggles and went upstairs, for what Rhoda called "our fifteen minutes of allotted sleep time."

Despite these misgivings, I set off for my first day of work with a great feeling of exhilaration. I wore a jade green Belle France dress with a tiny print and a white collar that I had managed to buy with a few days' break from everything but methadone when I worked in New York. I had noticed that Mary favored those kinds of dresses, and I was trying my best to do like the Romans.

The departing proofreader trained me, going over my work after I finished it, and the typesetter yelled at me for being stupid, but my worst problem was that I didn't have the stamina for an eight-hour shift. I was used to having drugs to give me an extra burst of energy when I flagged on the job. I called the house and told Julie that I missed the dope and wanted to get high. She told me that as time went on, I would find new ways to give myself an energy boost without drugs. I was dog-tired by the end of the day, and dragged myself back to the house in a near-stupor.

I signed in at the office, planning to ask if I could take a nap, but the counselors had a surprise for me. They had spent the day shifting all the women around to different rooms, and I had been assigned to share a room with Linda and Ethel, a woman who had recently come into the house pregnant and now had a newborn baby. I had been living in the big corner room for nine months. I was comfortable there, and my string-of-hearts, which my parents had brought from New York, was thriving in a sunny window. I considered its state of health a reflection of my own internal condition.

I groaned. "Why now?" I asked. "Why today? It's my first day of work, and I'm totally exhausted. How will I be able to work when the baby keeps me up all night?" I felt hurt and betrayed.

"That's the way life is," said Joanna. "You have to be ready for change at any time. Go in and eat dinner and then move your stuff. All the moving has to be finished by bedtime tonight."

By the same sheer effort of will that had gotten me home, I moved all my stuff into the new room. At least it was a pretty room, and I got along really well with Linda. But I nursed a resentment against staff. I thought they should support me during my first days of work, not sabotage my energy with more work and adjustments. Luckily I could count on understanding and sympathy from Rhoda when she got home. Both of us hated to move; it kicked up old painful feelings of being forcibly evicted from apartments we'd lived in for years. I'd already seen Rhoda through a few demoralizing room changes she'd had.

"Just think, Sue," she said. "One day we'll actually be out of treatment, and all this will be a distant memory. Not that I believe that myself. Personally I think we'll both be here till we're old and gray, still listening to presentations and moving our stuff from room to room in the middle of the night. It'll be 'the treatment that never ended.'"

The next day I confronted the typesetter about yelling at me my first day on the job, and she apologized. I continued my training with the departing proofreader, and at lunchtime I did a few Arica Psychocalisthenics exercises to try and generate some extra energy. I had to call the house every day from work to report in, and also at the end of the day to tell them I was on my way home. I felt a little better than I had the day before, and by the end of the week I was able to work a full day without any problem. I continued doing Psychocals and began taking vitamins, both ways to get extra energy without drugs. Some days when I got home, I was allowed to nap for half an hour or so, the height of luxury at Women, Inc.

Working outside the house was difficult, and I had to deal with my feelings every night with my peers. Without the drugs to buffer me from reality, I felt everything keenly. I was raw and vulnerable, with no emotional defense against the pressures, slights, aggravations, and frustrations that go with any job.

I had been working in my usual manner at the Ink Spot; I was accustomed to working in shops where my work was checked by a foreman and another proofreader. I worked quickly, getting through a large volume of work, and whatever mistakes I might miss would be caught on the next shift. At first Mary was pleased with my speed and that all the jobs would be read by the end of the day. After a few weeks, however, she called me to her office to complain that a customer had found ten errors in a brochure I read. I felt ashamed—inadequate and stupid—the same way I used to feel when my father criticized a job I had done. "This quality of work is unacceptable to me," Mary said, "and unless your work improves, I'll have to let you go."

Though I was defensive with Mary, blaming all my mistakes on the customer, inside I felt like a failure. I wondered if I had brain damage from the drugs and was no longer competent to proofread. I went to the ladies' room and cried, letting out my feelings of pain and humiliation. Then I got on my knees and prayed, asking God for strength and guidance to help me deal with this problem. I called Annemarie, my vocational counselor, to tell her I was certain I'd be fired from my job. She encouraged me to break the situation down into its components and deal with them one by one. I said that I had been used to reading for speed, sacrificing accuracy. She asked what I could do to improve my accuracy. Read more slowly, I said. Read the jobs several times over. But then I wouldn't have them all done at the end of the day. She told me to present the problem to Mary and ask which she preferred: speed or accuracy.

I put my pride in my back pocket and went to talk to Mary. She said that as I was the only proofreader in the company, it was essential for me to be absolutely accurate. I began reading each job through three or four times: once for specs, once for typos, and once for sense and a final check. I had jobs left over at the end of the day, but I hardly made any mistakes, and Mary came into my office at the end of the next week to tell me she was completely satisfied with the improvement in my work.

It was a new method of working for me and also another first: the first time I had ever found a solution to a problem at a job rather than give up in despair or defiance at the first sign of difficulty. I was beginning to apply the lessons I had learned in treatment to the outside world, and, by some miracle beyond my control or comprehension, they were working out there as well.

chapter eighteen

At the still point of the turning world. Neither
flesh nor fleshless;
Neither from nor towards; at the still point,
there the dance is...

T. S. Eliot,
"Burnt Norton"

FREE AT LAST—1987

The best thing about my job at the Ink Spot was that I worked alone in my own office, a wood-paneled room off the main reception area. The typesetters dropped new jobs to be read into a wire basket under an open window in the back. Light came from three outside windows on the front cinder-block wall. I kept the doors closed for quiet and worked at a large desk in the middle of the room, on a comfortable chair that leaned all the way back, smoking cigarettes and playing the radio to my heart's content.

After the noise and chaos of Women, Inc., I relished my privacy and the peace and quiet I had at my job. I needed it too. Not just to concentrate on the work at hand, but because inwardly I was in an almost constant state of emotional turmoil. Several times each day, I had to drop whatever I was doing and lock myself in the ladies' room to cry and pray. This was a real change for me. I had always spent lots of time in the ladies' room at my jobs, but before it had been for the purpose of getting high. Now I went there to deal with my feelings and pray that I wouldn't get high. The irony of this only slightly altered state of affairs was not lost on me.

Some days, of course, everything went smoothly and I worked in peace and harmony all day. But type shops are notoriously prone to crises and deadlines, and the Ink Spot was no exception. Some therapists say that we recreate the peculiar dysfunctions of our own families in all our relationships, and I certainly did this at my job. In my view Mary, my boss, was a workaholic obsessed with perfection. This particular set of qualities may well be indispensable for entrepreneurial success, but they reminded me so much of my father that I often related to Mary as I had to my father while growing up.

It was not uncommon for Mary to put in close to sixteen hours a day at work. The Ink Spot was her life, and she expected the same dedication from her employees. With my vision unclouded by drugs, I was able to put a hundred percent of my mental effort into my job. I came to work on time, tried to be pleasant, and worked hard to please Mary and get her approval. But I was still in treatment; my life was not my own; I simply could not afford to invest the amount of time and energy into the Ink Spot that she expected of me. So we were frequently at odds. And the typesetter, who was unpleasant but terrifically competent, was openly antagonistic to Mary's extra demands. The atmosphere at work was tense, with frequent blow-ups and silent, simmering feuds.

One day I came home from work exhausted and on the verge of tears. We had had a horrific day at work: too many jobs, too little time, and personality conflicts all day long. Mary had been in my office three times to complain about my work: I wasn't reading enough jobs; I wasn't putting in enough time; I had missed a few typos in a huge job for South Shore Bank. "They called me on the phone," said Mary, "and asked me, 'What's wrong with your proofreader? Is she sleeping on the job?'" It was a lie and I knew it, but still I felt hurt and ashamed. I barely managed to hold it together to the end of the day without screaming at Mary and quitting my job.

When I got home to Women, Inc., the first person I saw was Mollie. I greeted her with a smile, expecting her usual warmth and succor in return. "Don't even speak to me, Lucci," she said in a huff. "Today's my birthday, and where's my card? My feelings are hurt that you don't even have a card for me." I had meant to get her a card on my lunch hour, but it had been so busy at work, I forgot. I burst into tears and went to the office to sign in.

"What's wrong?" said Andrea.

"I had a horrible day at work," I sobbed. "I'm totally exhausted. I hate my boss. I hate my job. I keep making mistakes. I can't do anything right. Now Mollie's mad at me because I didn't get her a birthday card. I feel like giving up on everything. It's just too hard. I try my best to do everything right, and nothing works out. I'm fucked up."

"Of course you're fucked up," said Andrea. "That's normal. We told you this was going to be hard. You're out there naked, without any skin. You don't have the dope to protect you any more. And nobody outside gives a damn about your feelings; they couldn't care less how painful life is for a dope fiend without drugs. All the women get fucked up when they first go out to work. If you weren't fucked up, we'd really be worried about you. So let it go, baby. It's all right. You can have your feelings now."

I cried and cried in the office, sobbing out all my hurt and frustration and fear. I was like a newborn baby in the world, inadequate, scared, and vulnerable, and feeling all of it for the first time without dope to numb the feelings and take the edge off the pain.

Andrea held me while I cried. "Let it go," she said. "It's okay. You'll learn how to deal with it in time." When I finished crying, she smiled at me. "At least you're not fine," she said. "Be grateful for that." At Women, Inc., "fine" was an acronym for "fucked-up, insecure, neurotic, and emotionally disturbed." We were both laughing when Mollie came into the office.

"I'm sorry," I said. "I'll buy you a card tomorrow."

"You better, Lucci," she said. "If you know what's good for you." Then she gave me a big hug. I was home now, and safe.

Other times it was hard to come home from a full day of work and still be in treatment. At my job I made decisions all day long. I was paid to think, for my expertise in rewriting and correcting things. Then I came back to Women, Inc., and had to ask permission to take a nap. Sometimes the counselors refused. "I think," I would start to say, before they interrupted me. "Don't think," one of them would answer. "Your best fucking thinking got you right fucking here." It was humiliating.

My job took such intense concentration that by the end of the day I was burnt out. It was difficult enough to do my tighten-up and participate in weekly events like menu planning, but on many nights we'd have to sit up late listening to endless presentations. My only consolation at these times was when I'd look across the table and catch Rhoda's eye. We'd both roll our eyes at each other and suppress our giggles. It helped that somebody understood.

I felt that I had been able to survive at Women, Inc., only by shutting down whole parts of myself—taste, independence, intellect, discrimination—that would have interfered with my treatment. As I used these qualities at work, they quickly came back to life, and it was hard to suppress them again each night when I came home. I wasn't alone in this. It was quite common for women who worked at outside jobs to feel resentment toward Women, Inc., in their final phase of treatment, a natural result of the conflict between autonomy at work and dependence in the house. I felt like a rebellious teenager. I chafed under the rules and restrictions; I couldn't wait to get out of treatment and live on my own.

And of course this feeling got me into trouble. If I was rebellious at normal times, I was openly angry and defiant at the worst of times, right before my period, when PMS stripped my nerve endings raw and made me feel so edgy I wanted to crawl out of my skin. For about a week before my period, I cried easily and acquired a hair-trigger temper; I would blow up at the slightest provocation. It was hard for me to cope with even minor frustrations at work or in the house. I had often discussed these difficulties with staff, who advised me to proceed with utmost caution and deal with my feelings so that I wouldn't have to act on them.

But I didn't know how to deal with resentment. At this time there were four working women in the house: Rhoda, myself, Charlene, and BJ. One night we came home to find that the women had been given a group LE for failing to provide a recipe for a nutrition seminar. As none of us who worked had been involved in the seminars, we assumed we were exempt from the group LE. We asked coverage staff about it, but they were confused and didn't know. BJ decided to participate in the LE, a major cleanup of the downstairs day-care area; but Rhoda, Charlene, and I opted for what Rhoda liked to call "life on the sleazeball plan," the lazy way out.

The next morning I had terrible menstrual cramps. On my way out, I asked Julie if I could buy some Advil to bring to work. She said no. I argued with her, but she still refused. I bought the Advil anyway and kept it in my desk at work. That night, after morning meeting papers, I told Rhoda what I'd done. She sympathized with my reasons for doing it, but advised me to tell staff about it, rather than hold onto the guilt.

So I told Julie the next morning. On my lunch break, when I normally called Women, Inc., Joanna said Diane wanted to talk to me and that I should call back in a few hours. I was premenstrual and emotionally overwrought anyway, but by the time I spoke to Diane, my emotions had reached the breaking point.

"You know you're going to get consequences for that bottle of Advil, don't you?" she asked.

"Yes," I said miserably. I immediately envisioned having to clean the filthy, haunted basement by myself; the further along you were in treatment, the harder the LEs got.

"Why did you do it?" Diane asked me.

"I was afraid I wouldn't be able to work with such bad cramps," I said. "I'm scared of losing my job."

"Look, Suze," Diane said. "Losing that job wouldn't kill you, and keeping it isn't going to save your life. But not dealing with your feelings, that will kill you. What's the matter with you? Don't you trust us any more?"

At that I broke down in tears. I was on the office phone in the supply room. As my co-workers walked past, giving me puzzled looks, I sobbed out my hurt and resentment to Diane on the phone. "It hurt my feelings when you all made me change rooms my first night of work," I said. "I felt like staff didn't care about supporting me with my job. I've been feeling lost and alone. I was in pain when I asked Julie for the Advil, and I felt like she didn't care."

"Come on with it," Diane said. "Come on with all the feelings." I cried for fifteen minutes on the phone. I'd been feeling abandoned by Diane; I'd missed her caring and support. It was comforting to have her there again.

I felt tremendous relief when I got through crying. "Are you finished dealing with your feelings?" Diane asked. "Because if you are, I have something for you. You're going to do two LEs tonight when you get home from work. For buying the Advil, you have to strip, wash, and wax the dining room floor. But before you start that, you'll be cleaning the day-care classroom. That's for not participating in the group LE the other night. That really made me mad. Who do you think you are? I want you to ask yourself that question this afternoon, while you look forward to those two LEs tonight: Who do you think you are?" Then she hung up the phone.

I stood there for a minute, stunned. I was already exhausted and in pain. I would have to do a lot of explaining to Mary about that long, hysterical phone call in the middle of the afternoon. I still had several large jobs to read. And now I was going to be up all night cleaning, a prospect I faced with dread. I was angry too. I had been working now for a couple of months. Treatment was almost over for me. The thought crossed my mind to just not go home. On the way to the T after work, I was so tired that I wanted to lay down on the sidewalk and go to sleep right there. I hated Women, Inc., at that moment as much as I had ever hated anyone or anything in my life.

Diane smiled when she saw me walk into the dining room.

"You came home," she said.

"I thought about not coming; I'll tell you that," I answered.

"Oh, I knew you'd come," said Diane. "Where else do you have to go?"

Encouraged by her friendliness, I threw myself on her mercy. "Diane, I have to sleep at night. If I'm tired, I make mistakes, and if I make mistakes, I'll get fired. How am I supposed to do two LEs and then go to work in the morning?"

"You'll do it," she said. "Just put one foot in front of the other and keep going till it's done. You won't die from lack of sleep either, so don't even try that one on me. I'll see you tomorrow." She put on her coat and went home.

I ate dinner and went downstairs to start my LE. The classroom wasn't too bad. I was finished by ten. Then I started on the dining room. I stripped the floor with ammonia, washed it, and applied two coats of wax. I finished at two in the morning. Ramona, a recent graduate who worked as the nighttime counselor, came in and okayed the floor, and I went to bed.

The next day Diane called me at work. "Your LE was not accepted," she said. "The classroom was okay, but you didn't strip the dining room floor. So you have to do it again tonight. You can start after everyone goes to bed."

"I'm pissed," I said.

"That's okay," said Diane. "You can take it out on the floor."

I came home in even greater resentment and despair than I had the day before and wrote it all down on my morning meeting paper. After everyone had gone to bed, Undreea, a large, strapping woman who was as strong as any man and the most meticulous cleaner in the house, helped me break the tables down. "I don't see what's wrong with this floor," she said. "It looks good to me." I didn't either, but again I poured ammonia on it and started to mop up the wax I had put on the night before.

Ramona came into the dining room. "You're still not stripping the floor," she said.

"What are you talking about?" I asked, trying to control my sarcasm. I was almost choking on the ammonia fumes.

"You have to get the scraper from the office and scrape up the old wax on your hands and knees," she said.

Now I was totally enraged, but I didn't want to have to do the floor again the next night too, so I did as I was told. At two in the morning, I was still on my hands and knees with the scraper, feeling more and more hopeless by the minute. There was years' worth of accumulated wax on this floor, too much to do in one night. My hand ached, my mind was numb, and my body was moving on automatic pilot.

"Wax on. Wax off," I said to myself to keep going. I was thinking of the movie *The Karate Kid,* where the *sensei* trains his student in martial arts by giving him household chores to do. After several grueling days of polishing cars and painting fences, the student explodes in rage, accusing his teacher of exploiting him. But all the while he's been learning karate: practicing its movements in the repetitive domestic tasks.

All of a sudden, I had a flash of insight. What I was doing was like a Zen training. Women, Inc., with its scant financial resources, simply utilized the humble materials it had at hand, cleaning supplies and a big, funky house, to provide what was in essence a spiritual teaching. I looked down at the floor. Little by little the old wax was coming off. It wasn't hopeless at all. I saw that with a patient repetition of small efforts, even the largest task could be accomplished in time.

"They're trying to teach me patience," I thought to myself, and marveled at their brilliance. At that moment Ramona came in and told me I had scraped enough. "Put on the wax and go to bed," she said. I finished at four.

The next morning I was almost giddy with lack of sleep. Fortunately the work load was light, and I took advantage of the downtime to write in my notebook. For the first time since I had cleaned up from drugs, I felt my creativity take flight. It was a wonderful feeling. I kept on writing in my notebook, as I had in the old days at Dahl & Curry, high on the exhilaration and pure sweet pleasure of scribbling words on paper. I felt like I was witness to a miracle, one that had come about by totally unexpected means. "I'm writing!" I babbled to Julie when I called the house at lunchtime. "I'm writing again, in my notebook!"

Later that afternoon I called Diane to ask if my LE had been accepted. "What did you learn from it?" she asked.

"Patience," I said. "I learned that even the largest task can be accomplished bit by bit if you just keep at it."

"That's it," she said. "You learned the lesson. You all always think you accomplished something if the floor looks good. We don't give a damn how the floor looks. We care what you learn. That's why it's called a learning experience. Get it?"

"You're pretty clever," I said, "the way you use housework to teach these lessons."

"Does that mean you're over your resentment?" she asked.

"Yes," I said. "I'm tired but I feel fantastic. I'm writing again. It's a miracle. Thank you."

Diane laughed, a deep, throaty chuckle. "Did you ever think, in your wildest dreams, you'd be thanking me for giving you an LE?"

"No," I said. "But nothing is ever the way it appears."

"Well, Suze," said Diane. "You're at the end of your treatment. You're almost ready to leave the house. We know you can't wait to go, but without patience you'll never be able to stay clean. That was the piece that was missing from your survival kit. And humility. Who do you think you are? That's a question you should ask yourself a lot." Then she laughed again. "I know you're glad you don't have that floor to do tonight."

And I was.

Within a week staff had given me permission to look for an apartment. I felt somewhat daunted by the prospect. Rhoda had been looking for an apartment for months without success; that was why she was still in the house. "Why don't you look in Quincy, where you work?" Diane suggested.

"It's too white there," I said.

"Too white?" said Diane, "What are you?"

"I'm Jewish," I answered, "They hate me as much as they hate you."

"All right, then," said Diane. "Look wherever you like."

I didn't have any real idea where to look, but one Saturday I was out shopping at Dudley Station, and I picked up a paper. Rain was pouring down outside. I looked through the classifieds, and a listing in Mattapan jumped off the page at me. I had heard of Mattapan. Several women in the house came from there. It was a black neighborhood, considered slightly better than Dorchester/Roxbury, where we lived. I called the house and asked if I could go, and they gave me directions.

I rode the bus in the rain all the way down Blue Hill Avenue, almost to the end of the line, got off at Mattapan Square, and walked up a little curving street between a Brigham's ice cream store and a Shawmut Bank to a three-story brick building on a corner of Cummins Highway. The building manager, Mr. Baker, an ancient, toothless white man whose clothes smelled strongly of cats, took me to see the apartment that had been advertised in the paper, a dingy one-bedroom affair. "Do you have any others?" I asked. "A studio," he said.

We went upstairs to the third floor, and he opened the door to the studio, a large, round, corner room, painted white, with three good-sized windows and a nice wooden floor. The round room was light and airy; it reminded me of Candace's office. The kitchen was just big enough to eat in, cozy and charming. I liked the large black-and-white checkerboard squares of the floor and the way the double window looked up the street, over some treetops, and onto a big piece of sky. The rent was four hundred and fifty dollars a month, which I could manage.

Immediately I thought of the sunny, plant-filled place I'd envisioned during treatment. "I like it," I told Mr. Baker. "I like it a lot." He went to the window and called the owner, a Lebanese man, who came up with a rental application and said he would need $1,350 for me to move in. The apartment was available for September 1, three days from now. I sat in the round room for quite a while and filled out the application. I liked the apartment, but privately had my doubts that I could get it. Things just didn't move that fast at Women, Inc., particularly with Diane on vacation, as she currently was. Also, though I had money saved up from my job, I was a little short of $1,350. And it was the first place I had seen. But I told Mr. Baker, who seemed very friendly and pleased that I liked the apartment, that I would contact him Monday.

Diane was due back from vacation on Monday. There was a slim, outside chance I could get her attention when I called from work and ask for permission to take the apartment. I knew, however, it was far more likely that I wouldn't be able to get to her in time or that she would say no. So I didn't want to get my hopes up. I had some trepidation about telling Rhoda I'd found a place I liked when she had been looking for months. But she was happy for me and even volunteered to lend me the extra money I'd need. As much as I didn't want to set myself up for disappointment, I couldn't stop thinking about the apartment. I visualized myself living there, imagining where I'd put the furniture in the round room and how I'd decorate the kitchen. From the way my mind stubbornly refused to stray from these fantasies, I knew the place was perfect for me.

I went to work Monday morning in a state of high anxiety. At lunchtime I walked to the pay phone on Hancock Street and called Mr. Baker. "I want the apartment, but I don't know if I'll be able to tell you today," I said.

"I'll put off the owner as long as I can," he promised, "but you have to let me know soon."

Then I took a deep breath and called the house. "Can I speak to Diane?" I asked. I fully expected to be told that she was tied up in a meeting, but miraculously, her voice came on the phone. "Diane," I said, "I found this apartment I like."

"I heard," she said. "Where is it?"

"In Mattapan," I said.

"Mattapan would be okay for you," she said. "It's a little safer than Roxbury."

"It's available September 1," I said. She had given me a termination date in October, a month away.

"What are you asking?" said Diane. "Be direct."

"Can I get it?"

"You wouldn't be able to move right away," she said. "You might have to pay double rent for September. Would you be willing to do that?"

"Yes."

"Then it's yours."

"Oh, my God!" I just about yelled into the phone. "I don't believe it!"

"Why not?" she said. "We told you to look for an apartment."

"But I expected you to say no," I protested.

"I keep telling you, Suze," Diane said, "that you don't know everything. Now do you believe me?"

What I couldn't quite believe was that I was really going to leave treatment. Rhoda had her usual "mixed feelings" (the same ones she

wrote on her morning meeting paper each night) when I told her my incredible news. "I'm happy for you," she said, "but there's no way I could
stand to stay here with you gone. Fuck an apartment; I'm just going to
rent me a room and look for an apartment from there."

The next day, true to her word, she rented herself a room in a boarding house. Staff gave us the same termination date: September 16. We
could hardly contain our excitement, or our disbelief. We were sure
something horrible would happen before we could actually leave. Our
peers were envious, but they got over it. "I'm jealous," Michele said, "but
at least I can look at you two and know that there really is an end to this.
If you two can leave, someday so can I."

When I went back to Mattapan to bring Mr. Baker the money, he
gave me a big, smelly hug. "I'll tell you a little secret," he chuckled.
"Right after you looked at the apartment, I went to my daughter's. I
didn't answer the phone for three days. I didn't want anyone to have that
apartment but you."

Then he took me to the basement and showed me some furniture I
could have for very little money: a bed, dresser, table and chairs, almost
everything I needed. As it happened, there was also a bus that ran direct
from Mattapan to Quincy, so getting to work in the morning would be a
lot simpler than it was from Women, Inc. Things were falling nicely into
place, almost as if my life were being orchestrated by someone other
than myself. Could it be the Higher Power I had heard so much about in
meetings?

I wondered the same thing again a few days later when I went to register for school. A fine mist was falling in the early autumn twilight. I
walked through the Boston Public Gardens on my way to Beacon Street.
As if for the first time, I noticed the beauty of the weeping willows, the
gracefulness of the swans. I felt like I was in a state of grace myself. For
years I'd been wanting to study creative writing in school. I'd talked
about it, but my addiction wouldn't allow it. Now it was actually happening; I was becoming the woman I'd always wanted to be.

At the corner of the Public Gardens, on Beacon Street, I came upon
a Victorian statue of a beautiful angel with her wings outstretched. The
inscription on the statue read, "Cast thy bread upon the waters, for thou
shalt find it many days from now." It moved me to tears; not sad tears,
but tears of gratitude. I'd thrown away everything I had and knew, in

blind faith, that something better would come back to me. Now it had, in the fulfillment of one of my heart's desires. Somehow, mysteriously, I'd been blessed.

I went to register at school, and when I was done, I sat down under a willow tree and wrote a poem. I wanted to put these new, confusing feelings into words. My mood was so elated, I even felt good going back to the house.

Rhoda and I had a lot to do before our termination date. We had to arrange for utilities to be turned on, write budgets for our proposed moves, terminate with each of the counselors separately, and write lists of our short- and long-term goals. Plus we had to continue participating in treatment and going to work. In the midst of this, I had my one-year anniversary, celebrated in the house with a cake and a party. Despite all our busy work, the last few weeks of treatment seemed unbearably long. It reminded me of jail. I could stand being in jail with no end in sight, but the minute I knew I was being released, the last little remaining time dragged on interminably. So much was happening that I barely had time to sort out my feelings.

Finally the day arrived. We had terminations with all our peers around the table, much like introductions when a new woman arrived in the house. The reason for this, according to staff, was to learn how to end relationships and leave places gracefully, with no hard feelings. We left on a Tuesday night, so that we would have only one night to spend alone before we had to report to Re-entry group, which met each Wednesday evening. Rhoda and I had already been introduced to Re-entry the previous week, to make our transition easier. Now we were official grownups. My terminations with individual staff members had been both informative and emotionally charged. Much of the advice I'd received was ringing in my ears. In the long-term goals I had written for Diane, I said I hoped to be able to make a living from my writing, and to have a committed relationship with a man. Since I'd been secluded in an all-women's treatment center for nearly a year, sex was heavily on my mind, and I'd also included in my short-term goals my desire for some sort of sexual relationship.

"This really bothers me," said Diane. "All this focus on relationships. What will you do if you don't have one? It's possible, you know."

"I really want one," I said, "but if it doesn't happen, I'm not going to just lay down and die. I mean, I won't shoot dope over it."

"I hope not," said Diane. "Personally, I don't think you're ready to deal with men right now. But knowing you, you're going to do what you want anyway. So just be careful. You'll be really vulnerable just getting out of treatment. A lot of men at those meetings are looking for fresh meat, women who don't know any better. They'll use you and then they'll talk about you like a dog; yes, even in recovery. Just because they go to meetings, that doesn't mean they're well. There's a lot of AIDS out there too, so remember safe sex. If you have sex, use a rubber. And don't sell yourself cheap. You're a Women, Inc., woman. Have some respect for yourself. You deserve it."

I moved into my apartment. The first call I made on my new phone was to Tommy's brother in Minneapolis. Tommy wasn't there. "Where you at?" his brother asked me.

"I'm in Boston," I said. "I just got out of treatment. I've been clean for a year."

"Oh," he said, "and now you want to hook up with my brother and start the whole thing all over again, huh?"

I was speechless for a moment. What he'd said was exactly what one of my peers or counselors would have said; it gave me pause. "Just tell him I called," I said, "and give him this number."

I expected to feel happy being out of treatment, but the first few weeks were incredibly hard. I felt disoriented, lonely, and vulnerable, like I was walking around without any skin and everyone could see it. I didn't wait long to have sex, with a guy I'd been carrying on a flirtation with in meetings for months, and that, too, was disappointing. It bothered me that he wasn't Tommy. Without feelings, or drugs to conceal their lack, the sex felt empty and mechanical. And the great affair I'd fantasized having with this guy while I was in treatment never materialized; it turned out to be a one-night stand. Then I made the mistake of saying I was lonely in a meeting, and several men took it as an invitation to hit on me. I turned them down, but their come-ons made me feel cheap and sleazy, like I was still doing prostitution on the street. I missed the warmth and protection of Women, Inc., the feeling of community, the security of belonging. It was cold and lonely in the world outside, and my heart was heavy with sadness. As with all my other losses, I had to grieve for this one as well.

I went to the house three times a week to have my urine tested for drugs, and at first I tried to hide my feelings. "How is it, Lucci?" Michele asked me. "I bet it feels good to be out of here. You can do whatever you want, have sex, go to bed when you feel like it, eat what you like. It must be great."

"It's okay," I said, trying my best not to show the heartbreak and loneliness I felt inside. But I couldn't hide it from Diane. One Friday night, shortly after I had moved out of the house, I went with some of the women to a church nearby where Diane had set up a table to sell the jewelry she made in her spare time. "Let's go out and have a cigarette," she suggested to me. When we got outside, she put her arms around me, and I broke down in great shaking sobs. "It's not like you thought it would be, is it?" she asked gently.

"No," I answered.

"I know you were trying to act as if," she said. "But I saw you crying on the inside. Sometimes all it takes is a touch to bring out the real feelings."

The sadness and loneliness went on for quite a while. "As much as you hated all those women and couldn't wait to get away from them, you really got attached to them and you miss them now, don't you?" Diane asked me one day in the office, when I went to give a urine after work. "It's because you're a real human being, with real human feelings," she said. "Someday you'll even be grateful that you can have those feelings, no matter how much they hurt." The other women in Re-entry said they had felt sad and lonely for a long time after they left the house, too. We all talked to each other a lot on the phone, which was a help.

I got some consolation from an unexpected source: in my loneliness I discovered the solace of nature. My apartment was only a few short blocks away from the little bridge over the Neponset River, which separated Mattapan from Milton. I had to cross the bridge every morning to wait for the bus, and I got in the habit of saying my morning prayers to the river. The southernmost tip of Boston, where I lived, was very beautiful. It was close to the Blue Hills, which I could see from my bathroom window; the air was unexpectedly clear for a city; and the river was an ever-changing source of delight.

In the evenings, before dark, the sky turned a wonderful shade of crisp azure blue. The houses silhouetted in black, still lit with golden overtones from the fading sunlight, against this magnificent turquoise sky, looked exactly like a Maxfield Parrish painting. I was surprised to discover that Parrish, whose home was in New England, had actually painted from nature. I had always thought that his vivid shades of blue were a product of his imagination, part of the landscape of dreams, rather than reality. I had a large view of the darkening sky from my kitchen window, and I enjoyed it immensely.

Instead of having the romantic relationship I had envisioned for my new life outside treatment, I concentrated on having a relationship with myself, my surroundings, and my Higher Power, especially as it manifested in nature. Mollie and Kathy, the two Re-entry counselors, advised us to deal with loneliness by experiencing it; "the only way out is through" applied here as well. They told us not to run from loneliness or try to escape it with activity or men, but just to sit with the feeling until we were comfortable with it and no longer feared it. They promised that growth would come from following this simple path.

I had decorated my kitchen just as I had imagined, with an antique lace tablecloth over the windows, and a philodendron that eventually grew to surround them. I had a nice solid oak table, which Mr. Baker had given me, and I bought a wicker armchair from an antique shop in Quincy. The kitchen was where I cooked and ate, and also where I wrote. A man I knew in the Twelve-Step fellowship fixed my old red IBM Selectric for a ridiculously low price. It hadn't worked since Ninety-Fourth Street, and was the first of many things I was to retrieve from the ravages of my addiction. I had plants and hanging crystals in my bathroom window; my string-of-hearts was thriving for the first time since I had changed rooms at Women, Inc., and rainbows danced on my bathroom walls. I loved my apartment and was always happy to come home to it at the end of a day's work.

Shortly after we moved out of the house, Rhoda had found an inexpensive apartment in Dorchester. Both of us worried we would lose our apartments, lingering fears from evictions we'd both experienced when using drugs. It was overwhelming for us just to take care of our basic needs and responsibilities: go to work, pay bills, shop for groceries, do laundry, and show up at Women, Inc., for urines and Re-entry. We talked every night on the phone and still shared everything with each other. I went to meetings almost every night. As the weather got cold, it was a struggle to wait for the bus, take the train, and walk from the train to the meetings in the dark, cold, sometimes rainy nights. But as soon as I walked into the light and warmth of a meeting, I felt like I had come home. I made some friends in the fellowship and almost always managed to get a ride home. My support network was growing beyond Women, Inc.

I was still naive, however, about the men in the fellowship, and inclined to overlook Diane's warning. With money left over from my bills, I had bought myself some new clothes: black cotton leggings, fleece-lined ankle-high snow boots, and a beautiful bright red suede jacket I found on sale. I felt cute in these clothes, and it gave me the courage to flirt with some of the men I liked in the fellowship. There was a guy named John I had my eye on for about six months. He ran one of the outside meetings we'd attended from treatment. John was nice looking and soft spoken; he had always been kind and respectful to the women in our group. I considered him sensitive, intelligent, and serious about his recovery.

One night John gave me a ride home from a meeting, and I invited him up to my apartment for coffee. We sat in the kitchen talking for a while. When the talk got scary, old war stories from our desperado drug-using days, he asked me for a hug. The hug went on a little longer than the normal friendly fellowship embrace, but I didn't think much about it. Then he put his hand under my chin, lifted up my face to his, and kissed me. I thought about resisting, but it felt too good. We kissed for a long time. Long, slow, sensual kisses like those have been a lifetime weakness of mine. My resistance melted; my legs turned to jelly; and before too long, we were lying on my bed.

"I'm scared," I said. "This feels too good."

"I better go home," said John. "I don't think we should sleep together. It's too soon. I don't want to lose your friendship."

Then we started kissing again. I hadn't felt like this since I was a teenager in the fifties, when marathon make-out sessions were the adolescent norm. It felt deliciously romantic, better than actual sex.

"Now I'm scared," said John. "You're so soft. What do you think? Should I stay?"

"You might as well," I said. "The damage is already done." I meant that all that kissing had already brought up feelings in me that wouldn't be changed, one way or the other, by having or not having sex. At least that's what I thought I meant.

But the sex was disappointing. As a lover John was cold and detached. Once again I felt empty and used. And when I didn't hear from

John for days afterward, I was so upset I had to deal with my feelings in Re-entry.

I expected a confrontation, and I got it. "What, are you trying to sleep with every man in the fellowship?" said Mollie. "Are you that determined to get a reputation as a whore?"

I was crying as I talked, trying to explain myself through the shame and confusion. "All this self-empowerment is fine," I said, "except when it comes to men. He kissed me and I couldn't resist. I felt like I was powerless to stop."

"Bullshit," yelled Mollie. "Feelings aren't facts. You know that as well as anyone. If you can't say no to a man, Lucci, how the hell do you expect to turn down a bag of dope? Don't you know that man is a total sleaze? He's sleeping with four different women in the fellowship and bragging to all the men about what he's doing."

That made me cry all the harder. "I didn't know," I sobbed. "I thought he cared about me. I always think men care about who I really am inside when all they want is sex."

Kathy, the other Re-entry couselor, with whom I had not yet developed a relationship of trust, was surprisingly gentle. "Why don't you just get through your feelings, Susan, and then tell us what happened," she suggested.

I finished crying and told the story as best I remembered it. "We talked about it first," I said. "He said he thought it might be too soon for us to sleep together. I was the one who said we might as well because the damage was already done."

"What did you mean by that?" asked Kathy.

"That I already had feelings for him from the kissing," I said. A wave of shame washed over me, followed by a flash of recognition; some tiny familiar feeling was stirring deep inside my gut. "Maybe what I really meant," I said in a voice as small as the feeling, "is that I'm already so damaged, a little more sex wouldn't make any difference. I'm already damaged beyond repair." I burst into tears again, but this time my tears came from a deeper place, a wound so dark and buried that it hurt even to touch it. I was crying uncontrollably now, bent over, holding my stomach, and rocking back and forth so I wouldn't break apart in a million pieces.

"Stay with it," said Kathy. "Put some words to the feeling. When were you damaged beyond repair?"

"I don't know," I wailed. "I don't remember it. Maybe it never really happened. But it hurts so much I can hardly stand it. And I don't even know what happened."

"You were a little girl," said Kathy. "Isn't that right? A child. Did you feel like you had the right to say no?"

"No," I sobbed.

"And did you feel like you had the right to say no to this man you slept with the other night?"

"Not really," I answered.

"Think about this," said Kathy, her voice gentle as silk, "You can never really say yes until you give yourself the right to say no. You were a child when this all started. It wasn't your fault. You really were powerless then. I know how much this hurts. I know because it happened to me too. But I tell you this from the bottom of my heart, Susan: None of us is damaged beyond repair."

The next day at work I couldn't put out of my mind what had happened in Re-entry. I felt shaken and fragile, like a defenseless child. At lunchtime I went to walk in the woods near work to try to pull myself together. As I walked I thought about what I was beginning to identify as incest, everything I knew from beginning to end. After I asked my mother at Conifer Park if I had been molested as a child, she had told my sister Lorraine, who was three years younger than me. Although Lorraine and I had never once discussed this subject in our entire lives, she had, independently of me, come to the same conclusion about herself: that she had been sexually abused in childhood.

I had talked to Lorraine about it on the phone. "I don't really remember what happened," she said. "I know I was very young." She thought it had something to do with our alcoholic grandfather and his friends. "Another thing I know," she said, "is that you and I were probably together when it happened."

"What made you even suspect it?" I asked her.

"The terror I have around being trapped," she said. "My phobias. Feelings that come up during sex that I couldn't explain. How about you?"

"The same," I said. "Only with me it's shame. And other feelings that don't make any sense."

I thought about our conversation as I walked out of the woods, on my way back to work. We were somewhat distant now, but Lorraine and I had been inseparable as children. I was the older sister, and watched out for her, the younger. All of a sudden, I was overwhelmed with feelings. "Oh my God," I said out loud, "I couldn't even protect my baby sister." I was walking on Hancock Street, in plain view of all the passing traffic, but I couldn't hold back the tears that came in great, convulsive waves. I was sobbing so violently that I had to sit down on a low stone wall outside a house. I put my face in my hands and wept for Lorraine, for me, for the innocent children we'd been, and for the hidden, unfair pain we'd suffered ever since. "Oh, God," I cried. "She was my little sister. I was supposed to take care of her. And I couldn't even do it."

"Are you all right?" a voice said next to me. I looked up. The voice belonged to Renee, a young woman who'd come to work at the Ink Spot about a month before. I didn't particularly like her; she was loud and flaky and couldn't do her job. I suspected her of being an alcoholic and a drug user. "Take this tissue," she said. "You look like you could use it."

"I just need to cry this out," I said.

"That's okay," said Renee. "I'll sit here with you and wait till you're ready to go back to work."

I cried in my office that afternoon at work. Renee came in to see me. "I'm sorry," I said. "I can't stop crying."

"Don't apologize," she said. "It's awesome for me to see you like this. I feel like you're crying for my pain too. I have pain that big inside of me, but I don't know how to let it out. Maybe you can show me."

"I have to do this," I told Renee. "I'm a recovering drug addict, and I'm in a program that says if I don't have my feelings, I'll end up shooting dope again."

"How long have you been clean?" she asked me.

"Just over a year," I said.

"Go ahead and cry then," Renee said with a laugh. "You must be doing something right."

I cried on the bus going home from work and alone in my apartment as well. The next day, after crying on and off all day again at work, I went to see Diane in desperation.

"I can't stop crying," I told her. "It's this incest stuff. And the crazy thing is, I don't even know what happened. I don't even know if it happened. But these are some of the strongest feelings I've ever had. I feel like I'm falling apart, and I don't know what to do."

"Well," said Diane. "You may never know what happened. You might have to live with that uncertainty for the rest of your life. I know this incest stuff is painful, but I don't think that's all that's going on with you. What I think is that you're experiencing the total devastation of your self-esteem by the dope. I know you think you felt all that before, but it comes up more in relationships with men and around all your sexual issues. It hurts like a toothache now, I know, but in time you'll build your self-esteem back up. Slowly, bit by bit, you'll begin to feel better about yourself. And you do know what to do. Walk through the feeling. This too shall pass."

Every Monday night I went to school. I had found an old piece of writing I liked in the trunk of manuscripts that my father had brought from New York, and was expanding it into a story for class. I worried that my teacher and the other students wouldn't be interested in characters who were junkies; that my material would be judged shocking, distasteful, grim, or inappropriate. I had very little time to write. I was too tired when I got home from work, and on Saturdays I shopped for groceries and did laundry. So I usually only wrote on Sunday, the day before class. I was surprised to find that contrary to my expectations, the class loved my story-in-progress. I started out writing it in three-page segments, and at the end of my reading each week, everyone would be on the edge of their seats with excitement, hungry for more. Best of all, I was writing without drugs, a surprising and gratifying accomplishment.

I had felt insecure about my ability to write fiction, but as it turned out, many of the skills I had practiced for years in journalism—pacing, scenes, description, dialogue—translated very well to fiction. I had a lot to learn, but I was doing better than I had ever expected to do. The strangest thing for me was that as I went deeper into the story, I actually felt like I had entered into that part of my past; whole conversations and events I had believed forgotten returned to my mind crystal clear. The events I was writing about had been harrowing at the time, and it was somewhat unnerving and painful to relive them. Often on Sunday nights I went to a big meeting at Freeport Hall, and several times, after working on my story, I had to grab one of my peers out of the meeting and bring her into the ladies' room so I could cry on her shoulder.

I sent my writing in the mail to Shuna at college and to Tamara, still one of my oldest and closest friends, in San Francisco. Tamara and I had been corresponding regularly since she had found out where I was from

my sister Sheila. She had been a great source of encouragement and support for me, and as she was a writer as well, I trusted her literary judgment.

The further I got in my story, the more it began to obsess me. The
characters sort of took over my mind, and I thought about them constantly, wondering what would happen to them next. I was so preoccupied with my story that one dark, stormy night in November, as I walked
the mile from my job to the Quincy Center T-stop on my way home from
work, I stepped off a curb and fell flat on my face in the rain-soaked
street. As I laid in the street, a car full of teenagers pulled up to the light,
and one of them leaned out the window. "Ha, ha, ha, you stupid whore,"
he yelled. Despite the cold, I felt hot with shame.

I dragged myself up off the ground and gingerly put some weight on
my leg. My ankle hurt, but I could walk on it. I hobbled to the T and
went home on the bus. The next morning my ankle was swollen, black
and blue, throbbing with pain. I called Renee at work, and she came and
took me to the doctor, who diagnosed a minor sprain. The fall had aggra-
vated the disc problem in my lower back, which kept me out of work for
several weeks.

The accident turned out to be a blessing in disguise. I was able to stay
home and work on my story until it was finished to my satisfaction. Not
only did I end up with a sizable piece of work I liked, but I discovered
another benefit as well. Though I stayed by myself all day and couldn't go
out to meetings at night, so long as I was writing, I never felt lonely. The
cure for loneliness, I decided, was not in establishing a relationship with
someone else, but in improving my relationship with myself.

Shuna came to Boston for my forty-fourth birthday. Her hair was blue
and purple, like the feathers of an exotic bird-of-paradise. She brought a
friend with her from college. My apartment was not big enough to hold
three people, so we stayed with my friend Linda in Weston. Linda was an
old friend from New York Arica days. I had contacted her cautiously,
when I got Phase 3. The caution came from the fact that we had gotten
high together on many occasions in New York, and I didn't know if our
old relationship would survive the loss of drugs. To my surprise our
friendship was better than ever. I often spent time with Linda on weekends. One Sunday as we arrived at my house, a drug dealer who habitu-

ally hung out on the stoop outside my building asked us if we would like to buy some cocaine. We collapsed in giggles as we slammed the door behind us. "If he only knew," said Linda.

Through Linda I hooked up with the small Arica community in Boston, and sometimes participated in their meditations and parties. I still had to proceed with caution, turning down their invitations and going to meetings instead at the times I felt endangered. But I had been afraid I couldn't be in Arica and stay clean, and that fear turned out to be as groundless as the fear of not being able to write without drugs, another lie of the dope.

Shuna had spent a lot of time with Linda and her kids while they were all growing up in the Arica community, and we had something of a mini family reunion. I spent my birthday in Linda's light green living room, in the warmth of candlelight, surrounded by my blue-haired daughter, my old friend, and her daughter, Bhava, who had always been a favorite of mine. It was a sweet, quiet, nourishing time. I was touched that Shuna had come all the way to Boston to celebrate my birthday with me, and moved by the peacefulness of our small family gathering. I remembered countless other times when Linda and I had ignored our kids so that we could concentrate on getting high. This time all of us were really present, and the good feelings we had came from inside our hearts, rather than from the false stimulation of drugs.

I went to New York for Thanksgiving. I had to fight the Re-entry counselors for permission to go. "I haven't seen my brother and sister in over a year," I said. "And I live with drug-dealing right on my doorstep and don't get high, so I feel I can handle it."

"You'd better put protection around yourself by going to plenty of meetings," said Mollie.

She didn't have to worry about that. I was so frightened myself of being in New York City that the only way I would consent to have dinner with Mary Peacock, my *Village Voice* editor and longtime friend, was by planning to go to a meeting first and a meeting afterward.

I went to meetings on the Lower East Side. After the first one, I caught a cab to pick Mary up in Soho. As the cab passed the park on Houston and Allen where I had spent so much time copping Elegant, I felt a tugging at my heart so powerful that it was all I could do not to jump right out of the moving vehicle. My addiction worked overtime on that trip, trying to convince me to go look up my street friends, "just to say hi and see how they're doing," or drive by Second Street and Avenue B, "just to check it out." I resisted all the cravings, but it hurt like hell. I felt like a widow revisiting old familiar places for the first time since the funeral, keenly aware of the beloved's absence, alone and bereaved. Everything I saw there broke my heart.

After our dinner I went to a midnight meeting at the HOW club on St. Mark's Place. I had my hand up the whole time, but I didn't get to speak till they called for the burning desires. "It's a miracle for me to be here in a meeting on the Lower East Side," I said. "I always knew where this place was; I passed it every day of my life on my way to go get high. Now I'm inside it, clean. I don't have a habit, and by the grace of God, I never have to have one again, if I don't use drugs one day at a time. Thank you for being here in the midst of the battle."

I had a good time at my sister's house. I read my story, which I had named "Red Shoes with Heroin," to my brother, Ricky, one morning, while he sat across from me at the dining room table painting a water-color. Both of us were crying by the time I got through. I helped my sister with dinner for the first time since I could remember; I had always come four or five hours late to my family's Thanksgivings, because it was so hard to cop on major holidays. I played with Darryl, and Dani did my hair. Sheila went through her closet and sent me back to Boston in all new clothes. I had a lot to be thankful for.

When I went back to work, I noticed that Renee was becoming more and more erratic on the job. She frequently came in late, called in sick, or appeared looking so haggard and bedraggled that I wondered how she'd make it through the day. One morning I found her alone in the supply room. She was a pretty girl, but today she just looked tired and miserable. "Do you get high?" I asked her.

"Yeah," she said. "How'd you know?"

"I told you, I'm a drug addict," I said. "It takes one to know one." By this time I had grown to like Renee, and I didn't want to see her have to go through what I'd been through. "Look," I said, "if it gets too rough for you, and you want to stop, come talk to me. I'll take you to a meeting."

Renee became my first sponsee. She was young, only a few years older than Shuna, and sometimes I felt like I'd acquired another daughter. Other times I confided all my troubles to Renee, and came to value her feedback and advice. She reminded me a lot of myself. She was smart; "too smart for your own good," I told her, "just like me." And she was stubborn. It was difficult for her to get in touch with her feelings; she used her intelligence to rationalize them away. It drove me crazy when she refused to follow my advice. But to my amazement she got into recovery and continued to seek out my guidance. Now this was really something. Not only was I staying clean myself, but I was actually able to help someone else. I couldn't believe it.

"Every time I call you on the phone," Renee said one night, "you act like you're surprised I'm still sober."

"Yeah," I said. "'Cause I'm your sponsor. I'm used to fucking things up."

We saw each other often, even after she left the Ink Spot. Right before Christmas she snuck into my office and left me a gift and a card. "Dear Susie Sponsor," the card read. "Thank you for saving my life. I love you. Your pigeon, Renee."

I welcomed the first snow that fell that year. I wrapped myself up in a snowy cocoon of fluffy, white flakes and floated to the bridge to watch them melt and disappear in the swirling black waters of the river where I said my prayers. For some time now, I'd been aware that something was growing inside me. For maybe the first time in my life, I felt at peace. It wasn't happiness exactly, although in the past year I'd felt that too. There was a deep quiet space inside me that stayed the same through happiness and sorrow, elation and disappointment. It was there when I grieved and when I laughed out loud for joy. It was peace, plain and simple, as warm and welcoming as the lights of home. Somehow I knew that no matter what happened, I would be okay. I had come through the fire, and now I was free.

The snow swirled around me and hid me from view. I spread my arms out wide and slowly turned in circles, a dervish dance of celebration and of joy. I was on my own now; I could do as I pleased. I had earned my freedom from both the treadmill of addiction and the oppressiveness of treatment. What I felt, though, wasn't at all the giddy euphoria I'd imagined it would be; it was different, and maybe better. I felt peaceful: an unfamiliar feeling, hard to pin down. This peace was a puzzle: insubstantial as a feather yet solid as a rock. You couldn't buy it in a drugstore or cop it on the street. It was deeper than the love I'd ever felt with any man. I couldn't touch it, but I knew it was there. Best of all, it came from in me. It was part of me; I couldn't lose it. It was something I had earned, and no one, or nothing, could take it away.

chapter nineteen

> You don't have to yearn for love,
> You don't have to be alone,
> Somewheres in this universe
> There's a place that you can call home.
>
> Bob Dylan,
> "We Better Talk This Over"

THE MOTHER-CHILD REUNION—
FEBRUARY 1989

I was clean and serene, but I wasn't home free, because I hadn't yet recovered my bond with my daughter. Our relationship was in shreds and tatters. "To be a junkie mother is to know guilt," my old friend Tamara had told me years before. Clean, I felt it more keenly than ever.

Shuna's visits to Women, Inc., were difficult and painful for us both. We had no privacy. I was swamped with housework and responsibilities. I felt pressured and vulnerable, raw from all the grief and rage I'd been getting in touch with in my groups. And she was uncomfortable too. Just as I had learned to protect myself with a wall against hope, she defended herself with cynicism. She had hoped for my recovery and believed my lies about being clean too many times before. She didn't want to be abandoned again, and so she kept me at a distance. She was too angry to trust me, and she didn't really believe that I could change.

When I was living on my own in Boston, she visited me for several days at a time. As they had on other occasions, the tensions between us erupted into arguments. One day we quarreled at the restaurant where we had gone to get lunch. I drove my car to Wollaston beach and parked by the wall. There was a narrow strip of beach in front of us, and the blue waters of Quincy Bay and a vast open sky stretched out for miles to the horizon. I often went there at lunchtime to pray or think or sometimes to scream and cry inside my car when feelings overwhelmed me at my job.

"If you're angry at me," I said to Shuna, "why don't you just come right out with it. Scream, yell, get it out in the open. I can't stand it when you pick at me all the time."

"I'm not like you," she said coldly. "I can't just cry or get angry when you want me to, on command. I hold things in. Look, maybe things just can't be perfect between us right now. It's just too hard. We don't see each other for months at a time. Then when we do see each other, we're together every minute. It's too intense. There's no way for us to be normal."

"Then live with me," I said. "Come up here for the summer. I'll get a bigger apartment."

"I don't want to live with you," she said. "I don't think I could ever stand to live with you again."

I laid my head down on the steering wheel and wept. Shuna got out of the car and walked for a while on the beach. That night we went to a meeting together. We were quiet with each other, but some of the tension was gone. It was the last night of her visit. On our way home from the meeting, we were driving on River Street past the Star Market, toward Mattapan, where I lived.

"Can we stop at Brigham's?" Shuna asked me. "Peppermint ice cream with hot fudge?" We ate a sundae with two spoons, laughing at a joke someone had made at the meeting. All of a sudden, Shuna turned serious.

"You know, Mom," she said to me, "I think it's good we can fight and get over it. I feel like our relationship is healing. It's gonna take a long time, but it's happening. The sore isn't healed yet, but at least it has a scab on it now."

Shuna had been talking about moving to California since the previous summer, which she had spent in LA, babysitting for the son of some old Arica friends. In May I went to visit her at her school in New Paltz, and she told me she had completed the papers for transferring to the California College of Arts and Crafts in Oakland, and that she would go if she were accepted.

"Why don't you move back to California with me?" she said.

"I have to finish Re-entry first," I said. I was still in the graduate part of Women, Inc., which lasted for a year after residential treatment.

"Will you think about it?" she asked. "Promise me you'll think about it."

I thought about it a lot. I was worried about Shuna. She was drinking, and she told me she'd had blackouts that really scared her. I felt like she needed me, and that for my peace of mind, I had to do what I could to repair the damage to our relationship. I hadn't been able to be a mother in the later stages of my addiction, and now it didn't seem fair that I was in recovery and still couldn't mother her. I felt she needed to be in recovery too, for the sickness that had infected her as a result of growing up with a drug addict mother.

I was working on my eighth and ninth Steps, making amends. I knew that making amends to Shuna, who was at the top of my list, would involve more than just saying, "I'm sorry." I had heard a speaker at a convention say that he understood amends in the sense of amending, or changing, one's behavior. I felt that in order to make amends to Shuna, I would need to be around her, to be there for her, to be the mother the drugs had taken away. We couldn't live together in the same house, but perhaps we could live in the same area and see each other on a more normal basis.

But I was in early recovery, and I couldn't make a move without exploring all the possible options and consequences, and whether it would threaten my sobriety. I talked to Diane. She said she'd been wondering if I were going to move after graduation to be near my daughter anyway. She knew how concerned I was about her. I talked to my therapist. "It's a big chunk of unfinished business for you," she said. I asked my probation officer. "No problem," she said. "You've never given me any problem since I've known you." I talked to my sponsor. I shared in my meetings. And then I called my mother.

My parents were the only ones who didn't like the idea. "Oy," my mother said. "You're just getting settled in Boston. You're doing so well there now. Why take a chance on fucking things up?"

"To be near Shuna," I said.

"Shuna's in college," my mother said, "You can't go following her all over the country. What if she doesn't stay there?"

"California," my father said, with his usual sarcasm. "I guess you did so well there last time that you want to go back and do it again."

I hadn't lived in California for fourteen years. I knew I needed to go there and check out how I felt before I made such a big move. A journalist named Don Katz was writing a book about my family. A friend of my brother's, he had heard the family stories from him and decided that the Gordons embodied all the important trends of postwar American life. Don had suggested we go on a field trip. I called him.

"You know that field trip?" I said.

"Yeah," he said. "How about Vassar?"

"How about California?" I said. "I'll take you on a sixties tour of Berkeley."

"Fine," he said. "When do we leave?"

Shuna got accepted to CCAC and left for school in August. A week later I flew out to California. Tamara picked me up at the airport. When we got back to her house, there was a message for me on her answering machine.

"Hi, Mom," Shuna's voice said, "Welcome home."

It was, too. I saw some of my old friends from my Berkeley days. Suzy Nelson, who now owned the successful Fourth Street Grill, came to take me out to lunch. "Suzy," I said, "do you think I can find a place to live in Berkeley? Everyone says it's so hard these days." "Oh," she said, "do you want my apartment? I just put it in the paper today."

That was it. I went back to Boston, finished up Re-entry and the end of my three-years probation, gave notice at my job, and prepared to drive across the country.

The other day I made stuffed cabbage. It was on a Friday. That night I was supposed to speak at a program in Oakland called Group, Incorporated. Shuna had asked if she could come with me, but the meeting started at seven and she wouldn't finish work until six-thirty.

"Okay," I said, "I'll pick you up at your dorm at a quarter to seven. I'm making stuffed cabbage. I'll bring you some."

Stuffed cabbage used to take me all day to make, but I'd been cooking a lot lately, so I had the touch. The memory of how to roll up the stuffing inside the cabbage leaves is in my fingers anyway. It was imprinted on me as a child, when Mama Yetta let me help her in the kitchen. So the cooking was a pleasure, and the dish came out delicious. The sweet and sour sauce was perfectly balanced; the raisins plumped up just right; it was Jewish soul food at its soothing best. I ate some, put some more in a plastic container for Shuna, and went to pick her up.

In the months since I got here, Shuna's hair has changed color at least six times. She's also shaved the sides of her head. For a while she had a blue Mohawk. I didn't even have the satisfaction of wondering, "Where did I go wrong?" because I knew the answer: "Everywhere." Anyway it was cute, all the kids did it, and she was making a statement. "At least I don't do drugs," she would say when people stared at her on the street.

When I walked into Shuna's room in the dorm, she was slathering peanut butter on some bread. "Don't," I said. "I made you dinner. It's in the car."

"This is my mother," Shuna said to her roommate, Rosie. "She's Jewish."

"You don't have to be Jewish to want your kids to eat, do you, Rosie?" I asked.

"No," said Shuna, "but it helps."

"Don't eat in the car," I said. "Too messy. You can eat when we get to the meeting."

Group, Incorporated, is a long-term program, much like Women, Inc. They have a men's and a women's component, both of which get together for the Friday night meeting. I was nervous about speaking. Shuna took her stuffed cabbage and sat in the back of the room. I sat up front, and the meeting began. It was a candlelight meeting, and as soon as they turned out the lights, the energy in the room was transformed into a spiritual energy. I shared, as they say, my experience, strength, and hope. It was easy for me. I could relate. Not too long ago, I'd been sitting in a program just like this one, hoping, but not quite believing, that I too could have a better life. Now I was telling others just like me that it was possible. I was living proof. I knew just how they felt; I'd been there too.

I've shared at a lot of meetings in my recovery, but this was one of the best. I felt honored to be there, grateful for my experience and the opportunity to use it for a greater good. All the time I spoke, Shuna nodded and smiled at me from the back of the room. By the time I finished, I felt both humbled and elated. I was high in a way no drug could ever touch. They called a break, and the lights came on.

Shuna came right up to the front of the room and sat down on my lap. "Oh my God," she said, in her best Valley girl imitation, "that was absolutely the best food I ever ate in my life, ever. I had no idea. When you said, 'stuffed cabbage,' I thought to myself, 'So? Big deal.' Mom, how come you never made that before?"

"I did," I said. "I used to make it when I was pregnant with you. And I made it in Minnesota. It's my favorite dish in the world. I didn't know you never had it. I forgot."

"And your share, Mom," she said. "It was so great. Every time I hear you speak I'm amazed. You always tell such different stories. You related so well to the people here. I was so proud of you. You know, Mom, I feel really honored to be your daughter. Before, when people used to tell me, 'Your mother is a great woman,' I'd think to myself, 'Oh, sure. You don't know her like I do.' But now I see why they said it. You are a great woman. And I hope I grow up to be just like you." Then she kissed me on my cheek.

My eyes got misty. I didn't know what to say. "I never thought I'd live to see this day," I whispered, holding her close.

After the meeting a few of the women from the program came up to speak to me. "You're so lucky," one of them said, "to have your daughter here with you, supporting you in your recovery. I'd give anything to have someone in my family with me. You all are both lucky to have each other."

"Recovery is awesome," I told her, just as I'd been told so many times before, "beyond your wildest dreams. And this is one of its greatest gifts." Then I put my arm around Shuna, and we walked out into the moonlit night toward home.

The road of excess leads to the palace of wisdom.

William Blake,
"Proverbs of Hell"

DANCING LESSONS FROM GOD— SEPTEMBER 1992

After six years I finally had the courage to visit New York. Don Katz's book, *Home Fires,* was finished, and Shuna and I had been invited to appear on a TV show with my mother, my brother, and Don. "Should I go?" I asked one of my friends. "Why not?" he answered. "Strange travel instructions are dancing lessons from God." It was a line from Kurt Vonnegut's classic novel, *Cat's Cradle,* and one that had served almost as a coda for many of us during the sixties. I was still scared to go, so I got the kind of plane ticket that would allow me to leave at any time if things got rough. My experience of New York in the past was that my feet were always taking me places where my head didn't want me to go.

In my mind the present commingled with the past. I felt a mixture of longing and nostalgia, excitement and anticipation, sadness and resolution, a confusing emotional blend. I didn't know what it was going to be like to be in this city where I'd lived so much of my life, and from which I'd been so painfully exiled in the past.

As it happened, though, I loved it there. I ended up changing my plane ticket every day to stay longer because I was so energized and inspired by the city's vitality, which coursed through my body and barely let me sleep. I understood then that I had taken drugs in part as an attempt to deal with that energy, which made me crave excitement and movement just to try to burn it off. I was staying in Soho with my old friend Mary Peacock. Each day I put on my sneakers and jeans and flannel shirt—for comfort, and because it was what I knew best—and walked my old haunts, from Ninety-Fourth Street and Broadway to the Lower East Side. Shuna was staying at her father's, and sometimes we walked together.

Like a newcomer to the Twelve-Step programs, I planned my day around a meeting. Actually it was a relief to have my recovery again be about not taking drugs, because by now it's become so complicated with core issues of codependency and sexual abuse, work and self-esteem, that I normally don't even think about getting high. Shuna came with me to meetings, and it was healing for us to explore our past together, discuss it, and replace it with new associations of recovery and health.

Sometimes I view my recovery literally as a process of getting back—recovering—what I lost through the dope. My trip to New York seemed like a spiritual process of reclaiming lost territory; I wanted to revisit the scene of the crime. This time, when I walked the streets of the Lower East Side, I was surprised to find that I no longer felt the old familiar cravings, as I had on my first trip to New York from Women, Inc., so many years before. But I could only do that when I was feeling strong and secure; when I felt vulnerable or uncertain, I had to go to a meeting or avoid certain streets to stay safe. And I did have my moments.

One day I was walking down Houston Street on my way to meet Shuna for lunch, when I ran smack into my old connection Willie, on a hiatus between prison terms. "I thought you were dead," we both said in unison. I've seen all kinds of people from my past, at various types of reunions, and a lot of them say to me, "I'm really surprised to see you're still alive." I was glad that Willie was still alive, but I also was shaking in my shoes.

"Where you been?" he asked.

"I live in California," I said. "I've been clean for six years."

"Some people are just meant to clean up," he said. "But you better go right back to California today, because you won't stay clean here for even six minutes."

I told Willie he was in my book and asked him if he wanted me to change his name.

"What'd you say about me?" he asked.

"I said I had to wait for you a lot."

"Ain't nothing changed," he said. "There's people waiting for me on a corner right now."

I was glad I wasn't one of them. I had just passed a dope-fiend couple waiting on the street, looking desperate and wary; their eyes revealed a bottomless pit of misery. I was relieved not to be there anymore. But I was scared; this was the closest encounter I'd had with the dope yet.

What Willie had said made me angry too. "I'm sick of the dope keeping me from my home town," I thought to myself. And then the simple slogans of the program kicked in. "If you don't pick it up, you won't get high." Stuff like that. It was oddly comforting and let me know I had the strength to resist. I abruptly changed directions and headed uptown. I no longer wanted what Willie had. That old life was dead for me.

One night, on my way to a meeting on St. Mark's Place, I happened to pass by the synagogue on Sixth Street where I used to score my dope. In the early eighties, I sometimes copped from some crazy Ukrainian brothers who lived right near there with their aged father. Both the brothers are dead now; I don't know about the father, who was kind to me and often gave me some of his homemade pirogi to take to work for dinner. I would call the brothers on the phone, and one of them would meet me in front of the synagogue to hand over the dope. On the High Holy Days, the synagogue would be lit up with happy families going in and out, stopping to chat with their neighbors on the stoop. I'd be lurking outside in the shadows, waiting for one of the Ukrainian brothers, desperate with longing and burning with shame. The Tarot card called the five of Pentacles describes this feeling perfectly: its image is a crippled beggar and a barefoot woman in rags, who trudge through falling snow past a stained glass window. Inside the stained glass window there's light and warmth, but the beggars are outside it, separate from God, alone and unprotected in the cold, driving snow.

In those days I had sometimes thought that if I'd been brought up in a more religious family, I wouldn't have been such a mess. Given my rebellious nature, it's quite likely I would have felt stifled by the constraints of Orthodox Judaism, but I have always had an inexpressible longing for a connection with that tradition. When my old boyfriend Paul lived in a trade union co-op on the Lower East Side, I used to feel jealous of the Orthodox Jewish families I saw there. I had read Chaim Potok's novels about Hasidic and Orthodox families in Brooklyn, and no matter what the characters' conflicts, it seemed they were surrounded by such inclusive security and warmth that I imagined them perpetually wrapped in the holy light of the sabbath candles. I craved that kind of atmosphere with a palpable hunger.

I had spent years in a spiritual school, and so I knew what it was like to have an inner life and feel close to God. If there were one God, which I believed to be a nonnegotiable fact, then it wouldn't matter what you called or how you worshiped the Creator, so I felt no contradiction there. Upon reflection, it seems as though I wanted the connection with Judaism as much for identity as for spiritual sustenance; I needed to feel that I belonged somewhere. When I looked at those Jewish families, I was ashamed of what I'd become; this wasn't supposed to happen to a smart Jewish girl like me.

I felt like I'd sold my soul for the small amount of pleasure and relief that I got from the dope. But it wasn't enough. One day, standing on the subway platform waiting for the F train, I saw an old Hasid with a long beard, side curls, and a tall black hat. He could have been a *rebbe* or an ordinary Joe; it didn't really matter; he looked like a holy man to me. I followed him around the station, wishing I could absorb his sanctity and wisdom, somehow trade places with him. Whatever difficulties he had in his life, I wanted them more than I wanted mine.

I wish I could say that in recovery I've resolved my internal conflicts or satisfied my deepest spiritual longings, but it simply isn't so. I've explored different paths and participated in the rituals of various mystical traditions, but I've been unable to commit myself exclusively to any single one. The motivation for strict observance of Jewish law still eludes me. I like the freedom of the Twelve-Step programs, with their emphasis on a God of your own understanding. And through the practice of that simple and sort of *hamische,* homey, do-it-yourself spirituality, something has changed inside me, a subtle shift of consciousness that seems to manifest as an increase of compassion; with more self-acceptance, self-respect, and dignity; a greater reverence for all life, including my own. I don't know if this approach is right or particularly well-founded, but at the moment it seems to be working for me.

I stopped in front of that old synagogue on Sixth Street, surprised to find it lit up. It was the night before Yom Kippur, the Day of Atonement, the holiest day of the Jewish calendar year. A man was sitting outside on the steps. "Do you have to have a ticket to go in there?" I asked him. "Not tonight," he said. "Tomorrow you probably would." I was dressed in jeans and sneakers and carrying a small shopping bag, but I went up the stairs and into the temple anyway. One thing I know is that God cares more about what's in your heart than about your outward appearance. Still, I took a little lace doily from a box inside the entrance and placed it on my head as a gesture of respect. It was an Orthodox *shul;* women sat on one side, men on the other. A few women turned around to look at me, but without censure, only because they had never seen me before.

I sat in the back. I couldn't really understand the rabbi's Hebrew, but I knew when he got to the Kaddish, the prayer for the dead. My father says that Kaddish is like a chain that links all the generations of Jews together, back to the beginning of time. Sitting in that temple, I felt myself a link in that chain. I didn't judge myself or feel ashamed; I felt entitled to be there, present in the sight of God. I could hold my head up and be part of my tradition; I deserved my birthright and my place in humanity. Walking out of the temple after the service, I was smiling, and my step was light. Tears of gratitude filled my eyes. Somehow I knew I'd been blessed with grace, an undeserved reward. It seemed like a kind of redemption.

ACKNOWLEDGMENTS

More than most writers, I am indebted to my agent, David Black, because this book was his idea. My friend Ani Chamichian, of the Harper San Francisco marketing department, brought it to the attention of those publishers, where it found a home. I'm grateful to my editors, Tom Grady and Caroline Pincus, for helping to refine and shape the manuscript with skill and loving care and to Mimi Kusch for overseeing the book's production with patience and sensitivity.

Throughout my life I've been blessed with enriching, lasting friendships. Many of the people mentioned in this book are still in my life today. I've changed some names on request, or where an individual might be implicated in illegal activities, but used real names in most cases. My friends and family have provided me with a strong network of love and support. During the writing of this book, I've received aid from people too numerous to mention, but at the risk of sounding like an Academy Awards acceptance speech, I'd like to thank at least some of them by name.

For family remembrances I relied on Freddie Goldenberg, Blanche Teitelbaum, the late Sylvia Sternfield, the late Lou Samberg, Aunt Annie Samberg, and my cousins Jeffrey Samberg and Carole Paley. I had the benefit of long conversations with my sister, Lorraine Gordon Heard, and traded facts and chronology with Don Katz, author of *Home Fires*. Sheila Gordon Wolff, Ricky Ian Gordon, and Tom Piechowski read an earlier draft of the manuscript and offered invaluable comments, suggestions, and encouragement. My friends Mary Peacock and Ruhama Veltfort contributed their editing expertise to various sections of the book.

Thanks to Drs. Paul Walton and Robert Goble and the interns of Life Chiropractic College West for keeping me going; to Dr. Ellen Gunther, Emmett Marx, Lydia Garcia, Kenny Gong, and Guy Manybeads for medical, acupuncture, herbal, and homeopathic care; Lyle Poncher, Richard Maxwell, Roger Zim, David Pauker, and Camilo Wilson for technical and other support, and Bob Seidemann for taking the author photographs. Peter Mitchell kept my car on the road and shared his memories with me, as did Genie McNaughton, David Getz, Susan Kent Cakars, Deborah Michaelson Kolb, Christian Intemann, Anne Weills, Suzy Nelson, Kate Coleman, and Lee Ann Sandefer, among others. Maris Cakars, an important part of my life for many years, died suddenly of cirrhosis last spring; it saddens me that like so many others, known and unknown, he never made it to recovery.

Linda Vestal, Terry LaRue, Polly Frizzell, Karen Osborne, Marilyn Turner, Paddy Berne, Judy Moore, Terry Mercherson, and James Hill provided companionship, wisdom, humor, and love to leaven the years of a long and arduous project, and I am more grateful than I can say to the East Bay Fellowship for helping me through. I'd like to acknowledge the special help of my teacher, Oscar Ichazo, and the members of my Octagon, as well as the gift of heart I received from Hayat Stadlinger and Taner Vargonen. And of course, God, who makes all things possible. In the most graceful language I know, *mahalo nui loa;* many thanks.